EVANGELICAL THEOLOGY

EVANGELICAL THEOLOGY

A Course of Popular Lectures

A. A. HODGE

THE BANNER OF TRUTH TRUST

THE BANNER OF TRUTH TRUST
3 Murrayfield Road, Edinburgh EH12 6EL
PO Box 621, Carlisle, Pennsylvania 17013, USA

*

First published 1890
First Banner of Truth edition 1976

*

ISBN 0 85151 236 4

*

Printed and bound in Great Britain
by Hazell Watson & Viney Ltd
Aylesbury, Bucks

Preface.

———•———

WHEN Dr. A. A. Hodge was suddenly reft away by death, at the age of sixty-three, in the autumn of 1886, Principal Cairns of Edinburgh said truly—" The whole evangelical Church has lost in him a powerful and intrepid defender of its best and dearest beliefs." The sense of loss was naturally greatest in his own country, where his influence had just reached the meridian. President F. L. Patton, the successor of Dr. M'Cosh as head of the College of New Jersey, declared that " every element that entered into Dr. Hodge's eminent reputation had put on its best expression in the closing years of his life ; " and he and others have borne eloquent testimony to the importance of the place he occupied in the American Church, alike as a thinker and as a spiritual force. But the younger Hodge, like his distinguished father, had made the whole of evangelical Christendom his debtor, and when he died the Church of God on earth was poorer everywhere.

In the present volume we have Dr. A. A. Hodge's last legacy to the cause of truth. By it he, being dead, yet speaketh. And if we on this side of the Atlantic share the loss his death has brought, it is meet that we should also share the legacy.

These nineteen Lectures, which traverse with light but firm step the whole field of theology in its four great divisions, have, moreover, an interest and importance not altogether personal to their author. They strikingly illustrate, indeed, the aptness of Dr. Shedd's description of the younger Hodge, as "the popularizer of scientific theology;" for they were addressed, not to a theological class, but to a great and interested miscellaneous audience in a hall in Philadelphia. But popular as they are in form, and colloquial as they sometimes are in style, we have manifestly here on every page the work of a theological expert, who can illumine his theme without sacrificing his precision. And thus the Lectures have special value as a popular yet scientific presentation of the latest Princeton position on the great theological questions of the day.

Though the Princeton school of theology—so long a synonym for Calvinistic orthodoxy—has still its powerful living representatives, the mention of it will always be suggestive of the name of Hodge, father and son. The two were alike, yet different. They were especially alike in their absolute loyalty to the Word of God, but each had his own way of viewing truth and his own way of presenting it. It is well that the British reader should now be put in possession of a volume in which the Princeton system—already exhibited in more scholastic form in the other writings of the great leaders of the school—is presented in the freer manner of Hodge the younger.

This will be a most helpful and informing study for thoughtful laymen, as well as a stimulating and useful book for ministers and students of divinity. Some of the Lectures deal with what are living and even burning questions in our time. These they treat with full knowledge, complete honesty, marked independence, and rare felicity of illustrating power. What could be finer, for example, than the handling of Inspiration on page 78 ? what more discriminating than the remarks on Evolution in the middle of chapter eight ? Where will teaching more candid yet charitable on the subject of Church Unity be found than toward the close of chapter nine ? Where, taking the book as a whole, will a better illustration be found of the difference between a conservative and a narrow theology ?

The conclusions will not always be accepted by every reader; but no one can peruse these discussions without feeling that he is thereby brought into contact not only with a master in divinity, a thinker of vitalizing energy, a teacher of singular clearness and consistency, but with *a man* of profound convictions, whom it is good to know, and whose thoroughgoing enthusiasm for the truth he propounds is itself impressive in a too indifferent and negative age.

C. A. SALMOND.

CONTENTS.

BIOGRAPHY ix

I. GOD—HIS NATURE AND RELATION TO THE UNIVERSE 9

II. THE SCRIPTURE DOCTRINE OF DIVINE PROVIDENCE 29

III. MIRACLES 46

IV. THE HOLY SCRIPTURES—THE CANON AND INSPIRATION 61

V. PRAYER 84

VI. THE TRINITY OF PERSONS IN THE GODHEAD ... 97

VII. PREDESTINATION 118

VIII. THE ORIGINAL STATE OF MAN 139

IX. GOD'S COVENANTS WITH MAN—THE CHURCH ... 163

X. THE PERSON OF CHRIST 184

XI. THE OFFICES OF CHRIST 201

XII. THE KINGLY OFFICE OF CHRIST 223

XIII. THE KINGDOM OF CHRIST 249

XIV. THE LAW OF THE KINGDOM 271

XV. SANCTIFICATION AND GOOD WORKS.—HIGHER LIFE 290

XVI.	THE SACRAMENTS	...	...	...	...	313
XVII.	THE LORD'S SUPPER	...	...	...	...	339
XVIII.	THE STATE OF MAN AFTER DEATH AND THE RESURRECTION	...	...	...	...	364
XIX.	FINAL REWARDS AND PUNISHMENTS	...	...	...	383

ARCHIBALD ALEXANDER HODGE
A MEMORIAL DISCOURSE
by
FRANCIS L. PATTON*

I FEAR that I have little fitness for the service I have been so kindly invited to perform, beyond the fact that I had a share in Dr. Hodge's confidence, that I loved him dearly, and that during the short period of my acquaintance with him I had come to know him well. It has occurred to me more than once since the preparation of this Discourse was undertaken, that some one who had known him longer and whose record of memories reaches back to the years of a common boyhood would have done ampler justice to this occasion. For, when a great man dies, there is a natural, and surely a pardonable, curiosity on the part of all to know something of his early life. We love to study his history in the light of the facts that made up the totality of his career, and to read in stories of his childhood the promise of a greatness attained in later years. In the case of one like Dr. Hodge, whose personality was so unique, so manifold, and so manifestly marked by genius, we naturally suppose that those who have been his companions for a lifetime

*This address by Dr. Patton, Professor in Princeton Theological Seminary, was delivered in the Chambers Presbyterian Church, 21st December, 1886, in compliance with an invitation from the Philadelphia Presbyterian Ministerial Association. First published in 1887, it remains of enduring value and has therefore been added to this 1976 reprint of Hodge's *Evangelical Theology*. No full-length biography of A. A. Hodge has ever been written.

are in possession of reminiscences that would abundantly gratify this very natural desire. It may yet fall to the lot of one specially qualified, to do what obviously I cannot do. I must content myself with describing what I saw, and representing Dr. Hodge to you as he appeared to me. That we were engaged in kindred pursuits, that we had both taught from the same text-book, and had traversed in frequent conversations the leading topics embraced in Dr. Charles Hodge's *Systematic Theology*, may qualify me in a measure for forming a just estimate of his position in the theological world. This estimate I shall at least try to make, not in the form of fulsome eulogy—for a simple statement of the truth will be eulogy enough—but in tender regard for his precious memory and under the restrictions of sober fact.

The death of Dr. Hodge is such a sore bereavement to our entire Church, that a memorial service held in the midst of a larger community than that embraced in the University-town where the last years of his life were spent, seems eminently proper; and I know of no place where that service could be more appropriately held than in this city of his forefathers, the city that he loved above all others, and for which his last and ripest work was done. On this day of the week and at this hour of the day, many of you had hoped to hear his voice not many days hence as you heard it last winter, when he exhibited so clearly, with such aptness of illustration and characteristic affluence of expression, the great doctrines of our faith. How little any one dreamed that death would give such significance to his closing words when for the last time he addressed the large audience that had gathered week by week to hear him! How little did any one suppose that these closing words were to be treasured afterwards as the swan-song of the dying theologian!—" We shall meet together here no more. Let us pledge one another to reassemble in heaven. We part as pilgrims part upon the road. Let us take our way heavenward, for if we do we shall soon, some of us very soon, be at home with the Lord." His removal is God's strange work. We can only say : " I was dumb, I opened not my mouth because thou didst it." We bow submissively to our Father's will, and are here to-day to thank God for the life of ARCHIBALD ALEXANDER HODGE, to read afresh the record of that life, and in its lessons find new inspiration.

Philadelphia, as I have said, was the city of Dr. Hodge's ancestors. His great-grandfather, his grandfather, and his eminent uncle, lived and died here. His mother's ancestry, in several lines of descent, is still numerously represented here. His father was born here in 1797, and married here in 1822. Archibald Alexander was born in Princeton on the 18th day of July, 1823. An old frame-house on the corner of Witherspoon Street is still pointed out as the place where he first saw the light. He grew up in an intellectual atmosphere. During his boyhood his father's study was the meeting-place for all the great lights of Princeton. The Old and New School controversies, and the New Haven Divinity were discussed in his hearing by men like Dod, the Alexanders, John Maclean, and Charles Hodge. The *Princeton Review* began its career in his boyhood, and he was familiar with all the men who were active in its organization. If there is any advantage in breathing " the atmosphere of floating knowledge," which Dugald Stewart says is " around every seminary of learning," Archibald Hodge must have enjoyed it to the full. Yet he does not seem to have been a very studious boy or over-fond of books. I am inclined to think that boys, as a rule, do not care much for intellectual atmospheres, and that they do not profit so much by their environments as we might suppose. Books are too numerous to be counted luxuries by the sons of literary men, and literary men themselves come into too close contact with their sons to be their heroes. It is the boy who gets knowledge under difficulties, who buys his Virgil only by saving pennies, who has felt the pangs of book-hunger without the means of gratifying his appetite, that is more likely to

develop a love of reading and to devour libraries. Thirst for
knowledge young Archibald's environment did not give him.
But it gave him the air of one who is to the manner born. It
saved him from priggishness and conceit. It kept him from
displays of vanity and egotism that are so apt to mar the
greatness of men who have transcended the intellectual conditions of their childhood. In College he was one of Professor
Henry's most distinguished pupils. It was through the
influence of this eminent man that he developed the taste for
physical science that he retained through life ; and it is probable,
that, next to his own father, Professor Henry exerted a more
formative influence upon his mind than any other teacher he
ever had. He was graduated in 1841; he taught awhile at the
Lawrenceville School, and was for a year or two after that a
tutor in the College. In the Seminary he was one of a group
of students, consisting, besides himself, of Messrs. Lacy,
McPheeters, Phillips and Scott, who were specially interested
in the study of Systematic Theology. Dr. Charles Hodge was
then beginning to write his lectures. The members of this
group distributed among themselves the work of taking a
verbatim report of these lectures, which they were in the habit
of putting together in connected form after the lecture was
over. Besides this, they were required to read Turrettin and
present written answers to questions which Dr. Hodge himself
prepared every week. In these days of a crowded *curriculum*,
it could hardly be expected that students should devote so
much time to a department as important even as Systematic
Theology; and now that they can for the first part listen
indolently to lectures with a printed syllabus in their hands,
the labor of taking notes has been greatly reduced: but there
can be no doubt that those who were willing to work according
to the old method just described became thorough theologians.
It was through this method of study, taken in connection with
conversations with his father on theological subjects, that
Archibald Hodge laid the foundation for his own eminent

career, though no one would have prophesied—and least of all his father—that he would one day be a teacher of theology himself. On one occasion, however, he won a compliment from his father which he must have valued highly, for he has told me the story more than once. It seems that he had written an essay, and on reading it to Dr. Charles Hodge, that distinguished theologian looked up with an expression of pleased astonishment on his face, and said that Alexander must read the essay to the class. I would give a great deal to see that essay; for I doubt not that it would be another illustration of the well-known fact that a man's best and ripest thinking often consists in the development of ideas that are germinally manifested in early life. I am pretty confident that the subject of the essay was The Relation of God to the World—a topic which was the subject of Dr. Hodge's latest thought, and which he dealt with in a forth-coming article, the manuscript of which was placed in my hands only a few weeks before his death.*

Leaving the Seminary, Archibald Hodge offered himself to the Board of Foreign Missions, was accepted, married, and sailed for India in 1847. His stay in India was short, owing to his own illness and that of his wife. He rendered important service, however, to the Mission at Allahabad, harmonizing discordant elements and gaining personal influence and affection, which rendered his return a serious disappointment to his colleagues. But what was far more important, his experience in the mission-field enhanced his zeal for the mission-cause, gave him a grasp of the missionary problem, and an interest in missionaries that made him always the trusted counsellor of all those among his pupils who contemplated a missionary career. If the students wished advice, they went to him : if the Sunday evening missionary meeting was to be addressed, he was called upon : if, at the Monthly Concert, the expected speaker failed to arrive, he was called upon : if the son of a

*Presbyterian Review, January, 1887.

converted Brahmin was sent here to be educated, he was his guardian : if a penniless Oriental, bent on knowledge, and seeking it, that he might carry the gospel back to his countrymen, sought premature admission to the Seminary, he found an eager advocate in Dr. Hodge, if anything could be said in his behalf; and if, as sometimes happened, it was necessary to let him know that his coming had been a mistake, kind words from Dr. Hodge, and not infrequently a draft upon his exchequer, sent him away in peace: if the Inter-Seminary Missionary Conference held its meetings at Hartford, Dr. Hodge must make an address : if it met in Princeton, Dr. Hodge at least must pray.

Dr. Hodge returned from India with his wife and two children in 1850. In 1851, he settled in Lower West Nottingham, Md. It was a rural charge, and the salary—a little more than six hundred dollars a year—was very inadequate : but it was better than nothing, and it afforded him an opportunity to preach the gospel. He was not indifferent to pecuniary compensation, nor ignorant of the purchasing power of money. On the contrary, his action in this instance is admirably illustrative of the wise and cautious forethought in money-matters, which characterized his whole life. He did not put the call in his pocket and wait for an opportunity to compare it with another ; nor did he act like an auctioneer—using a bid from one church to stimulate a higher bid from another; nor did he get his friends to correspond with such vacant churches as he deemed worthy of being served by his gifts ; nor, going to West Nottingham, did he plan for a scale of expenditure exceeding his income, with the idea that when his necessities became known friends would rally to his support. He went there with a deliberate determination that, come what may, he would live on his salary and keep out of debt. He even took a few dollars that he had in his possession, and, providing against the direst contingency possible, secured a policy of life-insurance ; and actually lived without debt and paid his premiums—an example,

I think, to multitudes in the ministry and out of it, whose lack of thrift and forethought has far more to do with the distress of widows and orphans than is commonly supposed. I mention this, because there are men among us who remain unemployed simply because they will not take the churches they can get, and who seem to have the impression that if they bury themselves in small places remote from cities and away from railroads, God will not know how to find them when the great work is ready which he has for them to do. But He found Alexander Hodge when the church in Fredericksburg was vacant in 1855 ; He found him when Wilkes-Barré wanted a pastor in 1861 ; and He found him again when Allegheny Seminary stood in need of a systematic theologian in 1864— each step proving in the end to be a preparation for the work that Dr. Hodge was subsequently to do in the Chair of Didactic Theology in Princeton. Few men have the courage to seek obscurity for the sake of its advantages, but there can be no doubt of the intellectual advantages of a quiet country charge. When I hear men complain of the lack of stimulus in a rural parish, or find them longing for opportunity to preach to audiences more cultivated and worthy of their talents, I feel disposed to think that the poor quality of their intellectual fabrics is due not so much to lack of proper appliances, but rather to dearth of the raw material. Many a man will tell you that he owes all that he ever afterwards became, to the circumstance that, under God, he enjoyed the quiet of rural solitude, and had opportunity of uninterrupted thought and reading. Though not a prolific writer, Dr. Hodge was always busy with his pen, and it is worth while to remember that the " Outlines of Theology " was not the fruit of a leisurely professorship. It went out from the little study in the parsonage at Fredericksburg; and what has since that day become a text-book in theology in different languages was first of all preached to a congregation of Presbyterians in Virginia. It is said, sometimes, that we cannot preach theology. Here is a theology,

however, every word of which was preached, and not only
preached, but listened to with eagerness, first in Fredericksburg and afterwards in Wilkes-Barré. It was during his
Fredericksburg pastorate that Dr. Hodge became aware of his
power of extemporaneous address. From that time and
increasingly until his death he was pre-eminently a preacher.
When he went to Allegheny his gifts soon became known, and
he was in very general demand. Before long he accepted the
pastorate of a congregation there which soon built and organized what is known as the North Presbyterian Church; and
continued to perform the double function of pastor and professor until he came to Princeton. I have never heard that any one
found fault with him on the ground of "pluralities." It would
have been most unwise to do so. Dr. Hodge was not the less a
professor by being a pastor. He never would have been a man
of distinguished theological erudition, with the most abundant
leisure; for, though fond of reading, he had not the tastes of a
specialist. The two functions in his case acted and reacted in
favor of each other. His profound knowledge of theology, his
habit of pondering upon theological problems, his power of
minute analysis, and his determination to see every subject
with which he dealt in its various relations, made preaching a
very simple matter, and he fed his congregation with the finest
of the wheat. On the other hand, the necessity under which
he rested of presenting theological truth in forms suited to the
minds of ordinary people, fostered in him his natural gift for
illustration and saved him from becoming a mere dealer in the
dry formulas of scholasticism. Many a spark struck out in the
class-room was fanned into a flame of glowing illustration in the
pulpit; and many a popular sermon, I venture to say, served
to light up and lend fervor to the scientific discussions of the
class-room. There was an interchange of amenities, I doubt
not, between the pulpit and the professor's-chair, that was of
advantage to both; and the double duty he performed at
Allegheny had much to do with the superlative eminence he

afterwards achieved in doing what many will regard as, on the whole, the greatest work of his life.

In 1877, it became apparent that some relief should be afforded Dr. Charles Hodge, who, though entering upon his eightieth year, was still teaching both Didactic and Exegetical Theology. There could be no doubt respecting the man who was most conspicuously fit to be the associate and successor of Dr. Charles Hodge. It might seem like an ungracious act to bring him from Allegheny; but when the interests of the Church at large were taken into account, there could be no doubt that it was of paramount importance that the chair of Systematic Theology in Princeton should be filled by the best available man. Dr. A. A. Hodge was one of Princeton's noblest sons, and his *alma mater* exercised her natural right to summon him to her help in her hour of need. He was inaugurated on the 8th November, 1877. Referring to this occasion, a writer in the *Presbyterian* said: "During all the services, we noticed that many eyes were turned to a corner of the church, in which a venerable man sat apart communing with himself, with his heart, doubtless, filled with varying emotions." The reference, of course, is to Dr. Charles Hodge, of whom his biographer says : " His mind must have gone back to August 12, 1812, when he, a stripling lying on the rail of the gallery of the same church, looked down on the inauguration of Dr. A. Alexander to the same office. For from August 12, 1812, to November 18, 1877, for more than sixty-five years, there had been only two professors of Systematic Theology in Princeton, and Dr. Hodge received the office from a man he delighted to call father, and now transmitted it to his son."

The career of Dr. Charles Hodge was wonderful and beautiful beyond expression. During his long life of uninterrupted literary activity he had been brought into close relations with every active movement in what was a very active period of the Church's life. He had achieved eminence in every sphere of ministerial renown : preacher, debater, reviewer, exegete, ecclesiastic, historian, and systematic theologian—he was great in each of these dimensions of measurement. His plans ripened, and hopes that others entertained in his behalf were fully realized. He garnered the wisdom of his life and left his *Theology* as a legacy to the world. When old age came upon him he stood between two strong sons who lightened his labors and afterward divided between them the work that he left behind. He kept his faculties to the last, and taught his classes within a few weeks of his death. His death was as ideal as his life had been: and, therefore, when, one beautiful afternoon in June of 1878, his own sons took up their sad burden and carried him to his grave, we all felt that everything was exactly as we could have wished.

We must look now, however, upon a very different picture. The coming of Dr. A. A. Hodge brought new life to Princeton Seminary; and when his father died the work went on without abatement. He filled his father's place. In the pulpit, at the Conference, and in the classroom, he was a power, and was recognized as such by his colleagues and his pupils. We listened to him with pride and admiration, and derived from him intellectual refreshment and spiritual profit. We fondly hoped that many years of labor were before him, and that, like his father, by and by he would have a glorious sunset. Alas for us! his sun has gone down at noon; he has been taken away in the prime of his manhood, and when to all outward seeming he was physically and intellectually at his best. It is not strange that Princeton is in mourning. She has met as great a loss as she could possibly sustain. Dr. Hodge was emphatically a Princeton man. He was born there. It was his father's home, and he was bound to it by a net-work of domestic relationships. He was loyal beyond measure to the ideas with which Princeton is identified, and loved to refer to her traditions. His large heart embraced the world, but no one could mistake the special place that Princeton had in his affections. In the distribution of hypothetical millions of which, according to his habit of jocose exaggeration, he was so fond, it was Princeton College and Princeton Seminary that he always thought of. Sometimes, when my own heart yearns for the scenes of my childhood and the blue waters of my island-home, I can appreciate his affection for Princeton: it was home. I believe that it gratified his heart's desire when he went back there to live: and after that, to be his father's successor, to sit in his father's study, to walk under the shade of the elms that his father had planted, and, in the ways opened to him by Providence, to do the kind of work his father did, was his highest ambition. I do not know what his epitaph will be ; but I venture to say, that no words will so well convey the idea of what he would regard as a rounded life of realized desire as those which state the simple fact that he was Third Professor of Theology in Princeton Seminary. Of course, since Princeton was so dear to him, he was correspondingly dear to Princeton. A shock of personal bereavement was felt by every one and by all classes when word went out on the morning of the 12th November that Dr. A. A. Hodge was dead. A man may do excellent work in his department and not be generally known in a community as small even as Princeton. Were such a man to pass away, the public might acknowledge that a great light had gone out, but he would not be generally missed. Dr. Hodge, however, was a citizen and did his duty as such. Everybody knew him. He was public-spirited. He helped every good cause. We met him in social circles and at the house of mourning. He was a leading man in his church and a trustee of the College. In the Faculty he manifested the excellences without the faults or defects which sometimes show themselves when men are associated together. He was not opinionated, nor arrogant, nor reticent, nor indifferent. He pressed his views with manly confidence in their correctness, but could yield gracefully to an adverse decision. He was not simply attached to the Seminary. His life was grafted into its corporate existence, and he was always planning for its interests. He was frank, generous, full of good fellowship, and we were exceedingly filled with his company. His study-door, facing us as we went to and fro, was an invitation to turn in for a friendly chat. Ah! the echo of his familiar greeting lingers in my ear, and I seem to hear him tell me to "come again."

Men die, but institutions live. God, no doubt, will send a man worthy of the fourth place in this great succession.* He may be as great and in some respects even greater than his predecessors, but no matter what his attainments may be, it is not likely that he can be to us what Dr. Hodge has been. The glory has departed from Princeton Seminary and the Church at large has lost a leader. I claim for him no supremacy, of course, among contemporary theologians, but no one will hesitate to make ungrudging recognition of his greatness. It will be hard to appreciate the magnitude of the loss which the Church has sustained unless we consider the many lines of activity along which Dr. Hodge was working. I sometimes meet with a statement (which looks a little like jealousy of the professorial function), to the effect that the pastors and not the professors determine the theology of the Church. It is true that the pastors teach the people and in that sense determine the Church's theology : and from some of the specimens that have come under my eye of late, I should judge that it is very poor theology the people sometimes get. But who teach the pastors?

Think now of what Dr. Hodge was doing. Year by year he was sending forth men by forties and by fifties, into cities and towns, north and south, east and west, as settled pastors and as missionaries, to India, to the territories, to South America, and the islands of the sea—preaching a theology which he had taught them. His pen was busy defending truth and refuting error. As a watchman on the walls of Zion, he was sleepless,

*Dr. B. B. Warfield, of the Western Theological Seminary, Allegheny, Pa., has since received and accepted a call to this position.

vigilant, bold, clear-eyed, discriminating: not giving premature or unnecessary alarm, not allowing the citadel to be surprised: faithful to the last degree, and when he put the trumpet to his lips, giving no uncertain sound. He was writing, preaching, lecturing, making addresses, coming into contact with men, influencing them and, by doing so, widening the influence of truth. Men far and near corresponded with him and sought his counsel. He had the confidence of the Church as few men have. The North loved him; the South honored him. In Canada, in Great Britain, and over the wide missionary area, his judgments on theological matters were deferred to and quoted with respect. If a theological question was under debate, a few lines from his pen in a religious paper went the rounds of the press. Think now of the work that came to a stand-still when God's finger was laid upon that throbbing heart, and estimate, if you can, the loss that Christendom has sustained.

Dr. Hodge was in the zenith of his power when he died. Every element that entered into his eminent reputation put on its best expression in the closing years of his life. Let us seek to form a just estimate of him as a theologian and a man. We shall understand him better as a theologian if we know him as a man, for the elements of manhood gave form to his theology: and we shall not understand him as a man if we do not know him as a theologian, for theology was a large part of his manhood. His theology flashed into prismatic colors on the diamond-points of his manifold personality, and his manhood was warmed by a religious fervor that streamed like the fires of the opal from the theological convictions imbedded in the core of his being.

Systematic Theology is the most important, the most comprehensive and the most difficult of all the theological Disciplines. It is, in fact, the synthesis of them all. The ideal dogmatician should be a good philologist, a good exegete, and a thorough student of Biblical criticism. He should know the

history of opinion and should understand the forces, ecclesiastical and philosophical, that in the successive centuries
have been at work on doctrinal beliefs. He should be able to
prove the separate doctrines from Scripture, to defend them
against error, and then, looking at them with the eye of an
architect, build them into a system. It is, therefore, very
seldom that we find an ideal systematic theologian. It is
seldom that scholarship, erudition and philosophical acumen
meet in such proportions in any individual as to produce this
result. We must be contented, therefore, to find men in whom
the predominance of any one of these qualities implies a
relative deficiency of the other two. We must bear this in
mind when we undertake to form an estimate of Dr. A. A.
Hodge. When he entered the Theological Seminary he had
the education which the ordinary American college offered its
students forty years ago. He was generally well-informed,
fond of physical science, interested in metaphysical problems,
and possessed of fair classical attainments. He was a diligent
student of Systematic Theology in the Seminary, as we have
already seen, and went out well furnished with a theology that
he understood thoroughly, and could use with facility. In
after life, and through a professorial career of over twenty
years he devoted himself exclusively to this department. He
made himself acquainted with the creed-statements of the
Church, and knew both their contents and the history of their
formation. He was a diligent reader of the books that trace
the development of doctrine, and that discuss historically or
polemically the great systems of theological opinion. He was
a student of the Bible, and divine testimony was his test of
every doctrinal statement. We can see in his " Outlines "
how constantly he appeals to the Scriptures, and how much he
refers to the great Reformed theologians of the seventeenth
century. Yet he was not distinguished either for erudition
or scholarship. His distinguishing characteristic as a theologian—I mean, as compared with others of the class to which

he belongs—was his power as a thinker. He had a mind of singular acuteness, and though never a professed student of metaphysics, was essentially and by nature a metaphysician. He had great reverence for God's word, and was jealous of the intrusion of philosophy into theology : but he was, nevertheless, by temperament and by habit, a philosophical theologian. He loved the " high priori road," and might have been seen walking on it in many an hour of quiet contemplation. He loved sometimes to take short cuts to his conclusions, seeing in advance of special induction that, since this and that are so, this and that are also so. He would not manipulate texts, however, to serve the purposes of foregone conclusions, nor build towering structures of dogma upon the *obiter dicta* of inspired writers. He had broad and scientific ideas of what a dogmatic induction ought to be, though he did not have the patience requisite for minute exegetical investigation. He was always reasoning on the relations of doctrines to each other, and to the great scheme of grace. But he never ceased to affirm our entire dependence upon the Bible for the authority of doctrines ; and so distrustful was he of human reason, so conscious at the same time of the injury that has resulted from the alliance of theology with a false philosophy, that I believe he would hardly have liked it if I had called him a philosophical theologian. Yet, that is what he was. Theology was to him a revealed world-view. He would have said with Henry B. Smith, " Incarnation in order to Redemption," and thereby have expressed his philosophy of religion. He would also have said, "Redemption and Incarnation for the greater glory of God," and thereby have expressed his philosophy of history.

Think then of Dr. A. A. Hodge as having an acute mind ; interested in theological speculation ; rethinking independently the old questions ; analytic in his mental processes ; full of scholastic subtleties ; bold, confident, intense in his convictions ; filled with reverence for good traditions ; holding the Reformed faith as a sacred trust, and also as a personal posses-

sion ; pervaded by this faith and living on terms of easy
familiarity with it ; able to distinguish between essence and
accident, and knowing when harmless idiosyncrasy runs into
serious doctrinal divergence ; strong in his convictions, but not
litigious ; tenacious of principle, but never sticking in the
bark : a sturdy, robust thinker, always ready to defend the
faith : a brilliant thinker, so that, as circumstances required,
he could send truth out in the shining drapery of soft and
beautiful speech ; or shoot it forth like forked lightning, hot
and scathing, to leave on the face of error the scarred record of
its presence—think of him, I say, as exhibiting this many-
sided mental expression, and you have my conception of the
type of theologians to which Dr. Hodge belonged. Beyond
all question he takes his place among the great men of America
and the great theologians of the world.

As to the contents of Dr. Hodge's theology it is enough to
say, that it was the theology of the Reformed Confessions and
the Shorter Catechism : it was the theology of Paul and Augustine, of Anselm and Calvin, of Turrettin and Amesius, of
William Cunningham and Charles Hodge.   He had no peculiar
views, and no peculiar method of organizing theological
dogmas.   He was interested in the methods of other men, and
probably took more trouble to compare them with one
another than his father had ever done : but after all, he had no
taste for theological architecture ; and the old-fashioned four-
square house, consisting of Theology, Anthropology, Soteriology, and Eschatology, with all its obvious faults of logic,
pleased him by its roominess and simplicity.   He taught the
same theology that his father had taught before him ; but he
was independent as well as reverent, and I prefer his statements sometimes to his father's.   He saw that his father had
occasionally spoken on such topics as Imputation and Original
Sin, without full knowledge of the history of opinion, and he
was more ready than were those who had passed through the
heat of controversy to see that the doctrine of Original Sin is

more essential to Calvinism than the mode of explaining or accounting for it, whether that mode be Imputation, Realism, or Heredity. A strict *jure divino* Presbyterianism would have found in him a poor advocate, organization being in his view not of the essence of the Church. He knew that prelacy was old, but he abhorred Apostolic Succession. He was a Presbyterian by inheritance, and so far as the main principles of Presbyterianism go, by conviction. He regarded all man-made schemes for the reunion of Christendom as Utopian, whether proceeding on the basis of the prayer-book or of prelacy. But he loved to dwell upon the historic continuity of the Church through all the centuries; accordingly he loved the "Christian year," and the great liturgical formulas that bind the centuries together. He was opposed to the reunion of the Old and New School Presbyterian Churches, though I believe he voted for it at the last. It was impossible not to see that his sympathies were broadening year by year. In this he was in fact only giving further proof that, theologically speaking, the sun of analysis had set, and the sun of synthesis had begun to shine. He saw, moreover, that in the new issues coming or already here, the old men on both sides would now stand shoulder to shoulder. He was delighted with Dr. Henry B. Smith's *Systematic Theology*, and cordially commended it to his classes. In a generous article, begun but never finished, it is pleasant to see how fairly and appreciatively he puts the two theologies, Dr. Smith's and Dr. Hodge's, side by side, and, overlooking minor points, treats them as the two great cis-Atlantic defences of the Calvinistic system. There was a hot controversy in the old days between Dr. Charles Hodge and Dr. Park, but in his late debate Dr. Park has had no greater admirer than he of whom we speak. Dr. Hodge had an accurate eye for theological perspective and presented truth in proper proportions. He held the church-doctrine regarding eternal punishment, and had he lived would have put on record a reasoned protest against the new belief in a second probation. But he would not have given the doctrine of eternal punishment a place co-ordinate with the divinity of Christ, or the inspiration of the Scriptures. He was a champion of Calvinistic theology, but he rightly thought that the most important matter now is not the defence of Calvinism, but the defence of Christianity. Accordingly, in all his later writings, he affirms with ever increasing warmth the doctrine that the Scriptures are the very word of God, and the only infallible rule of faith and practice. He was impatient of any literary tampering with the Bible that would weaken its authority, or compromise its inspiration ; and he saw in the appeal to Christian consciousness, an attempt to overthrow the supreme authority of the Scriptures, and set up a sub-jective rule of faith under the sanctions of a pious plausibility. Dr. Charles Hodge took pride, I think, in saying on the occa-sion of his semi-centennial celebration, that Princeton had never originated a single new idea. We all understand the sense in which that remark is true : it is in that sense, therefore, that I am to be understood when I say that Dr. A. A. Hodge made no original contributions to the science of theology. If he did, it was in his very able article entitled *Ordo Salutis*, published in the *Princeton Review*, which I think he prob-ably regarded as the best piece of theological work he ever did.

I have been trying to show what Dr. Hodge was as a theo-logian. Perhaps I shall succeed better if I remind you of what he did. There were three modes in which Dr. Hodge declared himself as a theologian : by the Press, the Pulpit, and the Professor's-Chair.

Great talkers seldom write much. Dr. Hodge was a genius in oral expression, in this respect resembling Dr. Archibald Alexander. But he wrote easily and with a running pen. His style is very spontaneous. His sentences artless, unstudied, sometimes exquisitely beautiful, sometimes cumbrous and greatly needing the services of the file. He had, in fact, two styles. He was, on the one hand, a scholastic and full of scholastic distinctions, to which he attached great importance. He was very analytical, and when he wrote insisted on making these distinctions, and on marking them with formal exactness as he went along. So that it is not always an easy matter to thread our way through a thicket of lower-case letters, Arabic figures, and the same repeated in brackets, each serving to mark the heads and sub-heads of an analysis increasing in minuteness at every step. This, however, is the style which we find in his " Outlines " and in the " Commentary on the Confession of Faith." It is the style in which he liked to do his serious work, and the only one by which, until recently, he had made himself known. On the other hand, he had a poet's eye for metaphor and a poet's ear for rhythm ; and, had he chosen, could have excelled as a writer of English prose. Some of his shorter articles reveal his capacity in this respect. We all remember the characteristics of his style in these articles,— especially the long sentences, crowded with dependent clauses, cumulative, now arrested in their flow for the writer to make distinctions or guard against being misunderstood, now moving slowly on under a cumbrous weight of words, now sparkling with simile, and then ending in a torrent of strong superlative epithets that were equally expressive of his admiration or his scorn. I recall his article on Dean Stanley in the *Catholic Presbyterian*, and his notice of Farrar's Bampton Lectures in the last *Presbyterian Review* as illustrating what I mean ; though I think that for effective writing and as illustrating a more chastened style, he has done nothing that is quite equal to his Biography of his father. His first book and the one by which he is best known was his " Outlines of Theology," published in 1860, and at different intervals since republished in Great Britain and translated into Welsh, modern Greek and Hindustani.* Of course this work owed its first appearance to the relation of the author to his father ; but it is an independent

*A translation into Malagasy is in progress and one into Italian contemplated.

study of the topic with which it deals, and, particularly in the enlarged edition, is valuable for its concise and comprehensive definitions. Dr. Hodge's book on the Atonement was written during the agitation of the Reunion question, and is still one of the best treatises we have upon the subject. His *Commentary on the Confession of Faith* is a very useful book, full of clear thinking and compact statement. Dr. Hodge contributed also important articles to Encyclopedias—Johnson's, McClintock and Strong's, and also the Schaff-Herzog. He published several theological tracts and pamphlets, and was one of the founders of the *Presbyterian Review*, to the pages of which he was a constant contributor. He wrote the important article entitled *Ordo Salutis* to which I have just referred ; he wrote a valuable controversial article for the *North American ;* another on the reunion of Christendom for *The Century ;* and an admirably written paper from his pen on the subject of "Religion in the Public Schools " has appeared since his death in the *New Princeton Review*. But he was not distinctively a writer of Review-articles as were his father and the late Dr. Atwater : his literary activity seemed to flow more naturally in other channels.

Speaking of Dr. Hodge the other day, some one asked me if he was the pastor of a church or just a professor. I regarded the question as a naïve expression of the popular estimate of the class to which I belong : and it may be true that we are not always interesting preachers. Those who reproach us for this sometimes do it kindly and under the guise of compliment, saying that we are too learned and preach over the heads of the people ; or they use great plainness of speech, saying that we ride hobbies in the pulpit, and preach old sermons full of the bones of theology which, like those of Ezekiel's valley of vision, are very many and very dry. Dr. Hodge's preaching was not of this sort. He had been a pastor during most of his ministerial life and had been settled over four congregations. He therefore knew the people. He preached old sermons, but, as he did not read them, he went through the process of thinking them over as often as he preached them. It was the old metal, but it went to the melting-pot every time, and the red wine of divine truth was poured into a shapely cup of the brightest silver. It was easy for him to preach, and he could interest and instruct an audience with very little effort. His materials were always within easy reach. Philosophical thought, theological dogma, historical facts, scientific illustrations, poetic images, personal experiences, local allusions, and suggestions springing out of recent conversations, were ever ready to do his bidding. He had only to will it, and they set themselves in array and passed the portal of his lips, a shining company, marching to the rhythm of a solemn music in the service of the Lord. There were some sermons that he preached habitually. They were never written, and, I fear, can never be reproduced. These sermons had grown from small beginnings. They were never elaborated, nor were they deliberately planned as great efforts. When a topic was in the preacher's mind he brooded over it, then preached upon it. If the subject opened promisingly, he would preach the sermon again. In the process of repetition from time to time it would naturally expand, take more definite shape, and become possessed of greater literary charm. In this way the sermon on the Resurrection became one of Dr. Hodge's great discourses, and also that on the Person of Christ, and the Koinonia, and Miracles, and the Immanence of God, and—best of all, perhaps greatest of all—the sermon that he loved to preach so well, that has been listened to by so many congregations, that was preached in the Seminary Chapel and the College Chapel in Princeton, that was preached in this city, and New York, and Washington and Edinburgh : the sermon on "My Father's house of many mansions." There are few preachers like him. Indeed, he stood alone. To hear him when he was at his best was something never to be forgotten. All in all—in thought, expression and delivery, each of these great sermons was a wonderful combination : it was a union of theology, philosophy, Christian experience, knowledge of human nature, quaint humor, elaborate description, a metaphor dropped as a diamond unobserved might fall out of a casket, facile utterance, a disdain of elocution, few gestures, the face lighted up, the eye opened wide as though the speaker saw a vision of glory, the voice trembling when the Saviour's name is mentioned, the sensitive frame responding to the pressure of emotion, and emotion finding vent at last in involuntary tears.

Dr. Hodge was a man of wit and humor. He had a keen sense of the ludicrous. Had he chosen to make preaching a matter of Sunday-entertainment, he could have preached to packed audiences in our great cities. But with him preaching was a serious business ; he thought that the pulpit was no place for joke or witticism, and never preached without producing upon his audience an impression of solemnity. As words are commonly used among us, I feel that I am employing a tame expression when I say that he was a great preacher. I think he was one of the greatest preachers in this land ; and in comparison with some who, by their concessions to a popular demand for pulpit levity and meretricious rhetoric are feeding the multitudes who listen to them with that which is not bread, and are called great by the world, he was—I am tempted to use his own favorite extravagance of speech, and say that he was—" infinitely " great.

Yet let me not exaggerate : Dr. Hodge could be disappointing at times. Though he never failed to be instructive, the glow of enthusiasm was sometimes lacking ; and if anything occurred to interfere with his spontaneity, the weak voice and labored utterance formed a union hostile to oratorical effect. Nor do I doubt that he revealed the highest qualities of his mind most frequently in the professor's-chair. As a former pupil, now a Free Church minister in Glasgow, writes : " It was in the class-room that he shone, or in a company small enough or congenial enough for him ' to commit himself unto them.' "

It is possible to entertain several different views of what a professor's function ought to be. Much depends upon the department and not a little upon the man. According to one view, a professorship means an opportunity for special investigation and leisurely research, the results of which are communicated in the lecture-room to men who desire knowledge. The desire to know being presupposed, the matter and not the manner of presentation is the main thing. The subject is supposed to be treated completely. If the student does not intend to prosecute it further, it is probable that his best education in it is secured by his placing himself in contact with a living master and then reproducing in written form the substance of what he hears. If he intends to prosecute the subject by independent research, as good a preparation for it as he can have is probably of the kind described. According to another view, the academic lecture is intended to stimulate interest in the department to which it belongs. It may deal in outline with the whole department, or be a discussion of a single phase of it. In either case, it is the particular contribution that the professor brings to the advancement of his science. But it is not intended to be a substitute for independent reading, and that mastery of the subject which only independent reading can give. With this view of the purpose which it serves, a great deal depends upon its form : and, instead of being a series of paragraphs dictated to a class, or a compact and solid mass of fact or argument to be read slowly and transferred to note-books, it is written with some regard to the requirements of literary art as something addressed to the ear and intended to please as well as to inform. According to still another view, the professor's business is to see that a certain definite body of instruction is safely and surely transferred from his mind to the minds of those who hear him. He is not only or even chiefly to present truth that men may receive if they choose : he is to see that they receive it. Each type of professorial work, when it is of a high order, will secure good results, and it is not well to institute comparisons between methods that are so different. The teacher of the first class will reach those who, either by natural taste, or the pressure of sufficient motive, are willing to undergo the labor of diligent note-taking. The man of the second class will communicate less knowledge, but will, perhaps, make up for this by the enthusiasm which he awakens. Men will, at least, listen to him with interest, will be entertained, will absorb something, and a few·will be put upon the road of special investigation and independent inquiry. The man of the third class, being less intent on giving than on seeing that the students get what he gives, will succeed in filling the largest number of minds with his teaching. He will, perhaps, so emphasize his duty as a teacher, that his students will miss the charm of feeling that he is a fellow-laborer with them in fields which they are invited to enter, and which to comers even as late as they still hold out the promise of reward ; but he will succeed in incorporating the body of truth which he expounds into their mental life. He will give them what can never be forgotten : a $\chi\tau\tilde{\eta}\mu\alpha$ ἐς ἀεί— something that is their own, something indeed that is part of their very selfhood.· Now it is easy to see that since Systematic Theology constitutes the matter that men are to preach, it is very important that the teaching of this department should be of the kind last referred to ; and I regard Dr. Hodge as the greatest teacher of this type I ever knew. He was exacting and intolerant of indolence and irregularity. He was very far from being a simple hearer of recitations, but he insisted first of all that students should know the text-book—and they usually did. He made use of his father's Systematic Theology ; but that book in his hands was like an illuminated mediæval manuscript, and from title-page to colophon, it was filled with the bright, beautiful, quaint and sometimes grotesque creations of his fancy. The students saw every doctrine as it presented itself to his vision. They benefited by his power of concise statement and clear definition. He held up the representative systems of theology with such sharpness of outline and such accuracy of articulation, that they knew them as one knows the face of a familiar friend. They questioned him, and he answered their questions. They raised objections, and so woke in him the hot fires of his polemic. They failed sometimes to comprehend a dogma, and he swept the universe for illustrations, and poured them out so copiously and with such manifest spontaneity, that they overwhelmed him with their applause. "And yet," says one of his admiring pupils,* "he never confused simile and logic ; and although his wealth of happy imagery led him to support many of his arguments with an illustration, he often warned his students never to mistake a metaphor for an argument. His logic was the logic of the Westminster divines, admirably suited to its purpose, exact, straightforward, and not lacking in the warmth of intellectual and emotional enthusiasm." I cannot do better than continue the quotation : " His patience and intellectual charity were both large, and he allowed the greatest freedom of debate to his scholars. In these contests, he was always chivalrous, and dismounted to meet his adversary on equal terms. ... His many peculiarities of speech and manner never impaired his courtesy as a gentleman or his dignity as a professor. He had a powerful brain, a large heart, and the simple faith of a little child. He taught the knowledge of God with the learning of a scholar, the sympathy of a loving man, and the enthusiasm of a loving Christian."

" I was struck," says Dr. Shedd, " with his great directness and sincerity, intellectually as well as morally. His mind, like his heart, worked without ambiguity or drawback. Hence his energy in the perception and statement of truth—a quality that showed itself in his uncommon ability to popularize scientific theology." This is said in full appreciation of Dr.

*Rev. Paul van Dyke.

Hodge's position as a scientific theologian, as will appear from another passage, where the same eminent divine says: " His published works show both logical and theological power. While founding upon the massive and luminous system of his venerated father, he methodizes, condenses, and fortifies with an originality that evinces his competence to have made a system of his own."   And yet I think I am assigning Dr. A. A. Hodge his true place among contemporary theologians in this country and abroad if I say, in words suggested by the happy phrase of Dr. Shedd, that he is pre-eminently the popularizer of scientific theology.   No better illustration of his power in this respect need be asked for than his lectures delivered in this city last winter.   I have not alluded to them under any of the three categories to which reference has been made, for they are a combination of his powers in each of these three forms of manifestation, and are, indeed, the coronation of his public life.   They were addressed to eager ears in this city, but they were greeted, also, by eager eyes when they went out on their wider mission upon the wings of the newspaper press : and they will soon appear in a volume that will find a welcome, I hope, in many thousand households—and not in Presbyterian households only, for the truths declared in these lectures are, for the most part, the common inheritance of all who love the Lord; and by his defence of them Dr. Hodge has made Christendom his debtor.   He was building better than he knew.   I remember very well how his characteristic modesty showed itself in connection with the printing of these lectures : how it distressed him to have his own quaint and sometimes queer colloquialisms brought under his eye through the fidelity of a shorthand report ; and how, if he had acted upon his own impulses, he would have stripped these birds of paradise of half their plumage.   But I am glad that we shall have at least one volume that can be trusted as a faithful mirror of his mental life.   These lectures are not simply illustrations of his academic power, though his pupils will recognize in them the manner with which they are familiar. Nor are they simply sermons, though his ordinary pulpit discourse possessed many of the qualities that are present here. The preacher and the professor are alike visible in these lectures, and both in their best estate. Dr. Hodge was to have delivered another course of lectures in Philadelphia this winter. He was lecturing to large audiences in Orange, New Jersey, when taken ill ; and inquiries were already afoot respecting the possibility of having these lectures delivered in other cities. When I think of what he was doing, and of what, had his life been spared, he might have done, I am reminded of the day when Abelard lectured to vast audiences in Paris, waking a century from its intellectual lethargy, and filling the popular mind with enthusiasm for philosophical theology. And who can doubt that it is some work like that which Dr. Hodge was so well qualified to do, that our age and country need? I do not take a discouraged view of things. As I look along the rugged coast-line of the centuries, my eye falls upon no high-water mark above my head, telling me where the tide of religious life once reached. I believe we watch to-day a rising tide ; though at this moment, it may be, we are standing on the sand left wet by a receding wave. But when I think that the narrow strip exposed to view by this receding wave extends so far adown the shores of life, and that the interval between its crepitant retreat and its tumultuous rebound may involve the fortunes of a genera-tion, I have some sympathy with those who face the religious outlook with feelings bordering on fear. We see men turning away from God. They are drinking the wine of prosperity, and are intoxicated with worldly success ; or they have come to feel the hollowness of the world's promises, and have no refuge in a better life. We witness excess of luxury, and begin to apprehend the drying up of the channels of benevolence. We take the census of the church-going population, and find that our houses of worship are poorly filled in the morning and almost deserted at night. Men who have never investigated a single doctrine pride themselves on their intellectual independence, and fall easy victims to the fallacies of a shallow scepticism. Ministers of the gospel feel the burden that is placed upon them ; and, in order to escape the imputation of dealing in platitudes, or in their endeavor to lift the gospel chariot out of the rut of routine, sometimes secularize their holy calling, deal in pulpit flippancies, and ensnare their audiences into the hearing of the gospel by introducing it as a side-issue, and by way of remote allusions. We need a theological revival. We need an era of conviction. We need—if this appalling inertia and religious indifference is to be overcome—the outbreak of an epidemic of faith. We need a revolution of thought that shall reach the core of manhood and that shall make men see that they have forsaken God, the fountain of living waters, and have hewn out unto themselves cisterns, broken cisterns, that can hold no water. We need a prophet who can speak in words that shine and burn. Alas ! our Elijah has been taken away, and there is no one who can wear his mantle. We can only hope, that, by the blessing of God, a portion of his spirit may come upon his surviving colleagues, upon the ministers of this city who meet here to-day to do honor to his memory, and upon the whole Church that is bereft of his leadership.

It may seem to some of you that my admiration of Dr. Hodge has made me extravagant in his praise, and that standing in the shadow of a great sorrow I have supposed that this theological eclipse is visible over a wider area than it is. It is easy to fall into this mistake. But I believe that the judgments I have expressed are those of sober truth. From far and near, from other lands, and from all quarters of this land, the testimonies have come in that speak of the loss which Christendom has sustained in Dr. Hodge's death. Dr. Cairns, of Edinburgh, gives expression to a sentiment shared by multitudes, when in a letter to Mrs. Hodge, he says : " The whole Evangelical Church has lost in him a powerful and intrepid defender of its best and dearest beliefs ; and—strong as is the array of Presbyterians on your continent—he was a leader whom we could ill afford to lose."

In presenting Dr. Hodge as a theologian, I have already in great measure described the man ; and yet I think we must come a little closer to his personality to get a full impression of what he was, and to understand the charm that invested his public life. The blending of attributes in his case, and the interpenetration of his public and his private life, are very well appreciated by his pupil, Mr. Salmond, from whose letter I quoted a little while ago, when he says : " His courageous earnestness, with its other side of playful humor and quaint hyperbole, his burning sympathy with all that is good, and burning indignation at all that is false or mean ; his personal modesty, amounting even to shyness, with its counterpart of fearless and candid courage in defence of truth—qualities like these made him a model professor and an invaluable friend."

Dr. Hodge was a high-minded, warm-hearted Christian gentleman. He was cast in a unique mould and was *sui generis*. He could only have failed to be a gentleman through an entire suspension of the law of heredity ; for he was allied on both his father's and his mother's side, and for several generations, to some of the best and most distinguished families in this city and this land. Aristocratic sympathies were very strong in him, and they found expression sometimes in an extravagant avowal of Toryism that was partly jest, and partly based upon a real conservatism of sentiment respecting the philosophy of social life. Though not violating proprieties, he had no sedulous regard for artificial and meaningless con-ventionalities, and sometimes carried his indifference to what other people say and do, a little further than he need have done. Like all men of genius, he was eccentric ; and like most positive natures, he had violent likes and dislikes. If he was in an abstracted mood, he might wear an air of indifference, which was in no sense intended for coldness. But he made no effort at concealment if men were not congenial to him, and he recognized his right to " shut men out of his universe," as he used to express it, without feeling that he had abated any of their claims. He was not indifferent to the luxuries that money will purchase nor to the avenues of usefulness that it opens ; and when associated with refinement, he had great respect both for it and its possessor : but he hated the sordid temper that money-making so often begets, and he had an unmeasured contempt for the " gold that gilds the straitened forehead of the fool." I think, too, that he sometimes under-estimated the dimensions of the rich man's forehead. When his prejudices were not involved he could separate the chaff from the wheat in his estimates of men ; and I have known him to tolerate a great deal of chaff for the sake of a very little wheat. He was a quick interpreter of human nature, discriminating in his judgments, and only slow—by reason of his own superlative honesty—to see the presence of sinister motives. At the same time, I cannot say that he was eminently judicial : his blood was too warm for that. He had a keen sense of the ludicrous, was full of pleasantry, and, sometimes, when unbending after serious effort, would abandon himself to a lightness of manner and an Oriental luxuriance of speech, that I have no doubt have sometimes shocked those who regard the Professor of Theology as committed by his oath of office to a very sedate behaviour. I think he had somewhat against any man who could not appreciate a joke. He was full of persiflage, and was never happier than when he met his match in an encounter of wit. His imagination never slept. It was constantly weaving new fancies and coining new figures of speech. He lived, indeed, in his imagination and systematically kept the ideal clock in advance of local time. He was always foreseeing contingencies and providing against them. He crossed bridges before he came to them. Hence he was prompt, prudent and always beforehand. Hence, too, he suffered twice : suffered in the actual experience of pain, and suffered in anticipation of suffering. His imagination took hold of the possibilities of experience in dying and he shrank from them. The subject was often in his mind, and had been pondered, I doubt not, profoundly, although in his conversation on this and kindred themes, he would commonly veil the majestic depths of his nature by the ripples of pleasantry. He loved the beautiful, was fond of surrounding himself with beautiful things, and found no small share of his enjoyment in seeing how others enjoyed them. He was humble and had the most depreciative estimate of himself. He was capable of admiration, and I never knew a man who was so ready to give ungrudging praise. He loved with a large heart and a generous and most tender affection. Such a friend as he one rarely finds in this selfish world. I am glad to quote this testimony regarding him from one whom he greatly admired. Says Professor Young of Princeton: " I remember him as one of the most amusing, humorous and witty men I ever knew. He was one of the most affectionate and tender-hearted, one of the most imaginative and poetic, and also, as such men sometimes are not, one of the most transparently and purely sincere and truthful. ... I shall never forget some of our walks and talks when questions were raised and discussed relating to the incessant activity of God as the foundation of physical entities and forces ; or to the correspondence between revealed and humanly discovered truth, and the right relations and mutual respect to be observed between the interpreter of Scripture and the investigator of science ; or our debates as to the place and duties of earnest Christians in political society. I feel that I owe more to him intellectually and morally, for perhaps half a dozen hours of this sort, than to any but a very, very few of the instructors of my youth. He was broad and tolerant, an utter despiser of shams and conventionalities, and he went right to the bottom of things, penetrating almost instantly to the rocks and vacuums which equally limit our human powers of thought."

Dr. Hodge was a timid child, and perhaps would have made a poor soldier. But he had the courage of his convictions. He was sincere and scorned duplicity. He was honest and chivalrous, and hated everything that was sinister or mean. He was devoted to his work and showed no sign of self-seeking. Men sometimes serve God through their ambitions, but his ambition was to serve God. Dr. Hodge had been religious from childhood. The type of piety which he saw in his father, and in Dr. Archibald Alexander, whom he always reverenced as a saint and a sage, gave tone, I doubt not, to his religious experience. He had been chastened by sorrow. First his mother died, then the mother of his children passed away. He knew, therefore, how to interpret grief and to comfort others with the comfort wherewith he himself had been comforted of God. I shall never forget the prayer he made at the funeral of a Christian physician : how, taking the varied threads of human experience, he wove them into a veil of exquisite texture, and laid it across the face of death—how in the seeming medley of earth's music, through changing keys and in spite of discord, he traced the love of Christ and found in it the *motif* that unified it all—how he led us along the winding way of life, from light to dark, from dark to light again, until we entered the celestial city—and how he left us there alone with God.

Dr. Hodge was deeply interested in the spiritual welfare of both the College and the Seminary. He was not simply a theological professor ; he was a great spiritual force. In a note received yesterday, Dr. McCosh says : " I will be glad if, in your notice of our friend Dr. A. A. Hodge, you mention that he is nearly as much missed in the College as in the Seminary. He took the deepest interest in us. He often preached to us, and preached with great felicity of illustration. From time to time he addressed our students at their prayer-meetings, and ever brought the weightiest truths to bear practically on character and life. We all feel that we have lost a friend: a loss to us, a gain to heaven above." A loss indeed, to us, a gain to him and heaven. And so sweet thoughts are mingled with our sorrow. So are they comforted who called him father and to whom he was so dear. So finds she solace in her grief who wears to-day the drapery of widowhood. So they whose thought of him grows tender when memory brings back the far-off years, find resting-place for hope in the Father's house of many mansions. He said that heaven was the "consummate flower of the universe": he knows its beauty and its fragrance now. He likened its welcome to that which a fond parent gives a beautiful daughter whose school-days are over: he knows to-day how far the reality transcends even his most tender thought. Those who loved him best will grudge him least his welcome home ; and the pain of separation will be lessened when they think that it is only a little while, and then God's love shall set them at his side again.

Dear friend, farewell ! Thy going has made Heaven near. Full many a vase of comely phrase I keep among my treasures as witness to the cunning of thy hand. Thy loving words shall live in memory's garden like sweet forget-me-nots : and I will hold the broken thread of our high discourse until we meet again.

I

GOD—HIS NATURE AND RELATION TO THE UNIVERSE.

THREE questions obviously lie at the foundation, not only of all man's religious knowledge, but of every possible form of knowledge :—

1. Is there a God ?
2. What is God ?
3. What is God's relation to the universe ?

And if he does sustain a relation to the universe which is in any degree intelligible to us, a fourth question emerges :—

4. What is the sphere, nature, and extent of his providential action upon or in reference to his creatures ?

The answer to the first question, as to the fact of God's existence, we propose to assume as granted. The most certain of all truths is the existence of God.

I. *The second question*, therefore, presents itself : WHAT DO WE KNOW AS TO THE ESSENTIAL NATURE OF GOD ?

God reveals himself to us through the simultaneously concurrent action of two sources of knowledge, neither of which could give us the information separately. We are, each one, immediately conscious that we are intelligent, moral, voluntary agents and true causes. This, and all that this involves, comes to us by consciousness. It is the most immediate and certain of all knowledge, and that upon which all other knowledge rests ; and we give definite

expression to this self-knowledge when we call ourselves
spirits and persons. It is precisely this, and nothing else,
that we mean by the words " spirit " and " person." When
we come to look upon the course of external nature, to
reflect upon our own origin and history internal and external, and upon the history of the human race and the
life of the general community of which we form a part,
we immediately and indubitably discern everywhere the
presence and control of a Being like ourselves in kind. In
that intelligible order which pervades the infinite multiplicity and heterogeneity of events, and which makes
science possible, we see and certainly know the presence of
intelligence, of personal will, of moral character—that is, of
all that is connoted by our common term " personal spirit."
God is seen to be of common generic character with ourselves. The great difference we see is that, while we are
essentially limited in respect to time or space or knowledge
or power, God, the personal agent we see at work in
nature and history, is essentially unlimited in all these respects. The only reason that so many students of natural
science have found themselves unable to see God in nature,
is that their absorption in nature has made them lose sight
of their own essential personality. Hence they have attempted to interpret the phenomena of self-consciousness
in the terms of mechanical nature, instead of interpreting
nature under the light of self-conscious spirit. But the
scientist, after all, comes before his science, the reader before
the book he deciphers. And the intelligibility of nature
proves its intelligent source, and the essential likeness of
the Author of nature, who reveals himself in his work, and
of the interpreter of nature, who retraces his processes and
appreciates alike the intellectual and the artistic character
of his design.

Since God is infinite, of course a definition of him is
impossible. Obviously, no bounds can be drawn around

the boundless. God can be known only so far forth as he has chosen to reveal himself. And being essentially infinite, every side and element of his nature is infinite, and every glimpse we have of his being involves the outlying immensity or the transcendent perfection which cannot be known. But since we have been created in his likeness, and since we discern him in all his works as, like ourselves, an intelligent and moral personal spirit, we can define our idea of him by stating (1) the *genus,* or kind, to which he is known to belong, and (2) the *differentia,* or differences, which distinguish him from all other beings of that kind. The best definition of the idea of God ever given is constructed on this principle. First, as to his kind: God is a personal Spirit. Second, as to his difference from all other spirits: God is infinite, eternal, unchangeable, and in all his moral attributes absolutely perfect; and he is infinite, eternal, and unchangeable alike in his being, in his wisdom, in his power, etc., etc.

First, as to his kind. God is a personal Spirit. We mean by this precisely what we mean when we affirm that we ourselves are personal spirits. This conception comes wholly from consciousness, and it is absolutely certain. We see and know God, as manifested in his activities alike in the whole world within us and around us as far as the remotest star, to be another of the same kind with ourselves. We know ourselves to be intelligent causes. We see him likewise to be an intelligent Cause, and the original, the absolute, and the perfect One.

In applying this law in constructing our idea of God, we proceed according to three principles of judgment:—(1.) That of *causality.* We judge the nature of every cause from what we see of its effects; we judge the character of every author from what we read of his works. So the manifold works of God, past and present, physical and spiritual, reveal his nature as First Cause. (2.) That of *negation.*

We deny of him all those attributes and conditions the possession of which involves imperfection—for example, materiality, bodily parts or passions, the limitations of time or space.   (3.) That of *eminence*.   We attribute to him all that is found to be excellent in ourselves, in absolute perfection and in unlimited degree.

Second. This leads, necessarily, to the discrimination, in the second place, of those properties which distinguish God from all other personal spirits.

(1.) We know ourselves as causes : we can really originate new things.   But we are dependent and limited causes.   We did not originate, and we cannot sustain, ourselves.   We can put forth our causal energy only under certain conditions, and we can bring to pass only a very limited class of effects.   But God as a cause is absolutely independent and unlimited.   He is the uncaused First Cause of all things.   He is an eternal and necessary Being who has his own cause in himself.   He is not only the first link in the chain of causation, but he is the everywhere present sustaining and actuating basis of all dependent existence and the originating con-cause in all causation, because we and all other dependent causes act *only as we live and move and have all our being in him.*

(2.) We know ourselves always and necessarily as existing, thinking, and acting under the limitations of time and space ; we can think or act only under these limitations. But God necessarily transcends all these limitations, and condescends to them only on occasion, at his own pleasure, in the way of self-limitation.

We began to be at a definite period in the past.   We continue to exist and to think and to act through a ceaseless succession of moments, the present moment ever emerging out of the past and immerging into the future.   But God is without beginning or succession or end.   All duration, past, present, and future, is always equally comprehended in his infinite consciousness as the ETERNAL Now.

We are in space definitely, and are surrounded by it, and pass from one position to another through all the intermediate portions of space in succession. But God fills all space : not by extension, like the water of the sea or as the atmosphere ; not by multiplication, nor by rapid movement, like an ubiquitous general along the line of his army ; not as represented by his agents, as the head of an army or state may be said to be, and to act wherever his agents carry out his orders ; not by his knowledge or his power merely, as when an astronomer may be said to be in thought wherever his telescope points, or a great sovereign to reign wherever his laws are obeyed. But by reason of his own infinite perfection, Father, Son, and Holy Ghost are in their whole undivided being present at every point of space at every moment of time. The whole God is always everywhere : *within all things*, acting from within outward from the centre of every atom, and from the innermost springs of the life and thought and feeling and will of every spirit ; *without all things*, embracing them as an infinite abyss, and acting upon them in a thousand ways from without.

(3.) We know ourselves as possessing the spoiled and defaced lineaments of a moral character, the main elements of which are truth, purity, justice, benevolence. We know that God, who has revealed his character in the external physical world, in human history, and in the person of his Son Jesus Christ, is the absolutely perfect norm of our moral idea. Our morality is reflected, his is original and radiant. Ours is defective, his is absolute. It has become the mode of those who pose as the advanced thinkers of this luxurious age to emphasize the benevolence of God at the expense of his immaculate holiness and justice. They teach us that the cultured mind finds the old doctrines of expiation and perdition utterly inconsistent with its better idea of God. They think the great God "altogether such an one as themselves." The ground of this widely-advertised opinion is purely subjective—the Christian consciousness of the cultured *élite* in contradistinction to the historic Christian consciousness of the ages. The facts are all on the other side. The terrible record of him in history, blazed all along its line with the fires of judgment kindled by a sin-hating God, the death-throes of individuals and of nations, the answering cry of the human conscience uttered in the ceaseless rites of blood on altars and penitential stools—the entire voice of revelation, from the cherubim with the fiery sword driving out the homeless, helpless first pair from Eden, the frowning thunders and blasting lightnings of Sinai, the history of Canaan exterminated and of Israel chastised, the awful horrors of Gethsemane and Calvary, the destruction of Jerusalem and the dispersion and bondage of the Jews, to the final issue of the lake of fire set as the background of the picture of the Paradise regained, the eternal wailing and the smoke of torment ascending for ever and ever,—all these FACTS stand as the unquestionable evidence of the existence of *other* perfections in God besides benevolence.

II. *The third question* remains: WHAT RELATION DOES GOD SUSTAIN TO THE UNIVERSE HE HAS CALLED INTO BEING?

It is very evident that since we are able to comprehend neither God's essential being, nor his mode of existence superior to the limits of either time or space, nor the nature of his agency in creating, upholding in being or in governing his creatures, we cannot by any central principle or *a priori* mode of reasoning think out a perfect theory of his relation to the universe. We can only state severally the separate facts as we know them, leaving their complete elucidation and reconciliation to the future. And we are both assisted and confirmed in our efforts to present all the facts comprehended, by the circumstance that different heretical schools of thought emphasize one or another of these facts, while they deny or suppress the rest. Here we have a new and striking illustration of the universal principle that all heretical dogmas are partial truths— true in what they assert, false in what they deny or ignore. Orthodoxy is always catholic truth, embracing and integrating all the possibly separate and apparently incongruous parts and aspects of the truth. Thus in the present instance we have the Agnostics, who maintain that the Infinite is the Unknowable; the Deists, who set God apart from the world, separate upon his throne in heaven; and those who maintain exclusively the fact that God is immanent, or uniformly and universally present in all things, while they deny or ignore his equal transcendence above and over all things. True Christian Theism maintains all these partial truths as equally parts of the one truth. God is at once the unfathomable Abyss, the transcendent Father, King, and Judge, the immanent and vital Spirit.

First. God is unknowable, the infinite Abyss of darkness in which the universe floats as an atom. Herbert Spencer's philosophy emphasizes the truth that the more science advances, the more must the questions as to origin, first cause, ultimate force and end, be pushed back into darkness. If you light a spark in a starless night, it will fill a small sphere of illuminated space extending equidistant in all directions. If the spark becomes a candle, if the candle becomes a flame of gas, if the gas-flame becomes an electric arc, if the electric arc becomes a sun,—in every case the sphere of light will grow as the cube of its radius; and as the sphere of light becomes larger and larger, in exact proportion will it be enfolded within an ever-growing sphere of darkness. In this sense, the more we meditate upon him, God is ever beyond. In this sense, while the sphere of human knowledge is ever increasing, and will through eternity never cease to increase, God is always unknowable. And the sphere of a creature's knowledge, be it that of an infant, or of a man, or of a philosopher, or of a prophet, or of saint or archangel in heaven, will float as a point of light athwart the bosom of that God who is the infinite Abyss for ever.

This tremendous fact conditions all human knowledge in every stage of it. We can know anything only imperfectly, whether in science or in theology, because we know things only in parts, and can never comprehend the absolute whole. The botanist cannot comprehend a single flower except as he takes in the whole plant, nor the whole plant except as he takes in the whole species, nor the whole species except as he takes in the whole genus, nor the whole genus except as he takes in the whole system of organized life, the entire fauna and flora and all their history on the earth. The teacher may easily explain the laws and movements of the solar system to his class, but he knows them himself very partially, since he knows so little of the realities or of the history of the stellar universe of which the solar system is so small a dependency. All things go out into mystery. All our knowledge is conditioned upon the essential unknowableness of God. In all our knowing and in all our worship, the infinite God is always beyond.

This side of the truth is taught as clearly in the oldest word of revelation as it is in the latest word of science. " Canst thou by searching find out God ? canst thou find out the Almighty unto perfection ? It is as high as heaven ; what canst thou do ? deeper than hell ; what canst thou know ? The measure thereof is larger than the earth, and broader than the sea " (Job xi. 7–9).

Second. God is transcendent ; that is, he is a distinct Person, separate from the world and from all other persons —who speaks to us face to face, who commands our wills and regulates our lives from on high; who upon occasion, when he wills, acts upon the universe or any part of it from without. He is objective to each one of us, as a distinct Person, alike when he speaks to us and when we speak to him. He created all things out of nothing. The universe is not a modification of his essence, nor is it confused with his substance; he is essentially something other than any one of his creatures—the extramundane God. The relation he sustains to the universe, therefore, is analogous to that of a maker to his work, of a preserver and governor to a mechanism, of a father to his children, of a moral ruler to his intelligent and responsible subjects.

This view of the nature of God and of his relation to the world, and especially his relation to created spirits, is common to Deists and Christian Theists. It is denied utterly by Pantheists, and it is ignored in whole or in part by the modern special advocates of the immanence of God as containing all the essential truth related to our interests in the matter. Yet this view just presented of God's separate personality and agency and objectivity to man and transcendence above the world is true and infinitely important, although we concede that it is not the whole truth known to us on the subject. The view of God as extramundane is essentially the moral view of his relation to the world; that which recognizes his immanence is preeminently the religious view. If he be not extramundane, if he be not a separate transcendent Person revealing himself objectively, commanding from above and working upon his creatures from without, it follows that he cannot sustain either social or governmental relations to us. He cannot be truly our Father, our Lawgiver, or our moral Governor, or our Judge distributing rewards and punishments; he cannot come down at his will from without and work miracles of grace or power as signs and seals to his intelligent creatures.

This is the prominent view embraced by the mass of the worshippers in all theistic religions, Jews, Christians, and Mohammedans alike, among all historic bodies of Christians, Greeks, Romanists, and all classes of Protestants. It is realized in the consciousness of every repentant sinner and of every believing Christian. It is implied in all faith and obedience, in all prayer and praise, and hence in all the psalms, hymns, and prayers of the Church. It is taught equally in all Scriptures, the New Testament as well as the Old, which show forth Jehovah as sitting upon his throne in heaven, and as sending his messengers and as transmitting his energies and his judgments from heaven to earth, and as marshalling the hosts of heaven and the nations of the earth from afar. Above all, is this truth made patent as the sky, a matter of daily personal experience, in the personal incarnation of God in Christ. Christ is God. Christ is the same to-day and for ever as he was when he lived on earth. God is therefore a Person who is outside of and distinct from the world and all other persons; who speaks to us, and we speak to him; who hears us, and we hear him; who commands, leads, and guides us from without as another; and in whose personal society and under whose blessed reign we shall be transcendently happy for ever.

Third. God is immanent. He is everywhere present in every point of space and within the inmost constitution of all created things at the same time. God's activity springs up from the central seat of energy in all second causes, and acts from within through them as well as from without upon them. He reveals himself in us and to us through our own subjectivity, as well as objectively through the things presented to our senses. He is the universal present and active basis of all being and action, the First Cause ever living and acting in all second causes.

This is evident—(1.) From the essential nature of God

as omnipresent and as First Cause, the foundation of all dependent existence and the ultimate source of all energy. (2.) This is evident from what we see very plainly in the entire sphere and history of the physical universe. The impression made by the most transient observation is abundantly confirmed by science, that the continuity of physical causation through all worlds, through every sphere of mechanical, chemical, and vital action, and through all the succeeding ages, is absolutely unbroken. There are no broken links, no sudden emergencies of disconnected events, but a continuous sequence of cause and effect everywhere.

The deistical conception of God's relation to the universe is analogous to that of a human mechanist to the machinery he has made and operates. He sits outside his engine, feeds its forces, adjusts its parts, controls its action, and thus directs its energies upon the accomplishment of its appointed ends.

The conception of God and of his action as immanent in the universe, acting from within through the spontaneities of the things he has made, rather than upon them from without, is analogous rather to the action of the vital principle of a plant, which as a plastic architectonic energy is ever present within the germ from its first formation, and continues to control all the natural physical forces engaged in the upbuilding of the organism through all its organs during its entire life. The works of man are built up by the adding of part to part by external forces. The works of God grow continuously through the evolution of germs from within, by internal forces. Thus, in spite of the infinite number and diversity of the forces interacting in all the physical universe, and of all the wills interacting in human society, the history alike of the physical universe and of human society presents the absolutely continuous unfolding of a single plan.

The same great truth is illustrated in our religious

experience. A divine power not ourselves, working for righteousness, enters us on the side of our own subjectivity, and is confluent always with our most spontaneous and least deliberative exercises. Thus, regeneration is an effect of God's immediate working within the soul below our consciousness, giving a new character to all our conscious states and acts. God works within us constantly to will, and by willing to do, of his good pleasure. And thus also, while each book of Holy Scripture was written by a human author in the language and style peculiar to his age, his nation, and his personal character, and in the perfectly free exercise of all his faculties, yet all the books are the WORD OF GOD. His suggestive, elevative, and directive influence has so worked in them from within, mingling freely with their own spontaneities, that the writing is at once both God's and theirs, both supernatural and natural, because they, being men, wrote as they were moved by the immanent Spirit of God. Angels and men influence one another from without by objective presentations; God influences all from within by subjective impulses. Hence we realize the complementary truth that we live and move in him and have all our being in him. In some distant sense, as the birds draw their life and have their being in the air, God is the one essential, fundamental environment and life-condition of all creatures.

The consequences of this great fact of the divine immanence are :—

(1.) The whole universe exists in God. As the stars in the ether, as the clouds in the air, the whole universe floats on the pulsing bosom of God.

(2.) All the intelligence manifested in the physical universe, all that larger and timeless intelligence which embraces and directs the limited and transient intelligence of the human actors in the drama of history, is of

God. In the physical world we see an infinitude of
blind, unconscious forces, apparently independent in
their nature and source, working together harmoniously
to build upon a continuous and universal plan the most
intricate and harmonious results ; as the great cathedral
dedicated to St. Peter in Rome rose out of the marble
quarries of Italy through the agency of multitudes of
thoughtless men and beasts of labour working without
concert for many years, yet conspiring to balance harmoniously in the air a miracle of mechanical construc-
tion and of artistic beauty. It was because all the agents
in that work, of all kinds and during the entire period
of its development, were subject to the suggestive, elevative, and directive inspiration of the great Michael
Angelo.

(3.) Hence, also, in the third place, it follows that all
the effect-producing energy seen in the physical universe
is ultimately the efficiency of God. The First Cause
must be the efficient cause of all second causes and the
source of all the dependent energy they ever exercise.
As the sun's rays, shining on the tropic seas, raise by
evaporation the vast oceans of aërial vapours which, condensed by our northern cold, precipitate in rain and
generate the immense forces of our rivers and water-
falls ; as ultimately all the energies of nature distributed
from our central suns hold the worlds together in the
form of gravity, and are differentiated into the thousand
forms of vegetable and animal life, and into the mechanical movement of the currents of winds and tides and of
electric currents and of radiant light,—so all these issue
ceaselessly from their ultimate seat in God. What the
sun is to the solar system, what the furnace is to the
steamship, what the great centre of nerve-force is to our
bodies, that God is to his universe, and infinitely more.

(4.) Hence, lastly, it follows that everywhere the

universe reveals God.   The power of the indwelling
spirit to express its changing modes through the changes
of the body is a great mystery, and nevertheless is one
of the most obvious and constant of all facts.   Pallid
fear, raging passion, calm contemplation, assured confidence, radiant joy, determined purpose, have each their
universally recognized signs of expression current among
all nations of men and animal tribes.   So the constructive dream of the architect, the ideal of the sculptor and
painter, the high theme of the musician, are all expressed
in the several forms of their respective arts.   The great
artists are immortal, since they ever live, speaking and
singing in their works.   As our souls animate and
manifest their presence and their changing modes in
every part of our bodies, and as God is immanent and
active in all his works, so all nature and the course of
universal history reflect his thoughts.   All men always
recognize events of extraordinary character as expressions of the will of God.   Whatever is recognized by us
as providential expresses to us the divine thought.   Even
Shakespeare says that Providence "shapes our ends,
rough-hew them as we may."   The Christian recognizes
every event as providential.   Every hair of our head is
numbered, and not one sparrow falls to the ground except as our Father wills it.   He works in us all to will
and to do of his good pleasure in all things.   Hence every
flower is a thought of God.   The firmament reflects his
immensity, and the order of the stars his limitless intelligence, and the myriad-fold beauty of the world unveils
the secret chambers of his imagery.   The tempest is the
letting loose of his strength, and the thunder utters his
voice.   To the Christian the universe is not merely a
temple in which God is worshipped, but it is also the
ever-venerated countenance on which the affections of
our Lord toward his children are visibly expressed.

Everywhere we see God, and everywhere his ever-active and fecund benevolence toward us is articulated in smile and word and deed.

This view of God, which we signalize by the word "immanence," is not a new one, nor is it confined to philosophers or to theologians. The plainest and most practical Christians of all Churches live in the exercise of this faith every day. To the babes in Christ every event is providential, and marks the constant thought and care of God. Especially have evangelical Christians of the school of Augustine and Calvin always recognized the constant dependence of the creature and the constant inworking of the divine energy as the controlling source of all our spontaneous affections and actions. It is a first principle in their theology that the creature can act only as it is first acted upon by the First Cause. The doctrine of *prevenient* grace, which is the grand evangelical distinction, implies this. God must first move the sinner to good before the sinner can begin to co-operate with that grace which ever continues to prompt and assist him. Thus they argue for a previous, simultaneous, and determining *concursus*—that is, continuous co-working—of the ceaseless activities of God with the activities of his creatures. They hold that even the sinful actions of men originate in God as to their *matter*, while as to their *form* or moral quality they originate in the creature alone; as when a great artist handles an instrument out of tune, the sound that issues is due to the artist, but the discord which deforms it issues only from the unbalanced organism of the instrument, the unstrung cords or the unadjusted pipes.

The claim made by the advocates of the "New Departure" in theology, that this view of God as immanent and constantly active in all his works is new in the thoughts of Christians, is absolutely without shadow of evidence.

It has never been denied or seriously ignored; nor is it in the least inconsistent with the complementary view of his personal transcendence and objective presentation and working from without. The Church has always held both sides together of this double truth, as both equally essential and precious.

Neither is this view of the divine immanence to be confounded with Pantheism. They both alike emphasize the common truth that God is within us; that he is to be sought in the sphere of the subjective as well as of the objective; that he is the immediate basis of all created existence and the ultimate source of all the intelligence and energy manifested in the external world.

But Pantheism holds that the whole universe of extension and thought is one substance, and that substance God —that God exists only in the successive forms or events which constitute the universe. These forms are various, but God is one. They are successive, but God endures the same. He is not a person, but all persons are transient forms of his being. He has no existence other than that of the sum of all finite existence, and no consciousness nor intelligence other than the aggregate of the consciousness and intelligence of the transient creatures.

Hence Pantheism denies the freedom of man and the personality of God. It makes all events proceed by a law of absolute necessity. All evil, precisely as all good, comes immediately from God, and evil men are related to him precisely as are saints and angels. It confounds the doctrine of immanence with ontological identity, and it turns it into a heresy by denying the complementary truth of the divine transcendence. It allows no place for a heavenly Father beholding us complacently and providing for us benevolently. It makes no place for a moral Governor and Judge ruling over us, distributing rewards and punishments, teaching, disciplining, and acting upon us from without. It makes no place for a supernatural world, for revelations or supernatural truths, for miracles or supernatural works, for a "kingdom of God," a supernatural state, or for a future or supernatural life. Therefore *Pantheism* in its very essence renders all morality and religion alike impossible.

The Christian doctrine of the divine *immanence*, on the contrary, is the very essence of all religion. It admits and adjusts itself to the complementary doctrine of the divine transcendence. We begin, as we have shown above, with the conception of God as a distinct Person of absolute intellectual and moral perfection, self-conscious, self-determinate, absolutely free and sovereign, righteous and loving. This is our heavenly Father, the God and Father of our Lord and Saviour Jesus Christ. He created us in his likeness, rules us as our righteous moral Governor and Judge, and executes through all the universe and through all ages his all-perfect and immutable plan conceived in the infinitely wise and righteous counsel of his sovereign will.

This Being, moreover, transcends all the limitations of space and time. He is everywhere present in his eternal essence. The whole essence, with all its inherent properties, is present at every moment of time to every point of space. As First Cause he is the constant, abiding, supporting, and actuating basis of every second cause. All creatures exist, and act only as they exist, in him. At the same time, he acts through every atom from within and upon every atom from without. "In him all things live and move and have their being;" he turneth the hearts of men even as rivers of water are turned; he worketh in us to will and to do of his own good pleasure.

This is a function of the divine personality. The fact that the whole indivisible God is eternally in each point of space transcends our understanding, but it does not rationally necessitate the belief in many gods nor in a

divided God ; nor does it in any way invalidate the proof
we have establishing his personality. The Scriptures
clearly treat both truths together. The practical faith and
experience of all Christians embrace both of these truths
together in the same acts of trust and love. Both truths
are together implied in all religious experience, recognizing
God as our Father, speaking to him and listening to his
voice, obeying his word, trusting to his love, and at the
same time recognizing him as present everywhere and in
all things and events, recognizing his hand in every object
and occurrence, trusting him in everything, because all
nature executes his will, and hence reveals his presence
and expresses his thought.

The extension of our knowledge of the physical universe
effected by modern science, rendering visible to us the
absolute unity of the cosmos, the uninterrupted continuity
of the chain of cause and effect, as well as of design,
through all space and time, has not altered, but it has
greatly emphasized, this religious conception of " the divine
immanence." An eminent Christian scientist said to me
recently, " God is either in all or in none." It is not possible to believe, when looking upon the course of natural
creation and providence, that God comes down upon them
at disconnected intervals from without. In the miracle
he does that very thing, for " a miracle " is a sign the
essence of which is its articulate significance to the answering intelligence of man. But in the natural course of
providence the immanent God works continuously, without
interval, from within through the spontaneities of the
things themselves in which he dwells. He is not in one
object or event any more than in all others. The whole
course of the universe is divine in every part, except so far
as sin has marred it, and all the normal activities of men
and angels are religious—that is, have their source and
their end in God.

This view, therefore, evidently differs from Pantheism in that——(1.) It asserts the distinct personality of God as the Head of a moral government administered over free and responsible agents by a system of ideas and motives. (2.) It asserts the distinct personality and moral freedom and responsibility of men. (3.) It maintains the distinction of the human and the divine agency, although making the former depend upon the latter. (4.) It embraces and adjusts itself to the complementary doctrine of the divine transcendence, which Pantheism renders impossible. (5.) While Pantheism makes freedom, morality, and religion impossible, this view of the divine immanence in all things is the necessary basis of the highest freedom and of the most exalted morality and of the most vivid religion conceivable. (6.) This view, as held by Christians, not only admits, but affords the most rational basis attainable for the supernatural—that is, for the activity in the sphere of nature of that God who in himself infinitely transcends all nature.

III. In this catholic Christian doctrine of the relation of God to the universe we comprehend all the half-truths or heresies which have divided the schools. We recognize all the facts, and we reconcile the practical faith of Christians with the highest science, and we provide a rational basis alike for the natural and the supernatural, for the reign of law and for special miracle, for science and for practical religion.

Here we stand under the blended light of nature and of grace, of science and of revelation. God the infinite, and therefore the timeless and spaceless, the absolutely unknowable, remains ever the unfathomable Abyss. In all our knowing, God is always BEYOND us, hid in the light which is impenetrable.

At the same time, he is always ABOVE us, enthroned in heaven, commanding, revealing, ruling, showering myriad blessings from above.

. At the same time, the same infinite God is BEFORE us, looking upon us and speaking with us face to face. He is our heavenly Father. He has formed us in his own image. Our highest life and blessedness are found in his personal communion—that is, personal interchange of ideas and of affections, for our fellowship is with the Father and with his Son Jesus Christ.

At the same time, God is ever WITHIN us, the ultimate ground of our being and the unfailing source of our life, the wellspring of eternal life, the inspiration of all spiritual knowledge and beatitudes, springing up within us to the ages of the ages.

All these glimpses of this immeasurable mystery, of God's nature and of his relation to the universe, afforded by the light of nature, are reinforced and gloriously supplemented and illumined by the revealed truths of the Trinity of Persons and of the incarnation of the Eternal Word.

II.

THE SCRIPTURE DOCTRINE OF DIVINE PROVIDENCE.

WE shall now consider the general doctrine taught in the inspired Scriptures of the providence which God exercises over the world and its inhabitants. It is evident that this doctrine presupposes, and can be understood only in the light of what was ascertained in the previous lecture to be the facts of the case as to God's nature and his relation to the universe.

We then saw that there have prevailed among philosophers three partial views as to God's relation to the world, each presenting one side of the truth, but each radically erroneous, in so far as it was partial and denied the complementary truths presented by the others—(1) the agnostic, maintaining that God is unknowable; (2) the pantheistic or naturalistic, maintaining that God is ever present and active in every element of every created existence, whether spiritual or material; and (3) the deistical, which maintains the separate, extramundane existence of God, and his action at will upon all his creatures from without.

The element of truth in all of these alike is embraced and assimilated with the rest in Christian Theism. God is essentially unknowable. We can know only those parts of his nature, of his relations, or of his ways which he has chosen to reveal to us. And at the best the creature can know even that which he is permitted to know only in part. At the same time, God is essentially omnipresent and active at the same time and in unbroken continuity in all his creatures. Our dependent being exists in him, and our dependent energies are ceaselessly re-created from the inexhaustible fountain of his life. All nature and all human history evolve in unbroken continuity through his guiding, co-operating will, present in and working through the created dependent things themselves. None the less is God separate from the world, existing alike extensively and intensively infinitely above and beyond it.

All these views are essentially involved in all our practical, every-day religious experience. We all submit our intellects absolutely to him, as we reverently bow before the inscrutable mystery of his being who, although his essence is light, in his relations to us has " made darkness his secret place, and his pavilion round about him the dark waters and the thick clouds of the skies " (Ps. xviii. 11). We all instinctively recognize his presence and activity in all his creatures, and in all their changes, and in the innermost and most spontaneous exercises of our own souls. We all look up to him as our Father, speak to him and hear him speak to us in his word and providence. He deals with us as a person exterior to ourselves. He presides over the physical universe and over communities of men as a person exterior and superior to all. He controls all events by his interior confluent energies according to a plan, one and universal, formed before the beginning of the world. He has formed a great moral government over his intelligent creatures as men and angels, and governs them by commands and motives objectively presented, and by his providences and by his word. He at times, and for purposes evidently subsidiary to his general plan and to his ordinary methods, acts upon the system of second causes from without, working miracles, or signals to his intelligent children, thus arousing their attention, instructing their faith, and determining their action. He has revealed the great end of his whole system of works, to which all things, in all eras and in all spheres, work together, to be the giving of objective expression to the perfections of his own nature, or, as we usually phrase it, the manifestation of his own glory.

In all our religious experience, when we work, and when we study, and when we pray, God is always at once beyond us, and above us, and before us, and within us—at once the source of all life and movement, the authority binding all consciences, and the sublime object of all personal love and worship.

I. The word PROVIDENCE means, first, to see beforehand, and then to exercise all that care and control which God's infinite prevision of his own ends and his knowledge of his appointed instrumentalities may suggest.

The order of thought in theology is marked by the following commonplaces: *Deus existens*, God existing—his being, attributes, and threefold personality; *Deus volens*, God willing or forming his eternal plan; *Deus agens*, God in the successions of time executing the plan he had formed in eternity.

Our term "providence," then, includes generally the entire sum of all God's activities exterior to himself and subsequent to creation through all time. "God executes his decrees" or plan "in his works of creation and providence." Here "providence" evidently includes the entire sum of God's activities of all kinds with reference to his creatures previously brought into existence. It is the general term which includes all varieties or special kinds of the same. It includes the exercise in every mode of his *potestas ordinata*, or energy exercised along the lines of pre-established and uniform law, and his *potestas*

libera, or energy put forth independently of all established
sequences upon special occasion and as determined by his
personal will.   This includes his general or natural providence, embracing the universe as one system and operating through the uniformities of natural law, and his
special or supernatural providence, acting upon and modifying the action of second causes from without in the form
of miracle and of grace.

We should clearly apprehend and firmly hold the obvious truth that what we distinguish as the natural and
the supernatural providence of God — for example, his
ordinary providence, his gracious operations, and his miraculous interventions — are nevertheless inseparable parts
of one harmonious system in execution of one plan, and
the various manifestations of the energy of one God.
They run on together at the same time as the work of
one agent and the execution of one plan.   Ordinary providence is the constant fact which is never intermitted.
Grace always presupposes the ordinary providence, which
it simply supplements and perfects ; and the miracle always presupposes grace, which it subserves and confirms.
In the case of an apostolical miracle, as in that of the man
lame from his mother's womb healed at the gate of the
temple called " Beautiful " by Peter and John, all three of
these diverse modes of the divine activity were in operation at the same time, and as necessary parts of one
interdependent system :—(1.) There was the ordinary providence of God sustaining and directing the normal action
of the bodies and souls of all the parties engaged, and of
their physical and moral environment.   (2.) There was at
the same time the gracious operation of the divine Spirit
upon the souls of the apostle and of the subject of the
miraculous cure, producing their appropriate effects in
their sanctified affections.   (3.) There was at the same
time, and in perfect harmony with these, the miraculous

power of God exercised at the word of the apostles in the person of the man born lame.

As to the ultimate method of God's action upon or in concurrence with natural causes, either in the forms of ordinary providence, of grace, or of miracle, we absolutely know nothing. But it is important to observe that we do know very certainly (1) just as little of the one as of the other. The fact that we cannot understand the *modus operandi* of God in his works of grace or of miracle can be no objection to the admission of their reality to the man who believes in the reality of God's ordinary providence without being able to explain its method. (2.) We know that God's methods of operation, whether natural or supernatural, whether in the forms of ordinary providence, of grace, or of miracle, are all carried on simultaneously, are all mutually harmonious, are all the activities of one and the same infinite Agent, and in the execution of one all-comprehensive plan.

II. Whatever, however, may be the, to us, utterly un-known ultimate method of the divine operation, either in and through natural causes from within or upon them from without, it is intuitively certain, *a priori*, that they must in every case be consistent with what God has other-wise revealed to us of his own essential nature. It is simply impossible that God can deny himself, or ever in any form act in a manner incongruous with his own per-fections.

Hence it follows—1st. That the providence of God in all its modes, whether natural or supernatural, whether ordinary, gracious, or miraculous, must be, all and several, the execution of one single indivisible plan. There can be no real incongruities or antagonisms between the natural and the supernatural, or between ordinary providence and grace. God, being eternal and infinite in knowledge and wisdom, sees the end from the beginning. There can be with him no surprise, nor repentance, nor change of plan, nor divided counsel. All that he purposes must be one purpose; all that he does, of every various mode of activity, must be the execution of the one purpose, and must therefore constitute one harmonious system.

2nd. Hence it follows with equal certainty that the providence of God must be universal. It must comprehend in its grasp equally every agent and every event without the least discontinuity or exception. One event is never in any degree more providential than any other event. There prevails a very unintelligent and really irreligious habit among many true Christians of passing unnoticed the evidence of God's presence in the ordinary course of nature, and of recognizing it on the occasion of some event specially involving their supposed interests, as if it were special and unusual. They will say of some sudden, scarcely-hoped-for deliverance from danger, " Why, I think I may venture to say it was really providential." But would it have been any the less providential if they had been destroyed and not delivered ? Would it have been any the less providential if they had not been in jeopardy at all and had needed no deliverance ? The great Dr. Witherspoon lived at a country-seat called Tusculum, on Rocky Hill, two miles north of Princeton. One day a man rushed into his presence, crying, " Dr. Witherspoon, help me to thank God for his wonderful providence ! My horse ran away, my buggy was dashed to pieces on the rocks, and behold ! I am unharmed." The good doctor laughed benevolently at the inconsistent, half-way character of the man's religion. " Why," he answered, " I know a providence a thousand times better than that of yours. I have driven down that rocky road to Princeton hundreds of times, and my horse never ran away and my buggy was never dashed to pieces." Undoubtedly, the deliverance was providential, but just as much so also were the uneventful rides of the college president. God is in the atom just as really and effectually as in the planet. He is in the unobserved sighing of the wind in the wilderness as in the earthquake which overthrows a city full of living men, and his infinite wisdom and power are as much concerned in the one event as in the other.

There is a distinction to be observed between God's natural providence, which is universal and ordinary, and his supernatural providence, which is occasional and special. His natural providence is equally in every thing and event ; but his grace and his supernatural intervention are in one event and not in another, at one time and not at another. It is proper, therefore, to distinguish his natural providence as general, and his grace or his supernatural providence as special. But it is essential to understand that in the ordinary sense of *providence* relating to the course of events in our natural lives, the common distinction between general and special providence is unintelligent and irreligious. All God's providence is at the same time both general and special, and general because it is special, and special because it is general. It is general because it reaches by continuous action equally every element of the world and every event. It is special for the same reason, because, reaching equally to every particular, it reaches universally to all particulars and to their entire sum. That which controls every link controls the whole chain. That which controls the movement of every atom controls the whole world. That which controls the thought and volition of every man controls the entire course of human history. God does not come down from above upon the course of our lives in spots. His whole infinite being dwells everlastingly in each atom and each spirit. He is universally in all things, because he is ever equally in each thing. In every grain of sand, in every drop of water, in every pulse of air, in every flower that blows, in every infant soul, in every human thought and will and act, in the equable flow of natural law, in the great catastrophe of exploding worlds or of nations brought to judgment, in the fall of Adam, in the giving of the law on Sinai, in the redemption of man on Calvary, in the mission of the Holy Ghost, in the resurrection of the dead, and in the eternal judgment—however heterogeneous these agents and events in themselves, however incommensurate their significance to us, and however various is the method of the divine operation in them severally, yet in them all the one Jehovah is equally present with his absolute perfections and in his supreme potency. Events may be infinitely different in their significance as well as in their importance to us; yet the truly religious mind finds equally in all things, even the least significant and the least important, the presence and supreme control and the benevolent administration of our heavenly Father.

3rd. It is equally self-evident and certain that the whole of God's providence in every part of it must be an expression of his essential perfections, of infinite wisdom and power, and of absolute righteousness and benevolence. Nothing can be a surprise to his intelligence, or too complicated for his wisdom, or too difficult for his power, or inconsistent with his perfect righteousness or love.

These essential attributes of the great Ruler are abundantly manifested in all his works. The whole universe, and the entire course of its history as far as known to us, exhibit unquestioned evidence of limitless intelligence and power, and of unmistakable righteousness and benevolence. This is witnessed to by the entire volume of human literature, that of philosophers, scientists, and poets, as well as that of the special devotees of religion.

Nevertheless, the course of providence from the point of view of man unilluminated by a supernatural revelation is full of anomalies to him utterly insoluble. The question is not whether the face of nature and the course of providence give evidence of the intelligence, power, righteousness, and goodness of God,—this is admitted by all sober men,—but the true question is, as put by John Stuart Mill in his posthumously published *Essay on Theism :* Are the facts of nature and the history of events, as we know them, possibly reconcilable with the belief that the Creator and Controller of the world is at the same time infinite in his wisdom, and in his power, and in his righteousness, and in his goodness ? Mr. Mill is assured that this reconciliation is impossible in view of the awful prevalence of moral and physical evil. He is sure that God must be limited either in his wisdom or his power or his benevolence, and is inclined to think that he is limited in all, and upon the whole, with an imperfect standard and a limited ability, strives to do as well as he can.

The apparent incongruousness of the facts, and hence the difficulty of the problem, we admit. But we have seen God because we have seen Christ, and we have learned to read all the course of providence in the light of the Cross. Since the baptism of Pentecost we have been convicted of sin and of a guilt we are utterly unable to gainsay or remove. We have been convinced that the finite can never measure the Infinite, and that self-convicted sinners can never judge the integrity of the All-holy. In the light of Calvary we have an impregnable assurance that the Father of our Lord and Saviour Jesus Christ is unlimited in wisdom and in power, and that he can do no wrong. Bowing our heads in unquestioning submission to his sovereign rights, and with confidence in his absolute perfection, we exclaim, in the face of all apparent anomalies : " O the depth of the riches both of the wisdom and knowledge of God ! how unsearchable are his judgments, and his ways past finding out ! For who

hath known the mind of the Lord ? or who hath been his
counsellor ? or who hath first given to him, and it shall
be recompensed unto him again ?   For of him, and through
him, and to him, are all things : to whom be glory for
ever.   Amen " (Rom. xi. 33-36).

III. It is no less certain that, whatever be the ultimate
method of God's exercise of his energy in providence, it
must necessarily be in a manner perfectly congruous to the
nature of his creatures upon which and through which
he works, and with the laws of their action.   It is impossible to believe that the all-perfect Creator of all things
will in his subsequent control of their action violate the
properties with which he has endowed them, or the laws
he has imposed upon them.   The Scriptures everywhere
and constantly take for granted the principles of "natural
realism" which correspond to the instinctive judgments
and the spoken and written languages of all men.
Material and spiritual beings are real entities.   They
have real, substantial, objective existence.   Although they
are ever dependent upon their First Cause, they are nevertheless real active agents and causes.   God has endowed
them each and severally, according to their respective
kinds, with their essential properties and powers of action,
which, as far as we know, never change or fail.   We trace
an absolutely unbroken continuity in the action of these
second causes through the entire history of the world and
of mankind.   These elements, thus originally endowed
with unchangeable properties, act and react with invariable uniformity under the same conditions ; and as the
conditions change, they act differently, but always in a
way uniformly related to the conditions under which they
act.   As, therefore, the general adjustments or groupings
of second causes under which they act are for the most
part uniform from age to age, and change only locally and
slowly, the uniformity of action which results gives origin

to what are called " laws of nature," which continue absolutely uniform as long as the adjustments or groupings of
these causes remain unchanged. It is obvious that we
apply this only to the world of matter, and to certain
spheres of the natural actions of spirits. The spirit of
men in certain spheres of action is confessedly endowed
with the divine power of originating and directing its own
action independently of its external environment. But in
the sphere of purely natural causes men never seek to
attain their ends by violating the " laws of nature." On
the contrary, they seek by science to attain a definite
knowledge of those laws under all varieties of condition,
and then they so apply this knowledge, by varying the
conditions under which the natural causes act, that the
very laws of nature themselves, thus directed, work out
their purposes for them. Thus steam and electricity in
the hands of men obey the " laws of nature " as implicitly
as they do when nature is left to itself, only the same
causes naturally produce different effects under changed
conditions.

Now, men of pure science, habitually confining their
attention to the uniformities of nature's action under the
uniform conditions existing, regard the habit of religious
men in ascribing results to the action of a personal agent
having personal aims in view, and special reference to
human characters and necessities, as irrational and super-
stitious. And hence, on the other hand, many unintelligent religious men regard the point of view of men of
science as essentially irreligious. But it is obvious that
these contrasted views of the course of events in the
natural world are not mutually contradictory, but supplementary. They are the two equally true and real sides
of the one system of objects. If even men comparatively
ignorant and impotent can so wonderfully make the
powers and laws of nature subservient to their own pur-

poses without violating them, why cannot God at least do the same? Nay, why, since God's knowledge and power are alike absolutely limitless, should not the whole of nature be as plastic to his will as the air in the organs of a great musician, who articulates it into a fit expression of every thought and passion of his soaring soul? The reason that this analogy is not immediately conclusive to every mind is, that when man arranges the conditions so as to render the action of nature subservient to his purpose you can always trace his trail, see the visible marks of his interfering agency, while the course of nature flows on with mathematical precision of physical action, without the least trace of a providential interference *ab extra*. But it is forgotten that while man is always locally outside his work, and acts upon all elements from without, and in succession, a part at a time, God is simultaneously present and active within every ultimate element. His impulse is therefore through, not outside of, their own spontaneities. His control is neither partial nor successive, but simultaneously in the entire universe, thus co-ordinating all adjustments and all reactions in the execution of one plan and in the current of one issue.

There are two extreme tendencies to which different persons are inclined when regarding the course of events in the world, each of which is evidently false when exclusively indulged, but both of which together, when combined, lead to the true attitude which every Christian should cultivate: the view of the mere naturalist, in which the supernatural is altogether merged in the natural, and, conversely, the view of the pantheist, in which the natural is altogether merged in the supernatural. And these apparently opposite extremes virtually come to the same thing, because they both equally exclude a personal God and human freedom, and maintain a naturalistic fatalism. But both present a side of the one truth. The natural is the fixed and regulated method which the personal heavenly Father has laid down for his own guidance; the supernatural does neither exclude nor supersede the natural, but it is the self-revelation of the heavenly Father, who works through natural law, as the personal Agent who, having ordained law, uses it to accomplish his spiritual purposes. The universe has a personal basis. The laws of nature are the methods self-ordained of a personal Agent. The true scientists are the sons of God, who were not created for the laws of nature, but the laws of nature for them.

After the Charleston earthquake the Christian preachers endeavoured to enforce upon their hearers the scriptural lessons of the event viewed as a divine dispensation. The visiting scientists are represented as having scoffed contemptuously, maintaining that the preachers should have confined themselves to an exposition of the laws of nature, and drawn comfort from the proven exceptional character of such experiences. These men of mere science may have been able and useful in their narrow specialty, but they were certainly very absurd philosophers. They were perfectly right in confining their own investigations to the scientific aspects of the phenomena, and the preachers had an equal authority in calling the attention of the Christian people to the aspect which the light of the inspired Scriptures, when thrown upon the providential facts, presented. We say, advisedly, that the preachers' authority in the premises is limited to the application of the light of the inspired Scriptures to the current facts. They have no right to assume the *rôle* of prophets, as too many are at times inclined to do; and no man not the subject of plenary inspiration should dare to explain the ultimate divine purpose in any particular event, or its relation to human guilt. The Master himself said, "Suppose ye that those eighteen, upon whom the tower in Siloam fell, were

sinners above all men that dwelt in Jerusalem ? I tell
you, Nay : but, except ye repent, ye shall all likewise
perish " (Luke xiii. 4, 5).

IV. Providence, as made known to us in Scripture,
history, and our religious experience, includes two distinct
exercises of the divine energy—(1st) preservation, and
(2nd) government.

1st. *Preservation* is the continuous exercise of the
divine omnipotence through successive duration upholding
all creatures in being and in power.   This does not in the
least confound the Creator and Preserver with his works ;
nor does it invalidate the separate objective existence and
the real efficiency of these created elements as second
causes.   But it simply affirms that they are essentially
and continuously dependent existences and causes.   All
atoms of matter and all created spirits live and move and
have all their being and the unfailing spring of all their
energies in him only.   If he should withdraw his supporting power, the whole dependent universe would lapse into
non-being immediately.

2nd. *Government* includes God's control of all the
activities of all his creatures of every kind, and his
direction of them toward the fulfilling of his one eternal
plan.

(1.) That God has one universal plan which he executes
with undeviating purpose in all his works of creation and
of providence, is made very certain, *first*, from the fact that
he is an infinite Intelligence acting from eternity before all
worlds, and absolutely unconditioned by any facts or powers
external to himself. *Secondly*, from all that the Scriptures
teach us as to his sovereignty, eternal foreknowledge, and
as to making his own glory the single end of all things.
And *thirdly*, the same fact is obviously exhibited in the
unexceptional experience of all generations of men, and the
revelations of modern science, exhibiting the absolutely

unbroken continuity of thought and purpose and of divine
superintendence and control in the whole universe, in all
its parts and during all its successive ages. Of course this
general plan, although one and indivisible, has many subordinate systems successive and contemporaneous, and many
varieties of method. To us, of course, these appear very
various, and sometimes we make the mistake of regarding
them as mutually inconsistent. But while various, they are
only to be understood when conceived as the many articulated members of one consummate system, reaching through
all space and all time and all spheres.

Here we see that whatever is really true and significant in the famous but recent scientific doctrine of evolution had for many ages been anticipated by the Augustinian
theology. Whatever may eventually turn out to be the
facts with regard to genetic evolutions through successive
natural births, all must unite in recognizing the fact that
the universe in all its spheres and through all its history
is the continuous logical evolution of one purpose, to one
end, through the energies of one infallible and inexhaustible
Will.

(2.) God effectually governs all his creatures and all
their actions by a method to us inscrutable, but certainly
consistent with his own perfections and with their properties and laws. This government is revealed in the Scriptures and in our experience to be universal, certainly efficient,
holy, benevolent, and wise.

a. In matter God governs all things, apparently by the
distribution and adjustment of material particles under the
great categories of time, place, quantity, and quality. This
procedure leaves the properties and laws of matter entirely
unmodified, and it makes the omnipresent, omniscient, and
omnipotent God Lord of all.

b. The providence of God over his rational creatures
involves three elements : *First*, his working in the entire

sphere of their environment, presenting external motives
and influences, moulding character and stimulating to
action. *Secondly*, his working in their bodies and souls
through the natural laws of their organizations, through
the entire process of their growth. And *thirdly*, his immanent working within their will, whereby his directive
energy becomes confluent with their own spontaneity, and
" he turns the hearts of men as the rivers of water are
turned," and " works in us to will, and be willing to do, of
his own good pleasure."

The redeemed Christian is a child already at home
in his Father's house. All these beauties and all this
abundant wealth belong to our Father, and are set apart
for our use. All things whatsoever that come to pass,
however dark and enigmatical, are expressions of our
Father's will, and are wisely designed to promote our
welfare in the present, and to secure it with infallible
certainty in the great hereafter. The word " chance " expresses simply a relation. An event happens by " chance "
when the causes which produce it are so complex or so
unusual as to be incapable of rational explanation by us.
Hence, as far as God is concerned, there is absolutely no
such thing as chance. As far as we are concerned, all
events which lie beyond the reach of scientific prediction
fall into the category of chance. But by faith we embrace the infinitely wise will of God, and accept all events
as the excellent will of our heavenly Father. Creation
and providence are seen to be the preparatory work which
culminates in redemption. We read all the means in the
light of the glorious end. God is in every experience,
making " known unto us the mystery of his will, according
to his good pleasure which he hath purposed in himself :
that in the dispensation of the fulness of times he might
gather together in one all things in Christ, both which are
in heaven, and which are on earth ; even in him : in whom

also we have obtained an inheritance, being predestinated according to the purpose of him who worketh all things after the counsel of his own will : that we who first trusted in Christ should be to the praise of his glory."

" O the depth of the riches both of the wisdom and knowledge of God ! how unsearchable are his judgments, and his ways past finding out ! For of him, and through him, and to him, are all things : to whom be glory for ever. Amen."

III.

MIRACLES.

THESE are supernatural events implying a special and exceptional mode of God's providential action.

I. The first thing we have to do in discussing the nature and attributes of a particular class of phenomena is to settle between ourselves very distinctly a common understanding as to what particular class of phenomena we are talking about. The word "miracle" has been so vaguely and promiscuously used that, unless we come to an understanding as to the kind of events to which we agree to restrict its application in this discussion, we should only talk at cross-purposes.

It should be remembered that there are two kinds of definitions—(1) nominal or verbal, and (2) real. The former defines the thing by the etymology or the general usage of its name; the latter defines it by its own nature or relations.

In the present case it is essential to recognize the fact that a verbal definition of miracles, or a definition formed upon a study of the etymology or usage of the word "miracle," would be of not the least value. The word itself simply means a *wonder;* that is, it defines the events called "miracles" not by any essential characteristic of the events themselves, but simply by the effect they happen to produce upon the minds of some classes of beholders.

That this is absurd is easily shown by an illustration. A missionary in the use of a chemical apparatus turned water into solid ice in the presence of the king of Siam. To the missionary it was a common effect of a combination of natural causes ; to the king of Siam and his courtiers it was an unparalleled wonder. The like had never been a matter of previous experience in all the land or in all its history. Yet it was not a miracle to them. If they had regarded it as one, they would have been miserably deceived, and would soon have been brought to discredit all that had been associated with it in its assumed character.

These events are designated in Scripture by various descriptive titles which severally connote their various aspects and relations. Their true nature is represented adequately by no one of these names separately, but all collectively should be understood as describing rather than as defining the class. These names are in Hebrew אוֹת, *signum, portentum ;* פֶּלֶא, something separated, singular ; גְּבוּרָה, *power*, some extraordinary manifestation of divine power. Also, the Greek τέρατα, wonders ; δυνάμεις, powerful works, manifesting divine power ; σημεῖα, signs. All these words signify real properties or qualities of the " miracle," and especially the last. The " miracle " was distinctively God's " sign " to man.

Having thus dismissed, as profitless, the attempt to form a verbal definition of the " miracle," how shall we proceed to designate sharply the class of events to which, by common consent, the name should be restricted ?

We take the first step, then, when we point out the fact that the terms " miracle " and " the supernatural " are not coextensive. Every miracle is supernatural, but every supernatural event is by no means a miracle. The " supernatural " is the genus, while the " miracle " is a subordinate species of that genus.

The first thing, therefore, is to attempt to reach a clear,

distinct conception of the "supernatural." Supernatural events are of infinitely various kinds, yet they all have a common quality which renders them supernatural, and which distinguishes them from all kinds of events simply natural. What, then, is the common quality of all supernatural events?

"Nature" is from *nascor*, to be brought to the birth, to be produced, to become. The external world is the common type of pure nature. It is always becoming. Its process is genesis. In unbroken continuity the events of this moment proceed from the events of the last moment, and give birth to the events of the next moment. Viewed as a fecund cause, the whole external universe is the *natura naturans*—nature bringing forth; and viewed as a manifold effect, the same universe is every moment the *natura naturata*—nature just brought forth.

The *super*natural is, therefore, that which is above nature, which springs from, and therefore manifests, a higher cause. But scholars, philosophers, and theologians greatly differ as to where they draw the line between the natural and the supernatural.

1. Many draw it between matter and spirit, and hence just between the body and the soul of man. The body and the whole material world obey the law of necessity, while the soul moves spontaneously, and is self-determined in the light of reason and conscience. Hence Coleridge, Bushnell, and other high authorities, class the body and material world as natural, and the soul of man and the entire world of spirits as supernatural. Whatever reason there may be for this distinction, it is evident that it will not help us in this discussion. Men—their souls as well as their bodies—have their genesis, inherit natures, and their action and entire history are determined by their nature. Hence, by general consent, all that is human is natural.

2. Others draw the line between the natural and the supernatural just above men and between man and the angelic world. The *supernatural* is thus equivalent to the *superhuman.* This is a very common conception, and determines much of our current language. All that belongs to ghosts or disembodied spirits of dead men, and all that belongs to angels or devils, are called " supernatural." This is a legitimate use of the word. But it is not accurate or stable enough to suit our purpose. Evidently no action of angels or of devils could be classed as *supernatural* in the same sense that a *miracle*, in the Bible sense of that word, is. All created spirits, as well as all created worlds, have their genesis, all have their God-given natures, all are under law. Therefore every adequate sense of the word " nature " must take in the universe as a whole. It is one system, and cannot be divided into two separate parts, the one called " nature " and the other set apart as independent and styled " the supernatural." We consequently draw the line between the natural and the supernatural, in this discussion, between God and the universe, between the Creator and the creature, between the absolute and the relative and contingent. The " supernatural," therefore, is a peculiar kind or mode of God's action on and through his creatures. As far as we know, this supernatural action of God in nature is exercised in the modes of (1) special intervention in behalf of persons in the interest of a moral system ; (2) gracious operation in the souls of Christ's people ; (3) revelation of new truth, and inspiration controlling the communication of truth in the case of prophets, etc.; (4) " miracles," in the special and technical sense of that word.

It is common to regard creation as the type of the *supernatural* and of the *miracle*. But the distinction is obvious and important. Creation, or the bringing of the thing into existence, must differ from every mode of divine action *on* it or *through* it after it is existent.

Creation is God's bringing his creatures into existence.

Ordinary providence is God's sustaining and governing all his creatures and all their actions after they are created. This ordinary providence always works through natural causes, and according to the uniformities of natural law.

The *supernatural working of God* embraces all of his various modes of acting upon or through his creatures, which produce effects beyond their natural powers to produce, and different from the uniform method of natural law.

This includes special interventions, gracious operations, revelations, and, specifically, *miracles.*

" Miracle," as a technical word connoting a special matter in controversy, therefore refers only to a class of supernatural events alleged to have occurred in connection with the origin of the Jewish and of the Christian religion, which are recorded in the Old and New Testament Scriptures as a mode of divine attestation to the divine origin of these religions.

We exclude, therefore, from this discussion—

1. All spiritualistic phenomena—ghost-flitting, spirit-rapping, demoniac possession, or other manifestation of merely superhuman power.

2. Extraordinary providences, as the draught of fishes and the flight of quails mentioned in Scripture.

3. All possible special intervention and modification of the ordinary course of providence in the spiritual education of souls.

4. All the gracious acts of God in the spiritual sphere, regenerating and sanctifying the souls of his people.

5. His supernatural operations in the minds of his prophets, revealing truth, disclosing future events, and inspiring them as public teachers,

The " miracle," therefore, in the sense in which we now discuss it, should be defined thus :—

(1) An event (2) occurring in the material world, (3) obvious to the senses, (4) of such a nature that it can be rationally referred only to the immediate act of God as its direct cause, (5) accompanying a teacher of religion sent from God, (6) and designed to authenticate his divine commission.

When it is here said that a miracle is an event of such a nature that it can be rationally referred only to an immediate act of God as its direct cause, it is not meant that God is the only cause which operates in producing it. What is meant is that the direct intentional agency of God is always discerned to be one of its active causes, and that one which gives it its differentiating characteristics as a miracle. It is well known that the physical cause of any event in the physical world is never single ; it is always dual, if not manifold. All the necessary conditions upon which the event depends are its con-causes. The effect consists of these same conditions modified. If we kindle a fire, the con-causes are the fuel, the atmosphere, the flue, the match, and the agency of the person combining all these conditions. The effect is the change brought about in the person, the match, the flue, the air, and the fuel. In every miracle all surrounding and implicated natural bodies remain and act throughout the miracle in a manner perfectly true to nature under the peculiar conditions in which they are placed. But God, acting invisibly and from within, interpolates a new force, his own direct energy, into the plexus of con-causes naturally in operation, and the result is the miracle. It is God acting *from without and down upon and in nature*. When the iron was made to float in the water (2 Kings vi. 5), earth, air, water, and iron all remained acting according to the law of their nature under the circum

stances.   But God did invisibly and from within what
human agency in this case might have accomplished
visibly and from without—that is, he simply interpo-
lated a force acting in a direction contrary to gravity,
and equal in intensity to the difference of the weight of
the iron and of the weight of an equal bulk of water
which it displaced.

It is obvious that upon the assumptions of the deist,
the pantheist, or the atheist or materialist, a miracle would
be absolutely impossible.   In this discussion, therefore, we
necessarily assume as granted—(1) that there is a God; (2)
that he has access to the physical world, and can act upon
it at will; (3) that he is a moral Governor; (4) that men
are the subjects of his moral government, and also that
they are lost sinners in need of a redemption; (5) that he
has discovered a purpose of intervening redemptively in
man's behalf.

II. It is objected by sceptics that a miracle in the sense
just defined is an impossible event.

1. The first ground upon which this impossibility is
argued is that such an event would involve a violation of
natural law.   But the only three natural laws that science
has established as absolutely invariable are—(1) All substance possesses power : every substance is an active cause,
and acts as such invariably in the same way under the
same conditions; (2) all causes act uniformly under uniform
conditions, and their actions always change as their conditions change; (3) there is throughout all nature and during
all known time an absolutely unbroken continuity of causation : there is and can be no broken link.   Either in the
material or spiritual world, or in both together, the causes
of every event are to be found, and all the con-causes immediately co-operate in producing each event.   If by law
of nature be meant the ordinary sequence of natural events
occurring under ordinary conditions, then it is admitted that a

miracle does necessarily violate such a law ; but it is denied that natural law in *this* sense is necessarily uniform and immutable. The successions of day and night and of the seasons have changed, and will always continue to change, as the inclination of the earth's axis to the ecliptic, and other elements of the problem, vary.

But in every other sense of the phrase " law of nature " it is denied that the miracle violates it. It does not change the properties or powers of any natural substance. It does not annihilate or otherwise change any natural force. An act of God modifying the action of natural causes no more interrupts the law of physical continuity than an act of man doing the same thing. He only changes the conditions under which the entire plexus of natural con-causes acts. In all man's action in this world he uses his intelligence to bring the forces of nature into artificial combinations, and the result always is at the same time (*a*) natural, (*b*) yet a modified nature, and (*c*) an unquestionable evidence of man's direct agency. The electric current carrying messages through the ocean cable is as much an exhibition of natural law as an original stroke of forked lightning from the sky. But, in addition to this, it is moreover an immediate and intentional revelation of man. The same is true of the behaviour of all the natural forces implicated in a miracle, while at the same time the resultant action is an immediate and intentional revelation of God.

This is fully admitted by John Stuart Mill, the clearest-minded of the agnostic thinkers of this century, in the fourth part of his *Essay on Theism*, published since his death by his step-daughter, Helen Taylor : " The interference of the human will with the course of nature is only not an exception to law when we include among laws the relation of motive to volition : by the same rule interference by the divine will would not be an exception either, since we cannot but suppose Deity, in every one of its acts, to be determined by motives......It is true that human volition exercises power over objects in general indirectly through the direct power it possesses over human muscles. God, however, has direct power, not merely over one thing, but over all the objects he has made......Divine interference with nature could be proved if we had the same sort of evidence for it that we have for human interferences."

2. Sceptics declare miracles to be impossible because God is immutable, eternally perfect in wisdom and power, and therefore, it is argued, he can have no cause to change his plan or to modify his work. The machine invented and executed by man proves its excellence just in proportion as it is able to run on in its appointed way by itself, without any need of repair or correction at the hands of the maker. A machine that needs the direct intervention of its maker discovers thereby some defect either in his calculations or in his skill in execution. An absolutely wise and omnipotent God should have made a world which would have needed no intervention for ever. Theodore Parker said : " There is no whim in God, and therefore no miracle in nature."

This objection is absurdly irrelevant. The miracle involves no change in God's plan. Each miracle was foreseen and predetermined as an integral part of his eternal, all-comprehensive plan from the beginning. Neither does it imply any defect in his work. No miracle was ever designed to correct or regulate the action of the physical world (the machine). The *physical* world is controlled by forces and their interactions. The *moral* world is governed by ideas, reasons, motives, addressed to the will, and by discipline-forming character. A moral system involves free agency, and this independently of all theory as to its nature. The fact of personal self-determination cannot be doubted. Free agency involves liability to sin. Sin as an actual fact involves, necessitates, divine intervention either to punish or to redeem. Redemption involves the stupendous miracles of the incarnation and the resurrection, susceptible, both of them, of demonstrative proof ; and all other miracles are accompaniments of these. The physical world (the machine) is not an end in itself. It is the pedestal upon which God has erected his moral government, wherein he deals with a society of personal spirits. The physical world is the house in which the heavenly Father educates his children. He therefore uses the physical system as an instrument through which he makes " signs " to his children. The conditions of this " sign "-making are (1) the invariability of natural law ; (2) the infrequent and temporary interruption revealing his presence and purpose.

We admit that if there be no *moral* system of which the physical system of the world is only the foundation, there can be no miracle. But if there be a moral system, in which the moral and spiritual education of his children is the chief concern of our heavenly Father, miracles are not incredible, because not improbable.

III. It is asserted by sceptics that miracles are so violently improbable that even if they occurred, that occurrence could not be proved to non-witnesses by any amount of human testimony. This is one fallacy underlying the famous argument of David Hume against the credibility of miracles. We all would willingly agree to this principle, if the physical universe be separated from that moral system in which God is educating free personal spirits. In the physical system invariable law everywhere prevails. Uniformity of sequence is the rule in the experience of all men of all ages. From their very nature miracles must be to the last degree exceptional. If they were frequent, or if they could be accounted for by natural causes or analogies, they would cease to be miracles. Their frequent or sporadic occurrence would reduce the phenomenal world to chaos, would confuse the reason and paralyze the activity of man, and obscure the providence of God. But if the fact of a moral government is admitted, the facts of man's moral and spiritual condition and of his relation to God being what they are shown to be by natural religion, then a direct intervention of our heavenly Father in behalf of his bewildered and helpless children is in the highest degree probable. If God directly intervenes to instruct and educate his children, revelations and miracles must co-operate in that work. Each prophet sent to speak for God must be authenticated. Men sent bearing supernatural messages will reasonably be expected to possess supernatural phenomena. A detached, objectless miracle would indeed be unprovable. But a system of miracles mutually supporting one another, like those recorded in the Christian Scriptures, evidently bearing a divine redemptive character, and all constituting parts of one redemptive scheme, all issuing from one source and bearing upon one end, and associated with persons bearing the aspect of celestial messengers, teaching a spiritual doctrine self-evidencing itself as the word of God — such a system of miracles so supported becomes in the highest degree probable, and hence is to be received as true when supported by competent historical evidence.

IV. It is objected by sceptics that miracles, as above defined, even if they actually occurred, could not be certainly discriminated and recognized by us to be truly what they appear to be.

1. This is argued from the acknowledged fact that our knowledge of the powers and laws of nature is very limited, and therefore we are never competent, in view of any wonderful phenomenon transcending all past recorded experience, to say peremptorily that it transcends nature, and must have been caused by the direct action of God. This is true in part, but irrelevant. The question does not relate to the possible achievements of science in the future,

but to what was done through the agency of religious teachers in an obscure province of the Roman empire two thousand years ago. Besides, science secures its wonderful results by means of apparatus, by means of elaborately adjusted conditions, and never in any other way. But the miracle was always the response to a simple command in the name of God or of Christ. Besides all this, science has effectually shut some doors while it has opened many others. It is now scientifically certain that a man four days dead in a hot climate cannot be brought back to life by natural forces alone. If the events in question actually occurred, then it is scientifically certain that they reveal the "finger of God."

2. Sceptics argue that miracles, even if they occurred, could not be certainly recognized as such, because the phenomenon, although obviously transcending natural physical law, may, for aught we can tell, be produced by some unknown superhuman agency; as, for instance, by the devil or by his angels. This might be true so far as the isolated fact as a physical event goes, although we have no evidence that finite spirits of any kind have power of life or death over men. But the objection is wholly irrelevant. The miracles were professed "signs" of divine revelation and commission. Good spirits would not conspire to counterfeit God and deceive men; evil spirits could not, and would not be allowed to do so if they could. The prophet, his character, the doctrine, and the miracle, make one congruous whole, which in all its parts equally bears the unmistakable and uncounterfeitable sign-manual of God. Evil spirits could not conspire to build up the kingdom of God (Matt. xii. 25).

3. It is again argued against the credibility of miracles, that of the alleged phenomena we have only popular reports, and no evidence of their having been submitted to any adequate scientific test. We acknowledge that the

mass of people were then, as they are now, credulous and
inaccurate observers.   But in the case of the most important miracles recorded, the tests to which the phenomena
were subjected were all-sufficient.   The whole problem as
to the resurrection either of Lazarus or of Christ or of the
son of the widow of Nain is embraced in two definite and
easily ascertained facts.   They were really dead, and subsequently they were really alive again in the same bodies.
That Christ was really dead on Friday the entire educated
world, sceptical and believing, agree to be an ascertained
historical fact.   The fact that he was really alive again on
Sunday and afterward was tested in the strictest sense
scientifically, and especially by the apostle Thomas.   The
disciples used one sense to criticise and confirm the report
of another.   They saw, heard, and handled him, and thrust
their "hands into the print of the spear."   Many different
persons saw, heard, and handled him in many different
lights and in various situations through a space of six
weeks.   These persons were not deceived.   They were
intelligent and sober-minded men, as evidenced by all they
did and wrote.   They could not have conspired to deceive
us.   They consecrated their lives thenceforth " to preach
Jesus and the resurrection."   As conscious witnesses they
were true, for they sealed their testimony as martyrs.   As
unconscious witnesses they could not deceive, for their
unique experience transformed their characters and lives
from being Galilean fishermen to being world-compelling
apostles.

V. It is objected that the proof of which moral and
spiritual truths are susceptible is their own inherent self-
evidencing light ; that they are only worthily recognized
when they are seen and felt to be truth in their own light;
that miracles, consequently, even if real, are useless as
evidences of divine revelation, since moral and spiritual
truths cannot be established by any correlation with physical

phenomena; that the truth of a truth can never be established by the effects of even an infinite physical force.

But the gospel is not a disclosure of abstract moral or spiritual truths, but rather of a series of objective facts constituting the stupendous history of redemption. It is the history of God sending his own Son in the likeness of sinful flesh to condemn sin in the flesh, and afterward sending his Holy Spirit to apply and complete the work. No possible quickening of our intuitive consciousness would disclose these matters of historical fact. No self-evidence establishes them as historical realities except the evidence which history renders. And among the most convincing elements of this history is the witness it bears to the events we call " miracles." The incarnation, the crucifixion, the resurrection, are the very substance of Christianity and its saving power; the first and third of these are the central suns of the constellations of miracles recorded in the Bible. It is conceded that sporadic, inconsequent miracles could prove nothing, and would themselves be difficult to prove. But given a supernatural crisis, a supernatural teacher, and a supernatural doctrine, miracles are found to be in place like jewels on the state robes of a king. All the great miracles recorded in Scripture gather around two great foci in the history of redemption— the giving of the law through Moses, and the life and death of the incarnate God. Miracles in such connections are inevitable, and in the highest sense congruous. Their absence would have been unaccountable.

Besides this, the miracle, when found in this its normal relation to the character of the genuine prophet and to the nature of the genuine revelation, adds its own specific and indispensable quota of evidence. The miracle (the " sign ") is the seal of God. A seal detached, or attached accidentally to a rag or fraudulently to a fiction, has no legal value. Even a true document in many cases has only an incomplete value in the absence of the seal. But when the true seal is attached to the true document, the evidence is impregnable. The prophet, the message, and the miracle mutually authenticate one another. Separate, neither could be believed with confidence ; together, neither can be doubted. Faith is the highest reason, and therefore the most obligatory duty, while unbelief is alike irrational and sinful.

IV.

THE HOLY SCRIPTURES—THE CANON AND INSPIRATION.

LET us now consider the Bible, its genesis and its inspiration. The word "Bible" means book, the word "Scripture" means writing; and it is by the common consent of men that these words are applied to this one subject, because it is a Book of books, and because, beyond all comparison, it is the Writing of writings. It is the most important of all books, because, as a matter of historical fact, this book, more than any other force, has moulded the character of the great nations of the world and given birth to what we call the modern or Western civilization; because all historic Churches, with one accord, declare it to be the foundation of their creeds—declare that this book is the Word of God; because, in spite of all our divisions, the whole Church really accepts this book as the only infallible and divinely authoritative rule of our faith and practice; and because it is, between all Christians, the standard of appeal on all subjects of debate, the only common ground upon which we stand, the only court of last resort.

II. On what presuppositions does our doctrine rest? In every problem there are two elements—the *a priori* element of principle and the *a posteriori* element of fact. To this there is no exception in any of the problems of philosophy or of science or of theology. The *a priori* question of

principle must be taken first, and will condition the whole
argument. We must, before we take up the subject of the
Bible, first take up the questions : Is there a God ? Does
he exist ? What relation does he sustain to the universe ?
Can he reveal himself to man ? Has he made a revelation
of himself to man ? Are men capable of receiving a divine
revelation through the means of a book ?

Now, it is held, on the basis of all the presuppositions
of atheism, of materialism, of agnosticism, and even of
the old deism, that it is absolutely absurd to talk of any
supernatural revelation of God, or of any Bible as either
containing or *being* the Word of God. I want, however,
to assure the laymen who have not investigated these
questions, that nine-tenths of all the objections which men
are making now to the Scriptures, in which they claim
that the progress of knowledge, the progress of civilization,
the progress of science, the progress of critical investigation,
the vast aggregate of historical knowledge, all are sweeping
away the foundations of our ancient faith in the Bible—I
wish to assure them that these objections are totally untrue.
Those that are made are not founded upon facts, but simply
upon *a priori* philosophical principles. Neither science
nor history nor criticism bears any testimony against the
divine origin of the Bible. I appeal with confidence to
the *a priori* principles of a contrary philosophy. We
must meet them on their own ground, and appeal from the
postulates of a false philosophy to the postulates of a true.
We have as much right to believe our philosophy as they
have to believe theirs. Renan, for instance, begins his
discussion upon the Epistles with this assumption : " The
supernatural is impossible ; " therefore the supernatural is
unhistorical, and therefore any piece of literature that
claims to convey to us supernatural information must so
far forth be incorrect and be the subject of correction by
critical hands.

You see that this is a mere assumption, and the whole principle on which it rests is that which underlies the philosophy, atheistic, materialistic, agnostic, or deistic, of these errorists; and if this be swept away, not only all the foundations for such a claim, but all colour of presumption on which it rests, is swept away at once. Doubtless there are very many men of great ability who are perfectly honest who hold to this belief. They are thoroughly convinced of the principles of their *a priori* philosophy, and these principles are evidently inconsistent with the truths of Christianity.

But if we discard the unproved assumptions, we invalidate their conclusions. There are others who ought to be treated kindly : they are thoroughly convinced, but they are half-educated, timid souls who are confused in this babel of tongues, and who do not know the deceitfulness of materialistic belief—who are inclined to believe in the ancient faith, but are also under pressure from the arrogant claims of philosophy. For such we must have great consideration, and instead of repelling them by words, draw them to us by the spirit of Christ, and by showing that we not only believe intellectually, but that we have a ground of assurance in our inward experience, in the testimony of the Holy Ghost, which must excite respect and confidence in them.

Now, in beginning this argument, I wish to claim, first, the truth of all I have said in the three preceding lectures. You see, therefore, the logical reason for the order I adopted. I claim, as preliminary to the discussion of the doctrine of holy Scripture, the truths of the principles already established : to wit, there is a God ; this God possesses the attributes of omnipresence, omnipotence, infinitude, etc. ; he is everywhere present ; immanent in all things at all times ; working continuously and universally through all things from within. He is also transcendent

and extramundane, acting upon the world from without
on such points and at such times as he wills. The whole
order of providence and of moral government, whether
natural, supernatural, or gracious, is presupposed in this
argument.

If a man does not believe in God as omnipresent and as
active in all his creatures, if he does not believe that man
is a free moral agent under the moral government of God,
who is a holy, just, and benevolent Ruler, then this lecture
is not intended for him. But if a man does so believe, we
challenge him to present objections to the catholic doctrine
of the Word of God which will be at the same time rational
and consistent with Christian Theism.

III. *How do we ascertain the Constituent Parts of
Scripture?*—that is, how do we (1) ascertain the several
books which make up the canon? and (2) how do we
ascertain the words which make up the correct text of
those books? I can of course attempt only a very bare
sketch of what should be the full and critically-learned
answer to these questions. You all fully understand that
they fall outside of the particular department of study to
which my life has been devoted. The amount of the
highest talent and learning consecrated within the Christian Church to the defence and elucidation of the sacred
Scriptures would infinitely surprise the shallow critics who
are vociferously claiming that its pretensions have been
disproved. They should remember that a few frogs in a
swamp make incomparably more noise than all the herds
of cattle browsing upon a hundred hills. Yet none are
deceived, except the frogs themselves. In Princeton Theological Seminary the study of the subjects embraced within
this single lecture consumes the larger part of three years
of study, and the entire attention of four learned and able
professors.

(A) 1. *How do we ascertain what Books constitute the*

Canon of the Old Testament? The New Testament came into existence in an age in which a contemporaneous literature existed, thoroughly illuminated by the light of history. But the Old Testament contains the very oldest extant literature of the world. It inaugurates human history, and therefore cannot, in its earliest contents, be verified by contemporaneous testimonies. It is only in its later periods that it receives confirmation unquestionable from the monuments of Egypt and the cylinders of Assyria.

Nevertheless, we are certain that we have the very same canon which Christ recognized when he said to his disciples, and through them to us, " Search the Scriptures : ......they are they which testify of me." The very books which we have now are the very books to which Christ appealed. He cited them (1) by their classes, as " the Law," " the Law and the Prophets ; " and (2) he quoted the writings severally, and attributed them to their respective authors—-as to Moses, to David, and to Esaias. The same was done by the inspired writers of the New Testament. That the canon endorsed by Christ is the very canon we now possess we know to an absolute certainty— by the Septuagint translation, made nearly three hundred years before Christ; by the Hebrew Bible, jealously guarded by the Jews from the earliest ages to the present time; from the testimony of Philo and of Josephus, the great Jewish writers of the first Christian century ; and from the earliest Latin and Syriac translations.

As to this point, indeed, there is no controversy. The simple question remains, which to real Christians is no question, whether the testimony of Christ our Lord is sufficient to establish the fact.

2. *How do we ascertain the True Text of the Several Books which constitute this Canon?* Our reliance here also is upon the guarantee of Christ. We are sure that we possess the Masoretic text which was collected and

recorded by the Masorets from the fifth century onward.
These were great Jewish scholars, who searched all manu-
scripts open to them, not to form a new text, but to ascer-
tain the true text in the material that had descended to them.
The Targums and the Talmud also make it certain that
the text we now have is essentially the identical text
which Christ had, and which he virtually guarantees to us.
The same fact is proved to us by the Septuagint Greek
Version before referred to, and by the Peshito, the old
Syriac Version, made at the end of the second century.
The Septuagint, the Hebrew Bible, the Syriac Version, the
Vulgate, the Masoretic notes must embody the text as it
existed in the time of Christ. The agreement of all the
various sources of information is so close that the greatest
differences they suggest would not change a single doctrine
nor cast doubt upon a single historic fact of any importance. I am justified, therefore, in affirming that we stand
possessed to-day of the very same Old Testament Scriptures to which Christ appealed, and to which his authority
binds our obedience and our faith.

In these days you hear much of the ravages which a
learned criticism has made in the integrity of our traditional
Scriptures, and thus in the historical foundations of our
faith. Ordinary historical criticism is a perfectly legitimate and necessary process by which all the light, external
and internal, afforded by history, literature, and the intrinsic
characteristics of the books or texts in question is collected,
and we judge by means of all the best evidence we have
what conclusions we have to draw in reference to their
genuineness and their integrity, or the reverse. But there
is an arrogant phase of the " higher criticism " that is far
more ambitious, and attempts to correct, or even to recon-
struct, the existing text by wide inductions from the
history of the times, from the other writings, and from the
known or supposed character, knowledge, style, situation,

or subject of the writer. The whole historical situation is vividly conceived by the critic of this school, and he proceeds to infer therefrom what the writer must have said or could not have said. It is admitted that in some cases and within narrow limits such a process may be legitimate. When there is conflict or indefiniteness in the evidence afforded by direct explicit historical data of manuscript or version, it may be well to go further afield for collateral or for inferential evidence. But it is very plain that this process of "higher criticism" is liable to be coloured, and even wholly controlled, by the subjective conditions of the critic—by his sympathies, by his historical and philosophical and religious theories, and by his *a priori* judgments as to what the sacred writer ought to say. It is also very plain that the conclusions of this Criticism are of no value whatever when opposed to clearly-ascertained historical facts or documentary evidence.

In the case of "criticism" applied to the Old or New Testament Scriptures in a spirit hostile to the long-received faith of the Christian Church, it is notorious that it is the outgrowth of a false philosophy, of naturalistic views of God's relation to the world, and of *a priori* theories of evolution applied to history. When we remember, therefore, what can be clearly proved by historic fact and document, that Christ endorsed as the *Word of God* the very Old Testament Scriptures, book and text, which we now possess, when we remember that all the evidence attainable from Egyptian monuments and Assyrian cylinders corroborates the claims of this Hebrew Bible in all its parts, it is very evident that the claims of this "criticism" are groundless.

(B) 1. *How do we ascertain what Books of right belong to the New Testament Canon?* Here the case is different. Christ did not present us the collected books of the New Testament and guarantee their integrity. On the other hand, these books were written in the full light of an historically illuminated age, and come to us supported by a contemporaneous literature and followed by a copious consequent literature of their own creating.

The rule by which the canonicity of any New Testament book is determined is: any book written by an apostle, or received generally as canonical by the Church during the age in which it was presided over and instructed by the apostles, is to be regarded as canonical. Take, for instance, the Epistle to the Hebrews. If written by Paul, then it would have a right to a place in the canon for that reason. But if not written by Paul, if it was received generally as canonical by the Church during the lives of Paul and John, then its right must be admitted on that ground.

Of course, the facts in question must be determined by an examination of two classes of evidence——(1) the internal character of the writing; (2) the external historical evidence of its genuineness and of its recognition as canonical by the Church of the first century. No external evidence can prove a book to have come from God if its contents are morally bad or intellectually contemptible. Nevertheless, no matter what the contents of a book may be, we cannot admit that it belongs to the New Testament canon except on the ground of explicit and sufficient historical proof.

The kind of evidence by which we establish the canonicity of each of the books of the New Testament is precisely the same as that by which we prove the authenticity and genuineness of any ancient classic. The only difference is that in behalf of the books of the New Testament the evidence is incomparably more abundant. This evidence may be distributed under the following heads, each head representing copious literatures critically sifted and logically arranged——(1) quotations and references to

these books found in the writings of early Christians;
(2) early catalogues of the sacred books; (3) early translations; (4) general verdict of the Church; (5) internal
characteristics.

You hear a great deal to-day about the "Christian consciousness." The new critics, having destroyed the ancient
historical foundations of our Scriptures and of our faith,
wish now to build them up again upon a basis of Christian consciousness. Every book and every specific reading
is to be received which is approved by the subjective tests,
literary, scientific, æsthetic, religious, and fantastic, of self-
appointed Scripture-tasters in the nineteenth century. We
also believe in a Christian consciousness—that is, in a
human consciousness modified by religious experience and
the indwelling of the Holy Ghost. But the mouthpiece
of that consciousness is no self-appointed, self-conscious
group of cultured moderns. It is voiced only by the consensus of all Christians of all nations, all ecclesiastical folds
and ages. These very critics deny the growth of the
whole Church since St. Augustine, because its uniform
testimonies rebuke them. We, on the contrary, appeal
from the self-elected representatives of "Christian consciousness" to the thing itself—to the consensus of the whole
Church, ancient, mediæval, and modern, Greek, Roman,
Lutheran, and Reformed. We appeal to the historic and
abiding creeds, confessions, hymns, and liturgies of all
Christians. We appeal to the testimony of the Holy
Ghost, to the witness of all saints and martyrs, to all
reformations, revivals, and missions since Pentecost.

The progress of this controversy has been one unbroken
march of triumph for the integrity of our traditional canon.
The first destructive "critics" denied the authenticity and
historic validity of the fourth Gospel, and the originality
and accuracy of the synoptic Gospels; and they admitted
the genuineness of only four books—Romans, First and

Second Corinthians, and Galatians. These are admitted to have been the genuine writings of the apostle Paul by the general consent of the most destructive critics, and of all branches and ages of the Christian Church. This admission alone defeats the enemy, and establishes upon this rock of unquestionable historic fact the whole gospel system. The entire body of Christian doctrine can be shown to be taught in these four admitted original Christian documents—the entire person, office, and work of Christ; the entire salvation, temporal and eternal, of his believing followers. Since that time the originality and validity of the synoptical Gospels have been fully vindicated, and the genuineness of the fourth Gospel has been established beyond reasonable question, as is nobly admitted and maintained by the late Dr. Ezra Abbot, one of the most learned Unitarians America has ever produced.

2. *How do we ascertain the True Text of the Several Books of the New Testament?* You can easily understand that through the process of multiplying manuscripts by hand, which is laborious and involves an infinitude of independent details, an untold number of variations would creep into the text.

The *textus receptus* was formed in the age of the Reformation by a hasty and uncritical gathering and comparison of the manuscripts which were found lying ready to hand, without respect to their various age or authority. Cardinal Ximenes, in Complutum, Spain, printed the first edition, A.D. 1514, which, however, was not published till 1520 or 1521. The next edition was issued by Erasmus from Bâle, 1516, with succeeding editions of 1519, 1522, 1527, 1535; then that of Stephanus from Paris, 1546; then that of Beza from Geneva, 1565. Finally, the second Elzevir edition of 1633, Leyden, which claimed to give the *textus receptus*, was generally so received, and gave currency to that title. The text thus formed was the basis of the English version of King James and of all the New Testaments of all languages in modern times.

But during the present century the text of the New Testament has been carefully studied, a far wider collection of manuscripts has been gathered, the more ancient and valuable manuscripts have been made the basis of a corrected text, and a text nearly approximating to the original autographs of the sacred writers has been arrived at by a process of critical comparison and judgment of the immense material collected.

This is gathered—(1.) From ancient manuscripts : for example, the *Codex Alexandrinus* in the British Museum, dating from the beginning of the fifth century, from 400 to 450, after the birth of Christ; the *Codex Vaticanus,* dating from some time in the fourth century; the *Codex Sinaiticus,* believed by Tischendorf to be one of the fifty copies prepared by the order of Constantine by Eusebius, A.D. 331. (2.) From the numerous quotations from the New Testament writings found in the works of the early Fathers. (3.) From the early translations, such as the Peshito, or early Syriac, latter part of the second century; the Latin Vulgate of Jerome, A.D. 385 ; the Coptic, from the third century. From all these sources the new critical editions of the New Testament Greek text have been derived. The best of these in their order have been those of Griesbach, who died 1812 ; Lachmann, who died 1851 ; Tischendorf, who died 1874 ; and of Westcott and Hort, which was made the basis of the New Revision in 1880.

This much has been settled upon definite and sufficient historical evidence critically sifted. The testimony establishes the fact that these New Testament books constitute the second division of God's Word, and that the text in our possession is incomparably more accurate and more certain than that which is possessed of any other ancient

book in the world.   God has taken such care of his own
Word that the differences which you may observe between
the Revised Version and the Old Version of the Scriptures
are such as do not involve the stability of a single important historic fact, or of a single article of faith.   We are
brought by this process not only to the substance, but to
the form and shading, of the truth as it came from the
original organs of revelation.   We can almost recognize
the tone and inflection of the voice of Christ himself.

IV. *Our fourth question is, How was the Bible, this
Book of books, produced?   What was the true genesis of
these Scriptures?   Written evidently by men, how did they
become the Word of God?*

There are three distinct ways in which we can conceive
that God might produce a book to be read by man—(1.)
He could have produced it by his own immediate energy,
acting directly and alone, as he did when he wrote the
Ten Commandments with his own finger on tables of stone.
(2.) He might have used men as his amanuenses, not as
conscious and free penmen, but mechanically as his instruments of writing in simple obedience to his verbal dictation.
(3.) The third way is the infinitely better one which God
has chosen.   It is the God-like way, which is in analogy
with all his methods.   He first created man, and endowed
him constitutionally with all his rational, emotional, æsthetic,
moral, and volitional powers.   He then brought certain individual men into existence with the specific qualifications
necessary for writing certain parts of Scripture, and placed
them under their specific historical conditions, and in their
specific positions in the succession of sacred writers, and
gave them the precise degree and quality of religious experience, of natural providential guidance, of supernatural
revelation and inspiration, necessary to stimulate their free
activity and to determine the result as he would have it.

1. In the first place, the Bible is as intensely and

thoroughly a *human* book as ever existed. As Christ was a true man, tempted in all points as we are, yet without sin, because also divine, so the Bible is thoroughly human, yet without error, because also divine. God is infinite; yet his word, the Bible, is finite—that is, God's thought is expressed under all the limits of human thought and language, so that man may receive and profit by it. God is omniscient; but his word, the Bible, is not omniscient. It is narrowly limited in its range as a human book, produced by the instrumentality of human minds, and addressed to human minds of all classes; but within that range it is infallible, without any error. It has its limitations, as every human work has. It is based on human intuitions; it proceeds through the lines of human logic; it implies human feelings, tastes, experiences. Every separate book is a spontaneous work of human genius, and bears the marks of all the personal idiosyncrasies and of the historic situation of its author. The individuality of Peter, Paul, John, David, Isaiah, and Moses is as fully expressed in their writings as that of Shakespeare or of Milton in theirs. Each biblical writer wrought as freely and as spontaneously as any other. Each of these books was also a book of its time—bore the marks of its age, and was specifically adapted to accomplish its immediate end among its contemporaries. The provincialisms of thought and idiom proper to the situation of their writers are found in these books. They make no claim to eminent purity of language, or to high literary merit either in substance or form. Yet all these writings, severally and collectively, are books of all times, adapted perfectly to the edification and instruction of the Church of every age —of Moses, of David, of the prophets, of the time of Christ, of the ancient, mediæval, Reformation, and modern Church. Of all books, it is the most comprehensively human. Of all God's works, it is the most characteristi-

cally divine. It is, in one view, an entire national literature; in another view, it is two distinct volumes; in
another view, it is one single work, with one Author,
subject, method, and end.

2. In the second place, the Bible is a *divine* book, bearing the attributes of its Author, God. All along the line
of human authorship through which this wonderful book
grew to be, during at least sixteen hundred years, God
provided each specifically endowed and conditioned prophet for his appointed place in the succession, a place
prepared for him by all who had preceded; and on this
foundation, already provided, he proceeds to build up in
organic continuity, and in symmetrical proportion, the
system already inaugurated. To each prophet God has
communicated his specific item of revelation and his
specific impulse and direction through inspiration.

3. The result is that the whole is an organism, a whole
consisting of many parts exquisitely correlated and vitally
independent.

In this respect you may compare the Koran of Mo-
hammed with the Christian Bible. In the great debate
between the missionary Henry Martyn and the Persian
moulvies, the latter showed a great superiority of logical
and rhetorical power. They proved that the Koran was
written by a great genius; that it was an epoch-making
book, giving law to a language pre-eminent for elegance,
inexhaustible fulness, and precision, revolutionizing kingdoms, forming empires, and moulding civilization. Nevertheless, it was a single work, within the grasp of one great
man. But Henry Martyn proved that the Bible is one
single book, one single, intricate, organic whole, produced
by more than forty different writers of every variety of
culture and condition through sixteen centuries of time—
that is, through about fifty successive generations of mankind. As a great cathedral, erected by many hands

through many years, is born of one conceiving mind, and has had but one author, so only God can be the one Author of the whole Bible, for only he has been contemporaneous with all stages of its genesis; he only has been able to control and co-ordinate all the agents concerned in its production, so as to conceive and realize the incomparable result.

4. This book, whatever we may think of the propriety of it, unquestionably claims to be the *Word of God.* At the opening of the book it demands the implicit credence and obedience of every reader. Its instant order to every reader is, " Believe, on peril of your soul's life !" It does not point to evidence, nor plead before the bar of human reason. But it utters the voice of God and speaks by authority. What other book does this ? And this claim has been abundantly vindicated through the ages in the opinion of the wisest and best of mankind—(1) by its demonstrations of supernatural knowledge, (2) of supernatural works, (3) of supernatural power over the hearts and consciences of men; (4) by the accompanying witness of the Holy Ghost; (5) by its omnipresent beneficent influence through all Christian lands and ages.

What would you think if to-day at high noon the existence and the light and heat and life-giving radiance of the sun were brought into question ? How would you answer the sceptical denial of that self-evident fact by a blind man ? To all the living the sun is its own witness. So all who question the divinity of the Bible only condemn themselves. What a sorry appearance the grotesque herd make even now !

V. *What is God's part in bringing this Book of books into existence ?* This falls under several heads—namely, providence; the gracious work of his Spirit on the heart; revelation; inspiration.

1. *Providence.* In a previous lecture I showed that God

is to be conceived of as an infinite Spirit, presiding over all creatures and acting upon them from without at his will, but also as omnipresent, at every moment immanent in every ultimate element of every creature, and acting in and through all things from within.   Thus God's activities are everywhere confluent with our own spontaneities.   All creatures live and move and have their being in him.   He works in us to will as well as to do—that is, as free agents, though willing to do according to his good pleasure. A great musician elicits his most perfect music out of instruments and under conditions made for him beforehand by other men.   How much more completely would the artist be the sole creator of his work if he could at will first create his material with the very qualities he needs, then build and attune his instruments for his own purposes, and then bring out from them, thus prepared and adjusted, the very music in its fulness which his soul has designed from the first.   So God from the first designed and adapted every human writer employed in the genesis of Scripture.   Paul, John, Peter, David, Isaiah, have been made precisely what they were, and placed and conditioned precisely as they were, and then moved to write, and directed in writing precisely what they wrote. The revelation was in a large measure through an historical series of events, led along by a providential guidance largely natural, but surcharged, as a cloud with electricity, with supernatural elements all along its line. Thus, under God's providence, the Scriptures grew to be, all the conspiring forces which contributed to their formation acting under the providential control of the everpresent, ever-acting, immanent God.

    2. *Spiritual Illumination.*   This includes the whole sum of God's gracious dealing with the soul of his prophet, qualifying him to be the fit organ for the communication of religious truth.   In order to exhibit truth in its

comprehensive logical relations, God employed the logical and scholastically trained mind of Paul. In all his writing this natural and acquired faculty of Paul acted under God's guidance as spontaneously and naturally as the same faculty ever wrought in the case of any other writer. But in relation to spiritual truth the natural mind of man is blind and without feeling. Spiritual illumination by the Holy Ghost, a personal religious experience, was as necessary in the case of such writers as David, John, and Paul as æsthetic taste and genius are in the case of a poet or an artist. The spiritual intuition of John, the spiritualized understanding of Paul, the personal religious experience of David, have, by the superadded gift of inspiration, been rendered permanently typical and normal to the Church in all ages.

3. *Revelation.* Spiritual illumination opens the organ of spiritual vision, and clarifies it. Revelation, on the other hand, gives the additional light which nature does not supply. In every instance where supernatural knowledge of God, his attributes, his purposes, of the secrets of his grace or of the future of the Church in this world, of the life of body or of soul after death, came to be needed by a sacred writer, God immediately gave it to him by revelation. This was done in various ways, as by visions, dreams, direct mental suggestion, verbal dictation, and the like ; but whatever the method of communication, it was perfectly adequate to the occasion and congruous to the nature of the person to whom it was made. This, of course, was never furnished except on the occasions when it was needed : it appears more frequently in some portions of Scripture than in others ; but however frequent, it was an occasional and not a constant element of the Bible.

4. *Inspiration.* This was the absolutely constant attribute of every portion and of every element of the Scriptures, and that attribute which renders them infallible in

every utterance, and which thus constitutes their grand distinguishing trait, separating them by the whole heavens from all other books. Revelation supernaturally communicated to the sacred writer the truth which he needed, and which he did not possess, and could not attain by any natural means. Inspiration, on the other hand, is that influence of the immanent Holy Ghost which accompanied every thought, and feeling, and impulse, and action of the sacred writer involved in the function of writing the word, and which guided him in the selection and utterance of truth—that is, in its conception and in its verbal expression—so that the very mind of God in the premises was expressed with infallible accuracy. This influence was exerted from within the writer, not upon him from without. It in no degree constrains or forces; it directs through the writer's own spontaneity. It modifies action only so far as action would be otherwise divergent from the purpose of God or inadequate. It is like the directive agency of the plastic soul of the tree, which so directs the physical forces engaged in its erection that they spontaneously combine to form its intricate and voluminous organism. Or it is like the touch of the charioteer upon the reins which guide the courses of the racing steeds. Or it is like the touch of the hand of the steerer upon the rudder of the boat carried gently down the meandering stream by the currents of the air and water. These currents symbolize the natural powers and knowledge of the sacred writer, reinforced by revelation and by grace. The hand on the rudder symbolizes inspiration. It secures the fact that all things go right according to the will of the steersman. But it interferes only by gentle and alternate pressure, and thus only when otherwise the currents, if left to themselves, would not fulfil his will.

VI. *What is the doctrine of the Christian Church as to the extent to which the Scriptures are inspired?*

The two opinions which individual Christian men have severally maintained on this subject are represented respectively by the two alternative phrases, " The Scriptures *contain* the word of God," " The Scriptures *are* the Word of God."

The first is the loose formula of those who hold a low doctrine of inspiration. A river in India, " rolling down its golden sands," may be truly said to *contain* gold. But in that case we are left in doubt as to the relative proportion between the sand and the gold, and to our own resources to discriminate and separate the two. If the Bible only " contains the Word of God," it evidently can be no infallible rule of faith and practice, because we are confessedly left to the two very human and fallible instruments (1) of " higher criticism," and (2) of the " Christian consciousness," to determine what elements of the Scriptures are the very " word of God," and what elements are only the word of man. A law can have no infallibility beyond that of the court which interprets it. So in this view of the case the Bible has no infallibility beyond that of the criticism and consciousness of our self-appointed, self-complacent guides.

But the Church has always held that " the Scriptures are the Word of God." This means that, however these books may have been produced through human agency, God has (1) so controlled the process of their genesis, and (2) he so absolutely endorses the result, that the Bible in every book and every word, both in *matter and in form,* is the very *Word of God* uttered to us.

The phrase " verbal inspiration " applied to the Scriptures does not mean that the sacred writers were inspired or directed in their work by words dictated or suggested. But it means that the divine influence which we call inspiration, and which accompanied them throughout their entire work, extended to the verbal expression of every thought as well as to the thoughts themselves. This inspiration has extended equally to every part of Scripture, matter and form, thought and words, and renders the whole and every part inerrant.

Calvin, in the sixth, seventh, and eighth chapters of his *Institutes*, continually uses the phrases "Scripture," "the Scriptures," "the sacred volume," and "the Word of God" as synonymous. The first Reformed Confession of national authority, the *First Helvetic*, says, Art. i.: "Canonical Scripture *is the Word of God.*" The *Second Helvetic* Confession was the most widely recognized of all the Reformed Confessions in Switzerland, France, Hungary, Poland, Scotland, and highly honoured in England and Holland. It says: "We believe and confess that the canonical Scriptures of the holy prophets and apostles of both Testaments *are the Word of God*, and have plenary authority of themselves and not from men." Every Presbyterian minister and elder in England, Scotland, Ireland, Canada, and the United States, North and South, believes this, or he has forsworn himself. Each one has at his ordination solemnly declared, before God and man, that he *believes these Scriptures* "*to be the Word of God*" (Confession of Faith, Presbyterian Board of Publication, pp. 429, 434, 441). Thomas Cartwright, the father of English Presbyterianism, in his *Treatise of the Christian Religion; or, The Whole Body and Substance of Divinity* (London, A.D. 1616), has written his twelfth chapter "On the Word of God." This he identifies with the collection of canonical books, and accounts for their authority by saying, "for *God is the Author of them.*"

This is the doctrine of the whole historical Church of God. The Roman Catholic Church declares it *de fide* to believe that God is the Author of every part of both Testaments (*Can. Council of Trent*, sec. 4; *Dog. Decrees of Vatican*

Council, 1870, sec. 3, chap. 2). Also every branch of the Reformed Church—for example, *Belgic Confession,* Art. 3 ; *Second Helvetic Confession,* chap. 1 ; *Westminster Confession,* chap. 1. In this respect the late Professor Henry B. Smith, the noble representative of the theology of the New School Branch of the Presbyterian Church in the United States, precisely agrees with the late Professor Charles Hodge, who equally represented the theology of the Old School branch. In his sermon on *The Inspiration of the Holy Scriptures,* delivered before the Synod of New York and New Jersey, October 17, 1855, Dr. Smith said :—" All the divine revelations which are here recorded are also inspired, but all that is the subject of inspiration need not be conceived of as distinctly revealed. Inspiration designates that divine influence under which prophets or apostles spake or wrote as they were moved by the Holy Ghost. Christ is the great Revealer, the Holy Spirit inspires.

" Its function is to convey unto the world, through divinely-commissioned prophets and apostles, either orally or by writing, under the specific influence of the Holy Spirit, whatever has been thus revealed. *Its object is the communication of truth in an infallible manner, so that when rightfully interpreted no error is conveyed.*

" It comprises both the matter and the form of the Bible—the matter in the form in which it is conveyed and set forth. It extends even to the language—not in the mechanical sense that each word is dictated by the Holy Spirit, but in the sense that under divine guidance each writer spake in his own language according to the measure of his knowledge, acquired by personal experience, the testimony of others, or by immediate divine revelation.

" So wonderfully do the divine and human elements commingle in the Scriptures, as do the first and second causes also in the realm of providence, that it is vain to limit inspiration to doctrine and truth, excluding history from its sphere. The attempt is as unphilosophical as it is unscriptural. No analysis can detect such a line of separation. It is both invisible and not to be spiritually discerned.

"The theory of plenary inspiration, as we have already given it, comprises whatever is true in all these views, subordinate to the prime position *that the Bible not only contains, but is, the Word of God.*"

Dr. H. B. Smith's *Introduction to Christian Theology*: "Inspiration gives us a book, properly called the *Word of God, inspired in all its parts.* The inspiration is plenary in the sense of extending to all the parts and of *extending also to the words.*"

VII. *What is to be said as to alleged discrepancies?*

The above statement unquestionably truly represents the ancient and catholic faith of the historic Church of Christ. The hostile critics and theorists object that the Scriptures are full of inaccuracies and discrepancies of statement—(1) as between the statements of Scripture and modern science or undoubted history; (2) as between one statement or quotation of Scripture and another.

In answer to this we have space to say only—

1st. We freely admit that many errors have crept into the sacred text as it exists at present; although none of these errors, nor all of them together, obscure one Christian doctrine or important fact. In order to make good the objection of the critics, it is necessary that they show that the discrepancy exists when the clearly ascertained original text of Scripture is in question.

2nd. The Scriptures were not written from the scientific point of view, nor intended to anticipate science. A distinction should be clearly drawn and strongly held between the speculations of science and its ascertained facts.

The speculations of science are like the changing currents of the sea, while the Scriptures have breasted them like the rocks for two thousand years. The Scriptures speak of nature as it presents itself phenomenally. When this is remembered, the Bible contradicts no fact of science. On the contrary, the entire view of the genesis and order of the physical world presented by the Bible, in contrast with all the other ancient books whatsoever, is in correspondence with that presented by modern science to a degree perfectly miraculous. The men who press this objection are ignorant either of science or of the Bible, or, more probably, of both.

3rd. As to the alleged discrepancies with history, it must be remembered (*a*) that the most modern discoveries (from Egypt and Assyria) most wonderfully confirm the historical accuracy of Scripture; (*b*) that when only a part of an ancient situation is historically illuminated, different accounts may appear inconsistent which are really complementary to each other and mutually supporting.

4th. As to the discrepancies alleged to exist in certain passages between the Scriptures themselves, it is evident that the question is one of fact, which can be settled only by a thorough, learned, intelligent, and impartial investigation. Very few men are qualified to give an opinion. There is no possibility of commencing even an investigation in a popular lecture. It is sufficient for me that men like my learned colleagues in Princeton Seminary, who spend their lives in the special study of the Hebrew and Greek Scriptures, assure me *that one single instance of such discrepancy has never been proved.*

V.

PRAYER.

A COMPLETE treatise on the subject of prayer would necessarily include three special subdivisions—(1) prayer considered as a fact and an efficient agency in relation to God, to his eternal plans, and to the laws of the universe; (2) prayer considered as a Christian grace; (3) the manner in which prayer is to be practised and expressed, both as a private and as a public exercise. In this lecture we shall confine ourselves to the first subdivision—that is, to the consideration of prayer and its answer as a fact, and as an efficient agency in relation to God and to his eternal plans, and to the laws and natural forces of the universe.

All religion presupposes the personality of God, and springs from the personal relations subsisting between man and God. God can and does act upon men from within and below consciousness, turning the hearts of men even as rivers of water are turned. But he also acts upon us through our conscious acts of perception and feeling, called into exercise by his external intercourse with us as a Person speaking to persons. He is always face to face with us, our constant companion and guide and friend. From our creation he is constantly standing to us in the relation of our Father and of our moral Governor. And in these relations we have been sustaining intercourse with him ceaselessly all our lives. Sin consists in man's want of sympathy with God, his moral character, purposes, and mode of action in these relations. When we are born again by the Holy Ghost, we are brought into sympathy with him in all these respects, and thus intercourse with him becomes consciously active on our part, more and more intimate and tender, and a source of joy to us continually. To this conscious intercourse we assign the name "prayer," in the wide sense of that word, whether it is breathed in disconnected ejaculations or said or sung in connected sequences of thought or emotion. Prayer in this wider sense includes all the exercises proper to the relation our souls, as sinful yet redeemed and reconciled, sustain to God —for example, adoration, confession, thanksgiving, and supplication for ourselves and others.

The great design of God in this relation is to effect our education and government as rational and spiritual beings. He accomplishes these ends by revealing to us his perfections, by training our intellects to follow the great lines of thought developed in his plans and revealed in his works, and by training us to action in the exercise of all our faculties as co-workers with each other and with him in the execution of his plans.

In order to accomplish both these ends at once, the education of our thought and the training of our faculty by active exercise, God has established a comprehensive and unchangeable system of laws, of second causes working uniformly, of fixed sequences and established methods, by which he works, and by which he can train us to understand his working and to work with him. This careful adherence to the use of means, to the slow and circuitous operation of second causes and established laws, is surely not for God's sake. It cannot be necessary to him. It is ordained and rigidly adhered to only for our sake. And for us it is absolutely necessary. If means were not necessary to the attainment of ends; if God did not carefully confine his powers to the lines of established and known laws; if we lived in a world in which miracle, instead of being the infinite exception, was the rule, and God was constantly breaking forth with the exercise of supernatural power in unexpected places, and like the wild lightning eluding the most rapid thought as it dashes zigzag across the sky,—we should find all thought and intelligent action impossible. We could not understand God, because we could not trace the relation of means to ends in his action. If we could not understand him, we could not appreciate his wisdom, his righteousness, or his benevolence. We could not work with him, for we could not depend upon the operation of any means, we could not hope to effect any results. The universe would be a chaos, and the community of men a bedlam. In order to accomplish the necessary understanding between God and man, and in order to afford a secure basis for the exercise of human faculties in the education of man and the moulding of human character, the established fixed relations between cause and effect, uniform sequences of natural law, must be universal, continuous, perpetual, and absolutely uninterrupted, without any exception except for good and well-understood reasons. If there be miracles at all, they must explain themselves as divine signs by their connection with a new direct message from the heavenly Father to his children on the earth. In that case, and in that case only, the miracle brings God nearer to his children and makes his way more plain to them. In every other case a miracle is only a bewilderment and an offence, which darkens the face of God and effaces the evidence of his being and the traces of his wisdom and love.

Observe how patiently through the ages of ages God confines himself to the slow processes of natural law, and never impatiently cuts across the heavens to accomplish suddenly by miracle the results for which he works. Follow the long, long cycle of the geologic ages in which God, by slow natural processes, by the law of means adapted to ends, is preparing the world to be the fit habitation of man and the adjusted theatre of human history. Trace with your eyes the long, long cycle of human history preceding the advent of our Redeemer, while God is patiently governing his rebellious subjects, and by natural causes and historical methods evolving the plan of salvation and preparing the world for Christ, who never came until all things were ready and the fulness of the time was come. Look along the tedious course of the history of the Christian Church since the advent of Christ, and learn the lesson of God's methods by his use of second causes, by his slow following of the lines of natural law in the development of his kingdom, and his preparation for the second coming of our Lord. Each and all of these results God could have accomplished by miracle. But in that case his wisdom would have remained hidden in his own being, and his people would have failed utterly of education—neither knowing God or his way, nor trained to exercise all their faculties of head and heart and will as workers together with him.

There are two extreme and equally false views as to this framework of second causes and natural law in its relation to the action of God and to our intercourse with him through faith and prayer. The one view, that of deists and rationalists and agnostics, makes this framework of second causes and natural law, which men call Nature, an iron, impenetrable barrier, which utterly separates God and man, which makes prayer an empty form, and divine help and sympathy a delusion. The opposite view, just as false and pernicious, regards this framework of second causes and natural law as simply a stage, with natural scenery as a background, on which to exhibit startling and bewildering miracles, without system or meaning or evidential value. The true view of this framework of second causes and natural law is that (1) it reveals God and his perfections to man in a form he can understand and appreciate ; (2) it affords a practicable basis on which human faculties can be educated and men trained as intelligent co-workers with God ; (3) it presents an invariable course of action that we must follow. Nevertheless it is infinitely flexible, so that men everywhere are able, by the rational use of means, to accomplish their purposes. Thus, men following and using natural law plant and sow and raise crops, navigate the air with balloons and the sea with ships, tunnel mountains, erect buildings, and girdle the earth with the electric currents of thought and purpose. (4.) This great permanent framework of second causes and natural laws is, of course, incomparably more flexible in the hands of God than it can be in the hands of man. We know these laws partially and imperfectly: God knows them perfectly. We act upon these second causes externally : God acts upon them internally. We act upon them only at a few isolated points : God acts upon every point of the infinite system at the same time. Surely, therefore, while God can act through nature in a supernatural manner, he can also, like us, only infinitely more perfectly, act through nature and in accordance with natural law in accomplishing his purposes. He can answer prayer, send rain or sunshine, turn into new channels rivers of water or currents of air, just as he turns the hearts of men, without violating natural laws.

Using the word " prayer " in this discussion in the specific sense of " petition," " supplication for desired benefits, spiritual and material," we will proceed to discuss the following points :—

1. What are the true conditions of acceptable prayer ?

2. In what sense and under what limits are we to expect to have our prayers answered ?

3. Answer objection drawn from the previous certainty of events determined by God's eternal purpose.

4. Answer objection drawn from fixity of the laws of nature.

5. Show that the faith of the Christian Church in the efficacy of prayer is confirmed by uniform Christian experience.

I. What are the true conditions of acceptable prayer ?

1. The person offering the prayer must be in a state of reconciliation to God through Christ. This does not mean that God never answers the prayers of unregenerate persons ; but the promise can be claimed only by those who have accepted the conditions of salvation, and are loyal to their Christian engagements.

2. The prayer must be sincere, must express a real desire of the heart, and it must be offered and the answer sought only through the merits and intercession of Jesus Christ.

3. The prayer must be offered in absolute submission to the higher, broader knowledge, wisdom, and righteousness of God. It must follow our Saviour's "Not as I will, but as thou wilt." The only objects for which we have any warrant to press unconditional petitions are (1) our own sanctification, (2) the bringing on of the triumph of Christ's kingdom, because God has positively revealed both of these to be his "will." The unconditioned, unsubmissive demand for any other benefit, in relation to which the will of God is as yet unrevealed, is obviously a presumptuous sin, a ground of offence, and not an acceptable prayer.

4. In order that the prayer shall be acceptable, the person praying must in every case intelligently and diligently use the means provided by God himself in the

great framework of second causes and natural laws for the attainment of the end desired. If a man who prays for a crop neglects to sow the seed; or if a man who prays for learning neglects to study; or if a man who prays for the cure of disease neglects to take the appointed remedies; or if a man who prays for sanctification neglects to use the means of grace; or if a man who prays for the conversion of sinners neglects to work for it as far as his power or opportunity goes—then, in every case, he disobeys and insults God; his prayer is a mockery and an offence, and it can be answered only by rebuke and chastisement.

Means in relation to ends, and ends in dependence upon means, are as much an ordinance of God and as obligatory on us as prayer itself. If God shuts us up in a situation where no means are possible, we have a right to pray for what we want in the absence of all means; and God is perfectly able to give it to us without means, if it seem wisest and best to himself. But in every case in which means are available to us their use is commanded, and the poor fanatic who neglects them and petulantly cries for what he wants dishonours God, grieves rational Christians, and gives occasion to the devil and to his friends to triumph.

5. We must believe in the efficacy of prayer itself as a divinely-appointed means of attaining blessings. We must believe that we do and will obtain blessings by means of prayer which we would not attain without it.

II. In what sense and under what limits are we to expect to have our prayers answered?

Agnostic and naturalistic critics of the Christian faith have admitted that prayer might be a power in the spiritual sphere, and that in every case its subjective effects upon the person praying, upon his state of mind and character, would be beneficial; but that it is absurd to admit that prayer could have any effect upon the mind or purpose or act of God, or any influence upon the course of events in the material world.

It is true that prayer is a power in the spiritual world—that it does secure spiritual blessings, and that it does produce valuable subjective effects upon the state of mind and character of the person praying. But Christ commands us to ask for our daily bread, which includes all desired temporal and material benefits. If we are to pray honestly for daily bread, or for any other desired material good, it must be because we are assured that if we pray we may really and truly influence the mind of God to give it to us. To ask God for an objective material good, when we believe that the only possible effect of the asking is an internal and spiritual modification of our own feelings, is false and hypocritical, unworthy of either God or man, and sure to be of no effect.

The Scriptures assure us, and all Christians believe, that prayer for material as well as for spiritual good is as real a means of effecting the end sought as is sowing seed a means of getting a crop, or as is studying a means of getting learning, or as are praying and reading the Bible means of sanctification. But it is a moral, not a physical, cause. Its efficiency consists in its power of affecting the mind of God and disposing him to do for us what he would not do if we did not pray.

But it is plain that in order to be effectual in any given case, the prayer must have all the conditions or elements of true Christian prayer stated under the former head. The person praying must be in favour with God ; he must be sincere, must present his prayer only through Christ, and trust only in Christ's mediation. He must desire the thing sought, and ask for it only in complete submission to the wise and righteous will of God. There is nothing more contemptible than the presumptuous claim that God has subjected the government of the universe to our dicta-

tion.　Every really holy soul must prefer a million times
that God should reign absolutely, and do with him and
his as seems best in his sight.　What child of an earthly
father can judge in any case what upon the whole and in
the long run is best for itself?　How much more should
we insist upon leaving every decision at the disposal of our
heavenly Father!　And lastly, the person praying must
be diligent in using all the appointed means which are
available to him to secure the end.

When all the conditions are fulfilled, God will with
absolute certainty be moved to answer our prayer—to do
for us what he would not have done if we had not prayed.
He will, if he sees it best, give us precisely what we ask
for, at the precise time, in the precise manner.　Or he
may give it substantially in a different time and manner.
Or he may give us something better, something which we
ourselves would desire more if only we had the eyes to
see as God sees.　How do you treat your little ones when
they cry for unwholesome sweets?　God never will give
us a stone when we ask for bread, or a serpent when we
ask for an egg; but he often does give us bread when we
ignorantly ask for a stone, and an egg when we perversely
desire a serpent.

III. But it is objected that the doctrine of prayer is
absurd, because God has already from eternity determined
whatsoever comes to pass; every event is already fixed in
his eternal purpose; and this purpose is absolutely immutable and cannot be changed.　What, then, is the use
of asking him to do what we wish done?　If it is already
decreed, there is no need to ask for it; if it is not already
decreed, there is no use to ask for it.

We answer:—1. This is a theoretical objection hard to
answer, simply because the human mind cannot comprehend the relations of time to eternity.　But for practical
purposes the objection is absolutely senseless.　If God has

eternally decreed that you should live, what is the use of your breathing? If God has eternally decreed that you should talk, what is the use of your opening your mouth? If God has eternally decreed that you should reap a crop, what is the use of your sowing the seed? If God has eternally decreed that your stomach should contain food, what is the use of your eating? Prayer is only one means appointed by God for attaining our ends. In order to educate us, he demands that we should use the means, or go without the ends which depend upon them. There are plenty of fools who make the transcendental nature of eternity and of the relation of the eternal life of God to the time-life of man an excuse for neglecting prayer. But of all the many fools in the United States, there is not one absurd enough to make the same eternal decree an excuse for not chewing his food or for not voluntarily inflating his lungs.

2. The common difficulties men feel about the eternal and unchangeable decrees of God all arise from the absurd mistake of conceiving of God as determining the certain occurrence of a part separate from the whole, of an event separate from the causes and conditions upon which it depends. God's single decree determined the whole universe in all its successive ages as one whole. It has determined the cause and condition as well as the event. If a man will not believe, he shall not be saved; if he will not sow, he shall not reap. But if it is decreed that he shall reap, it is just as much decreed that he shall sow. If it be decreed that you shall have what you desire, it is decreed no less that you shall pray for it; and it is certain that you will not get it if you do not pray for it.

IV. But it is objected that the order of nature, the uniformities of natural laws, are fixed, and God will not violate them and so make the whole course of nature turn out of its way, in order to make way for a poor praying sinner like you or me.

We answer :—1. The whole order of material nature has been framed from the beginning for the very purpose of providing for the mutual intercourse of the praying children and of the prayer-hearing Father. It is a matter of universal experience that earthly fathers find the order of nature, when intelligently followed, no barrier but the most effective of conceivable instruments in providing for the wants and in answering the petitions of their children. How can the order of nature be a greater barrier to our heavenly Father ?

2. But it is answered that we can see our earthly parents use the order of nature so as to make it answer our petitions and provide for our wants, but we never see our heavenly Father so using nature. Our earthly parents leave their footprints while using means in our behalf, and in working for us always make chips which prove their work. But our heavenly Father never makes footprints, never leaves chips, so we have no visible evidence that he responds to our petitions or acts through the order of nature in our behalf.

We answer :—The sculptor cuts the statue out of the block of marble, piece by piece, from without, and so makes chips. So earthly fathers work upon material nature from without. But when the vital principle of a tree gathers nourishment from soil and air and builds it up from within, it leaves no footprints and makes no chips. Thus our heavenly Father acts not on spots of matter from without, but upon the whole frame of material nature from within, and the whole is as obedient to his touch as are the nerves of the human body to the human spirit which inhabits it.

All nature with its mechanical causes and fixed laws, and all human souls with their instincts, struggles, and articulate cries, form part of one eternally-designed system. Every prayer and every answer, every cause and every effect, every volition and every result, has been provided for from the first. But the relation between causes and effects is never disturbed. The effect immediately depends on the cause; the answer immediately depends on the prayer. If we do not work, we cannot eat; if we do not eat, we cannot live. If we do not pray, we will not gain what we desire.

V. What is the testimony of human experience as to the actual fact of God's answering prayer for temporal and material good ?

1. We appeal to the universal instinct of prayer inherent in men of all races and centuries. We claim the consent of all false religions with the true, and the involuntary testimony of dying infidels.

2. From the nature of the case, the testimony of mankind in general on such a subject is incompetent. Any scientific "prayer-test," as that proposed by Professor Tyndall, is most incongruous to the case, and therefore unphilosophical. Prayer is not a physical cause; it is a moral cause. It acts upon our heavenly Father, disposing him to attend to our wants in the exercise of infinite wisdom and love, and to use his loving and wise discretion in complying with or refusing our imperfect desires. Who can enter into this region of intimate personal relations between the praying child and the prayer-hearing Father except themselves ? More than a million Christians prayed for the life of President Garfield. The world laughed, and said our Father did not hear us. We know that he did hear and answer us in the best way possible : we are completely satisfied. Millions and millions of spiritual children of God have been ceaselessly trusting him, praying to him, and proving him, from Adam to Moses, from Moses to Christ, from Christ to the present. Our Father knows our hearts : we know and he knows the real meaning of our prayers. We know our Father's heart : we know that when we were " in distress we called upon him, and he answered us and

set us in a large place." The Christian is satisfied with what he knows as to the confidential relations between his prayer-hearing Father and himself. He can well afford to smile with pity when the stranger to the household criticises his Father's faithfulness, and tries to convince the child, against the witness of his own consciousness, that his Father does not hear and answer his prayers. What can the stranger know about it? He has never truly prayed, and therefore he has never experienced any answer to prayer. Would it not be more scientific if these agnostic critics should confine their remarks to the sphere of their own experience?

VI.

THE TRINITY OF PERSONS IN THE GODHEAD.

WE shall now discuss the revelation which God has made of himself in his inspired Word as three Persons. This we must do with bowed heads and reverent hearts, for the ground on which we stand is holy. The subject is transcendently sacred: it is the infinitely righteous and majestic God. It is immeasurably important as the foundation of all knowledge and faith. And for all our knowledge relating to it we are absolutely shut up to the matter which God himself has given us in his self-revelation in his Word. Consciousness, experience, observation, or speculation cannot in this exalted sphere advance our knowledge one scintilla. We can know only just as much of this subject of the Trinity as is definitely set forth in the Bible, and no more. Our office here is that, simply, of humble disciples—to observe and interpret the self-exhibition of the Triune God in Scripture.

This doctrine is properly a "mystery," and it is often by people not fully learned disparaged as such. These mistakenly understand by "mystery" some fact or principle of which we can have only a very vague notion—a sphere of assumption or of half-perceived shadow, in relation to which certainty is impossible, and which has no logical or practical relation to the great solid continent of human knowledge and of real life. But, on the other hand, the true meaning of the word "mystery" is, that which cannot be known through the processes of discovery or invention, or of speculation, but which can be made known only by revelation, and so far forth only as unveiled. Such were the secrets of the Greek societies, which were known only as they were discovered to the initiated, as the Eleusinian mysteries, and those of the Masonic fraternity, and of all the modern secret societies.

But when these otherwise undiscoverable secrets are once revealed, then just so far forth as they have been disclosed they become part of the real knowledge of those to whom the revelation has been made ; as much so as any other knowledge whatsoever which they possess, howsoever it may have been attained.

It is plain that as God is the Creator of all things, he must be the ultimate ground and centre of all things. Therefore our knowledge of God, no matter how we have gained it, must be fundamental and central to all our other knowledge of every kind. The fundamental questions in all science and philosophy, as well as in all religion, must always be—(1.) Is there a God ? (2.) What is God ? (3.) What relations does he sustain to the universe ? The Biblical answer to the second question includes two grand divisions : the nature of God is in the Scriptures revealed (1) through the attributes or energies, the perfections, of his essence as an infinite, rational, and righteous Spirit ; (2) as eternally existing as three Persons, one in substance, in the most intimate unity of thought and purpose. It is evident that if it is true that God does eternally exist as three Persons, that fact must underlie and give shape to all his counsels and to all his works in their execution. It must control his method of working in all spheres of creation and of providence and of grace ; so that this doctrine, if true, is a necessary postulate of all philosophy and of all science, as well as of all religion.

We affirm that, instead of this threefold personality of God as taught in Scripture being a burden to our faith and a mere puzzle to our understanding, it is, of all views of God ever presented to human consciousness, the most symmetrical and harmonious, the most satisfactory to the reason, the one which renders the moral perfections of God the most comprehensible, the one which brings him most nearly within the sphere of human sympathy; which is the most profound and fruitful in important consequences; which is the most practical in its applications within the sphere of man's religious experience and duty.

I. In maintaining that the doctrine of the Trinity, as held in common by the entire historical Christian Church, is conformable to right reason, we are mindful of the limited sphere of reason in relation to such questions, and of its liability to be abused. The frequent and disastrous abuse of reason has arisen (1) from its being made the *source* of all knowledge in relation to things concerning which we are entirely dependent upon a direct divine revelation, and (2) from its being made the *measure* and *standard* of that which transcends its measure, and which rests alone upon the authority of God. On the other hand, the important and necessary use of reason in such a study is (1) to apprehend the truth as the eye apprehends light, (2) to study and judge of the evidences or credentials of the revelation claiming to be divine, and (3) to judge of contradictions, if any such are involved. There is an evident difference between that which is *against* reason, or irrational, which can never be rightly believed, and that which is *above* reason, which all men do believe every day. The doctrine of the Trinity is above reason in respect to the facts (1) that it never could have been discovered, but rests entirely upon the authority of revelation; (2) that it cannot be fully understood or explained ; (3) that, like other *data* of revelation, it leads out into the region which transcends our knowledge on every side. But, on the other hand, this doctrine involves no element which contradicts reason. On the contrary, when received as presented in Scripture it is eminently agreeable to reason. It is found to coalesce harmoniously with all other known truths, and, above all, it is found to harmonize with the most profound and fruitful religious experience. Truly our fellowship is not only " with the Father," but equally with " his Son Jesus Christ " and with the Holy Ghost. And every experienced Christian has an experimental knowledge of his relations to each divine Person.

II. *The Scriptural Presentation of this Doctrine.* The entire Old and New Testaments are throughout perfectly in agreement as to the view which they present of the threefold personality of God. This disclosure is gradual and cumulative. The earlier instructions were so vague that, taken by themselves, they would never have suggested what we now signify by the term " trinity of Persons in the unity of the Godhead." But when the testimony of the Gospels and of the Epistles is gathered, and the light furnished is thrown back over the previous records of revelation, the obscure hint in the Old Testament is found to coincide fully with the fuller delineation in the New. It is one subject disclosed through a gradual process, unfolding itself continuously in the ever-increasing light. Taking the sum of these completed revelations together, we find Scripture clearly establishing the following points :—

1st. There is only one God. The testimony of Scripture here absolutely accords with the witness of our consciences, and with the obvious unity of the universe in all its provinces and successions. There is but one plan, and but a single administration—but one sovereign authority

either over consciences or worlds. There is but one infinite, self-existent Spirit, who reveals himself as the I AM,
from whom, and through whom, and to whom are all
things. The three Persons are declared to be ONE, identical in substance, one in the depths of a common consciousness, one in thought and purpose, and equal in power
and glory. This is a Trinitarian unity, which is moral
and full of life, not a barren, non-ethical Unitarian oneness, which has no significance to our understandings nor
attraction to our hearts.

2nd. The Scriptures teach with equal clearness that
" Father," " Son," and " Holy Ghost " are that one God.
In the case of the Father no one doubts that he is that
one God. In the case of the Son it is taught throughout
the Scriptures in every possible form of suggestion and of
assertion. Divine names and titles, attributes, prerogatives, works, and worship are ascribed to him constantly.
He is declared to be God, and from eternity to have been
with God—to be one with the Father, and to be in the
Father and the Father in him, so that he that hath seen
the Son hath seen the Father. In the case of the Holy
Ghost the fact that he is divine is not questioned; the
only point of doubt with any is as to his distinct personality. But Christ applies to him the pronouns " he " and
" him," and ascribes to him distinct personal will, sensibility, relations, and agency; and the inspired apostles
enrol his name with that of the Father and the Son as
a distinct and equal constituent with them of the one
Godhead.

3rd. But these titles, Father, Son, and Holy Ghost, all
applied equally to the one God, are not mere differing
titles of the same subject, as when God is called alter-
nately Creator, Preserver, or Father, but they are the
several titles of three different subjects or distinct persons.
We can know God only as his self-revelation presents him

in his inspired Word. This Word is a history in which God is set forth as acting in the creation of the world and of men, in the providential and moral government of the world and of men, and especially in the redemption of sinful men. In all these spheres of action God is represented as acting, speaking, hearing, judging. He stands before man face to face; he speaks to us, and we hear him; we speak to him, and he hears us. We regard him as an object of reverence and love, and he regards us with affections determined by our characters and personal relations to him.

In precisely the same manner the Father stands face to face with the Son as another person having distinct self-consciousness. They each look upon the other as a distinct object of love and thought. They each act upon the other as distinct agents. They use in reference to each other all cases of the personal pronouns. The Father loves the Son, speaks to him, speaks of him, gives him commandment, promises a reward for action, sends him, and receives him when he returns. The Son loves the Father, speaks to him, receives his commission, returns to him, and claims his reward. The Holy Ghost is sent by the Father and by the Son, acts for them as their agent, speaking of them, not of himself, and distributing their grace to men severally as he wills. The several functions of the divinity in relation to the universe in creation, providence, and redemption are distributed severally between these three as between separate though perfectly united and sympathizing agents.

4th. As to their mutual relations, of course we can know only the surface. There must be infinite depths in the conscious being of God to which no created thought can penetrate. It is plain, in the revelation God has made of himself in the history of redemption and in the record of it, that he exists eternally and constitutionally as three self-conscious Persons. But for aught we can know, in the depths of this infinite Being there may be a common consciousness which includes the whole Godhead, and a common personality. This may all be true ; but what belongs to us to deal with is the sure and obvious fact of revelation, that God exists from eternity as three self-conscious Persons, the Father, Son, and Holy Ghost, and that these sustain the following relations :—

(1.) They all are modes of existence of one indivisible spiritual substance. "They are the same in substance."

(2.) Hence they must be essentially equal in power and dignity and glory. There can be no temporal pre-existence, no dependence of one upon the will of the other, no superior authority to which the others are subject. Therefore they are to be regarded and treated by all their creatures with equal love, gratitude, reverence, confidence, and obedience.

(3.) Nevertheless, the Bible discovers a fixed order of existence and of operation between them. *As to existence*, the Father is first, the Son second, and the Spirit third. This order is of course not chronological, since all are alike eternal, but one of origin and consequence.

The Father eternally " begets " the Son, and the Spirit eternally " proceeds from " the Father and the Son. Hence the second Person is eternally the " Son " of the Father, who begets him, and the third Person is eternally " the Spirit," or breath of the Father and of the Son, from whom he proceeds. *The order of operation also from God* outward on his creatures is the same. The Father is the source of all movement. To him the decrees are principally referred in Scripture. He sends the Son, and the Father and the Son send the Spirit. In creation and providence all movement is habitually represented in Scripture as *from* the Father, *through* the Son, and *by* the Spirit. And in the return of man to God through the method of redemption it is always *to* the Father, *through* the Son, *by* the Spirit (Eph. ii. 18).

(4.) The terms "Father" and "Son" are reciprocal. We know these divine Persons in their personal distinctions and relations only so far as these are signified by these relative terms. The distinction of the personality of the first Person is that he is eternally the Father of the second Person; and the personal distinction of the second Person is that he is eternally the Son of the first. The personal titles of the second Person mutually throw light on one another. These are: ὁ λόγος, the Word; ὁ υἱός, the Son; ὁ μονογενής, the Only-begotten; εἰκὼν τοῦ Θεοῦ τοῦ ἀοράτου, πρωτότοκος πάσης κτίσεως, the image of the invisible God, the first-born of all creation; ἀπαύγασμα τῆς δόξης αὐτοῦ, the radiancy of his glory; and χαρακτὴρ τῆς ὑποστάσεως αὐτοῦ, the very image of his substance.

This divine Person, so designated as to his eternal and essential personal relations to the Father, has become incarnate by taking into his personality a germinant human nature in the womb of the Virgin Mary. Thus an eternal divine Person embraces in the unity of the one person a perfect human nature, so that he is both God and man in two distinct natures and one person for ever. This seems impossible. Nevertheless, it is an historical fact. We know that the one individual person, Jesus of Nazareth, was, and ever continues to be, at once perfect God and perfect man.

There is no more contrariety between the essential properties of the two natures than between matter and spirit. In our own persons—which we are certain are one and indivisible—we embrace both of these opposite substances in one. No act of consciousness, no analysis by microscope or chemical reagents, nor by knife, can penetrate to the dividing-line between soul and spirit. Both substances spontaneously conspire in one energy and coalesce in one consciousness. In some way like this the divine Spirit has penetrated the human nature and made it the obedient organ of its central personality. And everything done by him in execution of his mediatorial offices is due to the co-operating energies of both natures, divine and human.

There is no fourth Person added to the Trinity. The eternal second Person remains the same. On the inner side, that he presents to the Father and to the Holy Ghost, he is the same immutable divine Person. On the outer side, that he presents to mankind, the eternal Word has come down into time and space, and become visible and audible and tangible to us in the human nature he has taken into his Person. In him dwelleth all the fulness of the Godhead bodily, so that the apostles "heard it," and "saw it with their eyes," and "handled it with their hands" (1 John i. 1 ; Col. ii. 9).

(5.) The eternal third Person of the Trinity is always third in order. He proceeds from the Father and from the Son. He is eternally the "Spirit of the Father," and equally "the Spirit of the Son." He is the author of beauty in the physical world and of holiness in the moral and spiritual world. Wherever he is, there the Father and the Son are. He is in all spheres of action, whether of creation or of providence or of redemption, the executive of God.

III. That these three are really distinct Persons is thus manifested and illustrated in Scripture in the most definite and indubitable manner possible. No words or terms of definition could make the facts so clear and certain as they are made by the simple narratives of the mutual discourses and relative attitudes and actions of these three Persons in the Scriptures. We know nothing except through these scriptural representations. If these are delusive, we know nothing. And if these three are not distinct, self-conscious

Persons, then these evangelical narratives are utterly un-
trustworthy romances.

Moreover, we are the more ready to accept them as
accurate, inasmuch as they make the nature of God infinitely more intelligible to us.   The condition of our
knowing God at all is wholly that we were created in his
image.   Science, apart from our self-consciousness, which
reveals to us person and cause and end, does not give us
God.   Except as illumined by the reflected light of our
own self-consciousness, the immeasurable machine of the
material world gives no sign of God.   We are spirits,
persons, and causes; therefore we know God to be a personal spirit and first cause.   But we are no less essentially social beings, and to us all life and character, intellect,
moral or practical, is conceivable only under social conditions.   A unitarian, one-personed God might possibly
have existed, and if revealed as such it would have been
our duty to have acknowledged his lordship.   But, nevertheless, he would have always remained utterly inconceivable to us—one lone, fellowless, conscious being;
subject without object; conscious person without environment; righteous being without fellowship or moral relation
or sphere of right action.   Where would there be to him
a sphere of love, truth, trust; of sympathetic feeling?
Before creation, eternal darkness; after creation, only an
endless game of solitaire, with worlds for pawns.   But the
Scriptures declare that love is not only a possibility to God,
or an occasional mood, but his very essence.   If love be of
the essence of God, he must always love; and, being eternal, he must have possessed an eternal object of love; and,
being infinite, he must have eternally possessed an infinite
object of love.   This of course the eternal Persons find mutually in each other.   Nothing but this gives us a God and
Father whose nature we can comprehend, and with whom
we can sympathize.   A God essentially active—and active

in the forms of infinite intelligence and righteousness and love—can be found nowhere except in the mutual society of the Father and of the Son and of the Holy Ghost.

The least rational and moral of all theistic systems is that of a bare, bald unitarianism. The least intelligent and spiritual of all heretical perversions of catholic truth is the pale fallacy which substitutes the phenomenal and superficial distinctions of a model trinity in the place of the three self-conscious, loving, counselling Persons, Father, Son, and Holy Ghost, eternally one, yet eternally several and threefold. The most rational, illuminated, genial, and spiritually fruitful conception of God known among men is that conveyed by his self-revelation in the actual history of redemption as three Persons eternally loving and thinking and acting in the unity of one eternal Godhead.

IV. This catholic doctrine of the trinity of Persons in the one Godhead, moreover, fulfils another criterion of catholic truth, in that it embraces, combines, and reconciles all the half-truths of all the heresies which have ever attained to currency or power among thinking men, Christian or heathen.

The false systems of religion which have prevailed among men may in a general way be grouped under the general heads of Deism, Pantheism, Polytheism. These have various grades of merit, yet they all alike embrace some elements of important truth, and yet are all, upon the whole, false and injurious.

1st. The deistic view of God regards him as an exalted Person, who has created the universe, and now in a general and distant way governs it, but who exists essentially outside of the world, and acts upon it only from without, and almost exclusively through second causes and the utterly inflexible sequences of natural law. The world is a machine which is wholly inexorable in all its movements, shutting in the struggling souls of men, separating them from their absent Father, and holding them fast in the toils of fate.

2nd. The pantheistic view regards God as the omnipresent substance of which all things consist, the irresistible current of force which flows through all movement and all life. He is not a Person who knows and loves us, for he has no existence except as he exists in the things continually coming and going which constitute the phenomenal world. His only thought is the sum of the thoughts of all finite things, his only life the sum of all creature life. He works in all things from within, and he reveals himself to us only as he emerges in our own consciences, and reveals himself in us as essentially one with himself.

3rd. Even the gross fictions of polytheism have a tincture of truth to give them power over the human mind. If God is moral, there must be a personal distinction and a social basis in his essential nature. If the infinite and the absolute One is to exert a moral and educating influence on human life, he will appear to us self-limited under the conditions of time and space: "all the fulness of the Godhead" must appear to us "*bodily*."

It is easily seen how wonderfully the revealed doctrine of the Trinity comprehends in a harmonious and pure form all of the straggling and apparently conflicting rays of light preserved in these human systems of false religion. The Father sits apart as the distant and incommunicable God, the Origin and End of all things, the ultimate Source of all authority and power, but beyond all human thought and touch, separate on his eternal throne in the highest heavens. The truth of pantheism is realized in the Holy Ghost, who, while of the same substance as the Father, is revealed to us as immanent in all things, the basis of all existence, the tide of all life, springing up like a well of water from within us, giving form to chaos and inspiration to reason, the ever-present Executive of God, the Author of all beauty in the physical world, of all true philosophy, science, and theology in the world of thought, and of all holiness in the world of spirit. The eternal Son has stooped to a real and permanent incarnation, and has done sublimely what the incarnations of the heathen mythology have only caricatured. We have what the polytheists merely dreamed of, and never really saw—the unfolding of the ethical constitution of the Godhead, revealing his existence in a plurality of persons, the actual and permanent dwelling of the absolute God in the form of human flesh.

V. This perfect self-revelation of God as a trinity of co-equal Persons, moreover, completely fulfils, as none other can, all the demands of the highest philosophy and of the last suggestions of science. In the first lecture of this course we saw that when God was diligently sought, he was found in different directions and in different forms. These might be found to be mutually irreconcilable to human reason alone, while it was none the less the dictate of sound reason to persevere in the faith that in some higher region all these various aspects of the one God would be found to have a common ground. This common ground is evidently set before us by the revealed doctrine of the Trinity. Philosophy, natural religion, and science together give us God as the unfathomable Abyss, as the transcendent and ineffable extramundane Person, and as the omnipresent immanent Spirit who is the ground of all being and the source of all life. The inspired Word and the incarnate Christ of God give us the Father, Son, and Holy Ghost. The Father is the unknown and unknowable Source from which all things issue, and the End to which all things tend. The Son is the personal Jehovah who reveals the whole Godhead in himself—in whom we see and worship the Father, and through whom all things con-

sist.   The Holy Ghost is the God within us, whose movement in space gives us the order of the suns and stars, and
whose inspiration within us unveils the moral law and the
glory of the spiritual world.

VI. This transcendent truth can never be understood,
and can never be proved; but when once received as truth,
on the ground of the testimony of the divine Word, it may
be made clearer by felicitous illustration.   I therefore ask
you now to follow me while I present the PARABLE OF
LIGHT.

Before this is presented, I want to make two intro-
ductory remarks:—*First*, it would be foolish as well as
irreverent for mortals under our limited conditions to attempt to penetrate the awful secrets of the divine Being,
and to throw the rushlight of our poor understandings over
the impenetrable secrets of the inter-relations of the Father,
Son, and Holy Ghost as they exist together eternally in
the bosom of the one Godhead.   It is of course very different when we come to what God has himself condescended
to reveal to us as to the relations each divine Person severally sustains to the universe external to the Godhead, and
as to the work which they each perform in their co-oper-
ative agency in the economies of creation, providence, and
redemption.   Our illustration is confined to this distinctly
revealed region of the external relations of the different
Persons of the one Godhead to the universe.

In the *second* place, we claim that our right to illustrate
the revealed facts of the spiritual world by analogies drawn
from the physical creation is founded upon a right view of
the relation of the material and physical worlds as constituted by God.   The object of God in all his works has
been the manifestation of his own glorious perfections
through the medium of his works.   The heavens and the
earth and the whole course of providence are a veil through
which the perfections, designs, and methods of the several

Persons of the Godhead are more or less clearly shadowed forth to us. Hence our Saviour himself spoke in parables and metaphors. Both Old and New Testaments combine in making all nature a mirror reflecting the face and activities of God, the inmost operations of his grace being represented by such natural agencies as water, oil, salt, leaven, wind, fire, a hammer, a sword, and fuller's soap.

1st. Let it, then, be marked that light in its essence is absolutely invisible and passes all apprehension. Philosophers assume by hypothesis a great interstellar ocean of highly rarefied elastic matter called the ethereal medium, which no man has seen or can see. They tell us that light is a peculiar mode of motion transmitted in all directions illimitably in this ethereal medium. But whence comes this infinite throbbing, whose restless waves, traversing the celestial spaces, break ceaselessly on the revolving worlds? They flow down upon us from measureless space through measureless time, and no genius can imagine whence they come and whither they go. Light makes manifest all things from which it is radiated or upon which it is reflected, but is itself utterly invisible and unknown.

Thus it is with God the Father. Through infinite time he fills infinite space, and he is the Abyss from which all things flow and into which all things tend; yet no man hath or can see God at any time—the only-begotten Son, who is in the bosom of the Father, he hath declared him.

2nd. Light itself makes all things visible on which it falls and from which it is reflected, but it becomes itself visible only in a radiant point or disk, like that of the insufferable sun from which it floods the world. Suppose some angel or other inhabitant of an outlying province of creation, who had often heard of the wonders and splendours of light, though he had never seen them—suppose him to wander far afield through the nether darkness in search of this hitherto unseen wonder. If such an one suddenly should rise beyond the crest of some eclipsing shadow, and without transition stand face to face with our central sun, would he not with rapt wonder naturally hail the sun with language similar to that used in Scripture to express the essential relation of the eternal Word to God? —"All hail! thou art the very light I seek; thou art the Word of light, its uttered form; thou art its express image in which this invisible source of all life and knowledge may be beheld; thou art the radiancy of its inexhaustible glory. All its fulness dwells in thee bodily." Thus God the Father is never known except as he is seen in the Person of the Son. He that hath seen the Son hath seen the Father; and never otherwise or otherwhere is the Father ever seen. Angels and archangels, and all the other sons of God, who, impelled by a native aspiration, seek to know their Father, hear his voice only as it is uttered in his eternal Word, and see his image only as it is rendered visible in his express Image and is projected forth as the radiance or effulgence of his glory.

3rd. That which makes the energy and influence of the sun omnipresent is the inexhaustible volume of its rays flooding space in all directions. The rays of distant constellations come down to us through millenniums and centuries and years. The rays of our own sun flood the successive sides of the earth as it revolves daily on its axis, bearing down over the mountain-tops to the lowest valley, and over the broadest plains, heat, light, and actinic energy, the source of all life and movement. If these rays should by any reason cease, or if they should be cut off by the interposition of an opaque mass, the sun would, to us, virtually cease to exist. It would be utterly withdrawn from our consciousness, and it would entirely cease to be to us any more the source of light and life.

Thus the immanent Holy Ghost makes God the Father

and God the Son, and so Christ the God-man, now glorified in heaven, omnipresent to all the Church in heaven and on earth. If the Holy Ghost were withdrawn, the Christ would be absent and of none effect to us. But if the Holy Ghost is present and active in us, we dwell in the full flood of the light and of the life of God and of his Christ.

4th. The rays of light radiated or reflected from any surface to another never reveal themselves; they only make manifest or reproduce by reflection the surface from which they come. Thus every one sees by means of the rays radiated or reflected the very image of the sun and moon in the water and all the features of the landscape in the mirror. So it is always in the work of the Holy Ghost. He never speaks of himself, but he always receives of Christ and shows and communicates to us the Christ and his redemptive grace. The rays of light never picture themselves, but the stars from which they come. So the Holy Ghost never excites in our consciousness thoughts and emotions relating to himself, but always those which relate to the Godhead and to the incarnate Christ. Therefore it is that, although the Holy Ghost inspired the Scriptures, and although he is the immediately present and the constantly active Person of the Godhead in our hearts and lives, yet there is comparatively so little conspicuity given in Scripture and in Christian thought to the personality of the Holy Ghost. He is ever speaking, yet not of himself, but of Christ.

5th. *All* the fulness of light is exhibited and conveyed in the sun *bodily;* so *all* the fulness of the Godhead is exhibited and conveyed in the Person of the God-man bodily. The form is human, but all of God is here. The Infinite has kept back nothing, but has given us THE ALL in giving us his Son.

6th. The sun conveys his fulness to the attendant spheres only ray by ray in successive periods of time. So we live

only as we continue to live in God and receive from him
our life "grace for grace."   But the immeasurable ocean of
the interstellar ether ever contains in its depths, latent yet
potential, the infinite stores of historic light and heat.
Looking up athwart the evening sky, we see the inflowing
streams of radiance which have been invisibly pulsing in
the bosom of that ocean for years or centuries or millenniums.   All the secrets of the worlds from creation downward through the æons, all the heat or light of life-force
they have ever received or shed forth, are beating in the
depths of that impenetrable ether across the black bosom
of which we look out at night.   So is the eternal and
infinite Holy Ghost an absolutely measureless and inexhaustible source of light and life.   *In* him all the sources
of our life lie latent as in the being of God; *from* him all
the elements of the creature's life, and pre-eminently of the
Christian's life, spring in spontaneous freeness and in transcendent perfection.

7th. The fulness of the sun, brought out into the circle
of the dependent worlds by radiation, is brought into the
knowledge of the creature only by the refractions and
reflections to which this radiance is subjected in the worlds
themselves.   If we could place ourselves beyond the atmosphere, in the interplanetary space, we would on every side,
except that toward the sun itself, behold the whole hemisphere absolutely black, with the stars simply as points
without size—themselves visible, but spreading no light
around.   If we should turn and face the sun itself, we
should see only a dull blue disk of lambent flame.   It is
only after we have descended within the volume of the
atmosphere, and come to the surface of the earth itself,
that the hitherto latent myriad-hued beauties of the sun
first come out to view.   Refracted by every successive
stratum of the earth's atmosphere, and by the vapours of
various densities which canopy our hills and streams, this

hitherto latent radiance is broken and expanded into the infinitely varied hues of the rainbow and of the imperial retinue of clouds which attend the alternate rising and setting of the sun. And the whole earth, its hills and vales and plains, and all its innumerable tribes of plants and flowers and birds and beasts, reflect each one a separate colour or shade or tone of light, and by their infinite variety collectively articulate the incalculable beauties latent in the sun's radiance, which could not otherwise be known.

Thus it is that the radiance of the effulgent Image of the invisible God—that is, the ever-present Spirit of the Son of the Father—exhibits to us the infinite fulness and variety of his grace; not immediately in himself, but by refractions and reflections through the intelligent spirits in which he dwells—in no single Church or person, but in all the endlessly varied spiritual beauties and graces of all the saints of all nations and ages, and in the angels of all ranks. Thrones and dominions, principalities and powers, circle the throne and reflect the first gush of the white light. But all down the lines of vision, in interminable perspective, poets and philosophers, artists and musicians, prophets and priests, and all the saints of very various shade and tone, analyze and reflect all the perfections of their Lord, which otherwise no eye hath seen or can see.

8th. But the sun of our physical system is the inexhaustible source of all life as well as all light. When he moves southward toward the winter solstice, he leaves all our northern hemisphere comfortless and dead. The leaves wither and fall, the birds depart for the genial south, the springing fountains are sealed up, the whole earth freezes into solid, obdurate stone, and death reigns supreme. When again, at the vernal equinox, the sun returns and pours his warm rays over the world, then all nature is quickened to life and wakes, the fountains are unsealed, the softened mould is impregnated, and every germ unfolds, and the singing birds come back, and the trees blossom, and all the earth rejoices and bears fruit.

So when the Holy Spirit is withdrawn from our midst, and consequently God and Christ are absent, the fountains of our spirits close, our minds are darkened, our strength withers, and the winter of our souls enfolds us, and the whole Church with us, in death. But when the Holy Ghost returns again, and sets for us once more the returning sun in our sky, new life from on high thrills through our veins, our hearts sing, our eyes take the heavenly light, our hands are made strong, and the work of the Lord prospers everywhere.

9th. Once again : it belongs to the mystery of light that each ray tends to reproduce everywhere in the object upon which it falls the image of that from which it radiates. This general secret of photography was known ages before the time of Daguerre. Engravings reproduce themselves upon the blank paper which shades them from the light. The sun, striking the wind-ruffled river or lake with its radiance, reproduces on every one of the myriad wavelets a perfect image of himself. As we stand face to face, the image of each is reproduced on the eye and face of the other. This energy of light in the long run cuts deeper than the surface : in the sunny side of hospital wards it moulds anew the shrivelled limbs of the palsied, and like a sculptor fashions them after the forgotten ideal. So after long lives of mutual contemplation husbands and wives and familiar friends, however dissimilar at the first, come to look, as well as to think, alike under the plastic and assimilating power of light. Often has the mountain-traveller seen this miracle wrought in a lake between the forest-clad hills. The sky is cloudless ; the air as clear as crystal, and windless ; the water lying like glass, pure and placid as a mirror, under the bending skies. There you see the very heavens, the vast spaces, the great depths, the brilliant stars in their celestial perspective, all reproduced in the bosom of the lake. So when our souls lie in holy contemplation under the rays of Christ the heavenly Sun, our passions stilled, our hearts calm and purified from their lower springs, " we also, with open face beholding as in a glass the glory of the Lord, are changed into the same image from glory to glory, even as by the Spirit of the Lord " (2 Cor. iii. 18).

VII.

PREDESTINATION.

THIS is a subject which is very little understood, even by those Christians who profess to embrace it in their creed. This is due in part to the nature of the subject, to its profundity, and to the infinite range of its complications with other important truths. But it is also in large measure due to inattention, and to the general prevalence of a natural though an unfounded and ignorant prejudice. This prejudice has become in many quarters an epidemic irresistible to persons of more zeal than judgment. Now, I wish to urge a plea in favour of an earnest, frank, patient study of the subject. Vague prejudice unsupported by definite knowledge has no value. It is unquestionable that the Scriptures do teach some doctrine of predestination, and a very strict doctrine of unconditional election has been held by the greatest and most thoroughly biblical theologians, and by whole denominations of Christians most conspicuous for their evangelical character and fruitfulness. It will not do for any of us to dismiss such a subject with supercilious impatience. We should at the very least do our best to secure a clear conception of the doctrine, and of its relation to other doctrines, before we make ourselves sure that it is not true.

I. In the first place, it should be clearly understood that this great principle of divine predestination is held in two entirely different connections and interests. It has by a great many been discussed simply as a question of transcendental theology, as concerning the acts of God enacted in eternity in a sphere above and behind the external phenomena which are obvious to our senses. If there be a God, he necessarily exists in eternity, while the creation exists in the successions and limitations of time. The universe as a whole and all the parts of it originate in him and depend upon him, and therefore are determined by him. According to the precise language of the Westminster Shorter Catechism, Ques. 7, " The decrees of God are, his eternal purpose, according to the counsel of his will, whereby, for his own glory, he hath foreordained whatsoever comes to pass." This sweeps the whole universe, and is a proposition of the highest and most general speculative importance. This position is unquestionably, in this form, true and logically involved in all scriptural views of the doctrine of grace in all its elements. It is therefore rightly embraced in our Confession of Faith, and the present writer with all his heart believes it to be true. It is in this spirit and from this speculative point of view that Zwingle discusses this subject in his *De Providentia*. And it is this aspect of the question which is habitually considered by the general Christian public in their hostile criticisms of this doctrine. Now, I am perfectly free to confess that however true this view of the general principle of predestination is, and however much it is logically implicated in the essentials of the Christian doctrines of grace, nevertheless this transcendental way of conceiving of the matter is more speculative than practical. Although I heartily accord with the view in my own mind, I feel no disposition to insist upon the assent of any Christian brother as a matter of loyalty to the Christian faith. No element of the Creed is essential unless it practically determines the attitude of the soul in its relations to God through Christ.

And only those aspects and modes of conceiving Christian truth should be insisted upon and imposed upon others as obligatory which do directly determine this Godward attitude of our souls, or, in other words, which directly enter into and give form to our religious experience.

On the other hand, Calvin presents his characteristic doctrine of eternal election in living connection with the great practical experimental questions of personal salvation and of divine grace. If we are sinners, it is evident that the practically essential thing in religious experience is to appreciate truly our guilt, unworthiness, and helplessness before God, and God's free grace toward us to its full extent. If God is infinitely gracious and just, if at measureless expense he redeemed us at the cost of the pain, shame, and death of his Son, it follows that any failure in our appreciation of our own unworthiness and helplessness, or of God's gracious activity in our salvation, would be absolutely insufferable. To claim more for ourselves or to ascribe less to God than the facts of the case justify would be the greatest of all sins, and would be the very thing to make salvation impossible. The sense of our own guilt, pollution, and impotence, and of the absolute unconditioned freeness of the grace which saves us, is involved in every case of genuine religious experience.

The expiatory work of Christ which is sufficient for, adapted to, and freely offered to all men, being presupposed, the question of questions is, How—by what agencies and on what conditions—is it effectually applied to any individual ? The Scriptures make it plain that the condition of its effectual application is an act of faith, involving real spiritual repentance and the turning from sin and the acceptance and self-appropriation of Christ and of his redemption as the only remedy. But what will prompt a sinner in love with his sin, spiritually blind and callous, thus to repent and accept Christ as the cure of the sin he loves ? The first movement cannot begin with man. The sinner of himself cannot really desire deliverance from sin; of himself he cannot appreciate the attractive beauty, loveliness, or saving power of Christ. The dead man cannot spontaneously originate his own quickening, nor the creature his own creating, nor the infant his own begetting. Whatever man may do after regeneration, the first quickening of the dead must originate in the first instance with God. All Christians feel this as the most intimate conviction of their souls. Yet it involves necessarily this very doctrine of eternal predestination or election. If God begins the work, if our believing follows his quickening, then it is God, not man, who makes the difference between the quickened and the unquickened. If we believe, it is because we have been first quickened. If any man do not believe, it is because he is yet dead in his natural sin. God's eternal choice therefore cannot depend upon foreseen faith, but, on the contrary, faith must depend upon God's eternal choice.

As between the man who believes in Christ and the man who finally rejects him, the source of the difference is put by the Pelagian entirely in the inalienable, unassisted power of the human will. All that can be said in the case is that the one man has accepted Christ because he chose to do so, and the other man has rejected Christ because he chose to do so. Each has acted as he has done in the unfettered and unfetterable exercise of the human will. But Pelagianism makes no room for original sin nor for the necessity of divine grace. It is diametrically opposed to the Scriptures, to the religious experience of all Christians, and it has been rejected as anti-Christian by the unanimous consent of the whole historic Church.

The semi-Pelagian, admitting that man is morally sick, holds that every sinner must make the first movement Godward spontaneously in his own strength, after which, if his effort is sincere, however ineffectual, God will co-operate by his grace with him and make his effort successful. The Arminian, on the other hand, admitting that all men, being dead in trespasses and sins, are absolutely incapable of spontaneously originating any good desire or effort, yet holds that God gives the same sufficient grace to all men; and he makes the difference between the believer and the unbeliever to lie in the fact that the former co-operates, and thus renders the grace in his case effectual, and the other fails to co-operate with it, and thus renders it ineffectual. The Lutheran, who maintains that men are in such sense dead in sin that they are utterly unable to co-operate with grace before they have been themselves quickened to life by grace, yet makes the difference between the believer and the unbeliever to consist in the fact, that while no man can co-operate with grace previous to regeneration, every man is free to resist it. With the Lutheran, therefore, the believer is the non-resistant, the unbeliever is the resistant, subject of a common universal grace. The Calvinist, on the other hand, glorifies the free and sovereign grace of God by attributing to it alone all the efficiency in saving the believing sinner. It is God's grace which makes the believer all he is. He feels this; of this at least he is absolutely sure. He is nothing more than a poor wandering sheep. The Good Shepherd has sought him out, found him, and carried him back on his breast. In himself and of himself in his entire history he is no better than his fellow-men who are lost. It is only God's free grace, therefore, which has made the difference. The faith he has cannot have been the precondition of God's choice, but God's choice must have been the precedent cause of his faith.

In this form of the doctrine, we did not first choose him, but he first chose us. This truth enters into all genuine Christian experience. It is of the essence of the universal Christian sentiment. It finds its expression in the sacred hymns and in the prayers of our fellow-Christians who call themselves Arminians, as it does in the prayers and hymns of those commonly styled Calvinists. All alike wrestle in prayer as if God's grace determined the decision. All alike cry, " Make them willing, O God, in the day of thy power!" It is the common confession of all alike that it is God who in all things works in us to do, by " working in us to will, of his good pleasure." All alike ascribe to him the prerogative of turning the hearts of men even as rivers of water are turned. All Christians with one voice cry, " Not unto us, O Lord, not unto us, but unto thy name give glory, for thy mercy and for thy truth's sake." In the theology of the heart all Christians are Calvinists—that is, all Christians ascribe all their salvation unto God. And this is the only form in which the doctrine of sovereign predestination should be insisted upon as of vital religious interest.

II. The real question remains, What does the Word of God say upon the subject? In all matters of controversy between Christians the Scriptures constitute the single court of last resort. This is an historical principle. To-day it remains as true as ever, no matter what crude theories of inspiration some parties may proclaim. The Scriptures of the Old and New Testaments have been for eighteen centuries, are to-day, and always will remain, the only common authority of Christendom, acknowledged by all alike.

These Scriptures do certainly teach a divine election of persons and foreordination of events. This fact all educated persons acknowledge. The only controversy among Christians relates to the range of the foreordination, whether it comprehends all events or is limited to certain classes; and to the subjects, the objects, and the conditions of the election which the Scriptures teach.

1st. All Christians of course admit that the eternal

Creator of the world, in the very act of creation, intelligently comprehending the end from the beginning, really, immutably, and unconditionally determined all classes of events subsequently brought about by the necessary sequences of natural forces and laws. As far as the universe is a machine, God, in bringing it into being, and in implanting its forces, and in ordaining its laws, necessarily determined all movements of the machine and its results from the beginning to the end. But there has been a natural shrinking from attributing to the foreordination of God all the free acts of men and angels, and especially the sinful acts of men and devils.

Nevertheless, the Scriptures are very explicit upon these points. (1.) The foreordination of God does include the free actions of men and angels, as it does all other classes of events whatsoever. God works in man freely and spontaneously *to will* according to his good pleasure (Phil. ii. 13). Men and nations are the mere instruments (the axe, saw, rod) in the hand of God to do his will (Isa. x. 15). God definitely predicts the free actions of men ages before the men themselves exist (Isa. xliv. 28; xlv. 1–4). All prophecy implies foreknowledge; and all foreknowledge on the part of a God who has intelligently and of purpose created all things out of nothing, of course implies the foreordination of all the foreseen results of that creation. If even one so limited in knowledge and power as you or I should place in the hands of a dependant a horse that we certainly knew would run away on that road and in the hands of that man, beyond question we would predetermine that runaway and all of its foreseen results. (2.) The Scriptures go even further, and declare that even the sinful acts of men are foreordained by God. This does not mean that God regards the wicked acts with complacency, or that he will condone them, or that we are in any degree excusable for acting them, much less that God is their author or cause, directly or indirectly. It means, simply, that these wicked actions were a clearly foreknown part of a system of things which God freely chose, and the future existence of which he freely and righteously determined for good and sufficient reasons, the evil never being ordained as an end in itself, but always as a means to an infinitely greater and better end. Thus, in the history of Joseph (compare Gen. xxxvii. 28 with Gen. xlv. 7, 8; l. 20), Joseph said to his treacherous brethren who sold him into slavery, "So now it was not you that sent me hither, but God;" "But as for you, ye thought evil against me; but God meant it unto good." (Ps. xvii. 13, 14, and Isa. x. 5—15.) The greatest crime ever committed in the universe was the crucifixion of the Son of God. To accomplish this, Gentiles and Jews in vast numbers and of all classes freely conspired. Yet their wicked act was "determined beforehand to be done" by the determinate counsel and foreknowledge of God: "Him, being delivered by the determinate counsel and foreknowledge of God, ye have taken, and by wicked hands have crucified and slain" (Acts ii. 23). "For of a truth against thy holy child Jesus, whom thou hast anointed, both Herod, and Pontius Pilate, with the Gentiles, and the people of Israel, were gathered together, for to do whatsoever thy hand and thy counsel determined before to be done" (Acts iv. 27, 28; xiii. 29; 1 Pet. ii. 8; Jude iv.; Rev. xvii. 17).

2nd. As to the doctrine of election, and of the confessedly various "elections" which are asserted in Scripture, there have been very different opinions held among Christians. Those who lay emphasis upon what has been entitled the "theory of national election," as eminently the late Archbishop Sumner, maintain that the only election taught in Scripture concerning human salvation consists in the divine predestination of communities and nations to the knowledge of the true religion, and to the external privileges of the gospel. This form of election is an un-questionable biblical fact, and has been pre-eminently illus-trated in the people of Israel, in the ancient world, and in the great English-speaking nations of modern times.

Those who, like Mr. Stanley Faber and Archbishop Whately, emphasize what they call the " theory of ecclesi-astical individualism," hold that the only personal election taught in the Bible respects the election of individual men to membership in the external Church and the means of grace. This also is an unquestionable scriptural fact, realized in the experience of all the members of the Chris-tian community.

Both these types of election, both of nations and of individuals, to the external means of grace are obviously sovereign and unconditioned. Both men and nations are born to these privileges, irrespective of any previous merits or actions of their own. And as to these forms of God's sovereign election, there is no difference of opinion between Arminians and Calvinists or other Christians of whatever name.

But students of the Scriptures see that they do more-over teach explicitly that God does elect some individuals to eternal blessedness and to all the means thereof. Here the precise point of difference between Arminians and Cal-vinists comes in. The old Arminian statement was that God graciously elected the class of believers to everlasting life, and that if any individual man was included in the election it was because he was included in the class of believers. The more modern Arminian statement is to the same effect ; in other words, that God elected certain individuals to eternal life, on the ground of their faith as foreseen by him. But the question necessarily arises, Where did these individuals come by their faith ? If they got the faith of themselves, then their salvation is not entirely of grace and of God. If God gave them their faith, then it was in his purpose ; and if it was embraced in his purpose, it could not have been the condition on which it was suspended. But the Scriptures and Christian experience unite in affirming that "faith is the gift of God " (Eph. ii. 8 ; Acts v. 31 ; 1 Cor. iv. 7). The designed effect of this eternal election is " that we should be holy, and without blame before him in love " (Eph. i. 4 ; ii. 10 ; 2 Thess. ii. 13 ; 1 Pet. i. 2), and therefore that holy state could not have been the foreseen condition of his choice. The very gist of the election is that of the children who " neither had done good or evil," " that the purpose of God according to election might stand, not of works, but of him that calleth." God chose one and rejected the other. The very gist was that " the potter hath power over the clay, of the same lump to make one vessel unto honour, and another unto dishonour " (Rom. ix. 11–21). The order in which the Holy Spirit puts the matter is very clear : " As many as were ordained to eternal life believed " (Acts xiii. 48). It was the personal foreordination to eternal life which determined the believing, and not the foreseen believing which conditioned the foreordination.

The true comprehensive statement of the scriptural teaching as to election includes all those just stated. The purpose of God is sovereign, absolute, and all-comprehensive, relating to all classes of events whatsoever. All nations and communities and individuals have been predestined precisely to all the relations and means of grace they experience, and to all the results thereof. But besides this, the Scriptures explicitly teach an election (*a*) of individuals (*b*) to salvation, and to all the means and conditions thereof, (*c*) founded, not upon the foreseen faith of the persons elected, but upon the infinitely wise and sovereign purpose of God alone (Eph. i. 5–11 ; 2 Tim. i. 9 ; John xv. 16–19 ; Matt. xi. 25, 26 ; Rom. ix. 10–18).

III. The difficulty which all feel in attempting to receive this unquestionable truth of revelation, and assimilate it to the whole mass of our own thinking, respects (1) the freedom and responsibility of man, and (2) the holiness of God. How can man be free if from eternity all his actions have been certainly determined? And if God by his decree makes the future occurrence of each sin absolutely certain, how can he be holy? These combinations doubtless present puzzles of considerable difficulty to our minds in their present state of enlightenment. But these do not in any degree differ from a large class of problems which the imperfection and narrowness of our knowledge prevent us from solving. God's decree, it is obvious, is not an immediate efficient cause which interferes with natural causes or which brings anything into being. It is simply an immanent plan or purpose in the divine mind which determines the certain occurrence of the events to which it relates. The same precisely is true with respect to the divine foreknowledge. All Christians believe that God eternally foreknows whatsoever shall be in the future. If his knowledge is real knowledge, it is certain; and if it is certain as knowledge, the events to which it relates must be certainly future. If the difficulty of reconciling certainty with the freedom of man or with the holiness of God does not move us to abandon his foreknowledge, it cannot be a rational motive for our denying the truth of his universal predestination. A God without foreknowledge would be only a blind force. Every argument which establishes theism on the evident teleology of the universe by equal cogency establishes the divine foreknowledge. Without the foreknowledge of God there would be no intelligent creation, no wise moral government, no ground for religious trust, no confidence for the future, no basis for either the prophecies or the promises of God. The foreknowledge admitted, there is no logical reason for excepting to his foreordination.

1st. As to the bearing of this doctrine upon the freedom of man's will. It must be remembered that uncertainty is never essential to liberty. The essence of liberty is that the free act shall be self-originated and self-directed. The self-determination of an undeveloped child is uncertain. It is swayed every moment by external influences; and in just that proportion the child's action is uncertain, and lacks the highest quality of moral freedom. But the choices of the educated and thoroughly developed man in his ripe maturity are far more certain both to himself and to others. He is not open to external influence or liable to internal whim or change; and exactly in that proportion does he rise to the highest level of moral freedom. He thoroughly understands himself and his permanent needs and wishes. His character is formed, and freedom is the genuine and adequate expression of character. God's purposes and self-decisions are the most certain, and at the same time the most free, of any actions that are conceivable. A drifting boat at sea, swept hither and thither by the winds and waves, is an admirable type of action utterly devoid of freedom and of certainty. It has no self-control, and therefore its action is equally unfree and uncertain. But a great steamship, at the same time self-propelled and self-steered, is an admirable type both of freedom and of certainty. Its action is predetermined, foreseen, and may confidently be relied upon, because it is free—that is, in the intelligent will of its navigator, acting through its powerful machinery, it possesses in the highest degree self-control and intelligent self-direction.

The eternal foreordination of God, which determines at once the certainty and the freedom of man's free actions, can in no way interfere with man's freedom. The action is not free if it is determined from without, but it is free if determined from within a rational will. Now, this is precisely what God's foreordination of man's free action effects. The decree at the same time determines that man shall be a free agent, shall possess a certain character, shall be surrounded by a certain environment, shall be specifically solicited by certain external influences, shall be internally moved by certain spontaneous affections, shall deliberately canvass certain reasons, and shall freely make a certain choice. The man thus is, as far as a finite creature may be, entirely self-moved and self-determined, and therefore he is free. The fact that his act is also certain is, as we have seen, and as Richard Watson, the great theologian of the Wesleyan Arminians, admits, no ground of presumption that it is not also absolutely free.

2nd. As to the consistency of God's foreordination of sin with his holiness, we have nothing to say except to admit the mystery, and to affirm that there is no possible escape except in denying the fact either of the existence of God on the one hand, or of the existence of sin on the other. If the cause which produced the universe did not foresee the sin which the present system embraces, then that cause was a blind, unintelligent force, and not God. If he did foresee it, and notwithstanding proceeded to bring that system, involving these sins, into existence, then he made their occurrence certain; he foreordained them. God did with his eyes open choose, out of a myriad of other possible systems, this actual system involving sin. He nevertheless is holy. He hates, forbids, punishes, restrains, and overrules the sin for good. In the light of the cross of Christ, on which God lays upon his Son the penalty of human sin, in the light of the great white throne and of the Lamb which irradiates the eternal city, the mystery of the divine permission of sin loses its overwhelming force. We have no complete solution of the problem, and it is not to be expected in our present stage of education. But we do see the light underneath the curtain. We do possess pledges for the immaculate holiness of God, and for the future moral perfection of his realm, and for the moral vindication of his reign, which suffice for the perfect assurance of our faith.

IV. Everything depends, in all departments of human thought, upon the point of view. Every one knows that, when traversing the scenes of a great battle, what appears to be inextricable confusion to us while we are passing along the outskirts and through the lower grounds, falls into complete order and appears as clear as light when we overlook the whole field from the strategic centre from which the eye and mind of the field-marshal beheld and controlled the contest. We all know that the heavens continued through all past ages to be an insoluble riddle to all looking upon them from the exterior and shifting stand-point of the earth. The movements of the sun and moon and of the wandering planets could be reduced to no intelligible plan. But the moment that in imagination the great Copernicus transferred the point of view from the earth to the central sun, all the hosts of heaven fell into rank, and have ever since been seen to march onward in a symmetrical order absolutely divine. In the morning, if we look eastward over a vast landscape with the sun before us, we see all things obscurely on their shadowed side. But if we look from the same point eastward in the evening, with the sun behind us, we see all the objects contained in the vast panorama glorified on the sunlit side.

In like manner must it be with all men when looking over the vast reaches of Jehovah's plans or works from below. No matter how intellectual they may be personally, no matter how vast their knowledge otherwise, it is just a matter of course that, from their human, changing outlook, as they are themselves swept along in the current of events, the relations of all objects should be confused. And especially must the relation of the several parts to God be misconceived, seen as they are on their shadowed side.

But, on the contrary, if we take our mental stand at the centre, and from God's point of view look down upon the events of time from their common centre, with their eternal side illumined, as far as our vision goes we shall see them fall into perfect order, and especially will we discern their symmetrical relation as a whole to the Source from which they issue, and the presiding Authority by which they are marshalled on their way.

It is self-evident that if we look out at any time and from any point upon our environment, we must see things in the accidental relations in which they happen to group themselves along our line of vision as we sweep past on our course. We must also, by the same necessity, see things in partial groups detached from their surroundings. If we conceive of any one event being caused by any other single event, we are led to confusion, because all things that exist constitute one articulated system, and every event is determined not by one single antecedent cause, but by the whole system of things, the entire equilibrium of the universe, that precedes it. So if we conceive of God as absolutely foreordaining individual events disconnected from the entire system of causes, conditions, and consequents of which they form a part, we shall necessarily be embarrassed by contradictions. God could not certainly foreordain one event without foreordaining every event, without tearing the system to pieces and bringing utter confusion into natural law and human thought. For instance, a chronometer is a whole consisting of many parts rigidly articulated and exquisitely adjusted to each other. It would, evidently, be impossible for the most skilful mechanic to run his fingers into the plexus of the wheels and springs, with the intent of controlling the action of one part irrespective of the rest, without working confusion and ruin. Nevertheless, the chronometer as a whole, with all its contents freely working according to their law, undisturbed, may be lifted and carried round the world without changing the relation of interdependence of part on part. In like manner, if we will only make the effort to look upon the universe from God's point of view, as one all-comprehensive, complete system in itself, much of the apparent difficulty attending the principle of eternal predestination will disappear.

We can possibly conceive of the intelligence of God only so far forth as its laws are analogous to those of the intellect of man. We can only think of his mind as eternally teeming with all possible systems, embracing all possible creatures, grouped in all possible relations, and subject to all possible laws. By the " possible " we mean every existence that can be under the limits of God's infinitely wise and righteous nature. Out of all possible systems as wholes God chose the existing system of the universe, including all existence, spiritual and material, that has been, is, or will be, constituted as it is, with all its parts mutually interdependent as they are, as one whole. Viewed in this way, there is no conflict. The cause produces its effects, the event depends on its conditions ; necessary agents act according to their nature, and free agents exercise spontaneously their perfect freedom : all the parts of the system act according to their several kinds ; nevertheless, the system as a whole, including all its parts, has been from eternity made certain by the sovereign choice of God.

The point of view from which all difficulty disappears is infinitely higher and commands infinitely wider reaches of thought than the point of view from which foreordination and free-will are seen to be inconsistent. The new theology, asserting the narrowness of the old, is discarding the foreordination of Jehovah as a worn-out figment of the schools discredited by the advanced culture of to-day. This is not the first time that the owls, mistaking the shadow of a passing eclipse for their native night, have prematurely hooted at the eagles, convinced that what is invisible to them cannot possibly exist.

V. It is often objected to the biblical doctrine of predestination that, however much it may be apparently supported by the language of Scripture, it is utterly antagonized by all established truth in every other department of human thought—by all the united testimonies of philosophy and science. This preposterous claim is loudly voiced, even by some of the professed advocates of progress in theology. But the facts are all absolutely to the contrary. So much is this the case, so universally do all the real governing currents of modern thought outside of Christian theology run in the direction of universal determinism, rather than in that of the admission of the indeterminate, the contingent, the spontaneous and free, that many of us who are the stanchest Calvinists feel that the need of the hour is not to emphasize a foreordination, which no clear, comprehensive thinker doubts, but to unite with our Arminian brethren in putting all emphasis and concentrating all attention on the vital fact of human freedom. That our consciousness of personal freedom is reliable, that we in a true sense stand outside of the current of necessary causation and do truly originate and give direction to our own actions, is a principle fundamental to all morals and all religion. Its permanent vindication is the one only and effectual solvent of all pantheism and all materialism. So strong does the current set on all sides throughout the sphere of human speculation, in favour of the conviction of universal preordination, that we can afford to leave its vindication to others, while we support with our suffrages the neglected though essential counter-truth of the real freedom of the human soul.

All the philosophy and science of the century is deterministic. The great argument of Jonathan Edwards against the liberty of contingency and in favour of the liberty of certainty has been taken up and intensified by John Stuart Mill and Herbert Spencer to support the doctrine of necessity. The universally received scientific principle of continuity involves this principle of foreordination. The now almost universally prevalent scientific doctrine of evolution, in all its infinite variety of forms, and in every form alike, involves this principle of foreordination. The funniest reading accessible even in this humorous age is that in which a progressive theologian, committing himself everywhere to the evolution method, yet declares that the doctrine of divine foreordination is false because unscientific. All philosophies which are either materialistic in tendency or pantheistic or purely theistic necessarily involve the principle of foreordination.

Every conceivable philosophy must ultimately found the universe upon mechanism, chance, or upon personal intelligence and will. If mechanism be the ultimate self-existent principle out of which the universe is developed and operated, then fatalism is true. If chance be the ultimate principle, then accident, contingency, uncertainty must be in the method, and chaos the ultimate goal. If a personal, intelligent will be the ultimate principle, then Providence is the executive in time of an eternal purpose. All philosophies may be classified under these heads. All the possibilities of speculation must lie within these limits. Instead of our doctrine of foreordination being the same with the heathen doctrine of fate, it is its absolute opposite and only alternative. We are shut up to a choice between the two—either a fatalism which results from mechanical coaction, or a fatalism which results from a mindless and purposeless chance, or an all-controlling providence of a heavenly Father who, in the exercise of his own personal freedom, has made room for ours. All thinkers who understand themselves know that they run along one or other of these lines. The wiseacres who plead the authority of philosophy and science as inconsistent with the scriptural doctrine of predestination may be safely left to themselves. They will not be found to be dangerous enemies even behind our backs.

VI. Here, as everywhere else, there is essential truth on both sides of every controversy, and the real truth is the whole truth, its entire catholic body. Arminianism in the abstract as an historical scheme is a heresy, holding half the truth. Calvinism is an historical scheme which in its best representatives comprehends the whole truth with considerable completeness. But the case is essentially different when we come to consider the great co-existing bodies of Christian people calling themselves respectively Calvinists and Arminians. Each of these parties holds all essential truth, and therefore they hold actually very much the same truth. The Arminians think and speak very much like Calvinists when they come to talk with God in either the confession of sin or the supplication for grace. They both alike in that attitude recognize the sovereignty of God and the guilt and helplessness of men. Indeed, how could it be otherwise? What room is there for anything other than essential Calvinism on one's knees? On the other hand, the Calvinist thinks and speaks like the better class of Arminians when he addresses the consciences of men, and pleads with them, as free, responsible agents, to repent and believe in Christ, The difference between the best of either class is one of emphasis rather than of essential principle. Each is the complement of the other. Each is necessary to restrain, correct, and supply the one-sided strain of the other. They together give origin to the blended strain from which issues the perfect music which utters the perfect truth.

VII. It is now-a-days frequently predicted by men in high places that the distinctive doctrines of Calvinism are doomed. The future is uncertain; the *rôle* of prophet is unprofitable and unbecoming. But the history of the past stands fast. The doctrine of predestination, with its associated system of truths, has had a wonderful history. All world-movers have believed it surely and have taught it clearly—Paul, Augustine, all the Reformers without exception. During the eleven hundred years which elapsed from the time of Augustine to that of Luther, all the best of the schoolmen, all the great missionary movements, the revivals of true religion, the extension of popular education, and all great healthy political reforms, had their common inspiration in Augustinian theology. All the great national movements in France, Germany, Switzerland, Italy, and Britain in the era of the Reformation, and all the great national leaders, as Luther, Zwingle, Calvin, Cranmer, and Knox, were distinctively Augustinian, and were rooted in predestination. The most moral people of all history, the Puritans, Pietists, Huguenots, Reformed Dutch of Holland and German of the Palatinate, and the Scotch and the Scotch-Irish of Ulster and the United States, were all Calvinists. Calvin, William of Orange, Cromwell, and the Presbyterian and Congregational founders of the government of the United States, and all the great creators of modern civil liberty, were Calvinists. All modern provision for universal education sprang from the Scotch parochial school and the New England college. The patriots, free-state makers, martyrs, missionaries of all the modern era, have been, in nine hundred and ninety-nine parts out of the thousand, distinctively Calvinist.

This history is glorious and secure past all contradiction. It is natural also—a natural outgrowth of consequences out of principles. Predestination exalts God, and abases man before God. It makes all men low before God, but high and strong before kings. It founds on a basis of eternal rock one absolute Sovereign, to whose will there is no limit, but it levels all other sovereigns in the dust. It renders Christ great, and the believing sinner infinitely secure in him. It establishes the highest conceivable standard of righteousness, and secures the operation of the most effective motives to obedience. It extinguishes fear, it makes victory certain, it inspires with enthusiasm, it makes both the heart and the arm strong. The Ironsides of Cromwell made the decree of predestination their base; hence they never lost a battle, and always began the swelling chorus of victory from the first moment that the ranks were formed. The man to whom in all the universe there is no God is an atheist. The man to whom God is distant, and to whom the influence of God is vague and uncertain, is an Arminian. But he who altogether lives and moves and has all his being in the immanent Jehovah is a Calvinist.

VIII.

THE ORIGINAL STATE OF MAN.

THEOLOGY, as a science, has to do with the great questions which concern God and man and their relations. Consequently, it has been the habit of theologians to group these together under different classes, in this order. First, we have the topics which come under the head of Theology proper, which concern the being of God, the thinking or willing of God, and the acting of God. The second great province is that of Anthropology, which concerns man, his origin, his nature, his original condition, his apostasy, and the consequences thereof to the race. The third great division is that of Soteriology, which concerns God's plan of redemption, the divine Saviour whom he has provided, and his gracious work as our Prophet, Priest, and King. The fourth and last group is Eschatology, that which relates to the last things which remain still before the Church, such as the second coming of Christ, the millennium, the general judgment, the resurrection of the dead, the intermediate state, and the rewards of happiness and punishment which are to come after.

What we have had to say in the preceding seven lectures fell under the first great department of theology—Theology proper; to wit, God, his attributes, his relation to the universe, his providence, the method of it and the plan of it, and his constitution as a divine Person.

Now we begin the department of Anthropology, and of course the first question which emerges must be necessarily as to the original state of man. Those questions which concern man's origin and fall come under various heads, which might, if we had time, be discussed for many days— such as the origin of man, so called ; second, the nature of man—what elements constitute man, what constitutes the soul and body, or spirit, soul, and body, etc. Then as to the origin of the human soul itself : Is it created by God ? is it generated by the parent from the parent ? or is it from God, created by God, in each individual case ? And then the great question as to the unity of the human race, and whether all these great diversities, physical, intellectual, and moral, have been generated from the same parents — first from the original pair, Adam and Eve, and then from Noah and his family. And lastly, What was the original state of man ? what was his condition— the man who had no yesterday, who had no father and mother, who came to consciousness as an adult individual, without previous infancy and without education ?

The answer the Bible gives as to the origin of man is very explicit and very plain, and yet it does not satisfy all questions. And I want to say—and say it as a man who has devoted his life to systematic theology—if any class of men have ever erred in the direction which I am going to speak about to-day, systematic theologians have erred when they mapped it out so sharply. It is one thing to stand faithfully by what God says ; it is another thing to draw inferences from what God says. Our principles as Protestants make us deal with the Bible alone, and not with systems of divinity, and not with inferences from what the Bible says.

1. Now, the Bible asserts, in the first place, that God made the body of man out of the dust of the earth. The questions which arise are, What do we mean by " made " ?

and what do we mean by "dust of the earth"?   Obviously we do not mean absolute creation.   The only instance of this absolute creation that we find recorded in Scripture is in the first verse, "In the beginning"—in the absolute beginning, which marks the emergence of time out of eternity, which marks the first step in the order of creation under the conditions of time and space—"In the beginning God created," gave origin, being, to all the elements out of which the stellar universe is formed.   First it is the great Eternal ; afterward you have "chaos."

There is a wonderful accord between the general findings of modern science and the true meaning of revelation. You have first the creation of the elements out of nothing. You have then the abyss without form and void, the chaos ; and then you have the Spirit of God, the informing spirit of life and thought and power, operating over the face of the abyss ; and then you have, not the sudden, but the gradual movement of the elements; and from them the building up, through successive ages, by the power of God, of this wondrous cosmos, this harmonious universe.

The immediate creation is the making all things out of nothing by the word of his power; but the mediate creation is the making of new things out of old things ; that is, the building up of new things out of old elements —new entities, new species, the origination of new forms, new constitutions, out of the elements of which they are composed.   The Bible says God made man out of the dust of the earth.   He first makes dust, and then he makes man out of it.   So God is the entire maker of man.   It would be very childish to put a literal meaning to this word "dust," which is translated from the Hebrew, another language.   It does not mean simply "dust:" you could not make man out of common clay, because it does not contain all the elements which constitute man.   When you analyze the body of man you find it consists of lime, phosphorus, iron, carbon, nitrogen, hydrogen, and a great many other elements. These do not all exist in clay. What is meant is, that God made man out of pre-existing elements, which God had himself first created. These are everywhere—they are in the atmosphere, they are in the water, they are in the soil; and they were ever present from the time of the first creation, existing, possessing qualities with which God originally endowed them. And it is out of these pre-existing elements of the material universe that God formed, by his own power and will, the body of man.

2. The second point which is taught in Scripture clearly is that God breathed into man the breath of life, so that he became a living soul. Now the question is, of course, What is here meant by breathing, God's breathing, into man? There is a conception that God, as it is expressed, "breathed" into man a part of his own Spirit, and that the human soul, proceeding from God immediately, is a part or particle of God and of the divine Spirit. Now, I confess that seems to me metaphysically absurd, and also profane in its tendency. I do not like that idea. In the first place, God is a Spirit, and cannot be divided. It is of the very essence of matter that it has extension; that it has length and breadth and thickness; that it is composed of the union of elements, and that these elements can be united together or separated one from another, or that matter can be divided into its parts. It is not rational to believe that a spirit can be divided into parts; therefore it is not rational to believe that God breathed a part of his own Spirit into man. And besides this, reason teaches that the attributes are the active powers of the substance of spirit, and cannot be separated from it. Now, if God should give to me a part of his Spirit, I should have infinite attributes, the attributes of the Spirit of God. These are eternity, omniscience, omnipotence, and absolutely perfect and undeviating righteousness; therefore, if

the spirit of man were a part of the Spirit of God, the
spirit of man would be eternal, unchangeable, omniscient,
omnipotent, etc., which we know absolutely to be untrue,
and the very thought of which we reject. Or, God might
have created the spirit of man out of nothing. That is
what we believe; but the difference between soul and
body is just, of course, the essential difference between
matter and spirit. Matter consists of its parts, its
potency, its capability of position, its capability of division. The body can be built up part by part; the body
can be dissolved part by part. But the soul of man is an
absolute unit of consciousness. When my body acts, it
acts by reason of the organs which are external to one
another : my hand is in one place, and my foot in another;
my brain in one place, and my stomach in another. But
the whole soul of man, with its functions, is a single organ :
the one soul thinks, feels, wills, and acts, and therefore the
soul in its particular essence is indivisible ; therefore it
cannot be made. I cannot conceive how the soul can be
generated. The body is generated, but the soul is created.
This is the doctrine of the Church. God, at the moment
of conception, creates a new soul out of nothing by the
word of his power ; communicates to the germ new life,
and this soul, existing in the germ, builds up the body ; so
the body comes to be the expression of the soul. That is
the ground of physiology—that the body develops because
of the soul, and that the soul *ab initio* is the building
principle by which it is built up. Just as your tailor configures your coat to your body, so by the principles of
growth your soul configures your body ; so that your soul
is expressed in your body as the soul's instrument. That
is what is understood by God " breathing the breath of
life "—that is, creating a soul within us. You may ask
why use the word " breath " ? That can easily be answered. God must speak to man, not philosophically, but

according to the laws of humanity and the limits of human thought. Now, it is a remarkable fact that the word for "spirit" in all languages, so far as I know, was originally based upon the figure of breath. The Latin *spiritus*, the Greek *pneuma*, the Hebrew *ruah*, and our word "spirit," all mean breath ; and the reason for this is that men get their ideas from their conditions. Men originally were like children, and when they saw a man die the first thing they noticed was that he did not breathe. When they began to look around and to think, they found the only thing which indicated life or the absence of it was just the presence or absence of this fleeting breath. Thus men came very naturally, as the breath was invisible, to associate the thinking, feeling, and willing principle with the breath. To think and to breathe was to have a soul ; and to put the soul into man was therefore very naturally described as breathing into him the breath of life. Man is a living, breathing thing. But the points clearly taught are that God made the body by his power out of pre-existing material, and that he created the soul by his power and put it into the body.

3. There is a third point we have to consider at this time : The Bible teaches that, seeing Adam needed a companion, it was necessary that God, having made him male, should complete his being by making for him a wife, and that this should not be a new creation, because from the nature of man we constitute a race : there is a solidarity in our race. When Jesus Christ became incarnate, it would not answer to make him a body like man, for then he would not have been a human being. The only way Almighty God can make a human being is by generation. In order that there should not be two absolutely independent creations united together, God put a deep sleep upon Adam, and taking from him a rib, made out of it a woman. That is what the Bible says distinctly and clearly, and it

cannot be got rid of. Therefore I maintain that these three points are true: that the body of man was made out of pre-existing materials, that the soul of man was created by the mighty power of God, and that Eve was made from Adam by the miraculous power of God. And these are given here, not simply as so many facts, but they are inwrought into the whole subsequent scheme of redemption, and you cannot take them out. When I read the Bible I confess I am never absolutely convinced by one text. It is a habit of the mind perhaps, because the thought will arise, How do you know that text is sure? How do you know there is no error in the transcript? How do you know there is not some error in the interpretation? I do not believe God ever meant us to believe in a great doctrine upon a single text. But when the truth is interwoven and associated, as it is here, in the historical book as a condition of the history; when it is taken up and interwoven in the whole scheme of redemption, and afterward is the very basis of God's treatment of man under all conditions, under the covenant of works and man's apostasy, and the covenant of grace and its execution and application—why, I say, you cannot touch this truth without destroying the whole scheme of redemption; and it is just because it has been interwoven into the whole scheme.

You have heard a great deal in recent times about the application or the so-called application of the scientific doctrine of evolution to the question of the origin of man. This word "evolution," as used in the language of philosophers and scientists, does not mean necessarily to indicate always an opinion, but a certain tendency of thought, a way of looking at certain phenomena. But the word evolution has come to stay among us, no matter what we intend to do with it. It does represent a certain mode of thinking, which unquestionably you yourselves hold, and which men have always held more or less, and which is true. Now, the fundamental idea in the general experience of men in the present and past is just this—that the things which are have been produced by the things which were; and the things that are, are producing things that will be; and that this proceeds in lines of absolutely unbroken continuity and by stages almost imperceptible.

This is so, is it not? Remember, I am not advocating evolution, but I show to you what I believe; I want to put you in possession of the facts. The truth is just this: look around you; see the growing of the chicken out of the egg, the growing of the tree out of the acorn, the progress of the fœtus from the germ, the babe from the fœtus, the child from the babe, and the man from the child; the progress of the nation from the tribe, the progress of the tribe from the family,—and the gradual movement everywhere, just as I have shown you in the Bible, through successive stages. Why, the first book in the Bible is called Genesis. The Greek translation that gives us that title calls the work of creation " the genesis of the heavens and of the earth "—that is, the gradual procedure along the lines of unbroken continuity, and by changes of almost imperceptible degree, and this whole cosmos coming to be what it is from the original elements which God created by the word of his power.

And when you go out into the universe you see these things. You look up, and you see, for instance, the sun growing old, and certainly growing colder. And you see the light coming from Jupiter: Jupiter is nothing more than an old sun. And the earth, growing older and colder, is nothing but an old Jupiter; and the moon, grown colder through successive ages, is nothing but an old earth. The moon an old earth, the earth an old Jupiter, and Jupiter an old sun, and these by imperceptible degrees. The earth has been growing colder through time which can be historically traced. The fauna and flora of every zone have been gradually changing, and continually adjusting themselves to constantly changing physical conditions, and that in absolutely unbroken continuity, and by transitions almost imperceptible. The same thing has been going on in the human race. God created it; God made man, one man, and one woman out of the man, one simple family, like any other family; with this qualification, that they were made by an unbroken progress and by slight imperceptible changes, under the influence of climate and social and moral changes, into a human race which through ages has been differentiated into all the varieties of all the families, tribes, and nations that exist upon the face of the earth. The word "evolution" applies to this phenomenon.

Let us make the distinction between evolution as a working hypothesis of science and evolution as a philosophy.

What is science? Science is something which is very sure, but very narrow. Science has to deal simply with facts, phenomena—things to be seen and heard, etc.—and with their qualities, their likeness or unlikeness, whether they have a common existence, coexist, or have a succession. That is the whole of it. The reason science speaks with such authority is this: science is verifiable, and what is verified you must believe: you cannot get around facts. Science is verifiable, and therefore has authority; but it is very narrow. Now, there are a great many things you may call science which have not any science in them. Remember, therefore, that science is to be confined to phenomena, their likeness and unlikeness, their coexistence or succession; and that science has nothing whatever to do with causes, has nothing whatever to do with ends or objects. Science is authoritative within its sphere, because it can determine qualitatively what a thing is and quantitatively how much a thing is, and such results can be expressed in numbers. In this way science has gained its wide dissemination and its great authority. I feel I have a right to say what I shall say now, because I have been associated with a good many men of science who were also devout Christians. This doctrine of evolution, when it is confined to science as a working hypothesis, you may let alone, Christian friends, all of you. You need not be afraid of it. It cannot affect any of the questions of religion ; it cannot affect any questions of revelation ; it cannot lead you wrong, it must in the end go right. It has a narrow track on grooves, but truth is eternal and must prevail ; a lie cannot prevail.

On the other hand, what you have been accustomed to call evolution is not a science. Now, when Tyndall and Huxley go to a great scientific meeting, they talk science, they confine themselves to science. When they write books for the public and to circulate about, they give themselves to speculation ; and it is this doctrine of evolution run wild which is the evolution of the day, the general talk of the people. You hear it talked about in the newspapers, and find it discussed in all circles. It is only a philosophy. Philosophy is different from science. Science is applied to facts, philosophy has to do with causes. Now, I say, do not fear evolution in the department of science, but do fear and oppose evolution with all your might when it is given to you as a philosophy. As a philosophy it explains everything with one solvent ; with one theory it would explain universal being.

These men begin, for instance, with a postulate, the simple inorganic atom. Then by this postulate, which they know nothing about, and which science knows nothing about, they postulate that the living is evolved from the non-living. From that they infer the doctrine of spontaneous generation ; an inference, an hypothesis. Then this living thing is found to possess the property of heredity, the power of transmission, the power of variation, and so by constant transmission and constant variation it is held that from the original germ proceeded other germs, continually varying under the influence of habit; and thus they hold of all living things that they proceed from this original atom, self-generated out of non-living matter.

Now, this is not science, no matter what it teaches. It is nothing but speculation, and as a speculation it ought to be separated from science. Science confines itself to facts. This speculation in regard to evolution has no more authority than any other wild speculation that exists among men; it has no scientific facts to begin with. Science will tell you that there are absolutely no facts with regard to spontaneous generation. It will tell you, at the same time, that there is no missing link between the highest known order of creation and the lowest. You cannot, therefore, take this speculative evolution as a fact; the testimony of science thus far with regard to the facts is against it. It is a vain, vapid, pretentious philosophy of evolution, which has no scientific basis and is absolutely devoid of any scientific authority. You must oppose this, first, in the interest of the convictions of your own reason and of the fundamental principles of human thought and intuitions; secondly, in the interest of natural religion; thirdly, in the interest of revealed religion. It is to me intuitively certain that a thing cannot be evolved out of that which does not contain it. It is certain the chicken must be potentially in the egg before it can be hatched out of it, that the oak must be potentially in the acorn before it can be germinated out of it. You must have the thing that is to live in the seed or the germ. It would be a contradiction to the first principles of reason, an impossibility, to conceive of the living coming from the non-living (if it does come, God must be living in it), or of the conscious coming from the unconscious (if it does, God must be conscious in it), or of reason coming from the irrational (if it does, God must be the reason in it), or of the moral coming from that which is destitute of morality (if it does so come, it must have a moral sense in it). If it were found to be true that successive species have been produced by generation from existing species,—if it could be proved, as it cannot be,—it would follow that it was not the natural process, but there must have been a series of definite divine interventions all along the line. First, you would have life, then consciousness, then reason, then will, and last, the conscience; and thus you will determine that God has at last "made man in his own image."

Now, what do the learned men of science say about this?

1. First, as to the antiquity of man. Undoubtedly, human remains have been discovered under conditions in which it is impossible to believe that God created man only six thousand years ago. I have no doubt of that. I have no doubt you will have to extend the time of creation back further than six thousand years. But remember that God never said he created Adam six thousand years ago. Our chronology exists in two forms, that of Usher and that of Hales, and it differs by a thousand years. Two scholars taking up this chronology have made the difference simply by following out the genealogical tables.

Dr. Green of Princeton, as an interpreter of the Old Testament, is conservative and as much to be relied upon in the interest of historic truth as any man living. In a note to his book on the Pentateuch, he says: "The time between the creation of Adam and ourselves might have been, for all we know from the Bible to the contrary, much longer than it seems." I can well remember my father walking up and down his study when he heard this, and saying, "What a relief it is to me that he should have said that!" Professor Guyot lived in Princeton then; a man of great genius, as highly educated a man of science as I ever saw. He was for many years professor of history in the University of Lausanne, before he gave himself up to material science. He was one of the most devout Christians who ever kindled the flame of holy love from the light of nature and revelation ; he was absolutely a believer in the Bible as it stood in every way. He went to Europe about twelve years ago, and when he came back, after visiting the great museums, he said, " I was surprised at the amount of evidence I saw there of the antiquity of man ; still, I think that thirteen thousand years instead of six thousand would cover it." Now, what difference does it make ? Do you not know if you take history at all, with its chronology merely, that it is the most indifferent and utterly insignificant of all revelations ? The only questions which can be of importance are, Did a thing occur first or last, before or after ? Then of course it affects the question of cause and effect, and it becomes a question of great importance. Chronology in history is what perspective is in a great painting. When you stand before a great historical picture, a great painting—a battle-piece, for instance—you have the forefront of the picture presented to you in proportion, and you measure everything by the stature of men as they stand there, and so you form your judgment, as everything is in proportion ; but when you cast your eye into the background—the great background with life behind it—it makes little difference to you whether it is one mile or two miles, ten or twenty miles. Now, the Bible was written not for the sake of satisfying curiosity, not for the sake of addressing the intellects of men, but it was written for the purpose of giving us a history of redemption.

The first thing we see in the history of redemption begins with Abraham, and if you will look back of that time and see what the Bible says, it is merely the putting of chronological events into position. But begin with the birth of Abraham : after that we have biography, we have appointed times, we have history—a history that goes back only to the birth of Abraham. All before that is the

simple introduction crowded into some ten or twelve
chapters, designed to teach us these tremendous facts—
first, creation ; second, the fall ; thirdly, the general dealing
of God with men in preparation for redemption to come :
but these great facts are dropped in by the great artist of
revelation as an introduction merely to the history beginning with Abraham.   Everything back of this is piled
up like the background in front of which the history stands.
I say neither you nor I have any reason to know how long
it is since Adam was created.   There is no reason to believe
it was more than fifteen or sixteen thousand years ; but
whether more or less, revelation has not informed us.

2. The second question is, What has science found to
be the original condition of man ?

It is found by the testimony of men of science that wherever man is found he is a perfect man.   The most ancient
and primitive of skulls and of skeletons indicate intelligence
equal to any of the present barbarous races now existing
upon the face of the earth.   The whole testimony of history
is therefore not that we were developed out of animals, but
that when we began to exist it was in the fulness of our
organization, in the fulness of our powers.   On the other
hand, it is true that these skeletons indicate that men lived,
as far as they have been discovered, in a savage condition.
Now, the reason Guyot gave was to me perfectly satisfactory : he wished me to think that God created Adam
in his full capacity as a man, but not with habits matured
and formed.   Adam was created with faculties and powers
very much in the state of a child, capable of development
in the right direction, but without education.   Adam was
on trial of *faith*, and as soon as he fell his family are introduced in the narrative.   Cain sinned, and his family are
abandoned ; but the children of Seth were elected to salvation, and God introduced the covenant system into the
family.   Now, said Guyot, when you go out into the world

and find in one of the old caves the fossil remains of primitive men, you will find, of course, barbarians; not because the children of Adam were created barbarians, but the children of Cain necessarily *became* barbarians because they had sinned and were abandoned of God; but the children of Seth—you have their history in the Bible. The Bible is true, and it is given to be a simple history of the race. Therefore, as far as it alludes to primitive races it alludes to the history of those races who were subjects of redemption, who were the covenant people of God.

Now, what does the Bible teach as to the primitive condition?

1. First, the Bible teaches that Adam was brought into existence, not gradually, but suddenly and in a state of maturity. It is a very curious thing for you to consider. I never can understand it thoroughly, and it is because we have had no experience in it. You and I wake up men and women every morning—mature men and women. We wake up with a history—a history in which we can go back to years and years upon years with the assistance of the story of the generations which has come down to us. Then we came into existence as germs; we grew on our mother's breast until we became conscious; and then from early infancy we have been building up habits continuously. When Adam first waked he had no conscious destiny, for he had no history, he had no inheritance. You and I come into existence every morning, not only as men and women, but as Caucasians; and not only as Caucasians, but as Americans; not only as Americans, but as Philadelphians; and not only as Philadelphians, but as Smith or Jones,—and we have all the characteristics inherited from Adam. But when Adam waked he had no history, he had nothing behind him; he was just Adam, and he had no yesterday.

A case occurred which is nearly analogous to this.

There was a young lady in Western Pennsylvania. The history of the case has been written by Dr. Plumer, and was published in 1855 or 1856 in *Harper's Monthly Magazine* with great fulness and certainty, and I know it to be true. This lady, when she got to be twenty years of age, while away from home, waked up one morning with her mind absolutely disconnected with the past; she absolutely remembered nothing—did not know her father or mother. Undoubtedly there were retained by her in her natural consciousness certain habits which she had formed. She did not wake up a babe—she waked up a woman; but she knew absolutely nothing. She had to learn the language again; she had to learn the names of things; she had to learn words; she had to begin again at the beginning of knowledge. Now, when she woke up on that day she was like Adam in this, that she had no yesterday; she knew nothing; everything was fresh to her, just as it was to him. Yet, do you not see, he did not wake up to the consciousness of a babe; he waked up as a man—he came to consciousness as a man, and as a man of maturity. It seems to me unquestionable that God must have communicated something to him—communicated some knowledge for him to work on. I cannot conceive of anything else. I cannot conceive of Adam's mind without something in it. Adam waked up, and he began to speak to God. He had ideas about some things, just as I suppose this lady had. If Adam knew anything, God must have taught him; he could not have invented things himself; he could not have said, "This is so." If I understand it right, what knowledge he had God gave him. Then he gave to man a perfect body; he had a heart and a mind; he could talk and he could breathe. I do not know that he had higher qualities of a human body; I do not care. I *do* know that God gave Adam a good trial, and if he had not sinned he would not have died; and that is all the Bible says, and that is all that you and I have a right to make out of it.

2. The second fact is, the Bible says God made Adam in his own image. Now the word " image " here means two things, which you can easily see. There is a good deal taught in that saying, " Let us make man in our own image." There is a constitutional image of God, and there is a moral or accidental image. Now, when God made man in his own image, he made the spirit rational and moral, and he made it capable of free will; in doing so God made man in his own image. That image of God was not lost. Why, the sinner is in the image of God. The devil is in the image of God, because he is an intelligent spirit. Sometimes there are certain sinners who are in this respect more in the image of God than certain saints; that is, there is more of them—more will, more strength, and in that respect they are more like God. This constitutional image of God never was lost, and never will be lost. But, besides this, God created Adam in the moral image of God—that is, " in knowledge, righteousness, and true holiness," so that the new-created man was in the image of God. And when we take on the new man in Christ Jesus we take on his image, as in the creation—that is, by regeneration. It was the moral image of God which was implanted in the will which made Adam holy and good. The last point is his " dominion over all creatures." Now, this dominion over God's creatures is founded on two grounds : First, because of the constitutionality of it; even bad men can govern on the earth. But it is founded on the higher spiritual likeness to God, of which we have spoken, real although differentiated from the Creator, and which will never be completely developed until man adds to his constitutional likeness the original spiritual moral image of God which he

has lost: not until man becomes not only rational but holy can he regain this image.

Free-will is a question of great interest. I do not assert, nor is it necessary that I should, what are the essential elements of free agency. Men may differ about that. But we know we have a conscience, and that a person is not a mere machine—for that a machine cannot have an obligation, cannot be subject to command, is certainly proved; but that a person is subject to command, is subject to obligations of conscience, is a matter of universal consciousness. This is very true, more so than any fact of science. The most certain things in the world are not the things you can prove. You say, "I have proved this, and therefore I believe it to be true." The fact that you have got to *prove* things shows that there is doubt, for it is only doubtful things you have to prove. The things which you cannot prove are the eternal verities.

How do you prove things? You prove things by deducing the unknown from the known, the uncertain from the certain, by referring particulars to general laws—that is, you prove through a medium. But how do you prove the medium? Now, logic is a great thing. How does logic work? Of course, step by step. You know that in logic you cannot separate the links; if you get hold of one end of the chain, you keep following it up. But what is the force of the chain? You have got a chain of logic hanging down, and you climb up that chain link by link; but what supports the chain at the other end? Logic is like a ladder—by means of it you go up step by step. But how are you going to prove that the bottom of it is all right? The ladder rests on the ground; but what supports the ground? You prove this by that; but what proves *that?* You must have a starting-point, an ultimate fact, and these ultimate principles are the most sure, because if the ground is not steady the ladder is not steady; the ground must be more steady than the ladder. The things which you start from, which are the means of bringing us results, are more sure than other things which are proved by them. You and I know that we are free. You and I know that we are responsible. You and I have that assurance of knowledge which is before all science.

This matter of free-will underlies everything. If you bring it to question, it is infinitely more than Calvinism. I believe in Calvinism, and I say free-will stands before Calvinism. Everything is gone if free-will is gone; the moral system is gone if free-will is gone; you cannot escape, except by materialism on the one hand or pantheism on the other. Hold hard, therefore, to the doctrine of free-will. What is it? I say to my class, but I do not know whether it will do to say it here, " I have my will, but my will is not free; it is myself that is free." Now it makes a difference whether you have freedom of will or the freedom of man in willing. I am conscious that my will is free. But am I free when I will? That is what I mean to indicate. Consciousness tells me that I am free, therefore I am responsible. Then I have this freedom. It is not an abstract quality, it is not an abstract faculty; it has a whole meaning. It is the *I* that is free; the reason is free, as free as the consciousness. It is the *I* that is free, and has got a will; it is the *I* that is free, and has got a character.

Now, so understanding this freedom of the *I*, not of the will, but of the whole soul, what is freedom? I say it is just this, as far as I know anything about it, that it is just the self-originating, self-directing *I*, and that is the whole that it is. Let me illustrate. Suppose I should put upon your table, or you should see resting there, with nothing to interfere with it, a ball of something. It is a ball of yarn. Now suppose you begin to see the yarn moving; you

would be sure to say, "Some one is moving it." It is
yarn; nothing is more certain than that the thing cannot
move itself; if it moves, it moves by reason of some life
connected with it, and you settle that question right off.
You look again, and you say, "It is not a ball of yarn; it
is a mouse." The thing started itself; it could not move
unless it had life from within: that is self-originating
motion. Now, has the mouse free-will? No, because the
mouse has not reason and conscience; therefore I would
amend my definition. The mouse has self-originated action,
the mouse has self-electing action; but it has not reason and
conscience. I say it is self-originated, self-elected action,
with the illumination of reason and conscience, that makes
free-will.

You are sitting in a summer-house; you see something
darting about. What is it? It is nothing but a speck of
dust. That is not self-directed action; it is governed by
the wind. Suppose that you look and see that it is motion
directed from within, that this darting and stopping is self-
moved. Why, that is not governed by the wind; it is
governed by instinct, which is not reason or conscience.
Suppose that you or I at sea should observe a great ship
at a distance just carried about. We look at it; we take
our glasses, and you say, "It has no life about it," it is
moved by the current; and you say that it is an abandoned
thing that is carried about and swept along by controlling
circumstances and outside causes. But instead of this
object floating about, suppose we see a steamship. The
steam is on, the wheels are revolving, the action that you
see is controlled from within; and you have there self-
originated action—the action comes from within the ship.
A gale is blowing, and the waves are dashing against the
vessel; but you see the royal mail steamship fully manned
and equipped; the forces are all at work, and there is a
man at the helm; and there you have free-will in its

highest form——self-originated force, self-directed force, under the lead of reason and conscience : that I believe to be free-will.

Now, the second question is the influence of character on the will. A great many seem to think free-will a simple matter. I believe it is the greatest mystery of the world. Man has a fixed character which determines all in a certain track, and yet that man is free ; whereas, you say a man to be free ought to be perfectly uninfluenced. Suppose I bring up before you to-day in illustration a child. It has no past, no history. It can do what it pleases, of course ; and if I say to it, " Will you do this ? " it replies, " I will." The child does just what any one wishes it to do. Now, take a man of education and of character, a man of principle, a man of convictions, a man of purpose, a man of fixed habits, and you cannot make him do this or that. What he does is already determined by the character of the man, habits which have been crystallized into character. The child is unformed—— he can do anything ; but the character of the man is fixed, and he cannot do what is against his conscience, and he cannot do what is improper in his mind or view. It is uncertain what the child will do, but it is very certain what the man will do. Now, I ask you, Which is the more free ? Is it the child or the man ? Is the child free, or is the father free who can stand up in the most trying times, determined from within by the forces of his character and by the good habits of his life ? You take a man ——take a father and compare him with God : concede the father to be a man of high character, such as General Grant, and sanctified by the Spirit of God, firm as a rock. Yet, after all, the strongest human being may be tempted, may be overcome by seduction. But when you look up at Jehovah, whose character is not uncertain, whose character is eternal, who cannot do that which is foolish and who cannot do that which is wrong, which is the more free? Is Jehovah freer than man? Is the man freer than the child? Therefore, I hold that a man is free just in proportion to his convictions, just in proportion to his capability of determining his action from experience, just from his fixedness and crystallization of character. A man is free in proportion to the direction and development of his character. A holy character is the highest form of freedom.

I believe a sinful character leaves man responsible; for the sinner is just as free as the saint, the devil is just as free as Gabriel. Now, what is freedom? It is self-originated, self-directed action under the law of reason and conscience. But the devil has all that, just as much as Gabriel; the sinful man has all that, just as much as the saint. The difference is here. I have the power of willing as I prefer, but I have no power of creating a holy character for myself. If I have a holy character, my character coincides with my views, my judgment, my reason, my conscience, and my spontaneous affections; they all go in one direction. But if I am a sinner I have no right-directing heart. Reason says go one way, conscience says go the same way, the affections and the dispositions say go another way; and therefore the sinner, according to the language of the Bible, although really free and morally responsible, is in bondage to corruption; the impulses of his heart are in the wrong direction.

Apply that to the fourfold state of man. There are only four states, and there have been only two human beings who occupied all the four states—namely, Adam and Eve. There is the state of innocency, the state of sin, the state of grace, and the state of glory.

Now, we know what it is to be sinners; but can we cease to be sinners, and can we obey the law of holiness? We know what it is to be Christians through divine grace.

How was it with Adam ? Adam was created, according to the Bible, with a perfectly holy nature, without sin ; and yet he was able to sin, and he was able to do right. You have not had that experience. No one but Adam ever had that experience or ever can have it.

If you will read the ninth chapter of our Confession of Faith, on the " Freedom of the Will," you will find it one of the most wonderful treatises you have ever seen.

You are familiar with the fact that theologians always escape from difficulties by using the word " mystery," and that the mystery of mysteries is the origin of sin. The great mystery is a theological one. How is it possible that a God of infinite holiness, of infinite compassion, of infinite knowledge, of infinite power, ever allows sin to exist ? Why, sin is the very thing he hates. This is an absolutely insoluble mystery. How did sin begin ? Why did God permit it ? If we are all free, if we are created by God, and there is nothing which exists which God did not create except himself, how did sin come ? That is an insoluble mystery. St. Augustine attempted to account for it, and I believe his suggestion is the very nearest to it possible. It is that sin in its origin is not a positive entity, but it is a defect.

Take this for an illustration : Suppose you have a fiddle that has been out of tune : you hang it up on the wall, and a year after you come back and take it down, and the fiddle is all in tune. You know that the fiddle must have been put in tune ; it could not have got into tune spontaneously. But suppose your fiddle is perfectly in tune when you hang it up, and you go away, and when you return you find that it is out of tune. It does not follow that somebody did it. You do not say that somebody did it, but that it got out of tune. Now, in the case of Adam I have no doubt sin began in that way—not as sin, but it began to be through inattention, it began to be through defect in love, through defect in faith; it was an omission, and it was thus through a rift in the lute, through a crack here and another there, with a want of harmony. And with this want of harmony came the awful discord that has sent the world into a bedlam, and made a division between God and man. Adam sinned, and then we got into the condition with which we are familiar, with a will to sin, and with a power only to sin. And then, through the cross, we are lifted into a condition of grace, in which we have power to obey; and the power grows stronger and stronger, and the disposition and desire to sin grow weaker and weaker. That is before us. Thank God we shall come at last to the stature of perfect manhood in Christ Jesus, when the character, amplified and regenerated, shall come to its full divine crystalline beauty; and then we shall partake of the divine nature, and have a perfect freedom of will, as free as Adam, yet certain as God.

IX

GOD'S COVENANTS WITH MAN—THE CHURCH.

OUR present subject is a wide one. It comprehends the covenants of God—his covenant of works and covenant of grace. It is very obvious that because God is an intelligence he must have a plan. If he be an absolutely perfect intelligence, desiring and designing nothing but good—if he be an eternal and immutable intelligence, his plan must be one, eternal, all-comprehensive, immutable; that is, all things from his point of view must constitute one system and sustain a perfect logical relation in all its parts. Nevertheless, like all other comprehensive systems, it must itself be composed of an infinite number of subordinate systems. In this respect it is like these heavens which he has made, and which he has hung before our eyes as a type and pattern of his mode of thinking and planning in all providence. We know that in the solar system our earth is a satellite of one of the great suns, and of this particular system we have a knowledge because of our position; but we know that this system is only one of myriads, with variations, that have been launched in the great abyss of space. So we know that this great, all-comprehensive plan of God, considered as one system, must contain a great many subordinate systems which might be studied profitably, if we were in the position to do so, as self-contained wholes, separate from the rest.

Now, the great system of human redemption must in some respects stand alone, conspicuous and pre-eminent, above all other plans and systems of God. Even though God work through eternity, even though he work through infinity, God has but one Son. The incarnation of the Son of God cannot be repeated. This is an event, even in the annals of eternity and in the annals of the universe, without precedent, without parallel, without equal. And this incarnation of the Son of God, this taking upon himself the very nature of man, this uniting himself through the body of man with the whole material universe, and through the soul of man with the whole moral and spiritual universe, must in its very nature have wrought a change affecting universally and intimately all the provinces and kingdoms and all the individuals which it embraces. Besides this, a system which is worthy of the incarnation and the death of the Son of God must be something transcendently superior. I do believe that among all the commonwealths of the sons of God—and I believe these are infinite in number, in extent, and in variety—this commonwealth of redeemed humanity must occupy a central and interior position; that it is something unique, unparalleled, which cannot even in the universe of God be frequently experienced by any of his creatures. And this which seems to us to be possible and probable appears to be absolutely confirmed by the apostle Paul in his Epistle to the Ephesians, where he says, as you will remember, that in the fulness of time this great undiscovered secret, which God had hitherto kept to himself, he had now begun to unveil gradually and slowly through the gospel; to wit, his purpose to make men " accepted through the Beloved," his purpose to bring us under one Head in Christ, and to consolidate under one Head in Christ all things which are in heaven or upon the earth, " even in him."

Now, this plan is in effect a covenant. A great many,

comparatively recently, have come to doubt whether it is proper to apply terms so human to the transactions and relations of God. And yet I do believe that I can show to you that the very facts of the case justify this language, and that they implicitly and necessarily contain all these principles. The term " covenant " is not commonly found in ancient or mediæval theology. Hints of it—that is, the recognition of God's plan and purpose —began to appear in the century preceding the Reformation in the Roman Catholic Church, and then among the first Reformers. It was developed very distinctly afterward by one of the authors of the Heidelberg Catechism. That form of theology itself is generally attributed to the agency of Dutch theologians, who introduced it about the middle of the seventeenth century. But it is found in the early part of that century, in a book of great simplicity, called *The Body of Divinity* (compiled by Archbishop Usher, who was a man of very great learning), which, I believe, had more to do in forming the Catechism and Confession of Faith than any other book in the world ; because it is well known that, although Archbishop Usher was not himself present in the Westminster Assembly, he was twice invited to attend and sit there, and that this book, which he compiled as a young man, was in circulation in this Assembly among the individuals composing it. And if this is true, you could easily see how much of suggestion there is in it which was afterward carried into the Catechism—the Larger Catechism especially —of that Assembly.

Now, I believe that some foreign divines, and some in England, carried out this covenant form of theology in detail in a manner that might be called anthropomorphic. Yet it is evident that if God's dealings with man are ethical, if in their essential nature the system of redemption grew out of the relations of persons, and if the process consisted in the way of teaching, of commandments, of promises, of threatenings, of the presence of motives addressed to the will, and of determinate actions of form and character, then, in its last analysis, all the dealings of God must necessarily come back to this form of a covenant. What is the essence of a covenant between equals except a mutual understanding and the agreement of two wills ? What is the essential nature of a covenant formed between a superior and inferior but this—a conditional promise ? The promise is a reward on the condition of obedience, associated with threatening of punishment on the condition of disobedience. It follows from this, necessarily, that if you begin with an eternity, an eternal plan of God must be a mutual one in which the three Persons come to an understanding and knowledge of that common purpose in which they distribute among themselves reciprocally their several functions. Then when God comes to deal with any intelligent creature, whether it be an angel or a man, under any circumstances, if he commands or promises, or if he threatens, you have there all the elements of a covenant, because a covenant is simply a mutual understanding, and the covenant imposed by a superior upon an inferior is simply a conditional promise. Hence we have the covenant of works, the covenant of redemption, and the covenant of grace.

Now, the covenant of works is so called because its condition is the condition of works. It is called also, and just as legitimately, the covenant of life, because it promises life. It is called a legal covenant, because it proceeded, of course, upon the assumption of perfect obedience, conformity in character and action, to the perfect law of God. And it is no less a covenant of grace, because it was a covenant in which our heavenly Father, as a guardian of all the natural rights of his newly-created creatures, sought to provide for this race in his infinite wisdom and love and infinite grace through what we call a covenant of works. The covenant of grace is just as much and just as entire a covenant, receiving it as coming from an infinite superior to an inferior.

Now look precisely to the facts in the case. Let there be no speculation, let there be no inferences, but take the facts as they are. In the first place, God created man, as we saw in our last lecture, a newly-awakened being, intelligent, moral, with free-will, with a natural character through which he was able to do right, able to do wrong, apparently. In the second place, we know it to be a universal principle—and as it is of God, it seems to us to be a very just principle—that holy character is made to depend upon personal choice. But it does not seem to me that this is always and absolutely essential. We know that the immutable, holy character of God did not originate in personal choice; that God's existence is eternal; his existence is absolutely necessary, absolutely immutable, and that God is from eternity and essentially God, rational, holy, and wise. And yet it does seem as if God had determined to make the moral character of all the subjects of his moral government to depend upon personal choice; and it seems to us as if that was right. He made man, in the first place, holy and capable of doing right, but without a confirmed character he was liable to fall. Ought this confirmed character to result from and depend upon his own personal actions ?

I say that this seems to be God's plan everywhere, because we find it true, without exception, wherever we have any record of God's doings. In the first place, he created the angels, and gave the angels an opportunity of obedience or an opportunity of falling. Each one of them seems to have stood in his own person, and those who fell remained fallen. Those who maintained their first state continued afterward absolutely and eternally in the image of God. Then when God brings forth the gospel, his method is to preach the gospel to every creature, and to offer to all men this amazing gift of eternal life which covenants confirmed moral character, and which we may receive or refuse according to our personal choice.

Then, if this were so, obviously man must have had a probation—a probation in its very essence, because a time of trial and state of trial must be given. That is, God put man in a state of existence, in a state of moral equilibrium. He was in equilibrium because he was holy. His heart was disposed aright; his impulses were right. God endowed him thus with original righteousness; but he was in a state of freedom. His character was not confirmed; he was capable of either obeying or sinning. Now, it would have been an infinite loss to us, an inconceivable danger, if God had determined to keep us for ever, throughout all the unending ages of eternity, hanging thus upon the ragged edge of possible probation, and always in this unstable condition, this unstable equilibrium, able to do right, and liable also to fall; and, therefore, God offered to man in this gracious covenant of works an opportunity of accepting his grace and receiving his covenant gift of a confirmed, holy character, secured on the condition of personal choice.

God gave Adam and Eve the best chance he could, and he put them surely under absolutely the most favourable conditions that we can conceive of. He brought them into a new garden, and he introduced them under the most favourable circumstances, with one exception—he allowed the devil to go into the camp. Why he did that I do not know; but with that exception the conditions were the most favourable we can conceive of. Then he reduced the test to the simplest and easiest—the test simply of a personal violation of law, a test simply of loyal obedience. He did not make the condition, Thou shalt not lie; which, under the circumstances, would have been utterly impossible to Adam, who was a holy, honest man. He did not make the condition, Thou shalt not abuse thy wife Eve; which would have been impossible with Adam in his state as he was originally created. But he reduced the condition to one of specific obedience to a positive command, in itself absolutely distinct. Now, the only difficulty that seems to inhere in this view of man's original condition lies in the fact that the destinies of all Adam's descendants were made to be suspended upon his action. We all inherit what we call " original sin." And two questions here start up, the question as to *how* original sin comes upon us, and the question *why* original sin, under the government of a holy God, is allowed to come upon us.

These are two entirely distinct questions. You do not answer the question *why* when you explain the method by which original sin comes down to us in the order of generation; you must carry the question up to a higher plane and solve it in the light of divine choice. Undoubtedly, this bringing down upon each individual this original taint of our nature, which is the fontal source of all evils—moral, physical, temporal, eternal—is the greatest of all judgments, and it is either a tyrannical act of the Creator or it is a sublime act of justice. Every angel was created a spirit; every angel was constituted self-determining in his own person. But constituted as we are, possessing a responsible and moral nature like angels, which comes into existence in connection with propagated animal bodies, such an individual probation is absolutely impossible. From the very constitution of the human body, and from the nature of the case, anything that Adam did must determine his destiny and that of his children. As Hugh Miller says: " It is a universal law, just as wide as the providence of

God and as the history of man, that God has so constituted men everywhere that the free-will of the parent becomes the destiny of the child." If this be so, we must believe in the covenant of works, and that God has ordained this relation, not only in infinite wisdom and in infinite power, but in infinite justice and righteousness.

But this fact of the covenant of works does not stand by itself. It is a part of a great whole, and if you leave out any element of the system you will not get an understanding of the covenant. This covenant of works which God introduces, and the subject of which is the government of man and his whole career in this world, is part of that greater system which culminates in the covenant of grace, with its headship in the first Adam introducing us into the headship of the second Adam. There has been no Christ except among men. "Forasmuch then as the children are partakers of flesh and blood, he also himself likewise took part of the same......For verily not of angels doth he take hold, but he taketh hold of the seed of Abraham." Angels had a nature, but angels did not have a seed. Christ's relation to the seed of Abraham results from the generic nature of man, from the very constitution of the covenant of works. If there had been no covenant of works, there could have been no covenant of redemption; if there had been no fallen Adam, there could have been no redemption in Christ. You must study the covenant of works always in the light of that larger system wherein it is established that where sin abounded grace has infinitely more abounded.

Further: we say, then, that if the Father and Son and Holy Spirit constitute one Trinity, the plan must be a mutual one, and must contain within it all the elements of such a plan. According to the intimation of this plan given in the Bible, the Father must be an absolute God; the Son must represent his own people, whose nature he was to take. We know such an arrangement was made. Christ often speaks of the work which his Father, God, had sent him to do. He says, " This commandment have I received from my Father." Then he says, " All that the Father giveth me shall come to me." Here are all the elements of a covenant. There was an understanding between the Father and the Son as to the reward which the Son was to gain, so that we have all the elements of the covenant of redemption. The Father undertook all the providential conditions ; the Son was to do all the work in the world, and to that end the world is to be prepared for it, and that he might have the proper conditions of life, and afterward that he should see his seed and be satisfied with the results, with the crowning fruits that he should receive. Then the Son undertook, on behalf of his own people, to take upon himself their nature, to meet their obligations, and to suffer the penalty which had been pronounced upon them. The Holy Ghost undertook also afterward to apply these benefits, and undertook this part of the work because it is the covenant of three Persons, you must remember. He undertook the work of generating the body of the Son, of preparing his human nature, an entire human nature in its fulness, so as to render him, on the human side, a proper being. The Holy Ghost undertook to co-operate with him in every part of his earthly being, and then to constitute himself the other Advocate, which completes the whole work of redemption. He comes to us and takes the things of Christ and applies them to us. He makes continual intercession within us as Christ makes continual intercession for us.

Now, what is commonly called the covenant of grace as distinct from the covenant of redemption is just the human and external side of this eternal covenant of redemption.

Both the covenants are executed in our behalf, both under one name, the covenant of grace. It is better, however, to distinguish them, and to call the covenant between the Persons of the eternal Godhead, the covenant of redemption, which is eternally transcendent, and which is full of light and love, and life and power, the provisions and scope of whose grace transcend the imaginations of man or the tongues of angels. But the covenant of grace is just the human temporal side, which makes human redemption possible and gives its benefits freely to us. In the case of every one to whom the gospel comes, and to whom it gives salvation, it is done upon the condition of faith. Now, here is a covenant with a condition—whosoever believes shall be saved, whosoever believeth not shall be damned. Then the Lord Jesus Christ comes to view and is represented as the Mediator of the covenant, because it all depends upon his mediatorial work, and, above all, he is represented as the Surety. We promise and he indorses. You promise faith upon your knees, and the Lord Jesus Christ indorses for you. You promise service upon your knees, and the Lord Jesus Christ indorses for you. You see how much it is that God asks of you. He says you shall be saved. If we have no belief, we are utterly incompetent to attain to that salvation. Christ gives us faith : we promise trust, and Christ indorses it. We are offered salvation if we will serve; but we have no strength, no merit. Christ gives us the grace : we promise, since Christ indorses it. ·We are offered salvation if we fight the battle and persevere unto the end : we make our pledge, Christ indorses it. Thus our salvation is absolutely and infinitely secure.

Now, of course this covenant sustains to the whole work in the whole sphere of redemption the same relation as the constitution of a republic or of a limited monarchy sustains to the government of a land. Potentially, all the powers of government, all the elements of political society, are represented and granted in the provisions of our constitu-

tion; and so, potentially, all the elements of salvation, everything that can be experienced in the body of Christians in
the earth, everything that can be distinct to the soul of the
Christian on earth, everything that can be experienced
throughout all eternity, everything that can be realized in
the individual, everything that can be realized in the community, the whole body of the redeemed—all this is contained potentially in the provisions of the covenant of
grace. But this covenant, like all other covenants and
constitutions, must be administered; and there is a difference between the covenant and its administration. The
covenant is one; it is the administration which varies continually.

This is a form of language which it would have been
very well for the translators of our Bible to have adopted.
The Greek word *diatheke* means constitution as much as
anything else in the world. It is a constitution. In the
old classical language it was used to express that kind of a
constitution which a man makes when he makes a will, a
testament. You have the unalterable inheritance, and you
can never get rid of it. I prefer the old Latin word
"dispensation" to the words New Testament and Old Testament. These are not proper terms. The word *diatheke*
occurs dozens of times in the Bible; you can see the use of
it and determine the sense—the constitution, the administration of the constitution. That is, it is a covenant or it
is a dispensation of God. If you will then just go back to
your Greek concordance and take up your New Testament
where this word first occurs, and carry it through, you will
find how exactly it has this meaning. You see that covenant, or constitution of grace in the form of a covenant,
which provides for the salvation of man from the beginning
of the history of the human race to the present.

So there has been but one redemption, there has been
but one atonement and one offer of justification, there has

been but one offer of regeneration, there has been but one principle of sanctification, there has been but one operation of Father, Son, and Holy Ghost, from the time that the first gospel was preached to the woman in the garden, until the present day. But then this wonderful constitution has been administered in an infinite variety of ways, and it is capable of twofold unfolding. You take up this constitution, and subject it to a logical unfolding, and you have in it, of course, all possible theology. It has been shown over and over again how all the unfolding of God's plans, as far as those plans have been disclosed to us, and can be exhibited, makes manifest infinite variations and provisions for the redemption of men which can be exhibited under this form, logically and unvaryingly.

There is a second unfolding of the covenant of grace which is chronological : not only is it unfolded logically in itself, but it brings out all the different elements in time. It has been unfolded chronologically from the Garden of Eden up to the present time in the wonderful development of the Church of the first-born, the Church of the covenant, the Church purchased by Christ's blood.

THE CHURCH AND ITS UNITY.

What is the Church ? There is one thing certain about it : the Church has a great many attributes, but that which is absolutely essential is its absolute unity. There is no doubt if there be but one God, there is but one Church ; if there be but one Christ, there is but one Church ; if there be but one cross, there is but one Church ; if there be but one Holy Ghost, there is but one Church. This is absolutely settled—there can be but one Church. We have heard about the visible and invisible Church, as if there were two churches. There cannot be two churches, one that is visible and another that is invisible. There is but one Church, and that Church is visible or invisible just according to the eye that is looking, just according to the point of view taken.

Now, I take the true distinction to be, the Church as we see it, the normal Church, and the Church as God sees it. In respect to this matter our vision is limited in the way of discrimination. You and I cannot discriminate in regard to the Church; we have to take presumptions, we have to take the outward indications, when we make an examination. God's eye is absolutely discriminating. Looking down, he sees the line of demarcation which separates the Church and the world; his vision is sharp and keen. Then, again, our view is not very comprehensive; we see what we call the Church, and we conclude that it is the Church. I have often thought of this as an illustration. I ask a man, "Have you seen the planet, the Earth?" he would say, "Yes, I live on it." That is one of the reasons you never saw it. You never saw the planet Earth as you see the planet Jupiter; you never saw the planet Earth as you see its satellite, the moon. It is absolutely impossible; you are too near it; you see but one little segment of it; nothing but a fraction—a very little at a time. You must get away from the object in order to take it in as a whole, and you must have the advantage of perspective. So in regard to the Church: it is so vast, it has been gathering through the ages, through the centuries, through millenniums; its members come from the ends of the earth; and myriads, ten thousand times ten thousand and thousands of thousands beyond the calculations of angels, have been gathering there in white robes around the throne of Christ. Can you see it? We are too purblind, too earthly in our conditions; but we may see a part of it. What is called the invisible Church is the most conspicuous object in the universe; it has come to shine, to be like the sun, and like an army with banners. What is called the invisible Church

is the only Church that exists. We see parts of it; it
becomes visible to us in sections, in partial glimpses; but
yet it is the same Church. Now, the distinction I make
is, the Church as God sees it, and the Church as man
sees it.

There have been two distinct conceptions of the Church:
one is the theory that the Church consists of an organized
society which God has constituted, that identity consists
in its external form as well as in its spirit, and that its life
depends upon continuity of officers from generation to
generation. This is held by a great many able men, men
of intellect, and by many respectable, level-headed Christians as well.

I hold this to be simply impossible. The marks of
the Church are catholicity, apostolicity, infallibility, and
purity. Now, apply that to any corporation—to the
Church in Jerusalem or to the Church in Antioch; to the
Congregational Church, to the Presbyterian, or to the Prelatical Churches. I do not care as to the form; but there
never did exist, and there does not now exist, any organized
society upon the face of the earth of which these qualities
could be predicated. Not one of these societies has
apostolicity—that is, precisely the apostolic form as well as
the apostolic spirit; not one of these societies has had an
absolute organic continuity, or has, without modification,
preserved it. Societies, like the Church of Rome, which
are most conspicuous in claiming these marks for themselves, are most conspicuously unworthy of them, because
there is no comparison between their ritual of service, their
organization, and the apostolic Church with which they
claim to be identified.

The only possible definition of a Church is that it consists of what is termed "the body of Christ"—that is,
human souls regenerated by the presence and power of the
Holy Ghost, kept in immediate union with Christ. Of

this you can predicate apostolicity, catholicity, and the sanctifying power and perpetual presence of the Holy Ghost, which belongs to the Church of Christ. This is the true Church, which exists through all the successive generations of men, which is united to Christ, and which shares in the benefits of his redemption through the indwelling of the Holy Ghost. This great body is one because the Holy Ghost dwells in it and makes it one. This Church is apostolical, because it is unchanging as to apostolic doctrine; it is catholic, because it contains in one body all of God's people in all worlds and in all time; it unites all from the creation of the world to the coming of Christ, and all from the coming of Christ to the end of the world, in one body—absolutely one, both visible and invisible.

But you may ask me, as a good Presbyterian, a High-Church Presbyterian—because we have a High Church as well as a Low Church—you may ask me, Do you not think there is a visible Church? Yes, I believe the true Church is visible. It consists of men and women who are regenerated, who have divine life, and whose divine life is shown in their holy walk and conversation. You ask if the Church must not be organized? I say yes; but organization is never an essential of the Church. Organization is a simple accident; it is a necessary accident; it is a very important one with us; it is, according to our mode of thinking, obligatory, because it is commanded. By means of organization we have solidification and growth, and it is a great means of self-propagation in accomplishing the great missionary work of carrying the gospel to the ends of the earth. But Christ never did make organization needful in the sense that our being Presbyterians is an essential of the Church.

You and I believe that immortality is provided for all souls before birth, as well as after birth, and for infants that have not come to free moral agency, irrespective of their knowledge of Christ.   Now, think of the history of the world since Adam: all the souls of those that have died before birth or between birth and moral agency have been redeemed in Christ.   You see that organization cannot be the essence of the Church.   I tell you that the infinite majority of the spiritual Church of Jesus Christ come into existence outside of all organization.   Through all the ages, from Japan, from China, from India, from Africa, from the islands of the sea, age after age, multitudes flocking like birds have gone to heaven of this great company of redeemed infants of the Church of God; they go without organization.   Now this is demonstration: that if the great majority of the Church always has existed outside of organization, then organization, while of assistance, is not essential to the Church.   You may add church to church; these are but the incidental forms which the universal Church of God assumes on different occasions under the guidance of the Spirit, under the guidance of God's providence, as a great propaganda for the purpose of accomplishing the great and divine work of carrying the gospel to the ends of the earth.

The Church had its beginning in the family.   The plan of redemption assumes and presumes the original state of human beings as in the family.   How has the Church been logically and chronologically composed ?

In the first place, we have what is called the patriarchal administration in the original constitution of the race. There was no organization of the Church then; there was not much organization in the world, none of the state as distinct from the family.   The father was the sovereign; the great father—that is, the patriarch—was the head of the Church; and just as Adam had led his descendants away from God, so under the covenant of redemption did these patriarchal fathers, these prophets, priests, and kings, lead their people back to him.   In that age there was no priesthood, there were no sacraments. The next form was the Abrahamic dispensation, which was a more specific promise to the Church, the promise connected with the covenant of grace. There was more light, more doctrine, and we have here the specific sacrament of circumcision which was added to the specific covenant.

Then we come, in the third place, to the Mosaic dispensation. It is well recognized that the wonderful phenomena of this dispensation must be understood as presenting a threefold aspect or character, and it becomes very much more simple when we do this.

In the first place, these Jews were a people who, in their own time, constituted a distinct nation. God was their God, and a large portion of his providences toward them had reference simply to their temporal interests and to their relations as a specific people. They had a government which guarded the relations they sustained to other nations; therefore you must understand a great many of their laws with reference to this specific characteristic. The Jews were constituted a kingdom, and God was their God.

Another far more important aspect of the Jewish system was this: it was a promulgation of the covenant of works which was introduced at Sinai, and the design of this promulgation was to lead those generations to the gospel, for the gospel presupposes the law. The law has been from the beginning the schoolmaster to lead us to Christ. Therefore in this aspect it was a missionary institution, and must be understood as preparatory; it was the preaching of the doctrine of sin and condemnation in order to prepare man for the preaching of the doctrine of grace and salvation.

Then, again, it did most characteristically in the specific form of its administration outline the covenant of redemption; it was the setting forth of Christ—Christ as the Prophet, Priest, and King—in the method of his redemption and our personal reception of its benefits. The conditions of salvation were the same, and salvation was secured by the same plan. The Jew, if he believed in Christ's coming, was justified and received the Holy Ghost, although without understanding it, and was regenerated, sanctified, and justified; and being thus justified and sanctified, when he died he went to be, not with Christ—there was at that time no incarnate Christ; he did not exist—but he went into that happy place in which God gathered all his Old Testament people—in Abraham's bosom.

Now, how shall we regard the logical unfolding of the covenant from the time of Moses to the time of Christ? First, we have the breaking down of the middle wall of partition by the taking away of the limitation presented by the institution of the Church as a nation: it was confined under these circumstances to one people; it was incapable of being expanded among the nations of the earth. It is a remarkable fact that the Old Dispensation opened with the tower of Babel and the confusion of tongues, and the New opens with the Pentecost and the gift of tongues. The Old Dispensation began with the process of selection and exclusion: there was an election of the children of Israel out of all mankind, and a rejection of all the rest; a selection of the Israelites out of the Hebrews, and the rejection of the rest; and the selection of Judah out of Israel, and the rejection of the rest. But now see how the principle changes. Under the Old Dispensation it was exclusion and segregation; under the New Testament it is expansion and comprehension. The new Church begins in a little upper chamber in Jerusalem. The Church becomes the Church of the Jews; it becomes the Church of the Roman empire; it becomes the Church of Europe; it becomes the Church of the world.

Now, as to the unity of this Church I have something to say. A great many are agitated at present with regard to Church unity and its manifestations, and I think there is a great deal of confusion of thought as to the original conception of the Church itself. If the Church be an external society, then all deviation from that society is of the nature of schism; but if the Church be in its essence a great spiritual body, constituted by the indwelling of the Holy Ghost through all the ages and nations, uniting all to Christ, and if its external organization is only accidental and temporary, and subject to change and variation, then deviation of organization, unless touched by the spirit of schism, is not detrimental to the Church. I do believe that God's purpose, on the contrary, has been to differentiate his Church without end. You know that the very highest form of beauty of which you can conceive, the very highest form of order, is multiplicity in unity and unity in multiplicity; the higher the order of unity, the greater must be the multiplicity.

This is so everywhere. Go to the ocean: every drop of water is the repetition of every other drop, and there is union simply without diversity. Go to the desert of Sahara, and every grain of sand is the duplicate of every other grain of sand; but there is no unity, no life. You could not make a great cathedral by piling up simple identical rhomboids or cubes of stone. It is because you differentiate, and make every stone of a different form in order to perform a different function, and then build them up out of this multitudinous origination into the continuity and unity of the one plan or architectural idea, that you have your cathedral. You could not make a great piece of music by simply multiplying the same tone or sound. In order to obtain the harmony of a great orchestra, you get together a large number of musical instruments, or you have a great number of human voices in a choir, and you combine them; then you have an infinite variety of quality and infinite variety of tone. You combine them in the absolute unit of the one great musical idea which you seek to express.

But if this is true of such things, it is more true of Christ's Church. If God had followed our idea, how simple a thing it would have been to make a united Church descending from Adam and Eve! We might think that was all that could be done, and there would be then no stones of stumbling. You could then watch this Church, and it would go on indefinitely and without limit.

Now, what has God been doing? He has broken humanity up into infinite varieties. This has been his method. He has been driving it into every clime. He has been driving it into every age through the succession of centuries. He has been moulding human nature under every variety of influences through all time, until he has got men in every age, every tribe, every tongue, every nation, every colour, every fashion—in order to do what? Simply to build up a variety, to build up the rich, inexhaustible variety which constitutes the beauty in unity of this great infinite Church of the first-born, whose final dwelling-place is to be in heaven.

I say, under this dispensation God has left us free to form organizations. He has left us free to experience Christianity under all the conditions in which he has placed us; and the Christian religion which we receive takes various colours and tones from the nationality, from the tribe, and from the race. Undoubtedly, there is such a thing as schism. Schism is a great sin. But if the Church is a spiritual body, the sin is a sin against spiritual unity.

All high-churchism, all claims that our Church is the one Church and only Church, are of the essence of schism;

all pride and bigotry are of the essence of schism ; all want of universal love, all jealousy, and all attempts to take advantage of others in controversy cr in Church extension, are of the essence of schism. But surely it is not schism for each one of us to go out and develop in our own way. What is the result ? I trust in this I am not narrow. I am not making any claim for Presbyterianism ; I am talking of the whole Church of God that is truly loyal to Christ, animated by one spirit, comprehended in one body. On the other hand, I hold that it is our interest to have denominational differences in order to maintain what God has given us.

I believe the Church is like the world, and consists of many forms, many races. I say to every race, Maintain the integrity of your race ; and to every nation, Maintain the integrity of your nation, that it be not antagonized by other nations. This is the duty which God has historically devolved upon us. I say, then, if Presbyterianism be true, maintain the type which God has given you ; and I would say the same to our Baptist friends, and to our Episcopal friends and Methodist friends. I believe all our denominations are historically justified ; that they all represent great ideas, either theoretically or practically, which God commits to them, in order to have them act upon them ; that our duty is to maintain our true inheritance, and to prove true to the stock from which we came. We do desire comprehensively to work together toward unity, but mongrelism is not the way to get it. It is not by the uniting of types, but by the unity of the Spirit ; it is not by working from without, but from within outward ; by taking on more of Christ, more of the Spirit, that we will realize more and more the unity of the Church in our own happy experience.

X.

THE PERSON OF CHRIST.

IT is the grand distinction of Christianity that all its doctrines and all its forces centre in the Person of its Founder and Teacher. In the case of all the other founders of philosophical sects and religions, the entire interest of their mission centres in the doctrines they teach, the opinions they disseminate. This was obviously true in the case of Zoroaster, Confucius, and Buddha, of Plato, Aristotle, and Cicero, of Moses and Paul. In the case of each of them the question was not what they were, but what they taught. But in the case of Christianity, the entire system, from foundation to superstructure, rests upon and derives its life from the Person of its Founder. The question of questions is what he was, rather than what he taught.

This can be proved—(1.) From an examination of each of the doctrines of Christianity separately. All that the Scriptures teach of the Mosaic dispensation and its typical character; of the burden of all the prophets; of the new birth; of repentance and faith; of justification and sancti-fication; of holy living and of the Christian Church; of the state of the soul after death; of the resurrection from the dead; of the general judgment; and of heaven itself— takes its meaning and force from its relation to the person, offices, and work of Christ. (2.) From the experience of

Christians. We believe Moses and Paul, but we believe *in* Christ. To be a Christian is to be in Jesus. To live a Christian is to have fellowship with the Father and the Son. To die a Christian is to sleep in Jesus. (3.) The same is proved, in the third place, from the present attitude of the great controversy between Christianity and its opponents. In this age, in which secular philosophy oscillates between materialism and pantheism, when advanced thinkers disdain all the old questions of theology, natural or revealed, even the most inveterate sceptics acknowledge the necessity of presenting some solution of that miracle of all ages, the Person of Jesus of Nazareth. It is impossible to explain that unique phenomenon which emerged on the hills and valleys of Judea eighteen hundred years ago, whose life, character, and works are truly inexplicable unless we accept the account of his nature and his origin which is given to us in the Word of God. The press groans with *Ecce Homos* and Lives of Christ, and with new versions of rationalistic theories, mystical and legendary. Thus the infidel is constrained to unite with the believer in bearing testimony to the greatness of that mystery of godliness, God manifest in the flesh.

And here, in the very heart of our religion, all true Christians agree. The entire historical Church, in all its ages and in all its branches—Greek and Roman, Lutheran and Reformed, Calvinist and Arminian—are here entirely at one.

While this is true, as far as the public faith of the Church is concerned, as expressed in its great confessions, liturgies, and hymns, a great variety of opinion and diversity of speculation and definition have prevailed at different times among the various schools of theology. This diversity of speculation naturally arose from the following facts:—

1. The Person of the incarnate God is unique. His

birth has had no precedents and his existence no analogy. He cannot be explained by being referred to a class, nor can he be illustrated by an example.

2. The Scriptures, while clearly and fully revealing all the elements of his Person, yet never present in one formula an exhaustive definition of that Person, nor a connected statement of the elements which constitute it and their mutual relations. The impression is all the more vivid because it is made, as in a picture, by an exhibition of his Person in action—an exhibition in which the divinity and humanity are alike immediately demonstrated by the self-revelation of their attributes in action ; and

3. This unique personality, as it surpasses all analogy, also transcends all understanding. The proud intellect of man is constantly aspiring to remove all mysteries and to subject the whole sphere of existence to the daylight of rational explanation. Such attempts are constantly ending in the most grotesque failure. Even in the material world it is true that *omnia exeunt in mysterium.* If we cannot explain the relation which the immaterial soul sustains to the organized body in the person of man, why should we be surprised to find that all attempts to explain the intimate relations which the eternal Word and the human soul and body sustain to each other in the Person of Christ have miserably failed ?

Before proceeding to the historical illustration of this doctrine, I call your attention to the following general remarks :—

1. The doctrine of the Person of Christ is intimately associated with the doctrine of the Trinity. It is obviously impossible to hold the orthodox view with respect to the divine-human constitution of our Lord unless we first believe the orthodox doctrine that the one God exists as three eternal Persons, Father, Son, and Holy Ghost. At the same time, few hold the true doctrine as to the tri-personal con-

stitution of the Trinity without at the same time holding the corresponding catholic doctrine as to the Person of the God-man.

Indeed, I happen to know that the great objection which the most able and influential Unitarians entertain to the Trinitarian system is not originated by their difficulty with the Trinity, considered by itself, but because they regard the doctrine of the Trinity to be inseparable from that of the Person of Christ as held by the Church, which to them appears impossible to believe.

And undoubtedly we freely admit just here that in the constitution of the Person of the God-man lies the, to us, absolutely insoluble mystery of godliness. How is it possible that the same Person can be at the same time infinite and finite, ignorant and omniscient, omnipotent and helpless ? How can two complete spirits coalesce in one Person ? How can two consciousnesses, two understandings, two memories, two imaginations, two wills, constitute one Person ? All this is involved in the scriptural and Church doctrine of the Person of Christ. Yet no one can explain it. The numerous attempts made to explain or to expel this mystery have only filled the Church with heresies and obscured the faith of Christians.

2. The Scriptures do not in any one place, or by the means of distinct, comprehensive formulæ, give us complete definitions either of the doctrine of the Trinity or of that of the Person of Christ. They do give us, most explicitly and repeatedly, all the elements of both doctrines, and then leave us to put all the several teachings relating to the same subject together, and so to construct the entire doctrine by the synthesis of the elements.

Thus (1) *as to the Doctrine of the Trinity.* The Scriptures tell us, first, that there is but one God. Then we would naturally conclude that if there is but one God, there can be but one divine Person. But, again, the

Scriptures teach us that Father, Son, and Holy Ghost are that one God. Then, again, we would naturally conclude that the terms Father, Son, and Holy Ghost are only different names, qualitative or official, of one Person. But yet again the Scriptures prevent us, and teach us that these names designate different subjects and agents. The Father is objective to the Son, and the Son to the Father, and both to the Spirit. They love each other and are loved. They converse, using to and of each other the personal pronouns I, thou, he. The Father sends the Son, and the Father and Son send the Spirit, and they, in that order, act as agents, proceed from and return to, and report.

The Scriptures also teach that there is an eternal constitutional relation of order and origin between three Persons. The Father is the fountain of Godhead. He eternally begets the Son (the process is without beginning, or end, or succession), and the Father and Son eternally give origin to the Spirit. (2.) In the very same manner the Scriptures teach us all we know of the Person of Christ. Pointing to that unique phenomenon exhibited biographically in the four Gospels, the Scriptures affirm—(*a*) "He is God." Then we would naturally say, if he is God, he cannot be man; if he is infinite, he cannot be finite. But the Scriptures proceed to affirm, pointing to the same historical subject, "He is man." Then, again, we would naturally say, if that phenomenon is both God and man, he must be two Persons in reality, and one Person only in appearance. But yet again the Scriptures prevent us. In every possible way they set him before us as one Person. His divinity is never objective to his humanity, nor his humanity to his divinity. His divinity never loves, speaks to, nor sends his humanity, but both divinity and humanity act together as the common energies of one Person. All the attributes and all the acts of both natures are referred to the one Person. The same "I" possessed glory with

the Father before the world was, and laid down his life
for his sheep. Sometimes in a single proposition the title
is taken from the divine side of his Person, while the predicate is true only of his human side, as when it is said, "The
Church of God, which he hath purchased with his own
blood." The same Person is called God because of his
divinity, while it is affirmed that he shed his human blood
for his Church. Again : while standing among his disciples
on the earth, he says, "The Son of man, which *is in* heaven."
Here the same Person, who is called Son of man because
of his humanity, is declared to be omnipresent—that is, at
the same time on earth and in heaven—as to his divine
nature. This, of course, implies absolute singleness of
Person, including at once divine and human attributes.

Again : the Scriptures teach us that this amazing personality does not centre in his humanity, and that it is not
a composite one originated by the power of the Spirit when
he brought the two natures together in the womb of the
Virgin Mary. It was not made by adding manhood to
Godhead. The Trinity is eternal and unchangeable. A
new Person is not substituted for the second Person of the
Trinity, neither is a fourth Person added to the Trinity.
But the Person of Christ is just the one eternal Word, the
second Person of the Trinity, which in time, by the power
of the Holy Ghost, through the instrumentality of the
womb of the Virgin, took a human nature (not a man, but
the seed of man, humanity in the germ) into personal
union with himself. The Person is eternal and divine.
The humanity is introduced into it. The centre of the
personality always continues in the eternal personal Word
or Son of God.

Let me illustrate this by your personality and mine.
We consist of soul and body, two distinct substances, but
one person. This personality, however, is not composed
of the union of soul and body at birth. The personality

from the first to the last centres in the soul, and is only shared in by the body.

By soul we mean only one thing——that is, an incarnate spirit, a spirit with a body. Thus we never speak of the souls of angels. They are pure spirits, having no bodies. Put a spirit in a body, and the spirit becomes a soul, and the body is quickened into life and becomes a part of the person of the soul. Separate soul and body, as death does, and the soul becomes a ghost and the body becomes a corpse. When death takes place the body passes out of the personality, is called " it," and is placed in the grave ; while the soul, still continuing the person, goes at once to be judged of God. At the resurrection the same personal soul will return and take up the same body once discarded, and, receiving it again into its personality, will stand before God a complete man.

So the divine Word, which from eternity was the second Person of the Trinity, did eighteen hundred years ago take, not a human person, but a human nature into his eternal personality, which ever continues, not a human person nor a divine-human person, but the eternal second Person of the Trinity, with a human nature embraced in it as its personal organ.

3. There is one obvious respect in which the doctrines of the Trinity and of the Person of Christ agree, and one in which they no less obviously differ. They agree in that both alike utterly transcend all experience, all analogy, and all adequate grasp of human reason. But they differ in that, while the mystery of the Trinity is that one Spirit should exist eternally as three distinct Persons, the mystery of the Person of Christ is that two distinct spirits should for evermore constitute but one Person.

4. If you give due attention to the difficulties involved in each of these divinely revealed doctrines, you would be able *a priori* to anticipate all possible heresies which have

been evolved in the course of history. All truth is catholic; it embraces many elements, wide horizons, and therefore involves endless difficulties and apparent inconsistencies. The mind of man seeks for unity, and tends prematurely to force a unity in the sphere of his imperfect knowledge by sacrificing one element of the truth or other to the rest. This is eminently true of all rationalists. They are clear and logical at the expense of being superficial and half-orbed. Heresy, from the Greek αἵρεσις, means an act of choice, and hence division, the picking and choosing a part, instead of comprehensively embracing the whole of the truth. Almost all heresies are partial truths—true in what they affirm, but false in what they deny.

Take, for instance, the doctrine of the Trinity. One eternal Spirit exists eternally as Father, Son, and Holy Ghost, three distinct Persons. This the rationalists cannot understand, and therefore will not believe. They proceed, therefore, to deny one or other element of the whole truth, and try to hold the dead fragment remaining.

Thus (1) they attempted to cut the knot by denying the divinity of Christ, and had pure, lifeless Mohammedan Unitarianism left; (2) they pressed the unity so close that they had but one Person as well as one God, and the terms "Father," "Son," and "Holy Ghost" became different descriptive or official titles of the same Person: as Grant while in office was one person, and yet at the same time was husband and father, commander-in-chief of the army and navy, and President of the United States, so the Sabellians say Father, Son, and Holy Ghost are different titles of the same Person in different characters and functions; (3) or, lastly, they ran to the other side of the enclosure and pressed the distinction of Persons to such a degree that they had three Gods instead of the mystery of one God in three Persons.

Take, for another instance, in like manner, the doctrine

of the Person of Christ. The mystery is that two spirits —one divine, the other human—two minds, two wills, are so united that without confusion or change or absorption of one in the other they constitute but one Person. Scrutinize this, and you can predict beforehand all the possible heresies or one-sided half-truths. (1.) The Unitarian cuts the knot by denying half the facts of the case and leaving out the divinity. (2.) The Gnostics held that a man Jesus was temporarily possessed by the supernatural Æon or Angel Christ. (3.) The Docetæ cut the knot by denying the other half of the truth, that Christ was a man, holding that the reality was a simple divinity and the humanity a mere appearance. (4.) The Eutychians pressed the unity of the Person to such an extent that they confounded the natures, holding that the human was absorbed in the divine. (5.) The Nestorians went to the other extreme of emphasizing the integrity of the several natures after their union so very far as to dissolve the unity of the Person, and to set forth Christ, not as a God-man, but as a God and a man intimately united. These, if they do not cover, at least indicate the direction and spirit of all possible heresies relating to these two fundamental doctrines of Christianity.

Let us proceed to the historical development of the doctrine in the consciousness of the Church.

I. In the Council of Nice, A.D. 325, there were three parties. The Arians, led by Arius, maintained that the superhuman element in the Person of Christ was *heteroousion*—of a different substance from God the Father. The semi-Arians, led by the two bishops Eusebius, held that the superhuman element was *homoiousion*—of a like substance to that of the Father. The Orthodox, led by Athanasius, held that the divine nature of Christ was *homoousion*—of identically the same numerical substance with that of the Father. This last doctrine was embodied in the creed of that council, which, in the form afterward perfected at the end of the fourth century, is received by all Christians, Catholic and Protestant. From this time the doctrine of the Trinity and that of the absolute divinity of Christ have been universally held in the Church.

II. But from that time forth men began to question *how* the substance of God could be united in one Person with the substance of humanity.

Apollinaris, bishop of Laodicea, in all sincerity attempted, about A.D. 370, to maintain the truth by the following explanation, which really sacrifices an essential part of it. He supposed that the Scriptures (1 Thess. v. 23) and true philosophy teach that every natural human person is composed of three distinct elements — *soma*, body ; *psyche*, soul ; and *pneuma*, spirit—that the psyche is the seat of the animal life and appetites and the emotions and logical understanding, and the pneuma is the seat of the reason, the will, and the moral and spiritual nature. These three put in personal union make one complete human person. He held that in the Person of Christ the soma and psyche are human and the pneuma is divine.

But this view secures the unity and simplicity of Christ's Person at the expense of the integrity of his humanity. If Christ does not take a human pneuma— that is, a complete human nature—he cannot be our Saviour, our High Priest, who feels with us in all our infirmities, having been tempted like us. Indeed, the view of Apollinaris degrades the doctrine by maintaining that the eternal Word took not a complete human nature, but an irrational human animal into personal union with himself.

III. During the fourth and early part of the fifth centuries, theological speculation in the Eastern Church revolved around two great centres, Alexandria in Egypt and Antioch in Syria. The tendency of the Alexandrian school from Origen to Cyril and Eutychius was mystical and theosophical. With this school the divinity of Christ was everything, and into it the humanity was represented as absorbed. The tendency of the school of Antioch, whose great representatives were Theodore of Mopsuestia and Nestorius, patriarch of Constantinople, was to rationalistic clearness—to the emphasis of moral duties and of the distinctness and independence of the human will. The Alexandrian party generated Eutychianism, which absorbed the humanity in the divinity, in order to maintain the unity of the Person and absoluteness of the divinity; while the Antiochian party generated Nestorianism, in which the unity of the Person is sacrificed to the separate integrity of the natures, and especially of the human nature. Nestorianism was condemned by the ecumenical council held at Ephesus, A.D. 431, and Eutychianism was condemned by the council which met at Chalcedon, A.D. 451.

IV. In these decisions the whole Church, Eastern and Western, concurred. The advocates of Eutychianism endeavoured for a time to maintain, as a compromise position, that although the two natures in Christ remain entire and distinct, nevertheless that as they coalesce in Christ in one single Person, so that Person can possess but one will, divine-human, and not a divine and a human will combined in one personality. This party was then known as the Monothelite, the one-will party. After this heresy was condemned at the sixth ecumenical council, held in Constantinople in 681, the controversy was closed, and the faith of the Church remained as represented by the old definitions until the time of the Reformation.

V. After the Reformation the Lutherans, in order to establish their doctrine of the ubiquity of Christ's human nature in the Lord's Supper, introduced a new view as to his Person. The Eutychians taught that the humanity of Christ was absorbed in his divinity. The Lutherans taught that his humanity was exalted to an equality with the divinity. This they attempted to explain by the *Communicatio Idiomatum* — that is, the communication of attributes from one nature to the other, or the communion of one nature in the attributes of the other. The Lutherans held the formula *Communicatio idiomatum utriusque naturæ ad naturam*—that is, the communication of the attributes of each nature to the other nature. The Reformed Churches, on the other hand, admitted that the attributes of each nature are communicated only to the one Person, which was common to both natures. The Lutherans thus held that at the moment of the incarnation, in virtue of the union between the divine and human natures, the human nature of Christ became omniscient, omnipotent, and omnipresent.

This doctrine is evidently not supported in Scripture— is not consistent with the integrity of Christ's human nature; for that which is omniscient, omnipotent, and omnipresent is divine and not human, and is plainly inconsistent with all the facts related in the Gospels as to our Lord's earthly life. He is there represented in all respects, as to knowledge, power, and space, as literally finite as other babes and men.

This theory originated in the desire to lay a foundation for their doctrine that the body and blood of Christ are always present *in, with,* and *under* the bread and wine in the sacrament of the Lord's Supper. But it is evident that this foundation, instead of supporting, invalidates the sacramental presence. If his body and blood are omnipresent, then they are *in, with,* and *under* all food and drink, and indeed in and under all material forms of every kind in all worlds. What they needed was not essential, constant, universal omnipresence, but "voluntary multipresence"— that is, the power upon Christ's part of rendering his body and blood present at many places at the same time at his own good pleasure.

To reconcile their doctrine with these facts, one school of Lutheran theologians—namely, that of Tübingen, led by John Brentius—held that while on earth the human nature of Christ was really omnipotent and omnipresent, only that he hid the use of these attributes from man, like a king travelling *incognito*. Another school, that of Chemnitz, held that the use of these divine attributes of Christ's humanity was dependent upon his human will—that in his estate of humiliation on earth he voluntarily abstained from their use.

This speculation of the Lutherans was the latest and most elaborate attempt ever made by theologians to explain how the two natures of Christ can coalesce in one person.

VI. The Eutychians held that the human nature was absorbed in the divine ; the Lutherans, that the human nature was exalted to equality with the divine ; the Reformed held that the eternal divine Person humbled himself to be united with humanity ; ·the advocates of the modern German doctrine of Kenosis hold that the eternal Word himself *became* man—that Christ was and is both God and man, but that he is but one single nature as one single Person.   They build on such texts as John i. 14 and Phil. ii. 7, " He emptied himself."   *Kenosis* means the act of emptying or the state of being emptied.   They start with the orthodox doctrine that the Person of the Word, or Son, is eternally generated of his own substance by the Father.   This generation makes the Son partaker of all the fulness of the divine nature, and is, they say, dependent upon the will of the Son, his voluntary act conspiring with the act of the Father.   At the incarnation the eternal Son, of his voluntary act, emptied his person of the divine fulness, and became an unconscious human germ in the womb of the Virgin.   From that point, and under the ordinary conditions of human birth and life, this divine

germ developed through all the stages of human experience—infantine, youthful, and mature. After his death
and resurrection, this same nature, the self-emptied Word,
the divine germ, developed as a man, again expands into
infinity, and fills all things as God. His nature hence is
one, because from first to last it is the divine substance
communicated by the Father to the Son, who in turn
voluntarily empties himself of all except the merest point
of existence, which after his glorification expands again
into infinity. He is one Person because he is one single
nature. He is from first to last God as to substance, but
he has become, by passing through the womb of the Virgin
Mary, man as to form. Thus he ever continues God in
the form of man—always God, because he subsists of the
one eternal, self-existent Substance ; always man, because
retaining the human form and experience acquired on
earth.

This, confessedly, rests upon the assumption that the
divine nature is capable of taking upon itself humanity,
and that the human nature is capable of receiving the
properties of divinity. Hence it is evidently of a pure
pantheistic descent. God is immutable, incapable of becoming unconscious and of passing through the limitations
of the finite. To be man is to be finite and dependent ;
to be God is to be infinite and self-existent. Christ was
both at the same time, because his Person embraced two
distinct natures, the divine and the human.

VII. The common doctrine of the Church, then, is as
follows :—

1. As to the incarnation.

(1.) Substance is that which has objective existence, per-
manence, and power. Attributes are the active powers of
their respective substances, and are inseparable from them.
Only a divine substance can have divine attributes ; only
a human substance can have human attributes. In the

Godhead the one infinite divine Substance eternally exists in the form of three equal Persons.

(2.) In the incarnation the second Person of this Trinity established a personal union between itself and a human soul and body. These substances remain distinct, and their properties or active powers are inseparable from each substance respectively.

(3.) The union between them is not mechanical, as that between oxygen and nitrogen in our air; neither is it chemical, as that between oxygen and hydrogen when water is formed; neither is it organic, as that subsisting between our hearts and our brains: but it is a union more intimate, more profound, and more mysterious than any of these. It is *personal.* If we cannot understand the nature of the simpler unions, why should we complain because we cannot understand the nature of the most profound of all unions?

2. As to the *effects* of the incarnation.

(1.) The attributes of both natures belong to the one Person, which includes both.

(2.) The acts of both natures are the acts of the one Person.

(3.) The human nature is greatly exalted, and shares in the love, adoration, and glory of the divine nature. It all belongs to the one Person.

(4.) The human attributes of our Redeemer are the organ of his divine Person, and are, through the divinity, rendered virtually inexhaustible and ubiquitously available for us. When you put your babe to bed and leave him, to go your own way to a distant place, you say, "Love, fear not; Jesus will be with you while I am gone." You know Jesus will be with you also at the same time, and with all believers. By this you do not mean simply that Christ's divinity will be with you and the babe. You mean that the Person who is very man as well as very

God will be with you both. You want his human love and sympathy as well as his divine benevolence. If he were a mere man, he could be only at one place at one time, and his attention and sympathy would soon be over-whelmed by our demands. But he is at once God and man, and as such, in the wholeness and fulness of both natures, he is inexhaustible and accessible by all believers in heaven and on earth at once and for ever.

The best illustration of this mystery is afforded by the union of soul and body in the unity of our own persons. The body is matter, the soul is spirit. Matter and spirit are incompatible—as far as we understand as incompatible as divinity and humanity. Matter is inert, extended, and the vehicle of force; spirit is spontaneous, unextended, and the generator of force. Yet they form in us, under certain circumstances, one person. This is the person of the soul, not of the body, as shown before. The soul by this union is virtually confined to and extended in space, for wherever the body is, there the soul lives and feels through their union. The body, which is of itself inert and dead, is through its union with the soul palpitating with life, throbbing with feelings, and instinct with energy.

Every act of each nature is also the act of the one person, and both natures concur in our actions, organic and voluntary. Even digestion is possible to the body only through the indwelling of the soul. But in all our higher actions, when the orator speaks or when the singer pours forth his soul in melody, both soul and body penetrating each other, yet distinct, constituting one person, yet uncon-fused—both soul and body act together inseparably. As human voice and instrument blend in one harmony, as human soul and body blend in each act of feeling, thought, or speech, so, as far as we can know, divinity and humanity act together in the thought and heart and act of the one Christ.

I adore a Christ who is absolutely one—who is at the same time pure, unmixed, unchanged God, and pure, unmixed, unchanged man—and whose Person, in its wholeness and its fulness, is available throughout all space and throughout all time to those who trust him and love his appearing.

XI

THE OFFICES OF CHRIST.

HIS OFFICES OF PROPHET AND OF PRIEST.

I AM now to open the great subject of the Offices of Christ. In the last lecture we discussed the great mystery of his Person as God and man in two distinct natures and one Person for ever. These three—Christ's Person, his Office, and his Work—are absolutely inseparable. One of them cannot be understood as separated from the other two. He assumed humanity and became God and man in one Person in order that he might assume his office as Mediator between the holy God and sinful man, and his office and work are alike inconceivable except when viewed in connection with the unparalleled constitution and comprehensive range of his Person.

I. The office of Christ as Mediator is obviously one. He occupies the whole of it at the same time. He discharges exhaustively all the parts of it. All its parts have one end, and are mutually interdependent. The English word "office" unfortunately has come to have two meanings. In ordinary usage it stands for a concrete whole— a man occupying a position defined by law, involving many correlated functions, as the office of judge or of governor or of president. But, nevertheless, it continues to be used in its ancient classical meaning of function or duty, the exercise of which is involved in the office. This distinction is well marked by the Latin words *munus* and *officium*. The *munus* expresses the position defined by law, involving a destination and obligation to the accomplishment of a certain work. *Officium*, on the other hand, expresses the idea of function. Thus Christ undertook but one *munus* or office—that of Mediator between God and man—in order to secure the salvation of his elect. But in doing this he necessarily discharges all the *officia* or functions which the work necessarily involves. The *munus* or office of Mediator involves all the three functions of the prophet, of the priest, and of the king. These are not separate offices, as are those of president, chief-justice, and senator, but they are the several functions of the one office of Mediator. They are not separate functions capable of successive and isolated performance. They are rather like the several functions of the one living human body—as of the lungs in inhalation, as of the heart in blood circulation, and as of the brain and spinal column in innervation; they are functionally distinct, yet interdependent, and together they constitute one life. So the functions of prophet, priest, and king mutually imply one another: Christ is always a prophetical Priest and a priestly Prophet, and he is always a royal Priest and a priestly King, and together they accomplish one redemption, to which all are equally essential.

All these functions, moreover, equally involve the possession and exercise by Christ of the attributes of both his divine and his human nature. It was necessary that he should be God, in order that he should be the original Prophet of prophets and Teacher of teachers of the secrets of the divine will; that he should as Priest and Sacrifice render an obedience in the stead of men which he did not owe for himself, and render by his vicarious sufferings a satisfaction to the justice of God of expiatory value equal to the sufferings of all men to all eternity; and that as King he should reign in the hearts and over the lives and destinies of all his people. It was no less necessary that he should be man, in order that he should take man's place and obey and suffer in man's stead, and that he should become "a merciful and faithful High Priest in things pertaining to God, to make reconciliation for the sins of the people;" so that he himself, having suffered, being tempted, " is able to succour them that are tempted " (Heb. ii. 17, 18).

II. This office or *munus*, having for its end the complete salvation of sinful men, is designated in the New Testament by two comprehensive titles:—(1.) Μεσίτης, *Mediator.* This is applied in a lower sense to Moses, as a mere messenger or go-between, through whom the law was given to the Church from Sinai (Gal. iii. 19, 20). But it is applied in the highest sense to Christ, as the efficient Peacemaker, the Daysman, having full power to make the peace between God and man, and to deliver man efficaciously and with infallible certainty from all his dangers (1 Tim. ii. 5, 6). (2.) The second and more comprehensive title applied in Scripture to this great undertaking of Christ is Παράκλητος, *Paraclete.* The word *paraclete* is the Greek equivalent for the Latin *advocatus,* advocate. The words *ad-vocate* and παρά-κλητος mean *one called in to help.* The Roman " client," the poor and dependent man, called in his " patron " to help him in all his needs. The patron thought for, advised, directed, supported, defended, supplied the necessities of, restored, comforted his client in all his complications.

The client, however weak, with a powerful patron, was socially and politically secure for ever. We are lost, we have nothing, and we need everything. We are guilty, righteously condemned, held under sentence. We are ignorant, blind, weak, helpless. Christ undertakes for us just as we are, and he does everything for us as our Ad-

vocate or Paraclete, called in to help us and deliver us.
"If any man sin, he has a Paraclete with the Father, Jesus
Christ the righteous" (1 John ii. 1).   But even Christ
cannot do the whole work alone.   So when the Saviour,
having finished his earthly work, was ready to depart, he
said to his disciples, "I will pray the Father, and he shall
give you another παράκλητος [Paraclete, Advocate, unhappily
translated *Comforter*], that he may abide with you for
ever, even the Spirit of truth" (John xiv. 16, 26 ; xv. 26 ;
xvi. 7).   In this *munus* or office of saving men the incarnate God-man and the Holy Ghost work together, the
function of one being as essential as that of the other, and
mutually depending upon that of the other.   The God-man
is our Patron, who undertakes for us in the functions of
teaching, redeeming, and ruling.   The Holy Ghost is our
other or co-ordinate Paraclete or Advocate, who unites us
to Christ by dwelling in us, communicating his life to
us, and executing in us all the beneficial and sacrificially
merited stages and elements of Christ's salvation.   The
two are together our perfect Paraclete.   The one is our
objective, external, transcendent Paraclete, sitting in and
reigning from the heavens ; the other is our subjective,
internal, immanent Paraclete, dwelling in us and inspiring
in us a divine life and hope.

The essential parts of our salvation are regeneration,
justification, sanctification, resurrection, glorification.   These
obviously involve, upon the part of the two divine Persons
who together have undertaken the *munus* of our salvation,
the distinct offices or functions of making reconciliation by
atonement, of intercession and introduction to the Father,
of teaching, of reigning over and disciplining the individual
and the community of which he forms a part, and finally,
of quickening to life and communicating to the regenerate
sinner his part in the benefits of Christ's work, and pre-
serving and perfecting him therein.   These are distributed

under the heads of three-fold functions of the Christ as Prophet, as Priest, and as King, and of the functions of the Holy Ghost, the immanent Paraclete ever dwelling in the hearts of his people.

III. *The Function or Office of Christ as Prophet.*—A prophet is one who speaks for another. In religious concerns a prophet is one who speaks to men for God. Hence he must be for this purpose a seer—one who sees, and therefore knows, and hence is qualified to speak in God's name. The absolutely necessary qualifications for the office are competent information, adequate powers of expression, and unquestionable authority.

Every human prophet necessarily presupposes an infinite, eternal, divine Prophet from whom his knowledge is received, just as every stream presupposes a fountain from which it flows. As there must be a first mover in all movement, and a first cause in all efficient causation, so there must be a first Teacher of all teachers and a supreme Lord of all lords.

Father, Son, and Holy Ghost are equal in knowledge as well as in power and glory—equal, that is, both in the sense of originality and of universal comprehension. All things involved in the divine Being; all things spontaneously emergent in the divine imagination; all things embraced in the divine purpose; all things that have been or shall be actually existent in the past, present, or future—are all in their inmost essences, as well as in their phenomena, present within the universal sweep of the intuitional consciousness of God for ever. But it is the function of the second Person in the constitutional economy of the Trinity to communicate objectively any portion of this divine knowledge to his intelligent creatures. He is the eternal Word of God. He, as to his divine nature, is the express image of the Godhead, otherwise invisible, and he is the radiant glory of the divine essence. No man hath seen God at any time, save the Son, and he to whom the Son reveals him. He that hath seen Christ, the incarnate Word, hath seen the Father. He is at once the Word *in* God, for eternally the Word was with God, and he is the Word *from* God, exhibiting the glories of God in the whole range of creations, providences, and objective revelations. All the lights of nature, the broken fragments of tradition, the secrets of the ethnic temples, the wisdom of the schools, the crescent moons of philosophy, science, and the arts, the broader daylight of modern civilization—all these, and far more than these—the brightest constellations of supernatural revelation, the rising sun of the inspired Scriptures from the first dawn growing brighter and brighter to the perfect day, and the unparalleled radiance of the celestial throne within the circle of which the archangels stand,—all these are but the reflections of his inexhaustible light, whose function it is to make manifest the otherwise hidden light of God.

But as in all vision there must meet at once the complementary gifts of light and eyes—light the instrument and medium, eyes the organs—so in this communication of the light of God to his creatures, the complementary functions of Christ radiating the light, and of the Holy Ghost opening the intellectual and spiritual eyes, must meet together. And especially in the case of fallen men, where this spiritual vision has been lost, the subjective eye-opening work of the Spirit is the more necessary. And these two have been working together in this prophetical function of the work of human redemption from the first. Abraham saw the day of Christ, and all the prophets spoke of him. The priesthood of Aaron and of Melchizedek, the temple service in all its parts, were shadows of which his Person and work were the substance. The Spirit of Christ testified within all these holy prophets, and inspired their words and generated their religious experience, which in their immortal psalms have become normal to the Christians of all times. After his incarnation, Christ's human nature became the most effective organ through which his teaching function was wrought out. His all-perfect human life, standing alone, the conspicuous anomaly of all history, is the transcendent lesson he has taught us—a lesson, alike as to the nature and prerogatives of God, and as to the possibilities and responsibilities of man, which after the lapse of nearly two millenniums, remains the acknowledged lesson of all the ages, acknowledged as well by foe as by friend. In the appointed testimony of the twelve apostles, in the inspired text of the New Testament, in the special dispensation of grace which has led his Church forth through all the changes of two thousand years, in his general providence comprehending the evolution of all nations, in the ceaseless everywhere active operations of the Holy Ghost in our hearts, in the new light breaking in upon each wondering soul at death, and in the revelation of unutterable things in the third heaven of which Paul had a transient glimpse, which it is not lawful for a man on earth to utter—Christ has been fulfilling the teaching function of his great work as Redeemer. And throughout all the eternal ages he will never cease. In the New Jerusalem, the city of gold and crystal, wherein the unending career of God's perfected sons shall be continuously run, he will still continue the inexhaustible Source of all their knowing. For, for ever and for ever, " the Lamb is the light thereof."

Even in this life this precious office of Christ in behalf of his people surpasses all estimate. It is to be feared that while taking refuge under our Lord's mediation as Priest, Christians now-a-days make far too little of his function in them as Prophet. The condition of our experiencing the full measure of this benefit is, that we should implicitly submit our whole intellects to him as our Teacher; that we follow him without question in our thinking as much as in our acting; that the entire encyclopædia of human knowledge be brought under the regimen of his teaching; and that his doctrine in every department of thought be central and regulative to all other truth. On this condition, and on this condition only, he will grant us that unction from the Holy One whereby we shall know all things (1 John ii. 20). *Spiritual-mindedness* is the crowning grace of a Christian character, and is the unquestionable evidence of the presence of eternal life. A new and celestial light is let in broadly over the whole horizon of our thought. The entire rational world is transfigured. Even in the case of some of the intellectually least highly endowed of Christ's people, the telescope of faith reveals the deepest and most ravishing secrets of his kingdom. Just as in the material astronomy, the telescope of highest power takes into its field the narrowest segment of the sky, so in the disclosures our divine Prophet makes to his redeemed on earth often the intensest insight into the glowing centre of the heavenly world is vouchsafed to those whom the world regards pitifully as the unlearned and foolish, and whom even the Church recognizes as only babes in Christ.

IV. *The Office of Christ as Priest.*—The unity of the human race and the universal sense of sin are proved by the fact that in all ages and nations all historical religions provide a priesthood to stand between God and his worshipper. A priest is a man divinely chosen, qualified, and authorized to appear before God and to act in behalf of men. A prophet, we have seen, comes down from God manward. A priest goes up from man Godward. Bishop Butler (*Analogy*, Pt. ii., ch. 5) and Michaelis declare that the universal prevalence of priests and piacular sacrifices demonstrates the existence of a *sensus communis* essential to human nature as it now is, establishing the facts of human guilt, of divine justice, and of the absolute need of mediation and expiation. The entire state of the case stands pictured to us in the Jewish ritual with the utmost vividness as in a vast historical object lesson. God created man in his own likeness; a weak creature, but with the potency of the highest powers, with the possibilities of the grandest destinies, and consequently the responsibility of maintaining a record and of achieving a character in conformity to the law of absolute moral perfection, armed with the alternative sanctions of the blessing of God which is life, or the curse of God which is death. Man, abusing all the conditions of a favourable probation, sinned, and fell under the inexorable condemnation of the immutable law which sways the moral universe in all cycles and in all realms. The judgment of this law was immediately and consistently executed upon the entire existent human race, inwardly in the conscience of man and outwardly in the providence of God. Ashamed, conscious of his defilement and nakedness, afraid, conscious of his guilt and alienation from God, man was driven out of the garden to wrestle with the wild forces of nature for a living, under the frown of God. Death and pain seized him; and the farther he wandered through the continents and down the ages, the farther he went from God, the more corrupt his nature and hopeless his condition. All along this line the Spirit of God strove with men, and under his inspiration men chose their best and wisest, and sent them up to God as priests, with gifts and the blood of atoning sacrifices in their hands, if by any means peradventure God's justice could be satisfied and his just wrath appeased.

All this ritual of mediation and of expiation was gathered together into one divinely-ordered system in the Mosaic tabernacle and ceremonial institution made in all things according to the pattern God showed to Moses in the mount (Heb. viii. 5). All members of the human family, as such, were judicially excluded from the divine favour and presence. But as God graciously purposed to redeem men and restore them to life in union with himse¹f on certain conditions, he forthwith graciously selected the Israelites out of all the nations of the earth, and made them, in behalf of all nations, a priestly nation to represent all nations before God, and ultimately to be the organ of the reconciliation and restoration of all. Out of the nation of priests he chose the tribe of Levi to be a priestly tribe, to represent the whole nation before God, and to act as the organ of its communion with God. Out of the tribe of Levi he chose the family of Aaron to be in the strictest. sense the priestly order in successive generations ; and of this family of priests the head by the law of primogeniture was the one high priest, in whom the whole body of priests, and through them the whole tribe and nation, and through them all the families of man on earth, are ceremonially summed up—who is the one absolute priest, the one adequate type of Christ, able to perform in his own person every part of the typical service.

According to this symbolism, God, although he is omnipresent and everywhere active in his natural relation, yet as Moral Governor and Source of spiritual life is withdrawn from the world and sits apart. But to give visible objective expression to his willingness to have men brought back to his favour and fellowship, he directed Moses to erect a tabernacle, afterward rendered permanent in the magnificent Temple of Solomon—a place of meeting and communing between God and man (Ex. xxv. 22). This sanctuary was essentially a large parallelogram embracing three successive courts. The inner one of all, called the

Most Holy Place, was entirely enclosed, shut in darkness, a perfect cube. Here God sat alone, enthroned over the ark of the covenant, the foundation of his throne, containing the moral law expressed in the ten commandments, which were at once the foundation of his own government and his official indictment of all men as condemned sinners, and enthroned between the cherubim, or symbols of redeemed humanity as it will be in the end, when the true heavenly temple is consummated. This most holy seat of God holding aloof, yet willing to meet men on conditions consistent with his perfections, was separated from the next court by a close curtain, which none but the high priest, and he only once a year, could lift. Exterior to this was the Holy Place, which contained the table of shewbread, the golden candlestick, and the altar of incense, all symbolizing the Christian life redeemed, sanctified, and offered as an acceptable sacrifice to God. Exterior to this was the outer court, sacred to the Jews or to the priestly nation, from which the uncircumcised Gentiles were excluded. A believing Israelite, conscious of sin, proposing to return to God and seek eternal life in him, had his way of return distinctly marked out. He must come first to the altar of burnt-offering and make expiation, and then to the laver of regeneration and seek spiritual cleansing, and then approach through the Holy Place to the veil which divided it from the immediate presence of God. On every occasion of sin he was directed to obtain a lamb perfect in age, sex, and condition; take it to the priest before the altar; lay his hands upon its head, signifying the transference to it of his guilt or obligation to endure the penalty; give it to the priest, who then executed upon it, in the stead of the sinner who presented it as his substitute, the capital penalty of death. Then the blood of the victim was sprinkled upon the sinner and upon the horns of the altar, in token of the expiation of sin upon the one hand and the propitiation of God upon the other. The promised effect of this service was, as is constantly asserted (Lev. iv. 20 ; v. 10, 13, 16, 18, etc.), that "his sin shall be forgiven him."

On the great day of atonement, once every year, this priestly work was done, so as to exhibit the principle most perfectly. The high priest was the one whose office included and superseded that of all other priests. He represented the whole redeemed Church, the entire body of the elect, bearing the titles of all the tribes engraved upon his shoulders and upon his breast. He took two goats ceremonially perfect—two, yet constituting one sacrifice, to symbolize the entire function alike after and before death. On the head of the one goat he laid his hands and confessed all the sins of the whole people. The other goat he executed and sacrificed on the altar of burnt-offering. The first goat was then sent forth into the trackless wilderness, bearing into absolute and final oblivion the sins of the people, now expiated by the vicarious death of the other goat. With the blood of the second goat, and with a censer kindled with coals from off the altar of incense, the high priest now passed through the otherwise inviolable curtain into the presence of God enthroned over the mercy-seat between the cherubim. This blood was now spread over the golden lid covering the ark of the covenant, shutting out the vision of God looking down upon the tables of the law, witnessing against the sins of men. David hence sings of the blessedness of him "whose transgressions are forgiven, whose sins are covered"—that is, covered out of the sight of justice by sacrificial blood.

The high priest represented the people. What he did, they did in him. And he, and they through him, could at best pass that veil but once a year, and then only with the fresh blood of the goat judicially slain in their stead. This was because God is just, and without the shedding of blood there is absolutely no remission. The restrictions which limited it to the one day in a year and to the freshly-repeated sacrifice originated in the incompetency of the blood of bulls and goats really to expiate the guilt of sin. The sacrifices of bulls and goats were like token-money (as our paper promises to pay), accepted at their face value until the day of settlement. But the sacrifice of Christ was the gold which absolutely extinguishes all debt by its intrinsic value. When, therefore, Christ by the one sacrifice of his divine-human Person had put away sin (Heb. ix. 26 ; x. 10–12), the veil which shut off the Most Holy Place, the dwelling-place of God in the temple, "was rent from the top to the bottom"—that is, utterly and for ever removed (Matt. xxvii. 51), so that not high priests only, but every trusting Christian fleeing from sin and the wrath which follows it, have boldness to enter, not once a year, but in every instant of need, "into the holiest by the blood of Jesus, by a new and living way, which he hath consecrated for us, through the veil, that is to say, his flesh" (Heb. x. 20).

The entire religious life of the Jewish Church and of every individual believer centred in the priests, and pre-eminently in the high priest. He was the head of the nation and of the Church. He was the ever-living organ of their living union and fellowship with God. Cut off from the high priest, they were without God in the world, and without access or opportunity for any possible communication of prayer or sacrifice. But when in fellowship with the high priest, they not only had peace with God, but they were at once translated into the sphere of divine life and relations; their prayers and sacrifices were accepted, and the presence of the Holy Ghost made their whole sphere alive with spiritual fruitfulness and blessedness.

V. In all essential points this Mosaic ritual system was truly and designedly representative and expository of the mediatorial office, and especially of the priestly function, of Christ. The two correspond as shadow and substance, as token-money (paper promises to pay) and real money; as type—that is, prophetic symbol—and anti-type. 1st. Christ was a real Priest: (1.) He possessed all the qualifications really, intrinsically, and in the highest degree. He was absolutely righteous and holy; he had an absolute right of intimate access to God, and the right of bringing near to God; he possessed in his own person on its human side the most intrinsically valuable and acceptable of all offerings; he was divinely appointed to this end (Heb. ii. 16; iv. 15; v. 5, 6; vii. 26; ix. 11–24; John xvi. 28; xi. 42). (2.) He performed all the parts of the priest's official work: (*a*) he mediated, in the general sense of the word (John xiv. 6; 1 Tim. ii. 5); (*b*) he offered a propitiatory sacrifice (Eph. v. 2; Heb. ix. 26; x. 12; 1 John ii. 2); (*c*) he appeared in the true Most Holy Place, of which the inner court of the tabernacle was only the figure, and presented his sacrificed body *for us*, and ever liveth to make intercession *for us* (Heb. ix. 24; vii. 25; Rom. viii. 34; 1 John ii. 1). (3.) He was also the sacrificial victim. His characteristic designation is "the Lamb of God, which taketh away the sin of the world." The Lord laid upon him the iniquity of us all; he was made a sin-offering for us (2 Cor. v. 21). 2nd. The Mosaic ritual was designed to be expository of his method of saving men. He does essentially and exhaustively that which the ritual services only symbolized. These things "are a shadow of things to come; but the body is of Christ" (Col. ii. 17; Heb. viii. 5). The whole New Testament, and especially the Epistle to the Hebrews, is a continuous commentary upon the truth of this assertion. The same is conspicuously proved by the fact that the veil of the temple (the key to the entire ritual order) was "rent in twain from top to bottom" the moment Christ's real sacrifice was offered. The instant the debt was discharged by the real payment the token-money was cancelled. The instant the real expiation was "finished" the whole symbolical system provisionally representing it became necessarily *functum officio.* Soon afterward, consequently, the temple was razed to the ground and the ritual rendered for ever impossible.

VI. On the other hand, the perfect priesthood of Christ and his one intrinsically efficacious sacrifice infinitely and in manifold ways transcend all created and finite types. Thus Paul, having shown abundantly that the priesthood of Aaron is typical of that of Christ, proceeds to show that he was too large and perpetual a Priest to be one of a series included under the Aaronic order—that, on the contrary, he was an "everlasting Priest" after the order of Melchizedek, who was without predecessor or successor. The Aaronic priests came in succession, a series of many individuals. Christ abides a Priest for ever. The entire mediatorial and priestly work was, under the Mosaic system, distributed among many priests and Levites, each of whom did only his appointed part; while it was not the separate parts, but the coherent organic whole, which sufficed to effect the end designed. On the other hand, Christ discharges the entire priestly work alone, and he does it for all believers and during all time completely. "It is finished." Each of that series was morally impure, only ceremonially pure : Christ was absolutely pure and righteous. Each of that series was under the obligations of law, and owed obedience and expiation on his own account : Christ was God himself, above and personally independent of all legal responsibilities, able therefore to render a perfectly free vicarious service and penal suffering in the stead of others. The victim offered under the ceremonial institute had no intrinsic value : Christ is of infinite intrinsic value. The victim suffered without choice or conscious comprehension of the part it was taking in the drama of God's spiritual kingdom. In the case of Christ the real moral value of his expiating work as Priest, its power to make amends, to repair the offence of sin to the justice and law of Jehovah, did not reside in his mere sufferings, abstractly considered, either in their quantity or their quality, but in their connection with the moral attitude and exercises of the Person suffering. He in the sinner's place, and suffering the penalty due the sinner, he in the mortal agonies of his soul, justified God's justice. He consented to the law which condemned him vicariously. His cross was not, like the final lake of fire, a scene of mere capital execution, a Golgotha. On the contrary, it is a greater and more glorious Mount Sinai on which the absolutely perfect moral law is affirmed and made venerable. It is the great white throne on which the Moral Governor of the universe sits regnant, revealed in immaculate whiteness; it is the point wherein alone, in all the realms of space and all the successions of time, the inmost heart of the great Jehovah has been opened as through a wide window to the sight of his creatures; it is the focus in which all the divine perfections are blended in their most intense radiance. Here "mercy and truth are met together, righteousness and peace have kissed each other" (Ps. lxxxv. 10). And here the holy angels, the elder sons of God, experienced in all mysteries of the innermost "third heaven," gather in intense expectancy, and with faces veiled to shield them from the insufferable light "desire to look into" (1 Peter i. 12) this uncovered heart of God.

Besides, in the type the sinner was one party, the offended God another party, the mediating priest a third party, and the unwilling victim substituted in the place of the sinner is yet again a fourth party. From this the utter misconception has been inferred that Christ is a Friend of sinners, while God the Father is a stern, inimical Judge, determined to crush them according to the

forms of law—that Christ gives himself to suffer so as to
excite the compassion of the angry Father, and dispose him
to open a way of escape to the objects of his wrath. All
love and mercy are attributed to Christ, while all inexorable justice and wrath are attributed to the Father.
The Father is conceived of as relenting only in consequence of the effective satisfaction offered by the Son.
But the truth is, that the love and tenderness of the
Father is the cause, not the effect, of the sacrificial death
of his Son. "God so loved the world, that he gave his
only begotten Son, that whosoever believeth in him should
not perish, but have everlasting life." Christ in his single
Person unites the three parties of the offended God, the
mediating priest, and the substituted victim. It is not
one divine Person offering satisfaction to another divine
Person. But the divine nature in Christ, which is numerically one with that of the Father, is the very nature that
both demands and furnishes the satisfaction. The merciful
God out of his infinite compassion assumes to himself, and
inflicts upon himself in his own personal humanity, the
penalty in the stead of the sinner. "*Ipse deus, ipse
sacerdos, ipse hostia, pro se, de se, sibi satisfecit*" (John
Wessel, 1419–89): "Himself at once truly God, and truly
Priest, and truly sacrificial Victim, he made satisfaction
for the sins of men to himself, by himself, by means of
his own agonies." The Father, Son, and Holy Ghost equally
love the sinner, while they equally demand punishment
for the sin. The Father gives his well-beloved Son; the
Son voluntarily and *sui jure* puts himself in the sinner's
place to receive the judicial blow; and it is by the eternal
Spirit (sympathizing and co-operating) that he offered
himself without spot to God (Heb. ix. 14). The whole
Godhead in all the adorable Persons is revealed in this
transcendent act of human redemption. They exhibit a
common holiness tolerating no sin, and a common love

sparing no sacrifice to deliver the beloved object from destruction. But to us this is especially revealed in the divine-human Person of Christ. As he can the most fully sympathize with us because he is a man and has suffered, so we can most fully sympathize with him. In him we see the signs of sacrifice we understand—the bloody sweat, the crown of thorns, the pierced hands and feet and side. But he and the Father are one. The Person we see and love, the tears and blood we understand, are those of a man. But the man is God, and the blended righteousness and love which his death reveals are the righteousness and the love of God.

VII. *This Priesthood of Christ is absolutely perfect.*— 1st. He has been the medium of communication between God and man from the beginning, through all stages of human history. His kingdom was prepared from the foundation of the world (Matt. xxv. 34). He has been Priest ever since the foundation of the world (Heb. ix. 25, 26). He is the Lamb slain from the foundation of the world (Rev. xiii. 8). The gospel which Paul preached, and which we believe, is the mystery (secret) which from the beginning of the world had been hid in God, who created all things in Jesus Christ (Eph. iii. 9). Through him have all the scattered rays of true religion in all ages and to all people been revealed. In him all true believers of all dispensations have been accepted, and found the standing-place and life. Through his atonement not only all adult believers, but all dying in infancy, all idiots, and all who have been saved by any extraordinary means known only to God, are reconciled to God and stand absolved from guilt.

2nd. He is, in the complete and permanent and saving sense, the Priest only of his own people, his sheep, those from the beginning given him by the Father, those who believe on him through the effectual calling of his Spirit.

Nevertheless, it is true that in a very important sense he has always been the Priest of the whole historic human race. He is the second Adam. He took upon himself human nature, the seed of Abraham. He was made under the law, and fulfilled the obligations, preceptive and punitive, which rest upon all men alike. He arrested, in behalf of the whole race as a body, the immediate execution of the legal penalty. The whole course of human history, of all peoples and nations, of all religions and civilizations, has been evolved under the shield of his cross, under a dispensation of arrested judgment or forbearance secured through his mediation. He, by his expiation, removed utterly out of the way of all men alike the objective hindrances in the justice of God and in the judgment of the law which rendered their salvation absolutely impossible. In this general sense, Christ, as the man whom God has appointed Priest, is the common bond of the whole human race, and his meritorious service the common basis of all human history.

3rd. But while he, in his priestly work, has made the salvation of all men possible on the condition of their accepting it, he has made the salvation of those whom the Father has given him certain by purchasing for them that faith which is the condition of their personal participation in his work. He rendered his obedience and suffering in the stead of those whom he represented under a covenant with his Father. The Father from the beginning " gave to him " his sheep. · These, by the very act of Christ's atonement, are secured to him. When it pleased the Lord to make his soul an offering for sin, it was also provided that he should see his seed—that he should see of the travail of his soul, and should be satisfied (Isa. liii. 10, 11). Our Confession of Faith declares (ch. viii. § 5) : " The Lord Jesus, by his perfect obedience and sacrifice of himself, which he through the eternal Spirit once offered

up unto God, hath" not only "fully satisfied the justice of
the Father," but also "purchased not only reconciliation,
but an everlasting inheritance in the kingdom of heaven
for all those whom the Father hath given unto him." Not
merely forgiveness of sins, but all that we shall ever experience—regeneration, justification, the adoption of sons,
fatherly discipline, perseverance, increase of grace, deliverance in death, the resurrection of our bodies, and all the
unimaginable beatitudes of heaven,—all these, kingdom
and priesthood and glory, are parts of "the purchased
possession" secured for us through the priesthood of Christ.

4th. And the perfection of Christ's priesthood is this,
that he is a Priest for ever. We rest not upon an historic
fact long past, upon a priestly office transacted in our behalf two thousand years ago. But we rest upon a living
Priest, an absolutely immortal Priest, whose entire priestly
work, past, present, and future, is all one. We rest on a
Priest who is not only living, but who is the omnipresent,
immanent Source of eternal life to all who accept his
mediation. He is ever appearing in the presence of God
for us. He is ever making intercession for us. He sits
enthroned at the right hand of all power, making all things
work together for good to them that love him. He is at
the same time, through his Spirit, omnipresent as our Priest
in all hearts and throughout all lives—in our hearts and in
our lives, in our closets and in our homes, in our markets
and in our temples, making intercession for us, and making
intercession within us (Rom. viii. 26, 27).

And he is our only Priest. The Christian ministry is
not a priesthood. This is a fundamental doctrine. The
titles by which this ministry is called in the New Testament, and all the inspired definitions of the office to be
discharged by these ministers, fall under the two categories
of teaching and ruling. Absolutely nothing else is provided
for; absolutely nothing else is even hinted at; absolutely

no place is left for a New Testament priesthood. Christ occupies the office, and discharges all the functions of it exhaustively. Before Christ came, there was a place for a symbolical priesthood as types or prophetical settings-forth of his priesthood. But there is no place for the token-money when the gold has been paid. There is no place for the type when the antitype has come, no place for the shadow when the sun shines at noon. It is error to suppose that Christ's work can be rendered more complete, is supplemented, by an earthly priesthood. It is error to suppose that we need many or any other earthly mediators to go between us and Christ, who is our Brother, our own flesh and blood, within us and around us all the time.

Dear friends, take my advice in this. In maintaining our evangelical position against Romanists, Ritualists, and exclusive Churchmen, do not waste your force by laying emphasis upon any subordinate question as to Church government, liturgies, or parity of the clergy. Stand up only for essentials. Strike right at the heart of error. The three central dangerous errors of Romanism and Ritualism are these—(1) the perpetuity of the apostolate; (2) the priestly character and offices of Christian ministers; (3) the sacramental principle, or the depending upon the sacraments as the essential, initial, and ordinary channels of grace. These are three radical heresies which exclude the truth, derogate from the honour of Christ, and betray souls by inducing them to build upon false foundations. But if these three pestiferous roots of error are excluded, there can be no difference of radical importance between bodies of Christians who hold to the historic faith of "the holy catholic Church."

5th. Being a Priest for ever, he will be the organ of our communion with God, and his merits the foundation of our standing, during all eternity as well as upon earth. In the New Jerusalem the "Lamb shall be the light thereof." As a " Lamb that has been slain," he stands in " the midst of the throne." And of all the redeemed it is said that " the Lamb which is in the midst of the throne shall feed them, and shall lead them unto living fountains of waters " (Rev. vii. 17).

6th. And, finally, we are rendered complete in him, " for in him dwelleth all the fulness of the Godhead bodily, and in him ye are made full, who is the Head of all principality and power " (New Version, Col. ii. 9, 10). Having identified himself with us, he identifies us with himself. We are endowed with both the qualifications and prerogatives which distinguish himself in relation to God. We receive an unction from the Holy One, and know all things. We receive as the priests of God the right to draw near to the inmost heart of God, and to offer acceptable service and worship. We are delivered from all bondage, alike from the evil within us and from the evil without us; and we are set in the position of those who reign over all the subordinate powers alike of the material and of the spiritual world. He crowned us with his own crown, and made us to sit with himself on his own throne ; for we are, through the whole range of our being, and during the entire sweep of our existence, joint-heirs together with Christ. This truth is as sure as it is wonderful. Yet it utterly passeth understanding. Thought gives place to emotion and rises to adoring rapture : " Worthy is the Lamb that was slain to receive power, and riches, and wisdom, and strength, and honour, and glory, and blessing." " Blessing, and honour, and glory, and power, be unto him that sitteth upon the throne, and unto the Lamb for ever and ever." " For thou wast slain, and hast redeemed us to God by thy blood out of every kindred, and tongue, and people, and nation ; and hast made us unto our God kings and priests : and we shall reign on the earth."

XII.

THE KINGLY OFFICE OF CHRIST.

THAT the office of Mediator between God and sinful men must include the function of kingly dominion and control is self-evident. Christ's functions as Prophet and Priest would have been ineffective without it. That the promised Messiah of the Old Testament was to be a King, and that the historical incarnate God of the New Testament actually is a King in the highest sense, are witnessed to by almost every page of the whole Bible.

"There shall come a Star out of Jacob, and a Sceptre shall rise out of Israel" (Num. xxiv. 17). "His name shall be called Wonderful, Counsellor, The mighty God, The everlasting Father, The Prince of Peace" (Isa. ix. 6). I have "set my King upon my holy hill of Zion......Ask of me, and I shall give thee the heathen for thine inheritance, and the uttermost parts of the earth for thy possession. Thou shalt break them with a rod of iron; thou shalt dash them in pieces like a potter's vessel" (Ps. ii. 6–9). "One like the Son of man came with the clouds of heaven, and came to the Ancient of days. And there was given him dominion, and glory, and a kingdom, that all people, nations, and languages, should serve him; his dominion is an everlasting dominion, which shall not pass away, and his kingdom that which shall not be destroyed" (Dan. vii. 13, 14). The angel Gabriel, in the annunciation to the

Virgin Mary, said, "Thou shalt conceive in thy womb, and bring forth a son, and shalt call his name Jesus. He shall be great, and shall be called the Son of the Highest; and the Lord God shall give unto him the throne of his father David: and he shall reign over the house of Jacob for ever; and of his kingdom there shall be no end" (Luke i. 31–33). The universality and pre-eminence and absoluteness of his kingly authority is expressed in the Revelation when it is declared that the Lamb is "King of kings and Lord of lords." The ancient Hebrews in reading substituted "Adonai" for "Jehovah." The Septuagint translates Adonai by Κύριος, *Lord.* This latter word occurs between seven and eight hundred times in the New Testament, and in the vast majority of instances it is applied to Christ. The title which spontaneously springs to the lips of all men, even of the indifferent stranger, but with infinitely more meaning from the lips of all who have been made recipients of his love, is LORD, Jesus, Possessor, Master, Sovereign. It is universal over all, dominating the highest as well as the lowest, comprehending and bending to its own sway all lower authority and power—King of kings. It is absolute *in* all, knowing no limit in soul or body, in time or eternity—absolutely owning, possessing, and disposing to his own uses all we are and all we possess, each thing entirely, and all things in all relations.

1. And all this is predicated of him not merely as God, but as God-man in his work as Mediator between God and man. As the second Person of the Trinity, equal in power and glory to the eternal Father, the Word of God possesses an absolute, inherent sovereign dominion as King over the whole universe. This authority is intrinsic, underived, inalienable, and is the same yesterday, to-day, and for ever. During all the years of the earthly life of the God-man, alike while an unconscious babe in the manger and while hanging a dying victim on the cross, the eternal Son

of God was exercising his sovereign dominion over the entire universe.

But in his office as Mediator, and in his entire Person after the incarnation as God-man, he was constituted a King by the authority of the entire Godhead as represented in the Father. His mediatorial sovereignty is derived, as contradistinguished from his essential divine sovereignty as intrinsic. It is given to him by the Father as the reward of his obedience and suffering. " He emptied himself, taking the form of a servant, being made in the likeness of men ; and being found in fashion as a man, he humbled himself, becoming obedient even unto death, yea, the death of the cross. Wherefore also God highly exalted him, and gave unto him the name which is above every name ; that in the name of Jesus every knee should bow, of things in heaven, and things on earth, and things under the earth, and that every tongue should confess that Jesus Christ is LORD, to the glory of God the Father " (Phil. ii. 7–11). This authority, thus bestowed upon him by the Father, is special, having particular reference to the salvation of his own people, and, to that end, to the administration of all the provisions of the covenant of grace, of which he is the gracious executive. It attaches not to his divine nature exclusively, but to his entire Person as the God-man. A MAN sits upon the mediatorial throne of the universe. He who stood insulted, despised, condemned at Pilate's judgment-seat, now sitting at the right hand of God, rules all worlds, as he will hereafter, seated on the great white throne, judge all men. Our blood-Brother according to the flesh has "all power in heaven and in earth," that he may "make all things work together for good to them that love God." The attributes of both the divine and the human nature are together exercised in the administration of this kingly reign. All his kingly acts are infinitely wise, righteous, and powerful, because he is

God. But they are at the same time the acts of a man. They possess a truly human quality, for in all his administration he has a feeling for our infirmities as well as an eye for our interests.

2. Christ is already a King upon his throne in the full sweep of his kingly administration. He has, of course, as the eternal Word, been Mediator between God and sinful man ever since the fall of Adam. Otherwise, the sentence of the law must have been unconditionally executed immediately upon the apostasy. Ever since, we have been living, and human history has been evolved, under a system of forbearance involving an arrest of judgment. This was of course possible only as the human family has existed under the protection of a divine and competent Mediator. All the functions of the mediatorial office mutually imply one another. If he were "the Lamb slain from the foundation of the world" (Rev. xiii. 8), he must have been a Prophet before Moses, a Priest before Aaron, and a King before David. He was in these respects their predecessor and the ground from which they sprang, as well as their successor and antitype. A close inspection shows that the Jehovah of the Old Testament, who is also called the Angel of, or the one sent by, Jehovah, is the second Person of the Trinity, as is declared by the author of the Epistle to the Hebrews. (Compare Ps. xlv. 6, 7 and Heb. i. 8, 9; Gen. xxxi. 11, 13 and xlviii. 15, 16 and Hosea xii. 2–5; Ex. iii. 1–14 and Acts vii. 30–35.) He reigned over all human affairs, as the biblical history relates. He gave the law from Sinai, including the entire ceremonial ritual, as well as the Ten Commandments. He brought Israel out of Egypt through the wilderness and established them in the Holy Land "with a mighty hand, and with an outstretched arm, and with great terribleness, and with signs, and with wonders" (Deut. xxvi. 8). He fought their battles with the Philistines; established his types and representatives,

David and Solomon, upon their temporary symbolical thrones; and he directed the entire course of human history to the consummation of the fulness of times, in preparation for his own advent in the flesh.

But, on the other hand, in the strictest sense we must date the actual and formal assumption of his kingly office, in the full and visible exercise thereof, from the moment of his ascension into heaven from this earth and his session at the right hand of the Father. He could not have actually entered upon his kingly office as the God-man before he had become both God and man in the one Person through his incarnation. His function as Priest in a sense precedes his function as a King, as well as acts together with it. His atonement is the foundation of his royal right to his people and his royal administration in their behalf. When he was announced, it was "declared that the kingdom of heaven was at hand." He was received by his disciples and rejected by the Jews as one claiming to be a king. Pilate wrote the title of his kingship in three languages and attached it to his cross. "This man, after he had offered one sacrifice for sins for ever, sat down on the right hand of God; from henceforth expecting till his enemies be made his footstool" (Heb. x. 12, 13). His kingly office is essentially the royal dispensation of grace by him as a Saviour. In order that this may be universally and infallibly effectual and complete, he declares that now "all power is given to me in heaven and on earth," and he founds on this his great commission to his Church: "Go ye therefore, and disciple all nations." And Peter on the great day of Pentecost declared that when the prophet David recorded the sworn promise of God to raise up Christ to sit upon the throne, he spake of the resurrection of Christ: "This Jesus hath God raised up, whereof we all are witnesses. Therefore, being by the right hand of God exalted, and having received of the Father the promise of the Holy Ghost, he hath shed forth this. Therefore let all the house of Israel know assuredly, that God hath made that same Jesus, whom ye have crucified, both Lord and Christ " (Acts ii. 32–36).

3. The present mediatorial kingdom of the God-man is absolutely universal, embracing the whole universe and every department of it. This principle evidently involves the most momentous consequences. It has been disastrously abused by the Papal Church, and just as disastrously ignored by the Protestants. It follows logically from the Papal principles that the Church is an external visible organization of which the Pope, the vicegerent of Christ, is the head ; that if Christ is absolute Sovereign over the universe and all its departments, then the Pope, his vicar, is supreme governor at least over all bodies and affairs of mankind. But upon Protestant principles this atrocious consequence disappears. The Church is not a corporation or visible organization. Christ has no representative exercising vicariously his royal authority on earth. There is no question as to Church authority or union between Church and State involved. Protestants should shut out for ever all these dead issues and the prejudices which they excite, and open their minds to the scriptural evidence and to the stupendous and infinitely blessed practical consequences of the great principle I have stated—that the mediatorial kingdom of the God-man is absolutely universal, embracing in its rightful sway all God's creatures and all their actions.

This truth, nevertheless, is just as plainly and as certainly taught in the New Testament as any other article of our faith. In Ps. viii. God declares his purpose to put all things under the feet of man. This purpose Paul (Eph. i. 20–23) declares was fulfilled in Christ " when he raised him from the dead, and set him at his own right hand in heavenly places, far above all principality, and power, and might, and dominion, and every name that is named, not only in this world (*aiōn*), but also in that which is to come; and hath put all things under his feet, and gave him to be Head over all things to the Church." He declared to his disciples, as the ground of the commission he gave to them, "that all power had been given to him in heaven and on earth." In Phil. ii. 9, 10, Paul says, "God hath highly exalted him, and given him a name which is above every name : that at the name of Jesus every knee should bow, of things in heaven, and things in earth, and things under the earth." This absolutely and exhaustively includes the whole universe in all its categories of heaven, earth, and hell, just as the passage in Ephesians includes all duration, the *aiōn*, or world-age, which now is and that which is to come. And this is repeated and emphasized in the most forceful language in Heb. ii. 8, "For in that he put all things in subjection under him, he left nothing that is not put under him;" and in 1 Cor. xv. 27, he only "is excepted which did put all things under him"—that is, absolutely all things but God the Father. And all this is spoken, not of his authority as eternal God, but of his mediatorial authority as God-man : because (1) it is given to him by the Father; (2) it is given to him as the reward of his obedience and sufferings; (3) when the purpose for which it is given is fully accomplished, "when he has subdued all things unto himself," he shall deliver up this "given" kingdom over the universe "to God, even the Father," and become himself, as God-man, "subject unto him that put all things under him, that God may be all in all" (1 Cor. xv. 24–28).

Theologians have accordingly made a distinction, designed to classify the different aspects and methods of this vast administration of royal power, between Christ's kingdoms of power, of grace, and of glory. These, of course, are not absolutely different realms or spheres of government, since the kingdom of power includes the kingdom of grace, and the kingdom of grace precedes and prepares the way for the kingdom of glory. They are rather different methods of working and different special systems of administration, all comprehended in his universal reign as King.

I. *Christ's Kingdom of Power.*—This is the providential reign of the God-man over the whole universe, in the interests of his mediatorial work as Redeemer of his own people. The universe in all its provinces, material and spiritual, constitutes one system. The certain attainment of any end, the absolute control of any single department, necessarily involves the control and the co-ordinate administration of all the parts.

(1.) Hence Christ's universal kingdom of power must include, in the first instance, his providential control of the whole physical universe. The physical universe is the necessary basis of the intellectual, moral, and spiritual world. The higher cannot be adequately governed unless the lower is controlled. The laws of matter and the order of the material world remain the same as before, and no change takes place that can be discovered by science. Nevertheless, the glorious fact is that the God-man, as mediatorial King, has, during the present *aiōn*, or world-age, brought the whole mechanism of the material universe into requisition as means to secure the establishment of his mediatorial kingdom. He guides the marshalled hosts of heaven to that supreme result. The great currents of all the world-forces are directed to that end. The sweet influences of the Pleiades obey his voice, and the bands of Orion are in his hands. It is not the God absolute, but it is our kinsman Redeemer, the man who is also God, who orders the courses of the stars; " who covereth the heaven with clouds, who prepareth rain for the earth, who maketh grass to grow upon the mountains;

who giveth to the beast his food, and to the young ravens when they cry;" who "numbereth all the hairs of our head," and "will not allow any plague to come nigh our dwelling."

(2.) Christ's mediatorial kingdom of power includes the universal moral government of God over all his intelligent creatures. The moral government of God over the human family constitutes only one province of the immeasurable empire. Angels and devils, and whatever intelligent creatures may exist in other worlds, must constitute one systematic moral whole with the human race. The entire moral empire of God must be governed on the same general principles of righteousness. The will of God must be the common rule of all, his love their common motive, his glory their common end, his fellowship their common goal. Christ in this widest sense is King of kings and Lord of lords. God hath appointed his Son "heir of all things." He is placed "far above all principality, and power, and might, and dominion, and every name that is named." All in heaven and all on earth who are to bow at the name of Jesus, include all rational creatures. And all men and angels are to be gathered to his judgment seat. The devils "are reserved in everlasting chains under darkness unto the judgment of the great day" (Jude 6).

He exercises this universal moral government providentially in various ways, according to the various characters and conditions of his subjects, but always upon the same principles of essential righteousness. He employs angels as ministering spirits for his people at present, and he will employ them as his executive agents in the siftings of the great judgment. He restrains and controls the action of the devil and his angels, the spirits of the power of the air. He controls all events for the good of his people. Especially, he directs events to the end of effecting their complete discipline and education, and consequent preparation for the enjoyment of his glory. The end is the complete redemption of his people. But in order to secure this, all the members of the human family in their successive generations and in their various family and national groups must be dealt with as subjects of the same government. During the present world-age it is not God absolute, but our kinsman Redeemer, the God-man, who is the Lord, "the Governor among the nations." He speaks with authority to every conscience. He has a supreme right to control for his own ends the service of every life. He orders every political and social event, and the entire evolution of civilization and associated human activity, to the accomplishment of his supreme end. And at the close every tribe, and people, and tongue shall stand to be judged before his throne, and to have its destiny fixed by his decree.

II. *Christ's Kingdom of Grace.*—This spiritual kingdom, which is the special care of Christ, for the sake of which his government of the universe is undertaken, respects, *first*, his own spiritual people individually, and, *second*, his professed people collectively organized in the visible Church.

(1.) Christ reigns over his own individually, both from without and from within. From without, he subdues his and their enemies, restraining Satan, his angels, and wicked men. He strengthens them in weakness, defends them in danger, directs and co-operates with them in action, and gives them ultimately the victory in all their contests, and causes them always to persevere to the end, that they may receive the crown of life. He also, under the inspiration of his Spirit, brings his spiritual people into sympathy with one another, and stimulates and guides the great currents of sympathy and the large interdenominational movements of the catholic Church.

and all the various functions in which is manifested the " communion of saints."

From within, the God-man reigns supreme in every Christian heart. It is impossible to accept Christ as our Sacrifice and Priest without at the same time cordially accepting him as our Prophet, absolutely submitting our understanding to his teaching, and accepting him as our King, submitting implicitly our hearts and wills and lives to his sovereign control. Paul delights to call himself the δοῦλος, purchased servant, of Jesus Christ. Every Christian spontaneously calls him our *Lord* Jesus. His will is our law, his love our motive, his glory our end. To obey his will, to work in his service, to fight his battles, to triumph in his victories, is our whole life and joy.

(2.) Christ's kingdom of grace also embraces his visible Church. Although the true Church is constituted simply by the indwelling of the Holy Ghost, and although no organization is essential to its being or coextensive with its existence, nevertheless Christ wills that his true Church shall, for great practical ends, tend always spontaneously to organize itself in some form. Its forms are very various, determined in their differences by providential conditions, and they are of very different excellence; and yet they are all, whether better or worse, forms of the true Church, and therefore co-ordinate phases of the one Church. And Christ alone is the legitimate Head of this visible Church in any of its forms whatsoever. He has appointed no vicegerent. He has forbidden his servants to be called rabbi or master. He pronounces a curse upon those who lord it over his heritage, whether national sovereigns or universal patriarchs or popes. He has in his inspired Word and through his ever-indwelling Spirit provided for the government of this Church through all ages. He has therein ordained the conditions of membership, the laws, and offices, and he by his gracious providence leads to the selection of the right incumbents. There is no doctrine we are bound to believe which he has not clearly revealed in his Word, nor any duty we are bound to fulfil. The disciples of Christ are the Lord's freemen, discharged from all human bondage, because they are bound to render absolute obedience to him alone. It is to this principle that the Church of Scotland and her long line of martyrs, under Knox, Melville, and Chalmers, have borne such a noble testimony. The Covenant bound Scotland and Puritan England to live or to die by Christ's crown and covenant.

Christ declared that his kingdom is "not of this world" —that it is not one kingdom associated with the other kingdoms, with like organizations, laws, methods of administration, and ends. But it is a spiritual kingdom, embracing and interpenetrating all others, so different in method and ends from them that it cannot, when loyal to its Head, interfere with any of them, or enter into organic alliance with any of them. Its Head, members, laws, officers, methods, penalties, and rewards and ends are not of this world, but are spiritual—that is, they are revealed and applied by the Holy Ghost; and they bring man into relation to the great world of spiritual realities which is revealed in the Scriptures.

The kingdom of Christ therefore interpenetrates all the political commonwealths of this world, and all the political commonwealths of this world embrace the kingdom of Christ. Like different gases, the kingdom of Cæsar and the kingdom of Christ are vacuums to each other. They interpenetrate each other in occupying the same territory, and yet each retains its own identity and properties unchanged. They necessarily affect each other on certain sides, but when properly administered they do not interfere with one another. Having the same subjects, they nevertheless have entirely different ends, different agencies, different laws, and different methods.

III. *Christ's Kingdom of Glory.*—During the present age Christ is set forth principally as a conquering Captain, reigning at the head of his militant host, the Captain of our salvation (Heb. ii. 10), and the conqueror of his and our enemies, and the subduer of the world (Rev. xix. 11–16). But hereafter the Scriptures reveal a final consummation, when Christ's kingdom shall be complete in all its members, and shall be developed to its perfect state—when all the redeemed shall be gathered, the crisis of judgment past, the glorified bodies of the saints reunited to their perfected spirits : then " shall the Son of man sit in the throne of his glory," and " there shall be no more curse : but the throne of God and of the Lamb shall be in it ; and his servants shall serve him : and they shall see his face ; and his name shall be in their foreheads " (Rev. xxii. 3, 4).

IV. But if Christ's mediatorial kingdom is, as asserted, absolutely universal—especially if his direct authority embraces without exception every human being on the face of the earth during all ages, in all their relations and in all their actions—then the question necessarily arises, If Christ's kingdom embraces every human relation, how can there be any distinction between Church and State, between the things that belong unto Cæsar and the things that belong unto Christ ?

This is a question which, however simple in itself, has continued to puzzle the minds of men from the beginning ; and this confusion of thought has necessarily introduced confusion and conflict of action.

Among the Jews the State and the Church were one identical organism, discharging both secular and ecclesiastical functions, in part through the same officers, and in part and at times through distinct officers.

The answer given by the Papists, while admitting the distinction touching Church and State, is that as Christ is King of all men, and his authority is supreme in every sphere of human interest and action, the Pope, his vicar, reigns in his name supreme over all earthly sovereigns; that the Catholic Church, an external organized body, is in every land supreme over the State, the State being, in truth, only a subordinate and changeable organ of the Church for the purpose of executing the functions of temporal government.

The answer of the Erastians, of the State-Church systems, makes the State supreme over the Church, and the Church is practically regarded only as an organ of the State for the purpose of effecting the functions of religious institution and worship.

But the true principle has in this last age become generally recognized, that State and Church, considered as organized societies with laws and officers, have entirely distinct spheres, methods, and objects, and hence that they have no specific organic relation to one another whatever. They indeed embrace the same territory and the same personal constituents. The same men and women who in one relation constitute the State in another relation constitute the Church. The State deals with the persons and property of Church members and with the public property of ecclesiastical societies precisely as it deals with that of all other persons and voluntary societies, and the members of the Church and ecclesiastical societies owe precisely the same obedience to the State that is owed by all other citizens and associations.

All this is perfectly clear and true, but inferences have been drawn from these principles which absolutely divorce the State from all religion, and emancipate it entirely from the mediatorial authority of Jesus Christ. It is absurdly argued that if the State is absolutely free from any entangling alliances with the Church, it must be free from all religious qualities and obligations; that if it is free from the authority of the Church as an organized society, it must be free from the authority of Jesus Christ, the Head of the Church, and of the Bible, which contains his code of laws. It is argued that as no man has any right to impose his own religious convictions on others, so no body of men can possess any such right, and therefore that no majority of citizens has the right to impose by State legislation upon a recalcitrant minority obligations having a religious origin. These inferences, however unwarrantable and preposterous, are exceedingly prevalent, and are admitted, if not proclaimed, by many true Christians who are unconscious of their absurdity and utter disloyalty to the Lord that bought them, and whom they profess to serve as their King.

It is very evident that it does not follow, because the organized bodies we call " Churches " have no organic connection with the State, nor any right to pronounce judgment upon things purely within the jurisdiction of the State, that therefore the State has nothing to do with religious laws or obligations. There are three positions here of infinite importance to the Christian citizens of the United States :—

1st. As a matter of fact, every State in the world must have, and has had, a religion of some kind. The State is an association of human beings for the purpose of promoting and protecting the interests of society within the limits of secular life. The State is the people themselves acting in their organic capacity through the machinery of law. It is self-evident, therefore, that the State or collective body must have all the qualities which belong to its constituent members. A house is a great deal more than the wood or brick or stone or iron of which it is built; nevertheless, every house has the quality of its material, whether wood or brick or stone or iron, and will necessarily act, under given circumstances, as determined severally by the nature of its material. So every State is vastly more than the persons of whom it is composed; nevertheless, the character of the State must in every respect be determined by the character of the people who constitute it. If the people are rational, the State will be rational; if moral, then moral; if rich or energetic, then it will possess those qualities; and, none the less, if the people be religious, will the State they compose be religious. It is simply absurd that a man can be thoroughly convinced that God exists, and that he is a Moral Governor who will demand an account for all the deeds done in the body, that he can have his heart full of loyal affection and devotion to God as an individual, while engaged in private business, and then be perfectly oblivious of the existence and of the claims of God as soon as he begins to act politically as a citizen of the State. If a man knows that God has forbidden theft, or incest, or divorce except on certain conditions, or the pursuit of worldly business on the weekly Sabbath, he cannot as a citizen do otherwise than make and execute laws in conformity to the known will of God. If a State in its public law acts atheistically, it can only be because a majority of its citizens are in heart atheists, no matter what religious professions they may make. Middle ground, a negative position, is absolutely impossible. God is either recognized or denied, he is either carefully obeyed or rebelliously disobeyed; and this impossibility of a negative position is just as true in political societies and in their conduct as in any other department of human life. Every nation has a religion, or is positively, aggressively atheistic; indifference is antagonism.

2nd. Every Christian must believe that the State ought to be obedient to the revealed law of Christ. This is so because—(1.) The Word of God explicitly declares that "the powers that be are ordained of God;" that "rulers are ministers of God to us for good;" that "whoever resisteth the power, resisteth the ordinance of God" (Rom. xiii. 1–4). (2.) Because Christ himself explicitly declared that to him as Mediator all power (ἐξουσία, right of dominion) in heaven and on earth had been committed (Matt. xxviii. 18). He is thus made "Lord of lords and King of kings." (3.) Because the Christian revelation expressed in the inspired Scriptures expresses the will of Christ upon many subjects in which it can be carried out only through the agency of the State and of her laws and officers. The State must pronounce her will as to the rest of the Sabbath day, as to marriage and divorce, as to the rights of property and the relations of capital and labour, as to capital punishment, and as to the education of the young. The ground covered by these subjects the State cannot possibly avoid. And it is equally impossible for a Christian man, who knows the will of Christ as to the points in question, to ignore or disobey that will when acting in the capacity of a citizen of the State. If he does do so, he is consciously guilty of direct disloyalty to his Lord. All intelligent and honest Christians must seek to bring all the action of the political society to which they belong obedient to the revealed will of Christ, the supreme King, the Ruler among the nations. The Church and the State are mutually, entirely independent. The officers and the laws of the one have no jurisdiction within the sphere of the other. Nevertheless, Christ is the common King of each, and his Bible is the common statute-book of each. The only difference is, that under the one and selfsame King, Christ, the light of nature is the primary, the word of Scripture the supplementary, law of the State; while the word of revelation is the primary, and the light of nature the supplementary, law of the Church. But Christ and conscience and the Bible rule equally in each sphere.

3rd. These United States of North America are, and from the beginning were, of law, of right, and of actual fact, a Christian nation. The original colonies were settled by bodies of men of conspicuous Christian character, who emigrated from their European homes for religious reasons. They were Puritans, Huguenots, Scotch, Scotch-Irish, Dutch, and German Presbyterians, Quakers, Episcopalians, and Roman Catholics, but all alike Christians. Beyond any other equally various and numerous set of men known in human history, they were earnest Christians; and they came here for the very purpose of crystallizing their faith in imperishable institutions. These men subdued the wilderness, founded the nation, and laid all the foundation stones of our constitutional law. The common law of England, the creature of Christianity, is the common law of nine-tenths of our States and Territories. Christian denominations, Episcopal or Independent, were established by law in almost all the early colonies. Theism is recognized explicitly in almost all our State constitutions, and Christianity in many of them. Christianity has been recognized from the first by explicit action in the appointment of chaplains for Congress and for the army and navy of the United States, and for the legislatures and prisons of the several States; by the appointment of fast-days and of thanksgiving-days by the supreme magistrates of the several States and of the nation; and by the enactment of the Sabbath laws and of the laws for the suppression of blasphemy. What was true at the first has been becoming more and more true to the actual fact ever since. Nearly one-half of all the actual adult population of the country are communicants in the Christian churches. The ratio of the communicants in our evangelical churches to the whole population was in 1800 as 1 to every 14.50 of all ages; in 1850 it was as 1 to every 6.57; in 1870, as 1 to every 5.78; and in 1880, 1 to every 5 of the total inhabitants; while in the meantime between six and seven millions of our Roman Catholic fellow-Christians have come into existence. From 1800 to 1880 the whole population of the nation has increased 9.46-fold, while in the same time the communicants of our evangelical churches have increased 27.52-fold.

There are not two laws for individuals and for communities. The obligations which bind individuals necessarily bind all the communities which these individuals constitute. Every human being is bound to be Christian, therefore every community of human beings is bound to obey the law of Christ. The United States, as a matter of historic fact, have always professed to be a Christian State, and we are therefore doubly bound to this allegiance—(1) by virtue of the common obligation which binds all men; (2) by virtue of the special opportunities and covenants of our ancestors, which descend upon us by natural inheritance.

V. The overwhelming importance of this principle and weight of this obligation appear in the clearest light the moment the nation claims to regulate the supreme function of education. It is insisted upon that the right of self-preservation is the highest law of States as well as of individuals; that if the suffrage is universal, all holders of that suffrage must be educated in order to secure the safety of the State; that in consequence of the heterogeneous character of our population and the divisions of the Christian Church, there is no agency in existence competent to educate the whole body of the holders of the universal suffrage except the State herself.

The situation, therefore, stands thus :—

1st. The tendency of the entire system, in which already vast progress has been made, is to centralization. Each State governs her own system of common schools by a central agency, which brings them, for the sake of greater efficiency, into uniformity of method and rules. These schools are graded and supplemented by normal schools, high schools, and crowned by the State university. The tendency is to unite all these school systems of the several States in one uniform national system, providing with all the abundant resources of the nation for the entire education of its citizens in every department of human knowledge, and in doing this to establish a uniform curriculum of study, uniform standards for the selection of teachers, and a uniform school literary apparatus of text-books, etc.

2nd. The tendency is to hold that this system must be altogether secular. The atheistic doctrine is gaining currency, even among professed Christians and even among some bewildered Christian ministers, that an education provided by the common government for the children of diverse religious parties should be entirely emptied of all religious character. The Protestants object to the government schools being used for the purpose of inculcating the doctrines of the Catholic church, and Romanists object to the use of the Protestant version of the Bible and to the inculcation of the peculiar doctrines of the Protestant churches. The Jews protest against the schools being used to inculcate Christianity in any form, and the atheists and agnostics protest against any teaching that implies the existence and moral government of God. It is capable of exact demonstration that if every party in the State has the right of excluding from the public schools whatever he does not believe to be true, then he that believes most must give way to him that believes least, and then he that believes least must give way to him that believes absolutely nothing, no matter in how small a minority the atheists or the agnostics may be. It is self-evident that on this scheme, if it is consistently and persistently carried out in all parts of the country, the United States system of national popular education will be the most efficient and wide instrument for the propagation of atheism which the world has ever seen.

3rd. The claim of impartiality between positions as directly contradictory as that of Jews, Mohammedans, and Christians, and especially as that of theists and of atheists, is evidently absurd. And no less is the claim absurd and impossible that a system of education can be indifferent on these fundamental subjects. There is no possible branch of human knowledge which is not purely formal, like abstract logic or mathematics, which can be known or taught in a spirit of entire indifferency between theism and atheism. Every department which deals with realities, either principles, objective things, or substances, or with events, must be in reality one or the other: if it be not positively and confessedly theistic, it must be really and in full effect atheistic. The physical as well as the moral universe must be conceived either in a theistic or an atheistic light. It must originate in and develop through intelligent will—that is, in a person—or in atoms, force, or chance. Teleology must be acknowledged everywhere or be denied everywhere. Philosophy, ethics, jurisprudence, political and social science, can be conceived of and treated only from a theistic or from an atheistic point of view. The proposal to treat them from a neutral point of view is ignorant and absurd. English common law is unintelligible if not read in the light of that religion in which it had its genesis. The English language cannot be sympathetically understood or taught by a mind blind to the everywhere-present current of religious thought and life which expresses itself through its terms. The history of Christendom, especially the history of the English-speaking races, and the philosophy of history in general, will prove an utterly insoluble riddle to all who attempt to read it in any non-theistic, religiously-indifferent sense. It is certain that throughout the entire range of the higher education a position of entire indifferentism is an absolute impossibility—that along the entire line the relation of man and of the universe to the ever-present God, the supreme Lord of the conscience and heart, the non-affirmation of the truth, is entirely equivalent to the affirmation at every point of its opposite.

The prevalent superstition that men can be educated for good citizenship, or for any other use under heaven, without religion, is as unscientific and unphilosophical as it is irreligious. It deliberately leaves out of view the most essential and controlling elements of human character : that man is constitutionally as religious (that is, loyally or disloyally) as he is rational ; that morals are impossible when dissociated from the religious basis out of which they grow ; that, as a matter of fact, human liberty and stable republican institutions, and every practically successful scheme of universal education in all past history, have originated in the active ministries of the Christian religion, and in these alone. This miserable superstition rests upon no facts of experience, and, on the contrary, is maintained on purely theoretical grounds in opposition to all the lessons which the past history of our race furnishes on the subject.

It is no answer to say that the deficiency of the national system of education in this regard will be adequately supplied by the activities of the Christian churches. No court would admit in excuse for the diffusion of poison the plea that the poisoner knew of another agent actively employed in diffusing an antidote. Moreover, the churches, divided and without national recognition, would be able very inadequately to counteract the deadly evil done by the public schools of the State with all the resources and prestige of the government. But, more than all, atheism taught in the school cannot be counteracted by theism taught in the Church. Theism and atheism cannot coalesce to make anything. All truth in all spheres is organically one and vitally inseparable. It is impossible for different agencies independently to discuss and inculcate the religious and the purely naturalistic sides of truth respectively. They cannot be separated. In some degree they must recognize each other, and be taught together, as they are experienced in their natural relations.

I am as sure as I am of the fact of Christ's reign that a comprehensive and centralized system of national education separated from religion, as is now commonly proposed, will prove the most appalling enginery for the propagation of anti-Christian and atheistic unbelief, and of anti-social, nihilistic ethics, individual, social, and political, which this sin-rent world has ever seen.

VI. The allegiance we owe is not to a doctrine, but to a Person, the God-man, our mediatorial King. We are bound to obey the Bible in all our actions and relations as citizens as well as church-members, because it is the law he has promulgated as the rule of our action, and because he is our supreme Lord and Master. The foundation of his authority is not our election, but the facts that he is absolutely perfect and worthy of absolute trust and obedience, and that he has created us, continues to uphold us in being, supplies us with all that makes existence desirable, and that he redeemed us from the wrath of God by his blood. His authority therefore does not depend upon our faith or our profession. It binds the atheist and the debauchee as much as the believer or the saint. No man can plead immunity because he is an unbeliever. Nor can we who are believers be excused from the consistent ordering of our whole lives according to his revealed will because the majority of our fellow-citizens disagree with us. Let others do as they will; as for us and for our houses, we will serve the Lord.

And if Christ is Lord of lords, and King of kings, if he

is really the Ruler among the nations, then all nations are
in a higher sense one nation, under one King, one law,
having one interest and one end. There cannot be two
laws for Christians—one to govern the relations of individuals, and the other the relations of nations. We
must love our neighbour-man as ourselves, so the Master
says; therefore we must love our neighbour-nation as our
own. The rivalries, jealousies, antagonisms, and cruel
wars between nations are all hideous fratricidal contests
and satanic rebellions against Christ our common King.
How miserably small and narrow and selfish is the form
of so-called patriotism which our poor children are taught
is so great a virtue, in comparison with that holy, up-
lifting passion which comprehends all nations as inseparable parts of the one living, universal kingdom of our
Lord and Saviour Jesus Christ! Suppose your enterprise
in the great competitions of manufacture and trade surpasses theirs, and you grow rich and gild your palaces
with the spoils of their poverty; suppose your sinews of
war or your personal prowess and valour surpass theirs,
and your empire grows great out of the ruins of their
commonwealth—what are you, after all, but the betrayer
of your brother's peace, or the destroyer of your brother's
life, and the disloyal render of the body of your common
Lord? Alas, that we have yet to learn that the so-called
code of honour among nations is just as mean and vulgar
a thing as the code of honour among individuals!

And if Christ is really King, exercising original and
immediate jurisdiction over the State as really as he does
over the Church, it follows necessarily that the general
denial or neglect of his rightful lordship, any prevalent
refusal to obey that Bible which is the open lawbook of
his kingdom, must be followed by political and social as
well as by moral and religious ruin. If professing Christians are unfaithful to the authority of their Lord in their

capacity as citizens of the State, they cannot expect to be blessed by the indwelling of the Holy Ghost in their capacity as members of the Church. The kingdom of Christ is one, and cannot be divided in life or in death. If the Church languishes, the State cannot be in health; and if the State rebels against its Lord and King, the Church cannot enjoy his favour. If the Holy Ghost is withdrawn from the Church, he is not present in the State; and if he, the only " Lord, the Giver of life," be absent, then all order is impossible, and the elements of society lapse backward to primeval night and chaos.

Who is responsible for the unholy laws and customs of divorce which have been in late years growing rapidly, like a constitutional cancer, through all our social fabric? Who is responsible for the rapidly-increasing, almost universal, desecration of our ancestral Sabbath? Who is responsible for the prevalent corruptions in trade which loosen the bands of faith and transform the halls of the honest trader into the gambler's den? Who is responsible for the new doctrines of secular education which hand over the very baptized children of the Church to a monstrous propagandism of naturalism and atheism? Who is responsible for the new doctrine that the State is not a creature of God, and owes him no allegiance, thus making the mediatorial Headship of Christ an unsubstantial shadow and his kingdom an unreal dream?

Whence come these portentous upheavals of the ancient primitive rock upon which society has always rested? Whence comes this socialistic earthquake, arraying capital and labour in irreconcilable conflict like oxygen and fire? Whence come these mad, nihilistic, anarchical ravings, the wild presages of a universal deluge which will blot out at once the family, the school, the church, the home, all civilization and religion, in one sea of ruin?

In the name of your own interests I plead with you; in

the name of your treasure-houses and barns, of your rich farms and cities, of your accumulations in the past and your hopes in the future—I charge you, you never will be secure if you do not faithfully maintain all the crown rights of Jesus, the King of men. In the name of your children and their inheritance of the precious Christian civilization you in turn have received from your sires; in the name of the Christian Church—I charge you, that its sacred franchise, religious liberty, cannot be retained by men who in civil matters deny their allegiance to the King. In the name of your own soul and its salvation; in the name of the adorable Victim of that bloody and agonizing sacrifice whence you draw all your hopes of salvation; by Gethsemane and Calvary—I charge you, citizens of the United States, afloat on your wide wild sea of politics, THERE IS ANOTHER KING, ONE JESUS: THE SAFETY OF THE STATE CAN BE SECURED ONLY IN THE WAY OF HUMBLE AND WHOLE-SOULED LOYALTY TO HIS PERSON AND OF OBEDIENCE TO HIS LAW.

"I charge thee in the sight of God, who quickeneth all things, and of Christ Jesus, who before Pontius Pilate witnessed the good confession; that thou keep the commandment, without spot, without reproach, until the appearing of our Lord Jesus Christ: which in its own times he shall shew, who is the blessed and only Potentate, the King of kings, and Lord of lords; who only hath immortality, dwelling in light unapproachable; whom no man hath seen, nor can see: to whom be honour and power eternal. Amen" (1 Tim. vi. 13–16).

XIII.

THE KINGDOM OF CHRIST.

WE are now to examine what is revealed in Scripture as to the nature and destiny of the kingdom of our Lord and Saviour Jesus Christ. The mediatorial King must of necessity have a kingdom, and the discussion of the kingdom appropriately succeeds the discussion of the royal office of the King.

There is but one kingdom or spiritual realm in which Christ-reigns for ever, and which in the end shall be eternally glorious in the perfect glory of her King; yet in Scripture there are three distinct names used to set forth the excellences and the blessedness of that realm in various aspects. Let it be remembered that while these different names are never to be confounded, since they differ from one another in flexibility and range of usage, and in the aspect in which they severally set forth the one subject, yet they are related to one and the selfsame subject. Therefore, the variety of the names and their usage should never lead to any confusion as to the identity and singleness of the object to which they relate. They should, on the contrary, by their variety illustrate the many-sided perfections and relations of the one kingdom, growing more glorious and powerful through all the successions of time.

These several names used in Scripture to designate this

one transcendent object on its different sides and relations are, the "Kingdom," the "Church," and the "City of God."

I. The word "kingdom" is the first in the order of its use. It is the characteristic word used for this purpose almost exclusively in the Old Testament. In the New Testament the word "kingdom" appears to pass out of frequent and prominent use precisely in proportion as the word "church" is advanced in these respects. "Kingdom" is used fifty times in Matthew, and one hundred and seventeen times in the four Gospels, only eight times in the Acts of the Apostles, and only twenty-four times in all the Epistles and Revelation; while, on the other hand, the word "church" occurs only three times in all the Gospels, and one hundred and five times in the Acts, Epistles, and Revelation. The word "kingdom" primarily signifies dominion, control, and obedience to law. The Greek word "church" primarily signifies election, redemption out of the mass of sinful and lost men. The words "city of God" primarily emphasize the kingdom as central, as an absolute unit, as having reached the consummate light of civilization, wealth, and power.

Of all these terms, the word "kingdom" is the most flexible, and has the widest range in its New Testament usage. It is naturally and properly used in three special senses. (1.) In the sense of "realm," or sphere of dominion. Thus we habitually use the phrase "the kingdom of England" when we intend to signify the geographical division with its known political boundaries and its inhabitants. In this way the New Testament habitually uses the phrase "the kingdom of God," or "of Christ," or "of heaven," to signify the realm over which the government of Christ extends, the subjects of his kingdom in their relation to his government. In this sense men are said to enter the kingdom—that is, to become subjects of it and participants of the benefits which belong to all its loyal subjects. In this sense of "realm," or subjects of Christ's dominion, the word kingdom is coincident in its meaning with the word church in its strictest sense and widest comprehension. (2.) The word kingdom is habitually used alike in the language of Scripture and of secular life in the sense of "reign," or of the exercise of royal authority. Thus when Charles I. was deposed in England, and the office of king abolished, and the protectorate of Oliver Cromwell set up in its place, historians say that "the kingdom" was abolished and the commonwealth set up. Again, when Oliver died, and his son and successor was forced to abdicate, and Charles II. was brought back and set upon his inherited throne, historians say the commonwealth was abolished and "the kingdom" was restored. Thus, in this sense of "reign," the Scriptures use the word kingdom when they say "the kingdom of heaven is at hand," or when we are taught to pray, "Thy kingdom come." And (3) alike in the usage of Scripture and of that of daily life we use the word kingdom to signify the benefits or blessings which result from the beneficent exercise of royal authority. Thus, while preparing for the *coup d'état*, Napoleon III. said in a public address at Lyons, "The empire is peace"—that is, universal peace will be the policy and effect of the imperial *régime* which I propose to introduce. In like manner Paul uses the word when he says (Rom. xiv. 17), "For the kingdom of God is not meat and drink"—that is, the reign of Christ does not express itself in that kind of activity—"but righteousness, and peace, and joy in the Holy Ghost:" these are the characters of his realm because the results of his reign.

II. The first question here is concerning the nature and extent of this "kingdom" and the method of its "coming." After that we will consider the biblical doctrine of "the church," and lastly that of the "city of God."

If Adam had not apostatized, the entire course of human history would have been a normal development in fellowship with God. The central principle of loyalty to God having been preserved intact, the whole moral nature of man would have grown healthily, and all his faculties in all their exercises, and all his relations with his fellows, would have been correspondingly normal. But since sin introduced rebellion against the supreme authority of God, the human character has been radically corrupted and human society disorganized. This has subjected the entire race in all spheres of its activity to the dominion of a malign spiritual empire comprehending the whole world, over which presides " the prince of the power of the air," the " prince or god of this world." And, being thus alienated from the centre of all life, the entire subsequent course of the development of man's moral character and social condition has been, in the absence of a supernatural intervention, continuously in the direction of greater and greater corruption and disorder.

In consequence of this state of facts, the God of heaven has set up a kingdom in antagonism to the kingdom of Satan, and to all temporal kingdoms organized in Satan's interest; which kingdom shall never be destroyed, but, breaking in pieces all its antagonists, shall stand for ever. This kingdom of the God of heaven was introduced immediately after the Fall, and is to be consummated in the eternal city of God which shall descend out of heaven at the last day. It has been mediatorial from the beginning, administered at first in the hand of the unincarnate eternal Word of God, and afterward in the hands of the incarnate Word. It was symbolized in the throne of David in Jerusalem and the Jewish theocracy, and it was visibly set up in its higher spiritual form when the long-promised Son of David, having redeemed his people on the cross, rose from the dead, ascended to the heavens, and sat down at the right hand of God. This kingdom is not one among the many competing kingdoms of the earth. It is antagonistic to the kingdom of Satan only : all the natural kingdoms of men, except in so far as they are compromised with the kingdom of Satan, are penetrated, and assimilated, and rendered subservient to its own ends by the kingdom of God. All other kingdoms have their rise, progress, maturity, and decadence ; while this kingdom alone is eternal, growing broader and waxing stronger through all ages until its consummation in the city of God.

It is essentially distinguished from all the kingdoms of the world whatsoever by its origin, its nature, its end, its method of development, its eternal continuance. (1.) It necessarily rests upon a basis of redemption by blood. The atonement on Calvary is its essential pre-requisite, for in its highest development " a Lamb as it had been slain " stood in the midst of the throne. (2.) It is built up and constituted not by natural forces, but by the supernatural power of the Holy Ghost directing, using, and overruling all natural forces to the accomplishment of his own ends. (3.) The sphere of this divine reign is not in the first instance external relations and conduct, but primarily the essential character, the permanent state of the heart in its ultimate springs of action as discerned by the all-seeing eye of God. And it extends to all external relations and actions whatsoever, as these are the streams which proceed from and reveal the essential state of the heart. (4.) The central principle of this kingdom, which determines all its other conditions and requirements, is the absolute loyalty of the hearts of all its subjects to the person of the King. Any service rendered from any inferior motive than this is essential rebellion. But this supreme motive is to take possession of the entire person, and to absorb all his life. If any man would be a subject of this kingdom, " and hate not his father and mother, and wife and children, and brethren and sisters, yea, and his own life also," he cannot be accepted as such. And this all-absorbing principle of absolute loyalty is to dominate all other springs of action, and mould the entire life and all the relations which the individual sustains to the whole body. (5.) It is essentially a kingdom of righteousness. On the foundation of supreme loyalty to God its reign effects the establishment of all righteousness in all the relations the individual sustains to God and to his fellows. Rooted in the theological virtues of faith, hope, love, it enforces all the moral virtues known among heathen or Christian men—true manhood in all its elements of truth, bravery, purity, generosity, magnanimity. It embraces the man and woman as individuals, and the perfectly ordered family and community, and all ecclesiastical and political societies. It comprehends all the virtues, and sets its seal of reprobation upon all moral evil ; its demands in all the departments of moral character or action never fall short of absolute perfection. (6.) Its condition of citizenship is the new birth or spiritual regeneration of each subject by the re-creative power of the Holy Ghost. The King himself has said, " Except a man be born again, he cannot see the kingdom of God." This supernatural change of nature is in each case the origin of a supernatural life, both internal of faith and love, and external of holy obedience. (7.) This kingdom is neither a republic nor a democracy, but an absolute monarchy and an ordered aristocracy. The King possesses all perfections, human and divine, in absolute fulness. All authority and dominion, alike legislative and executive, descend upon the subject from above. The Sovereign selects his subjects, and not the subjects the Sovereign. Each subject in the economy of the kingdom will have his own peculiar grade, status, and function. As in the heavens one star differeth from another star in glory, so will it be in the resurrection (1 Cor. xv. 41).

The members of the one body include the hands and the
feet and the head. Some shall sit with their Lord on
thrones judging the twelve tribes of Israel. (8.) But the
conditions of reward in this kingdom and of promotion to
influence and power will be the opposite of all those which
have prevailed in the kingdoms of this world. It is " not
by blood, nor of the will of the flesh, nor of the will of
man, but of God." The King has said, " Ye know that the
princes of the Gentiles exercise dominion over them, and
they that are great exercise authority upon them. But it
shall not be so among you : but whosoever will be great
among you, let him be your minister ; and whosoever will
be chief among you, let him be your servant : even as the
Son of man came not to be ministered unto, but to minister, and to give his life a ransom for many " (Matt. xx.
25-28). The baleful doctrine of human rights which is
now turning all political societies into pandemoniums is
never admitted in the kingdom of God. But the sublime
doctrine of human duties in its stead binds all hearts and
lives in beautiful harmony to the throne of the Prince, and
to the happiness of all his subjects. (9.) This kingdom is
to endure for ever, gradually to embrace all the inhabitants of the earth, and finally the entire moral government
of God in heaven and on earth. The little stone which
breaks the image will become a great mountain and fill the
whole earth (Dan. ii. 35). This gospel of the kingdom is
to be preached to all nations. Then all the kingdoms of
this world shall become the kingdoms of our Lord, and of
his Christ ; and he shall reign for ever and ever. And in
the dispensation of the fulness of times all things, both
which are in heaven and which are on earth, are to be
gathered together in one in Christ ; who is set at the right
hand of God in heavenly places, far above all principality,
and power, and might, and dominion, and every name that
is named, not only in this world, but also in that which is

to come ; and all things are put under his feet, he only being excepted that did put all things under him (Eph. i. 10, 20, 21 ; 1 Cor. xv. 27).

III. The process by which this kingdom grows through its successive stages toward its ultimate completion can of course be very inadequately understood by us. It implies the ceaseless operation of the mighty power of God working through all the forces and laws of nature, and culminating in the supernatural manifestations of grace and of miracle. The Holy Ghost is everywhere present, and he works directly alike in the ways we distinguish as natural and as supernatural—alike through appointed instruments and agencies, and immediately by his direct personal power. The special agency for the building up of this kingdom is the organized Christian Church, with its regular ministry, providing for the preaching of the gospel and the administration of the sacraments. The special work of the Holy Ghost in building up this kingdom is performed in the regeneration and sanctification of individuals through the ministry of the Church. But beyond this the omnipresent Holy Ghost works to the same end, directly and indirectly, in every sphere of nature and of human life, causing all the historic movements of peoples and nations, of civilization and of science, of political and ecclesiastical societies, to broaden and deepen the foundations and to advance the growth and perfection of his kingdom. Thus this kingdom from the beginning and in the whole circle of human history has been always coming. Its coming has been marked by great epochs, when new revelations and new communications of divine power have been imported from without into the current of human history. The chiefest of these have been the giving of the law; the incarnation, crucifixion, resurrection, ascension, and session of the King on the right hand of the Father ; and the mission of the Holy Ghost. Yet the kingdom has been always coming every moment of all the years that have passed. In all the growing of the seeds and all the blowing of the winds; in every event, even the least significant, which has advanced the interests of the human family either in respect to their bodies or their souls, and thus made their lives better or worthier; in all the breaking of fetters; in all the bringing in of light; in the noiseless triumphs of peace; in the dying out of barbarisms; and in the colonization of great continents with new populations and free states,—the kingdom is coming. Above all, in the multiplication of the myriad centres of Christian missions and of the myriad hosts of Christian workers, each in the spirit of the King seeking the very lowest and most degraded, everywhere lifting upward what Satan's kingdom has borne down, the kingdom is coming. Its process is like that of the constructive power of the kingdom of nature, silent and invisible, yet omnipresent and omnipotent, like the rain and the dew, and the zephyr and the sunlight. The kingdom comes intensively in each heart, like the leaven, which penetrates the whole mass silently yet irresistibly until all is leavened. It comes extensively, like the growth of the mustard-seed, which from the least beginnings unfolds itself until it shoots out great branches and shelters the fowls of heaven. In this world the wheat and the tares, the good and the evil, grow together to the end. The net gathers in fish good and bad. One field brings forth thirty, another forty, and another an hundredfold. In the end the tares shall be gathered and burned, and the pure wheat gathered without mixture in the eternal garner of the Lord. In the whole history of its coming the kingdom of God "cometh not with observation; neither shall they say, Lo, here! or, Lo, there! for, behold, the kingdom of God is within you." But its consummation shall be ushered in suddenly and with overwhelming demonstrations of glory: "For as the lightning, that lighteneth

out of the one part under heaven, shineth unto the other
part under heaven; so shall also the Son of man be in his
day." For the present the King is absent, gathering together in his grasp the reins of his empire: we are left to be
diligently employed with the doing the utmost for his cause
possible within our respective spheres against his coming.
When he comes he will be revealed as a King of kings, followed by great retinues of royal princes sitting on thrones
and reigning over cities in his name and through his grace.

IV. We now come to the word for this subject characteristic of the New Testament——THE CHURCH. It must
be remembered that this does not present a different subject, but a different phase of the same subject. The word
"kingdom" expresses chiefly the ideas of dominion and of
loyal obedience. The word for "church" expresses chiefly
the ideas of sovereign election and of free and efficacious
salvation. The New Testament word represented by the
word "church" is ἐκκλησία (*ecclesia*), which precisely means
the body of the elect——the elect, the effectually called by
the power of the Holy Ghost. And phenomenally the elect
are believers. Their specific mark is faith. When the
Lamb shall gain his victories over his enemies and be manifested Lord of lords and King of kings, those who accom-
pany him will be the "called," the "elect," "believers"
(Rev. xvii. 14). This is the sense of the word *ecclesia*——
the body of "the elect," "the effectually called" by the
Holy Ghost, "the body, the fulness of Christ," "the bride,
the Lamb's wife." All its real members are saved. None
are saved who are not really its members. It is absolutely
one, no matter how its members may appear to be separated
by differences of time, place, creed, or outward form, for "by
one Spirit are we all baptized into one body, whether we
be Jews or Gentiles, whether we be bond or free." The
unity of the Church is the one absolutely essential element
of its existence which is never absent, and which can never

be lost. And, however much this essential unity may be disguised by the varying fortunes or by the passions of human life, it will be conspicuously exhibited in its glorified form at the last day.

But the laws of human thought and language have made it inevitable that the transient forms in which parts of this great body are temporarily organized should be confounded with the essential being of that body which transcends and survives them all, and that the name which designates the whole should be applied to all its constituent parts. Accordingly, in the New Testament and in our current language the word church is applied to the local congregation, to the collected congregations of a city or a province, or to some special denomination distinguished by a particular creed or form of organization or ceremonial of worship. Thus we read constantly of the church in the house of Aquila and Priscilla, "the church in Corinth," "the churches of Asia," and of the Reformed, of the Presbyterian, and of the Episcopal churches.

Here two points are to be distinctly borne in mind :—
1st. The whole Church in its totality, the holy catholic Church in which we all profess to believe, is not made up as a general sum by adding all the particular Christian denominations together, as adding the Presbyterians to the Baptists, and these to the Methodists, and these to the Anglicans and Romanists, etc. This is self-evident, because all of these outward organizations contain many members which have no part nor lot in the essential Church of which Christ is the Head ; and also because the whole body of those dying in infancy outside of the visible Church, which constitute the vast majority of the essential Church, never formed any part of these particular denominations. You might as well attempt to reach an adequate survey of the whole surface of the round earth, with its oceans and mountains, by adding together the surveyed

farms of Europe and America, as to present an adequate
survey of the Church, which is the body of Christ and the
heir of the promises, by summing up in one table the
statistics of our several organized denominations.   The
essential Church is like the all-investing atmosphere; the
several phenomenal organizations, which we call churches,
are like the visible clouds which float in various forms and
variable proportions in its bosom.

2nd. There are not two churches, the one visible and
the other invisible.   There is, and can be ever, but one
single, indivisible Church of Jesus Christ.   This is always
visible in its exact definition and in its widest comprehension to the omniscient eye of God.   It is always visible,
although imperfectly, even to the eye of the human observer.
It consists in its essential nature of men and women living
in the flesh, and as far as they are distinguished as the
possessors of a peculiar spiritual nature: by the very force
of their saintship they are set apart in contrast to the
mass of mankind as " the salt of the earth" and " the light
of the world."   Moreover, it belongs to the essential nature
of the spiritual Church, as composed of intrinsically social
beings, who, by reason of their saintship, are loyal servants
of their Master in a hostile world, that it always and
everywhere tends to express itself in some external organized form, and so render itself the more definitely visible.
When it is finally consummated, this Church will be the
most conspicuously visible of all created objects, "fair as
the moon, clear as the sun, and terrible as an army with
banners."

On the other hand, in contrast with external ecclesiastical societies, called churches by us, the one holy catholic
Church is relatively invisible to the eyes of men.   This
relative invisibility is due to two facts: *First*, that, because
the true members of the Church in this world are inex-
tricably mixed with false professors and unbelievers, it is

impossible for human observers in this life accurately to discriminate the members of this body from its environment. And, *secondly,* since this one Church comprehends all the centuries and members in all the communities embraced in the whole course of human history, a part being glorified in heaven, while a part is struggling with the conditions of this life, it follows that this Church is too vast to be comprehended in its unity in one human vision. As a whole, it is invisible because its proportions transcend vision. It is seen in its parts successively and imperfectly, but it will be seen completely only when the city of God descends from heaven " prepared as a bride adorned for her husband."

V. There are possible only two generically distinct theories as to the nature of the Church. The first maintains that it is essentially an outwardly organized society, like the Church of Rome or of England ; its outward form as well as its informing spirit being determined by the constitution originally imposed upon it by Christ, through a succession of offices, in unbroken organic continuity from the days of the apostles until now.

The second doctrine maintains that the Church is a general term for the whole body of regenerated men, whether of past, present, or future generations. These are constituted one spiritual body by the indwelling of the Holy Ghost, which unites them to Christ their Head, as all the various elements and members of our natural bodies are constituted one by the indwelling of a common soul. The many members of this body, being many, are *one* body ; and it is all the more one because of the infinitely various relations which the several members sustain to our Lord and to each other, determined by their various natural faculties, historical conditions, and gracious endowments.

A very slight knowledge either of the Bible or of ecclesiastical history proves that the doctrine of the Church first stated is impossible. The claim is that such organizations as the Greek, Roman, and Anglican churches are identical, as external corporations, with the church of the original apostles. This is simply absurd on the face of it. It is admitted by the first scholars of the Church of England * that "nothing like modern episcopacy existed before the close of the first century." The office of the twelve apostles was in its essence incapable of transmission, and as a matter of fact has not been transmitted. No living man can follow Paul's example in presenting the "signs of an apostle." It has been proved hundreds of times, and never with clearer demonstration than by Bishop Lightfoot in his *Commentary on the Epistle to the Philippians,* that the idea of a clerical priesthood was unknown in the early church. Nothing like the Roman or Anglican hierarchy can be read between the lines of New Testament history without the most grotesque incongruity. Nothing like their vestments or elaborate liturgies can be conceived of as belonging to the church of that period. Most of these are demonstrably comparatively modern, and bear marks of Jewish, of heathen, and of secular origin.

Besides, the claim that the original external corporations have remained intact through all intervening generations without break in the absolutely continuous transmission of authority can in no case be proved, and in most cases is conspicuously false. The Church of Rome ridicules the claims of the Greeks and Anglicans alike. The contestant apostles of Romanism and Anglicanism excommunicate each other, and claim exclusive authority in dioceses embracing the same territory over half the world, and utterly irrespective of any claims to priority of occupation on either side—for example, the claims of the Romanists in New York and Virginia, and of the Anglicans in Canada, Louisiana, and California. The more thoroughly, there-

---

* Dean Stanley, Bishop Lightfoot, etc.

fore, the first theory of the Church, or that which regards it as a visible corporation, is put to the test, the more inconsistent it is shown to be with all the providential facts of the case.

On the other hand, it is evident that the second doctrine of the Church, or that which regards it as a collective name for the whole body of the saved in all ages, is the one which alone justifies the application to it of the common predicates of "unity," "apostolicity," "catholicity," "infallibility," "perpetuity," and "sanctity." The spiritual body is always faithful to its genuine apostolic doctrine in all its essentials; is infallibly preserved from all fatal errors of faith and practice; is set apart from the world as consecrated and morally pure; and endures through all conflicts and changes as indestructible and unchangeably one and catholic, embracing in one spiritual union all saints in all parts of the world, in all successive generations.

Nevertheless, this spiritual body, always consisting of men and women whose natures are essentially social, must ever spontaneously and universally tend to organize itself under all historical conditions. All the various forms which thence result have been comprehended in God's design, and are necessary for the spiritual development of the Church, and for the accomplishment of the great tasks it has been commissioned to perform. Yet the permanent results of biblical interpretation unite with the history of Christ's providential and gracious guidance of the churches in proving that he never intended to impose upon the Church as a whole any particular form of organization. Neither he nor his apostles ever went beyond the suggestion of general principles and actual inauguration of a few rudimentary forms. The history of the churches during all subsequent ages shows that these rudimentary forms have been ever changing in correspondence with the

changes in their historical conditions. And in exact proportion to the freedom and fruitfulness of the Church's
activity in the service of its Master are these organic
forms rapidly and flexibly adapted to the conditions of the
sphere in which their especial work is appointed. These
various denominational forms of the living Church are all
one in their essentials, and differ only in their accidents.
These accidents have been determined in each case by
conditions peculiar to itself, especially by those resulting
from national character and from political, social, educational, and geographical circumstances. Some have sprung
from transient conditions, some from the idiosyncrasies of
their founders, and some even from the follies and sins of
selfish partisans. Other differences are rooted in far more
permanent distinctions of nations and classes, and represent
persistent rival tendencies in the thoughts and tastes and
habits of men. All of these, since they exist and are
used as instruments of the Holy Ghost, have in that fact
a providential justification. And each one, even the least
significant, emphasizes some otherwise too much neglected
side of the truth, and is therefore, in its day, necessary to
the completeness of the whole.

It is evident, therefore, that while the Church of Christ
necessarily tends to self-organization under ordinary conditions, and to different forms of organization under different
conditions, nevertheless organization itself is not of its
essence. The Church exists antecedently to and independently of any organization; and its far larger part,
embracing all mankind of all centuries dying in infancy,
extends indefinitely beyond all organizations. All the
more it is certain that no special form can be essential to
the existence, or even to the integrity, of the Church.

As the outward form should express the true character
of the informing spirit, of course in an ideally perfect
state the essential unity of the Church, as well as all

other permanent characteristics, must find expression. All radical diversities, all irreconcilable oppositions, all bigotry, jealousy, alienation, and strife, must be eliminated. But all unity implies relation, and all relations imply differences, and the sublime unity of the catholic Church of all peoples and of all generations implies the harmony of incalculable varieties. The principle of the union is spiritual and vital, and hence must be the result of an internal growth. The more perfect the inward life, the more perfect will be its outward expression in form. The final external form of the holy catholic Church will never be reached by adding denomination to denomination. It will come, as all growth into organized form, alike in the physiological and in the social world, comes, by the spontaneous action of central vital forces from within.

All living unity implies diversity, and just in proportion to the elevated type and significance of the unity will be the variety of the elements it comprehends. In the barren desert each grain of sand is of precisely the same form with every other grain, and therefore there is no organic whole. The life of the world results from the correlation of earth and sky, of land and sea, of mountains and plains. All social unity springs out of the differences between man and woman, parent and child, men of thought and men of action, the men who possess and the men who need. No number of similar stones would constitute a great cathedral. No number of repetitions of the same musical sound would generate music. Always where the most profound and perfect unity is effected it is the result of the greatest variety and complexity of parts. This law holds true through all varieties of vegetable, animal, and social organisms, and is revealed equally through all the pages of the geologic records.

Certainly, God appears to be preparing to make the ultimate unity of the Church the richest and most comprehensive of created forms in the number and variety of its profound harmonies. It would have been a very simple thing at the first to form a homogeneous society out of the undifferentiated family of Adam numerically multiplied. But for thousands of years God has been breaking up that family into a multitude of varieties passing all enumeration. In arctic, torrid, and temperate zones; on mountains, valleys, coasts, continents, and islands; in endlessly drawn-out successions of ages; under the influence of every possible variety of inherited institution; in every stage of civilization, and under every political, social, and religious constitution; through all possible complications of personal idiosyncrasy and of external environment,—God has been drawing human nature through endless modifications. All these varieties enter into and contribute to the marvellous riches of the Christian Church; for her members are "redeemed out of every kindred, and tongue, and people, and nation." And all these are further combined into all the endless varieties of ecclesiastical organizations, monarchical, aristocratical, republican, and democratic, which the ingenuity of man, assisted by all complications of theological controversy and of social and political life, has been able to invent.

Who, then, shall guide all these multitudinous constituents in their re-combination into the higher unity? Shall it be accomplished by a process of absorption into some ancient society claiming to be *the Church?* Shall it be helped forward by the volunteered offices of some self-authorized "Church congress"? A time can never come when many of these differences so evidently designed will be obliterated. But undoubtedly a time is soon coming when the law of differentiation, so long dominant, shall be subordinated to the law of integration—when all these differences, so arduously won, shall be wrought into the harmony of the perfect whole. The comprehension of so vast a variety of interacting forces must be left to God. His methods are always historical and his instruments are all second causes. He alone has been contemporaneous with the Church under all dispensations, and omnipresent with the churches of every nation and tribe; and with him " a thousand years are as one day."

The sin of schism is unquestionably very common and very heinous. In its essence it is a sin against the unity of the Church. If this unity were external and mechanical, then all organic division or variety would be schism. But since the principle of unity is the immanent Holy Ghost, binding all the members in one life to Christ its source, schism must consist in some violation of the ties which bind us to the Holy Ghost or to Christ or to our fellow-members.

Hence all denial of the supreme Godhead and lordship of Christ is schism. All denial of the body of catholic doctrine common to the whole confessing Church and embraced in the great ecumenical creeds is schism. All sin against the Holy Ghost, every breach of the law of holiness and every defect in spiritual-mindedness, tend to the marring and dividing of the body of Christ. All pride, bigotry, and exclusive-churchism all claim that the true Church is essentially identical with a certain external organization or form of organization or with a definite external succession of officers, all denial of the validity of the ministry and sacraments of any bodies professing the true faith and bearing evidence of the presence of the Holy Spirit, are schisms. All party spirit, jealousy, and selfish rivalry, all unnecessary multiplication of denominational organizations, all want of the spirit of fraternal love and co-operation in the service of the common Master, tend to the marring and dividing of the body of Christ.

If this be true, it is evident that the real union of the

churches can best be cultivated by promoting the central spiritual unity of the Church which comprehends them all. For this end all who call themselves Christians must with one purpose seek to bring their whole mind and thought more and more into perfect conformity to the Word of God speaking through the sacred Scriptures, and their whole life and activity more and more into subjection to the Holy Ghost dwelling in the whole body and in all its members alike. This process must, of course, proceed entirely from within outward, never in the reverse direction. Organic unity will be the result of the co-operation through long ages of an infinite variety of forces. It cannot be brought about by any system of means working toward it directly as an end in itself. All such unionistic enterprises are prompted by many mixed motives, some of them essentially partisan, and therefore wholly divisive in their real effects. But hereafter, in God's good time, the result will come as an incidental effect of the ripening of all churches in knowledge and love and in all the graces, and especially of a whole-souled, self-forgetful consecration of all to the service and glory of their common Lord.

VI. The CITY OF GOD.

The most sublime picture presented in the entire past history of the Christian Church since Pentecost is that presented by St. Augustine, the grandest of all uninspired Church teachers, when, during the years A.D. 413 to 426, from the very midst of the conflagration of ancient Rome, the so-called "eternal city" of the pagans, he uttered in trumpet tones his argument and prophecy of the superior strength and beauty, and of the absolutely immortal life and glory, of the city of God, in his *De Civitate Dei*. The Teutonic barbarians had already taken Rome and shaken to its foundations the ancient universal empire, upon which civilization and order and the hopes of mankind appeared to depend. The minds of men were in a state of chaotic confusion. The future was utterly dark. Even Christians began to despair. Then Augustine made all men see the difference between the " city of the world," called eternal, which was passing away, and the pure and rainbowed " city of God," the goal of contest, but the realm of peace and love, which shall abide secure and radiant, like the incorruptible stars, for ever and ever.

A city differs from a kingdom only in being its condensed essence, its central seat. What Paris is to France, what the city of Rome was to the empire of the same name, suggests the use of the title " city of God " for the consummate and glorified form of the kingdom. It is the kingdom comprised in its absolute unity, raised to its highest condition of culture, refinement, wealth, and power.

Isaiah saw the " city of God " (Isa. lx. 10–22) when he said : " The sons of strangers shall build up thy walls, and their kings shall minister unto thee......Therefore thy gates shall be open continually ; they shall not be shut day nor night ; that men may bring unto thee the forces of the Gentiles, and that their kings may be brought." " The Gentiles shall come to thy light, and kings to the brightness of thy rising. Lift up thine eyes round about, and see : all they gather themselves together......the abundance of the sea shall be converted unto thee, the forces of the Gentiles shall come unto thee."

The author of Hebrews saw that " city of God " when he said (Heb. xii. 22, *seq.*) : " Ye are come unto mount Sion, and unto the city of the living God, the heavenly Jerusalem, and to an innumerable company of angels, to the general assembly and church of the firstborn, which are written in heaven, and to God the Judge of all, and to the spirits of just men made perfect, and to Jesus the mediator of the new covenant, and to the blood of sprinkling, that speaketh better things than that of Abel."

And the apocalyptic prophet closes the volume of divine disclosures with the prophetic picture of the kingdom consummated in the form of this "city of God" descending from heaven: "And I John saw the holy city, new Jerusalem, coming down from God out of heaven, prepared as a bride adorned for her husband. And I heard a great voice out of heaven saying, Behold, the tabernacle of God is with men, and he will dwell with them, and they shall be his people, and God himself shall be with them, and be their God. And God shall wipe away all tears from their eyes; and there shall be no more death, neither sorrow, nor crying, neither shall there be any more pain: for the former things are passed away." For the city has "the glory of God: and her light was like unto a stone most precious, even like a jasper stone, clear as crystal...... And I saw no temple therein: for the Lord God Almighty and the Lamb are the temple of it. And the city had no need of the sun, neither of the moon, to shine in it: for the glory of God did lighten it, and the Lamb is the light thereof......And the gates of it shall not be shut at all by day: for there shall be no night there. And they shall bring the glory and honour of the nations into it. And there shall in no wise enter into it any thing that defileth, neither whatsoever worketh abomination, or maketh a lie: but they which are written in the Lamb's book of life." "He which testifieth these things saith, Surely I come quickly. Amen. Even so, come, Lord Jesus" (Rev. xxi., xxii.).

XIV.

THE LAW OF THE KINGDOM.

WE have seen that the great end in which all the providential activities of God culminate in this world is the establishment of a universal kingdom of righteousness, which is to embrace all men and angels, and to endure for ever in absolute perfection and blessedness. This kingdom, viewed as a reign, must be administered by law; and, viewed as a realm, must be brought into perfect subjection to law in all its elements. This law can be nothing lower than the law of absolute and immutable moral perfection, which, having its seat in the moral nature of God, embraces the whole moral universe in its sway.

This divine institution, under its title of "Church," is too habitually regarded as simply the sphere of a divine redemption. The member of the Church is looked upon as a beneficiary unconditionally delivered from condemnation, whose happiness is rendered infallibly secure for ever. But the essential idea of the kingdom is a community of men in communion with God, whose whole nature and life are dominated by the law of righteousness, where every individual is holy as our Father in heaven is holy, and where all spontaneously perform to perfection all the duties which grow out of their several relations.

There are here two opposite and equally false conceptions of the nature of the kingdom of God which must be discriminated and rejected—that which makes its righteousness consist of natural morality divorced from religion; and that which makes it consist of religious sentiments and observances, morality being unemphasized.

I. It is a characteristic position of the modern rationalists, who maintain the perfectibility of human society through a process of natural evolution, that a morality which provides for all the duties which man owes to his fellows may be cultivated to perfection independent of any religious motives. It is maintained, even, that religious faith is injurious to pure morality—(1) because it diverts the thoughts and efforts of men from their fellow-men and from the present life, which they insist is the only sphere of moral relations and obligations, and directs them toward an invisible, spiritual world, and to a future world of which we can know nothing certainly, and to which we can, at least in our present condition, owe no duties. And (2) they hold that the motives which religion presents in the future reward or punishment of the individual are purely selfish, and therefore can never prompt to a genuinely moral and noble character or course of conduct. They insist that the moral relations of men are necessarily confined to their fellow-men and to the present life, and that all genuine morality is prompted by the natural sense of justice which regards our fellows, and by the natural sympathies which bind us to them. And (3) they point triumphantly to the degrading superstitions and the cruel fanaticisms which in the course of human history have been associated with all forms of religion.

On the contrary, we are able to show that neither degrading superstition nor cruel fanaticism has any source or encouragement in the principles of genuine Christianity; that these evils spring, like all other vile things, from the corrupt hearts of sinful men; that they have existed during all periods of human history independent of all forms of religion; and that their association with any of the doctrines or institutions of Christianity has been only accidental and temporary. We maintain that the pleas for the separation of morality and religion are rational only on the supposition that atheism is true. On the other hand, if the existence of God is admitted, then conscience instantly proclaims itself to be his voice in the soul, and speaks in his name. All morality, personal and social, must have a theistic basis to give it depth, authority, and power. The morality of these boasting opponents of religion is superficial in the extreme. The noblest motives they present are those of sympathy and compassion for others. They have no eternal moral Governor, no heavenly Father, no divine elder Brother, no indwelling Holy Ghost; no infinite sanctions of eternal rewards or punishments. Their pale and languid lives prove that their vaunted altruistic morality is supported by no faith in its truth and no enthusiasm for its beauty. It has done nothing for the world beyond what is rationally referred to natural amiability, a passing cant of the hour, a self-admiring desire for human recognition. How miserably poor do the best showings of the ephemeral flower of non-religious morality appear when laid in the effacing radiance of the life and cross of Christ, and of that immense company of his humble disciples who through all ages and in all spheres of human life have followed his example of self-sacrifice in the interests of humanity and of heroic devotion to the will and service of his heavenly Father! All true morality has its root and ground in, and derives its only adequate motives from, the doctrines of Christianity and from the fellowship of God with man which Christ secures. A rebel against supreme and fundamental obligation cannot possibly be righteous in any relation, however subordinate. And the only motives which render any action completely righteous are supreme love to God, and love to man for

God's sake; for "whether we eat, or drink, or whatsoever we do," if we would claim the meed of the righteous, we must "do all for the glory of God."

II. The danger most easily besetting many apparently zealous Christians lies in the opposite direction, of holding to the validity of a religious experience, the immediate effect of which is anything short of the love and practice of all righteousness. The gratuitous justification of a sinner on the ground of another's righteousness, imputed to him freely without respect to his personal past character or record, is legitimately the root and necessary precondition of the most perfect morality. Nevertheless, this doctrine in the hands of ignorant and impure men is capable of the most serious abuse. And even among orthodox Christians, who are theoretically all right in their acknowledgment of all moral obligations, the least lapse of watchfulness will bring us in danger of a comfortable resting in the security of our position in Christ, while we neglect the full performance of all the moral obligations which spring out of our relations as Christians alike to God and man. The very end for which the stupendous enginery of redemption was devised and executed, including the incarnation, crucifixion, resurrection of the Son of God, and the mission of the Holy Ghost, is to establish a community of regenerated and sanctified men, absolutely perfect in righteousness. The very conception of an immoral Christian is monstrous. And however imperfect the Christian may be at any stage of his spiritual growth, he can make no compromise with any sin; he must put forth all his powers in ceaseless efforts after absolute moral perfection in all directions. He must include all the duties which spring out of our relations to God, and all those which spring out of all our relations to our fellow-men of every kind. There can be nothing over-looked, much less willingly neglected. He must include not only the theological graces and the cardinal moral virtues, but the bloom and symmetry of moral excellence which result from the perfect harmony of all the virtues. He must be pure in thought as well as in life, magnanimous and generous in feeling and impulse, as well as just in his transactions. A narrow - minded, conceited, and selfish Christian is an incongruity as real, though not quite so shocking, as an immoral Christian. Whatsoever things are pure, whatsoever things are of good report, whatsoever things are edifying, whatsoever things are spiritually beautiful, whatsoever things are Christ-like, all these things are involved in the righteousness of all saints. To be a gentleman or a lady in the essential, not the conventional sense, is the very least demanded in the moral character and conduct of any Christian. Anything beneath that is out of the question. But beyond that the Christian hero and heroine must ever aspire to the heights of moral and spiritual excellence and beauty, such as will be realized perfectly only in the spirits of just men made perfect in the holy city.

III. The sublime source of this law is the uncreated, absolute, and immutable moral perfections of the divine nature. This nature is presupposed in the divine volition, the self-existent nature being immanent in the will. This perfection is absolute; it admits of no qualifications or degrees. Every, even the least, element of duty is imperative. Every, even the least, shortcoming in that which is right is of the essential nature of sin and guilt. This law, having its seat in the nature of the supreme moral Governor, must be at the same time original, supreme, absolute, universal, and immutable. It must have been one in all ages and in all realms, over all orders of creatures of all degrees of knowledge and power, over the heights of heaven and over the pit of hell. The specific duties may vary indefinitely, but the principle of duty— the absolute obligation to all that is right and to the rejection of all that is not right—is universal and immutable.

The absolute obligation of all moral excellence is universal and immutable, but specific duties grow out of relations immediately when those relations are constituted. (1.) The obligation of universal love and of absolute truth binds all God's moral creatures equally everywhere, because these are absolutely demanded by the unchangeable nature of God, and because they are results under the universal law of moral perfection, from the essential relations which all moral agents sustain to God and to each other. (2.) There is another very large class of duties which immediately spring out of the permanent relations which God has sovereignly established in the constitution of human society in this world. These are expressed by the commandments, "Thou shalt not steal," "Thou shalt not kill," "Thou shalt not commit adultery." These would have no meaning in a state of relations in which there was no property, no mortal life, and no sexual constitution. But as soon as these relations exist, the moral obligations necessarily exist. (3.) A third large class of duties spring for a time from certain temporary relations which God has constituted among a particular people and during a particular dispensation or constitutional period: as, for instance, the judicial laws of the Jews, many of which appear to us so peculiar, grew necessarily from the application of the eternal principles of right to the very peculiar social, governmental, and ecclesiastical conditions which God, for wise purposes, had at that time established among them. The specific laws last as long as the special reasons for them continue, and pass into desuetude as soon as these reasons cease to exist. (4.) A fourth class of duties spring from the simple sovereign volition of God. He is of course always rational and righteous in all his decrees. But the reasons which determine him may be utterly unknown to us; and whether we see or appreciate the reason or not, the sovereign volition of God binds us by a perfect moral obligation to obey, because he is our Owner and Lord. Thus, the command to observe as holy the first day of the week as the Christian Sabbath has two parts—the one invariable, because it rests upon the general nature of man, physical and spiritual, which needs a day of rest; and the other variable, because it is positive purely, resting only on the volition of God, who has set apart one day in seven, and a particular one of the seven, to be that day of rest, which otherwise would have been a matter of indifference.

Hence the moral law of the kingdom is absolute and perfect and universal, descending from above, never ascending from below. It is immutably one, yet always comprehending new conditions, and generating an indefinite variety of new special obligations out of the changing relations constantly developed under the sovereign guidance of the great King. We never elected God. The united power of all his creatures can never limit or condition his will. No rebellious barons will ever coerce from him a charter which will limit the absolute autocracy of his reign. There is, in all the ages and in all the provinces of his kingdom, no such thing as human rights to disturb his government or to distract righteousness. No creature, from the very nature of the case, can possess any rights over against Him who causes him to exist and to be what he is. Nor can any creature possess any rights over against any other creature, except such as are given by God. If I possess a right relative to my brother, my brother owes it to God to render it to me, and my possession of it creates a new obligation on me to God. Thus, all so-called human rights are divine appointments for our benefit, creating special duties on all sides, which all the parties concerned owe directly to God. The universe is an absolute monarchy in which absolute moral perfection, interpreted by infinite wisdom and executed by infinite power, sits upon the throne. In this realm there are no rights but universal honour and blessedness secured by the mutual discharge of all duties, all which spring ultimately from the will of God, and hence are all duties owed to him. The King of the kingdom is the incarnate God, who has redeemed us by his blood, as well as created us by his power. The only ultimate right is his right to us, and the only source of law is the moral perfection of the divine nature expressed in his will. All service is worship; all righteousness is service to him rendered out of love and gratitude for his redemption. The obligation which descends upon us from his absolute right and sovereign will is loyally accepted by us, and rendered back in our loving service as the spontaneous tribute of our hearts. "To the only wise God, our Saviour, be glory and majesty, dominion and power, now and for ever."

IV. This divine law is made known to the subjects of the kingdom through many different channels. All these mutually supplement and corroborate the testimony of one another. The fundamental fact upon which all others of this order depend is that man in his moral nature, as in his intellectual, was created in "the likeness of God." Our nature is essentially finite and contingent, and our knowledge imperfect and variable; whereas God's knowledge is infinite, and his nature essentially perfect and absolute. Nevertheless, the immanent, spontaneous moral law of our intrinsic nature corresponds, as an imperfect reflection, to the transcendent moral perfection of God's nature, and answers obediently to every indication of his will. Sin has perverted and deteriorated this law, but the voice of God can always arouse it to intense action; and the regenerating and sanctifying power of the Holy Ghost restores it to its original purity and vigour; and as our whole nature is developed into perfect manhood, into the measure of the stature of the fulness of Christ, "the moral law within us" will be more and more assimilated to the divine standard. The light of nature, as reflected even in the outward physical and lower animal world, and pre-eminently as witnessed in the providential course of human history, testifies to the same eternal principles of righteousness. "For the invisible things of him from the creation of the world are clearly seen, being understood by the things that are made, even his eternal power and Godhead." For even the Gentiles, who are without the supernaturally revealed law, and "do by nature the things contained in the law, these, having not the law, are a law unto themselves: which show the work of the law written in their hearts, their conscience also bearing witness, and their thoughts the meanwhile accusing or else excusing one another."

But such has been the deteriorating influence of sin that "the law written on the heart" and "the light of nature," although these remain, no longer suffice as the organ of signifying God's will to man. A supernatural revelation has been necessary to reveal the law of duty, as well as to reveal the method of salvation through redemption. For this purpose God has at sundry times and in divers manners spoken unto the fathers by the prophets, and afterward by his Son, whom he hath appointed heir of all things; "who being the brightness of his glory, and the express image of his person, and upholding all things by the word of his power, when he had by himself purged our sins, sat down at the right hand of the Majesty on high."

The entire mass of this prophetical testimony, and, above all, this personal self-revelation of God in Christ, as represented by the pen of inspiration in the sacred Scriptures, constitute the volume of the supernaturally revealed will of God. This is the divinely authoritative and infallible rule of all duty as well as of all faith. All the principles of duty binding us are herein contained. Nothing not in principle commanded in the Bible can be held to be obligatory on any Christian, and all that is thus enjoined is obligatory upon every Christian. The will of God, as indicated in the current leadings of providence and in the dealings of his Holy Spirit with our hearts, never imposes new principles of duty, but only applies the general principles already revealed in the Bible to the changing conditions of our providentially guided lives. The Bible, the Holy Ghost dwelling in us, and providence, the two latter always read in the light of the former, constitute the Christian's complete organ of knowing the will of his Lord. A summary of this moral law, including, in general principle, all the duties which grow out of our relations to God and to our fellow-men, is presented in the Ten Commandments, engraved by the finger of God on two tablets of stone on Mount Sinai.

And all the members of the kingdom of God are under equal obligations to obey this law absolutely. There are no classes of subjects, no allowed degrees of saintship. We are all alike redeemed by one price, and under the same moral obligations and sanctions. The ordained minister is no more bound to consecrate his powers to the Lord than the most secular layman. The missionary and the martyr owe no higher measure of duty than the most self-indulgent professor. If a man does not open his conscience to every indication of the divine will, and if he is not prompt to obey, he is an alien and not a subject; and if he is found masquerading under false colours, he is in danger of being arrested as a spy.

This law, moreover, demands instant and absolute obedience, not only from all classes of Christians, but also in every sphere of human life equally. A Christian is just as much under obligation to obey God's will in the most secular of his daily businesses as he is in his closet or at the communion table. He has no right to separate his life into two realms, and acknowledge different moral codes in each respectively—to say the Bible is a good rule for Sunday, but this is a week-day question; or the Scriptures are the right rule in matters of religion, but this is a question of business or of politics. God reigns over all everywhere. His will is the supreme law in all relations and actions. His inspired Word, loyally read, will inform us of his will in every relation and act of life, secular as well as religious; and the man is a traitor who refuses to walk therein with scrupulous care. The kingdom of God includes all sides of human life, and it is a kingdom of absolute righteousness. You are either a loyal subject or a traitor. When the King comes, how will he find you doing?

V. If we are asking for the conditions of salvation alone, the law and the gospel mutually exclude each other. For what the law could not do, in that it was weak through the flesh, God has accomplished in the flesh of his own Son, whom he sent for that purpose in the likeness of sinful flesh. And yet in this work both the law and the gospel co-operate in different ways to one end. *What, then, are the uses of the moral law under the gospel dispensation?*

If man had never fallen, his obedience would have been wholly spontaneous, and his knowledge of the will of God for the most part intuitive. But after man sinned, it was necessary that God should reveal his will supernaturally by his inspired spokesmen, and vindicate it by terrible demonstrations of power and judgment. So, when Jehovah proceeded to introduce his kingdom in a visible form under the old economy through the ministry of Moses, he prefaced the institution of the ceremonial system, which is a shadow of the gospel, by a most striking re-promulgation of his moral law amidst the awful thunders and lightnings and earthquakes of Sinai. Never are the exalted holiness and inexorable justice of that law so emphasized as when the law is shown in connection with human redemption, as that which extorts expiation at such a dreadful cost as on Calvary, and as that which demands that the whole of human life must be raised to the height of such an inexorable standard of righteousness as on Sinai.

That the moral law still binds the unregenerate, and must be enforced upon them rigorously, has always been clearly admitted by Christians. But there grew up a controversy in the second generation of the Lutheran theologians, chiefly resulting from misunderstanding of the terms employed relating to what was called among them the "third use of the Law." This all resulted in a very luminous answer being given to the question in the *Formula of Concord,* which has since been accepted as true and wise by the whole Church. This statement recognizes these three uses of the law under the gospel dispensation :—

1st. Its primary use by its commands and its terrible penalties is to restrain wicked men, and thus make human society possible in this state of probation.

2nd. Its second use is to convince men of sin by revealing to their eyes the awful whiteness of the divine holiness. In this light they see· their own moral vileness and the true measure of their guilt. This is the instrument the Holy Spirit uses in bringing us to genuine repentance, and to the humble, sincere embracing of Christ as our Saviour. It is thus that the moral law, even more efficiently than the ceremonial law, becomes our "schoolmaster (tutor or disciplinarian) to bring us to Christ."

3rd. The third use of the law, which is as essential as either of the others, is that it should ever continue in this life to the regenerated and progressively sanctified Christian the transcendent measure and test of right, the standard of character, and the stimulus to effort. To live

up to this standard of excellence is the goal to which the
Christian runs, the prize for which he fights. The all-
perfect law, embodying the righteousness of God, continually reveals our shortcomings, condemns our corruptions,
evokes our repentance, and drives us to endeavour. In
the case of the Christian the law remains, although the
motives to obedience are changed. Our obedience is
spontaneous, our motive is love ; yet all the while the
law towers above, like the white glistening peaks of the
Alps, forbidding us to loiter, summoning us to the skies.
Our obedience is possible, because the Holy Ghost of Christ
has been sent to dwell in our hearts for this very end.
The obediences we render are the " fruits of the Spirit."
We are not discouraged. We press onward to the absolute
fulfilment of all righteousness ; for all things are possible
to him in whom the Spirit of Him dwells who, in our
stead and in our behalf, has " fulfilled the law in the flesh."

VI. Since the kingdom of God on earth is not confined
to the mere ecclesiastical sphere, but aims at absolute
universality, and extends its supreme reign over every
department of human life, it follows that it is the duty
of every loyal subject to endeavour to bring all human
society, social and political, as well as ecclesiastical, into
obedience to its law of righteousness. It is our duty, as
far as lies in our power, immediately to organize human
society and all its institutions and organs upon a distinctively Christian basis. Indifference or impartiality
here between the law of the kingdom and the law of the
world, or of its prince, the devil, is utter treason to the
King of Righteousness. The Bible, the great statute-book
of the kingdom, explicitly lays down principles which,
when candidly applied, will regulate the action of every
human being in all relations. There can be no compromise. The King said, with regard to all descriptions
of moral agents in all spheres of activity, " He that is not

with me is against me." If the national life in general
is organized upon non-Christian principles, the churches
which are embraced within the universal assimilating
power of that nation will not long be able to preserve
their integrity.

Population increases geometrically, and food only arith-
metically. Capital seeks aggregation in masses; labour
becomes more plentiful and cheaper. The weaker goes to
the wall, and the stronger survives. The masses crowd
into vast cities, forced by the irresistible pressure up into
garrets and under ground into cellars. Capital is massed
as never dreamed of before into hundreds of millions.
Vast corporations aggregate and perpetuate the wealth of
kingdoms through succeeding generations. Machinery
takes the place of human labour in cultivating the earth,
and in the manufacture and distribution of all commodi-
ties. The terrible struggle of competition, directed by
science and whipped into intensity by steam and electricity, is assuming proportions never conceived of before
by the wildest dreamer. The pressure of the advancing
column is overwhelming; the weakling has no possibility
of maintaining his ground. Combinations are increasing
and assuming a more threatening aspect every year. In
the old monarchical nations of Europe the ships of state
labour terribly in the storm. The experienced navigators
propose to lighten their ships and relieve their strain by
throwing overboard obnoxious institutions. They would
grant the principles of "nationalities," of "home rule," of
land distributed among the multitude of small proprietors;
they would abolish class distinctions, aristocracy, and
monarchy. And all this may relieve the stress of the
contest in Europe for a generation. But, alas! all this
has already been long done in our America, and yet the
war has not slackened. There remain no more lumbering
abuses for us to sacrifice in the forms of our institutions.

For a free republic like ours there is no salvation except in obedience to the principles of the kingdom of God.

That kingdom rests ultimately upon the Fatherhood of God, the Elder Brotherhood and the redeeming blood of Christ, and the universal brotherhood of men. Its principle is love; its law is duty. It appeals not to the right of the weak, but to the love and duty of the strong. Brothers are never all equal; but true brothers respect, sympathize with, and love one another. The interest of one is the interest of all, and the anguish or the joy of one is experienced alike by all. This human brotherhood is essential; it is eternal. The earthly conditions which separate us are accidental and transient. There is no gulf of ignorance, or poverty, or vice which should cut off or modify our expressions of tender love and sympathy. Even the very least of these humble ones Christ calls brethren. We must not keep them at arm's-length : we must not neglect their interests; we must not, in the competitions of trade, push them to the wall. We must love them, and make them know we love them, and help them in their struggles with poverty and sin.

The kingdom of God embraces all classes, but it recognizes no class distinctions. We know neither capitalists nor labourers, neither rich nor poor, as such, but only men as men, men as brothers in Christ Jesus. If the rich operator, under the pressure of competition, obeying the so-called " laws of trade," pays starvation wages, we warn him, not as a rich man, but as a brother, that he is sinning against the law of the kingdom. Our brothers should, in spite of all the laws and competitions of trade, be enabled to live as becomes our brethren while they do our work. Charity degrades the lazy receiver. So the withholding a full share in the profit of the common business degrades the man hastening to get rich. If the poor brother joins the association to fight capital, we warn him, not as a poor man, but as a brother, of the duty which he owes to his employer, and of their mutual responsibilities in the common enterprise. If capitalists combine to fight labour, labourers will combine to fight capital ; and one is as right as the other, and, whatever may be hoped for from a mutual recognition of their rights, more is imperatively necessary. But if all will open their hearts to the love of Christ, and submit their wills absolutely to the reign of righteousness, and devote themselves to the performance of duty instead of the vindication of rights, then the strong will bear the burden of the weak, and we will all together enjoy a common prosperity, in which the sympathy of all multiplies the happiness of each. It is said that socialism is opposed to religion and the inviolable sacredness of the family tie. If so, then religion and the holiness of the marriage bond are the great weapons with which to fight socialism. Carry the cross and the love of Christ into every home. Practically recognize the brotherhood in Christ of every man. Prohibit divorce, hold sacred the marriage tie. Consecrate your personal service and all your wealth to the Master's cause. And the dark clouds of threatened anarchy will melt away into the clear sky. It is too late to go back. In this free republic repression of the monster of social chaos by sheer force is impossible. In the grant of universal suffrage we have burned our ships behind us. There lie before us now only the two alternatives—either a war between the forces, which will shatter the social fabric and end in anarchy, or the supremacy of the reign of the kingdom of God.

VII. And to us and to our fellow-countrymen of this generation God has committed this tremendous trust of forwarding or of retarding by centuries the coming of the kingdom of heaven in all the world. He has placed us in the centre of the field, and at the crisis of the battle on which the fate of the kingdom for ages turns.

When human society was reconstructed after the destruction by the Flood, the laws of differentiation and dispersion prevailed for millenniums. At the Tower of Babel the languages were confused and multiplied, and the children of men driven in all directions over the face of the earth. The different divisions were isolated from one another by physical barriers, pre-eminently by the Souliman Mountains in Asia and the great Desert of Sahara in Africa. Thus, after the lapse of ages, through the influence of climate and other providential conditions, different permanent varieties of the human family were generated, which may be grouped under three great types—the Mongolian of Eastern Asia and Oceania; the African; and the Caucasian of Western Asia and Europe. The Caucasian race, itself divided by mountain-chains and seas, and distributed on peninsulas, generated innumerable races and national varieties, as the Celt, the Teuton, the Sclav, the Russian, the French, the Anglo-Saxon. Under the Old Dispensation every epoch-making movement was divisive. The children of Eber were chosen, and the rest of mankind rejected. Out of the Hebrews were selected the Israelites, and out of the Israelites the Jews.

But when Christ assumed the reins of his kingdom at the right hand of the Majesty on high, the tendency was instantly reversed. His commission was, " Go, disciple all nations, baptizing them, teaching them ; and, lo, I am with you to the end of the ages." The banner of the kingdom was set up in Jerusalem and carried throughout the Roman empire, then throughout Europe, thence throughout the world. Always the standards of the kingdom have followed the course of empire westward. But beyond the shores of our Pacific there is no more west. There the Occident and the Orient stand face to face. The whole continent is ours, and it stands with all its mountain-chains running north and south, its immense plains, including all zones from the tropics to the poles, open to the free access of all nations and races, facing the western migration of all the inhabitants of Europe and Africa on our eastern side, and the eastern migration of the multitudinous Mongolians on our western side. Celts, Teutons, Sclavs, Russians, Germans, Frenchmen, Anglo-Saxons, are all incorporated in our population. Africans, Mongolians, Caucasians— Africa, Asia, Europe, all pour their tides of superfluous population into our wide areas. Here the kingdom is to be consummated in the reunion of all the varieties of the long-rent family of man. Here, where the multitudinous hosts rally, is the very eye of the battle-field. To-day is the day of fate, the crisis of the world's history.

At the beginning God sifted the foremost nations of Christendom and sowed our soil with the finest of the wheat. The Puritans, Huguenots, Dutch, Scotch-Irish, Episcopalians, German Reformed of the old Palatine stock, and the best of the Roman Catholics, laid the foundations of our empire. During the first ages religion controlled the development of the State. It was established at first in nearly all the colonies in some definite form of church government. It was recognized in the colonial charters and in the constitutions of the first States. For nearly two hundred years every college and almost every academy was founded and administered by Calvinists.

During the first two centuries our growth was slow, the elements brought in by immigration were homogeneous, and the process of assimilation to the original type was rapid and complete. In the first one hundred and sixty years, from the colonization of Plymouth Bay to the Revolutionary War, the population only grew to be three millions. It required nearly fifty years more to raise it to ten millions; while in the last fifty years it has increased thirty-seven millions, and at present it advances at the rate of considerably more than a million a year. It is estimated that during the fifty years preceding 1847 the number of immigrants did not amount to one million, while in the forty years since that time more than ten millions have been received. In the single year 1882 nearly eight hundred thousand were received. At present, Dr. Strong, in his wonderful book entitled *Our Country*, estimates the foreign population, consisting of the foreign born and of their children, at fifteen millions. He calculates that at the present rates of progression the foreign population will in 1900 amount to not far from forty millions. During the first one hundred and sixty years only thirteen colonies were organized. These multiplied to sixteen in 1800, to twenty-six in 1840, and to thirty-eight in 1880. Others of immense size are demanding recognition, and many of the new States are much larger than all the New England States together. There is no question that the moral and spiritual destiny of the world depends upon the moral and religious character ultimately assumed by the population of the United States. There is no more room to question the obvious fact that the moral and religious character of the populations filling the States and Territories of the great West, which must soon control the whole nation, is rapidly forming now, and must take its permanent stamp for ages within the next thirty or forty years.

Men of this generation, from the pyramid top of opportunity on which God has set us we look down on forty centuries! We stretch our hand into the future with power to mould the destinies of unborn millions. We of this generation occupy the Gibraltar of the ages which commands the world's future.

> "We are living, we are dwelling,
>   In a grand and awful time,
>   In an age on ages telling—
>   To be living is sublime!"

XV.

SANCTIFICATION AND GOOD WORKS.—
HIGHER LIFE.

IT is a great blessing to be able to recognize the fact
that all the great historical branches of the Christian
Church are very much united in their faith as to the
essentials of the gospel. As to who Christ was, as to what
Christ did, as to his Person and as to his offices, as to his
supreme Lordship over the whole Church and over the
whole universe as mediatorial King, Catholics and Protestants of every name agree. The differences chiefly
relate to the application of Christ's redemption, to the
method of its application, and to the order in which the
great benefits of salvation are communicated to us and
realized in the experience and life of the believer.

In the first place, I would say that rationalists generally
—and by this term I include all of a rationalizing tendency,
all who would be comprehended generally in theological
language as of a Pelagianizing or semi-Pelagianizing tendency—maintain the principle that God's favour depends
directly and immediately upon man's moral character : that
as long as man is good God is favourable to him ; that as
soon as man sins God comes into opposition to him ; and
that the only condition required for restoration to the
divine favour is genuine repentance and reformation.

The principle universally recognized by this class of

thinkers is that becoming good is the necessary pre-requisite of being received again into favour with God.

Romanists in general, of course, are free from this Pelagianizing and rationalistic spirit. The tendency of Romanism is to make everything supernatural. The tendency of rationalism is to make everything natural.

The Romanists' doctrine, in the first place, differs from Pelagianizing and rationalistic notions by maintaining that salvation wrought by Jesus Christ our Lord is applied only by a supernatural operation of the Holy Ghost working through certain sacraments which he has appointed as means and instrumentalities. Their doctrine is, that without the sacrament there is no grace, and that all grace can be obtained through the sacrament without the knowledge of the truth, and very much without the co-operation of the subject.

The Society of Friends, as you know, go to the extreme, as we think it, of holding that grace may be adequately experienced without the use of this class of appointed means.

The position taken by the great historical Churches since the Reformation is one intermediate between these two extremes.

We believe thoroughly that the grace may be given through the sovereign pleasure of God, and by an exercise of divine power experienced without the sacrament; but we believe the sacraments are also divine institutions of his appointment, and that they are therefore universally obligatory and necessary because of the obligation of precept, and that beyond this they are in their adaptation to our constitution and our condition very admirably fitted to be efficient means of grace when intelligently received in connection with the truth and accompanied with the gracious power of the Holy Ghost.

On the other side, the Romanist agrees in certain respects with the rationalist. This comes out in the historical fact that they confound the ideas which we emphasize by the words justification and sanctification.

The Romanist word *justificatio*, which has come down in the literature of the Roman Catholic Church, combines in its meaning all these ideas—to wit, the forgiveness of sins, the establishment of a state of favour, the removal of indwelling sin, and the communication of indwelling grace; that is, all that is embraced in our terms justification, regeneration, and sanctification. In the nomenclature of the Roman Catholic Church all these are embraced under one word, justification; and this opinion coincides with that which I have stated to be the common opinion of rationalists in general, though they differ from rationalists so much on the other side in regard to the position that the making of a man good must precede as a condition his reception into divine favour.

There are two principles, then, in which the Roman Catholic doctrine as to the application of redemption stands in direct contrast and opposition to what we call the doctrine of the Reformers—what we now call the evangelical doctrine.

The Romanist holds that every individual must be first united to the Church, and through the Church to Christ. The evangelical believer holds that every individual must be spiritually united to Christ, and through union with Christ united to the Church. The Romanist holds that through the grace of God we are to be made good, and then, being made good, we are to seek divine favour. Whereas the Protestant evangelical position is, that we must first be received into the divine favour, and in consequence of that reception be made good.

The Roman doctrine of justification is that its *final* cause is the glory of God; its *efficient* cause is the powerful operation of the Holy Spirit; its *formal* cause, that in which it consists, the remission of sins and infusion of grace; its *meritorious* cause, the passion, death, and merits of our Lord Jesus Christ ; and that its *instrumental* cause is baptism.

The sacrament acts as an *opus operatum*—that is, by the simple grace inherent in the sacramental act itself. In every case in which the subject does not consciously and intelligently oppose an obstacle to the grace-effecting power of the sacrament, all sin is removed and saving grace is infused. Only *concupiscence* remains, which they deny to be true sin properly so called, and regard only as the ashes or cinders, the result of past sin and the cause of future sin. But in every instance, and under all ordinary conditions, they admit that men do sin after baptism ; and then they provide for them what they call their second justification, which is accomplished always through the instrumentality of the sacrament of penance.

If any of you want intelligently to form an opinion in regard to the Roman Catholic theology, you must remember the very first necessity is to recognize the fact that words are used in a different sense in the two systems. You would do them great injustice and bring to yourself great confusion if you should take, for instance, *justification* and give the Protestant definition of it, and then the Roman Catholic definition of it, and put those in opposition one to the other.

The analogue of our doctrine of justification is the Roman Catholic doctrine of penance. Romanists hold that when a man has sinned after baptism, the condition of his being forgiven is that he shall experience and perform repentance.

Now, repentance, as an experience, may be defined as a virtue. That is, it is just what we call repentance, a grace wrought by the power of the Holy Spirit. But penance as a sacrament consists of three parts : it is confession made to the party having jurisdiction ; it is an undergoing of satisfaction as defined and appointed by him ; it is then, finally, receiving absolution. Romanists hold that upon a perfect confession and repentance, and upon due and adequate and legally appointed satisfaction, the absolution, which, as pronounced, is not declarative simply, but is efficient, really removes liability to the punishment of sin. They hold that God awards to all human sins two distinct penalties, one eternal and one temporal. Their doctrine of the eternal penalty of sin is that it has already been suffered and paid by Jesus Christ our Lord, and therefore removed absolutely and for ever from all these members ; but the temporal penalty is retained, which must be endured proportionately by each sinner for himself. And thus God is represented as keeping a debit-and-credit account with all Christians, wherein their sins in their various degrees of turpitude shall be debit, and wherein their acts of benevolence of various degrees, either in this life or in purgatory, represent the credit, and a balance is struck between these ; and in every case it must be finally adjusted on the side of credit to the individual before the final day of judgment.

We come now to the Protestant or evangelical position. The first principle that we hold is that all spiritual life in the creature is conditioned upon his intimate relation to and fellowship with God. If God is angry with us, we are cut off from him, and spiritual life is impossible. If spiritual life is to be restored, it must be upon the condition that God shall be first reconciled to us, and then we shall be restored to his love.

The doctrine of the evangelical Church is that a man must first become reconciled to God, and be brought back into the sphere of divine favour, before he can receive the Holy Spirit and be brought into union with God and made spiritually good ; that is, the favour of God is the essential precondition of grace and holiness.

Now, this is expressed by saying that justification must

precede regeneration, and that regeneration must precede sanctification. All these graces are defined with wonderful precision and fulness in our Catechism, which is familiar to you all. Justification is there declared to be an act of God, accomplished by one single divine volition, completed by one single act in each instance. It is declared also to be an act—a forensic act; that is, an act of a Judge, not an act of God as Sovereign. It is not performed in the exercise of prerogative or of right as a Sovereign, but in the exercise of his infinite wisdom and justice in judging of objective facts. It is an act of God pronouncing that with respect to this person the law has no penal demands—that all its demands in the covenant of salvation have been satisfied. And this act of God proceeds upon his previous act of accrediting to the believer, as the ground of his acceptance, the righteousness —that is, all the result of the penal suffering and all the merit of the vicarious obedience—wrought out by our Lord Jesus Christ.

It consequently changes the relation of the justified person to the law, not only with regard to the past, not only with regard to the present, but with regard to the whole future. So that obedience to the law is no longer the condition of our acceptance. We are received into the favour of God for ever, and on the condition of righteousness which has already been achieved, and which has already been made ours, not simply in the purposes and covenants, but in the actual act of God in putting it to our account and making it actually ours.

Now, regeneration follows immediately upon this. It is also an act of God, wherein he exercises his mighty power in one single volition; but it is not the act of God as Judge. It is an act of divine creative power, analogous to that which he put forth when he created man originally, when he said, " Let there be light, and there was light," or when our Lord Jesus Christ called Lazarus out of the grave. It is an act in which he communicates to us in the centre of our soul a new spiritual life, which, acting from within, involves the whole nature and communicates a new principle of activity and a new mode of action to all the faculties in all their functions and in all their relations.

Sanctification necessarily begins with, and indefinitely continues as a consequent of, regeneration. It is not an *act* but a *work* of God's grace, wherein he sustains and develops, perfects and continues, the work which he has commenced. He himself teaches us the relation of these graces, one to the other, by metaphors and analogies between the natural and the spiritual life. Regeneration is begetting, or, on the other hand, it is the new birth, and therein we are born babes in Christ. Sanctification is a growth under the sustaining and supporting influences of the Holy Spirit dwelling within us. It proceeds in a two-fold process—in the mortification of the old man, and in the vivification of the new man. All that remains of the old corruption is subdued, and the principle of life which has been implanted in us is gradually developed in us in every faculty and in every function. It involves the intellect, because sin is blindness. The new birth involves spiritual relations, and the process of sanctification is a process of illumination, whereby we come more and more to understand the revelations of God as they illuminate both hemispheres—both the earthly and the spiritual horizon.

Hence it involves the affections. These new affections go forth to new objects; and gradually these affections, in their entirety, and in all their exercise, and in all their functions, are made pure and spiritual. It involves also the voluntary faculties, the desires, the affections, all the faculties of connation which go out to their object and issue in volition, in choice, and purpose. A man is thus enabled to choose the highest end and to resist the evil, so that he gradually becomes, not only more illuminated with it, but more and more in love with it in his affections, and he becomes stronger and stronger in the habitual understanding, detection, and rejection of all evil, and in the choice and in the achievement of all good.

Now, every Christian who really has experienced the grace of Christ must, unless very greatly prejudiced, recognize the fact that this work of sanctification is the *end* and the *crown* of the whole process of salvation. We insist upon and put forward distinctly the great doctrine of justification as a means to an end. It is absolutely necessary as the condition of that faith which is the necessary source of regeneration and sanctification; and every person who is a Christian must recognize the fact that not only will it issue in sanctification, but it must begin in sanctification. This element must be recognized as characteristic of the Christian experience from the first to the last. And any man who thinks that he is a Christian, and that he has accepted Christ for justification when he did not at the same time accept Christ for sanctification, is miserably deluded in that very experience. He is in danger of falling under that judgment of which Paul admonishes when he speaks of the wrath of God coming down from heaven upon all ungodliness and unrighteousness of men, and with special reference to those who " hold the truth in unrighteousness."

Now, this process, however, from its very nature, must be a gradual process. Of course, I would not deny that just as God might take a pebble and make a man out of it, so he might take the greatest sinner in the world and, by the exercise of his mighty power, make him in an instant the greatest saint in the world. But I do say, from all we do know of God, either in the works of creation or in the works of providence, or in the Bible that any such conception is utterly incongruous and outside of all analogy and all probability. All God's working, so far as we know anything about it, is historico-genetic. He works by means. He works according to the lines and sequences of natural law.

Now, that justification should be an *act*, that it should be begun and accomplished by one divine volition, is very natural, because it is unavoidable. There can be no degree between condemnation as a sinner and acceptance as a justified man through the righteousness of Christ. If I stand before God in my own right, I am utterly condemned. If I stand represented in the vicarious righteousness of Jesus Christ, then in one instant I stand divinely justified, and far beyond what I would have been if Adam had kept his first estate and sin had never invaded this world.

If Adam had not fallen, we would have been justified by Adamic righteousness. Angels and archangels now stand before God justified by angelic righteousness. But Jehovah *Tsidkenu*—Jehovah is our righteousness. It is not what you or I have done or will do, it is not our services in the past or promises for the future, but it is what the eternal Son of God, in the likeness of sinful flesh, did suffer and accomplish in the flesh, which is the ground of our justification and of our acceptance before God. And therefore it is that, the instant the sinner believes and trusts in the pardoning Lord, *his* righteousness becomes his, and it is by one instant act which cannot be divided, in a moment which cannot be analyzed into degrees, that the condemned sinner becomes a justified saint.

The same must be true, from its very nature, of regeneration. There must have been an absolute commencement somewhere when God was moved to come forth out of the solitude and isolation of his infinitude to lay the foundations of the heavens and the earth. There must have been an absolute beginning ; there must have been one instant when the energy of God went forth from without and acted in the objective world, and brought something into existence that was not there before. So regeneration must be an instant act. There must be a time, an instant, when the soul is dead. There must be another instant when the soul is living. You know how it is expressed in the divine Word. It is creation—that is, an instant act. It is a begetting—that is, an instant act. It is a new birth ; it is a quickening of the dead—that is, an instantaneous act. But when this new life is implanted in us, is it not evident to all men that unless God shall work, nothing of this kind can take place ? This, then, is a simple act of his power, and from the very nature of the case must be instantaneous. But after it is implanted in us, there must be a gradual process by which that grace that is implanted in us, exhibiting itself as an energy in every one of the faculties, takes possession of the whole being, shows its gradual and repeated action in all the habits of the life, and at last comes forth in its spontaneity as a complete and finished result.

The same is clear from the precepts of God wherein he commands us to work out our own salvation with fear and trembling ; in which he commands us to avail ourselves of all the means of grace which he has especially appointed as the great means of sanctification.

The truth of God acts upon us, of course, in every way according to the nature of the truth which acts. The commands act upon us in one way, the threatenings act upon us in another way, and the promises act upon us in another way, and the glimpses of divine glory act upon us in another way. Retrospects of the past and the prospects of the future all act upon the regenerated Christian and stimulate his activity in various ways. And so it is with the providences of God. The Lord leads us, you know, by devious ways through our pilgrimage, and he appoints for us all our changes.

Now, under all these conditions, God is carrying on the process of sanctification. We are gradually growing up and adding grace to grace, going from one degree of knowledge to another, from the acquisition of one increment of strength to another, from the development of one faculty to another, just as a child grows, just as Jesus grew himself in wisdom and stature. First we are babes in Christ, and come at last to the measure of the stature of perfect manhood in Christ.

But every one can see that a Christian, while he recognizes that this work must be a growth, recognizes that we cannot compromise with any evil. It is perfectly evident that the standard of sanctification in the Christian life, which is at once placed before him when he first receives Christ, is the standard of infinite and of absolute perfection. There can be, from the very nature of the case, no compromise here, and it must be recognized as such from the first.

This results from the nature of moral principle and moral obligation. It is very plain that all that is moral is obligatory. That is what the word means. If a thing is right, it ought to be ; and if it is right in its entirety, then it ought to be in its entirety.

St. Augustine said fourteen hundred years ago—and the language has never been improved—"Every lesser good has an essential element of sin." Now, for instance, suppose that you love God ; suppose that there is nothing in your heart but love to God. It does not follow that you do not sin. You say, "I love God, and there is nothing in my heart but love to God. Is not love right ?" Yes, if you love God with all your heart, with all your mind, and with all your strength, and with all your manhood. But if there be in this love any defect—if it come short in quality, if it come short in quantity—then it partakes of the nature of sin ; for every lesser good, as well as every degree of good short of perfection, is of the essential nature of sin itself. Therefore, if any Christian should say, " Why, we cannot be perfect; that is impossible. Nobody is perfect. I will not succeed if I try, and therefore I will sit down with a qualified obedience; I will mix water with my milk; I will mix half-heartedness with my endeavour; I will compromise the standard, because the perfect standard is absolutely impossible,"—why, that man is selling his soul to the devil in doing this; he is making a compact with sin in the very nature of it. Any permitted sin, any sitting down willingly to imperfectness, is of the nature of sin, and unallowable.

The Perfectionists, all of them, confound justification and sanctification miserably, just as Roman Catholics do, only they do it in an informal, illogical way; but they do it.

They hold that the Lord Jesus Christ, or that God, for the sake of the Lord Jesus Christ, has graciously lowered the demands of the law. They admit that we cannot fulfil the Adamic law under which God created man; but they say that we can fulfil the gospel law, that we can render a perfect love, and the evangelical standard is lowered to conform to our standard. This is an act of substitution of a new thing. That is a miserable lowering of the standard. It is putting a new and lower standard in the place of the old and higher standard.

Now, the truth is that this law has never been lowered, the principle of the law by which moral character is to be measured having its norm in the absolutely perfect moral constitution of God himself. God's law is an utterance, it is an expression of God himself in the forms of human thought and language; it reveals to man the infinitely perfect moral nature of God himself. And when God's law is altered, and so altered and modified that God is compromised, that moral character has been modified, and has been compromised in the very throne of the universe itself. It is true that the law has been satisfied for us for our justification, that the Lord Jesus Christ has been substituted in our place. But the law was not lowered—it was magnified, it was made honourable; so that what a man could not do, in that he was weak through the flesh, God has done by giving his Son in the flesh. But it was by perfect obedience and by the vicarious sufferings of Jesus Christ that this debt was paid, and fully paid by the terms of the law. But this refers to the law as a covenant of salvation; it does not refer to the law as a moral standard of character. St. Paul said, in his Epistle to the Romans (vi. 14), "Sin shall not have dominion over you: because you are not under the law, but under grace." He is referring to justification; he is not referring to sanctification. He does not say that the Lord Jesus Christ satisfied the law in your behalf, and that therefore the law has no more demands upon you; but he says the Lord Jesus Christ satisfied the law as a covenant in your behalf. But the law, as a standard of character, remains the same infinite, perfect law, having its ground and norm in the infinite and perfect, in the absolutely unchangeable, nature of God himself.

The same thing is proved by the fact that the Bible tells us that God himself is the standard. How can anybody claim to be perfect when God is the standard, or claim that the law is to be lowered? We are to be holy as our Father in heaven is holy. We are told to lay aside every weight, and the sin that doth most easily beset us, and run with patience the race that is set before us, looking unto Jesus as our standard and our aim and glory. Then, as Christ's perfection was an absolute perfection, why of course the perfection of the Christian can be nothing less than absolute perfection. As Christians, therefore, we cannot compromise with sin. No man can serve God and mammon. No service is admitted from the first, not even in the recruits, from those who come with a divided heart. We are to leave the things which are behind, and to reach forward always to the things which are before, in order that we may apprehend and realize that whereunto we have been apprehended in the purposes and in the design of Christ.

Especially is it our privilege and duty to go forward to the attainment of perfect assurance, making our calling and election sure.

There are two different positions occupied in Christendom on this subject of faith and assurance. Some have held that assurance is of the essence of faith, and that a man, if he is a Christian at all, will know that he is a Christian. This was a form of thinking very prevalent at the time of the Reformation. It grew out of the fact that they were more earnest, spontaneous men than they were reflective Christian divines. It is a matter of fact that at that period of Church history there were men in whom this grace of assurance of salvation was very prominent. They did have it; and God gave it to them, because he gave them an herculean work to do which demanded heroes for its performance.

In direct opposition to this the Romanists take the position that assurance of personal salvation is impossible, and they take it on this ground : assurance means absolute certitude, grounded upon divine revelation. The Romanists point out the fact that there is no text in the Bible where it is said that John Smith is a Christian ; the fact that any man is a Christian is not a matter of divine revelation.

Now, our Confession of Faith takes the middle ground, and I think the right ground, that assurance is not of the essence of faith. And this is very plain, because the Bible makes the distinction between the assurance of faith and the assurance of hope. Assurance of faith is strong, full faith; assurance of hope is an inference from that. Faith terminates on the ground of assurance; hope terminates upon the object desired. Faith is the foundation of hope, but faith and hope are not the same thing; they do not go out in parallel lines with one another and take hold of the same object. Assurance of faith is assured faith; but assurance of hope is the conviction that we are Christians, and that we are objects of divine love and heirs of divine glory. It can be put, like any other point of reasoning, in the form of a syllogism. It is a matter of absolute revelation that he that believes in Christ is saved. This is the major proposition of the syllogism. The minor proposition is, "I believe." That has no need of revelation; it belongs to the inner consciousness. Am I not just as sure that I believe as I am sure that my pulses beat? You put the minor under the major proposition, and the infallible conclusion is, "Therefore I am saved."

Our Confession says that this infallible assurance springs up in the heart in consequence of three elements meeting together. The first is, strong faith in the Word of God; second, the consciousness of the possession of those graces to which the promises are annexed. It is not simply faith. The Bible is full of promises, and they are addressed, not to persons named, but to characters—whosoever loveth, whosoever believeth, whosoever obeyeth, whosoever trusteth, whosoever hopeth. Well, if I hope and trust and obey and love, the consciousness of possessing these graces gives me the assurance of the promises which God has annexed to the graces. Then, in the third place, there is that mysterious and royal gift, the witness together with our spirit of the Holy Spirit.

Like all similar truths, this may be abused fanatically and claimed ignorantly by very stupid persons to whom it does not apply. But it is in the Word of God; it does belong to some person, and there must be a way of finding out and testing this. It is the witnessing together of our spirit with the Spirit of God. You cannot confound these two personalities: my spirit and Jehovah's Spirit—we are two. But if the Spirit of God as a Person comes to my spirit as a person, and bears witness together with my spirit that I am a child of God, I have the utmost certitude. Of course we must guard against misconception; there is no point in which it is more necessary for us to apply critical tests. There is no state of mind which is more to be desired, which more immediately tends to sanctification, which develops more power, and is in a wider sense the precondition of great usefulness, than that which is characterized by the words assurance of hope, and which results from the witnessing with our spirit of the Spirit of God. *Per contra*, there is no state of mind so dangerous and profane, and which leads more to sin, than that wicked, conceited assumption which we meet sometimes in unholy and godless persons, when they claim to know that they are the favourites of Heaven, because they have conceived they had the witness of the Spirit. We are all liable to this abuse; we are moved to it by the natural operation of self-love. We all want to be " the sons of God, and joint-heirs with Jesus Christ." We all want to have the question settled.

Then, again, it is not only the tendency of an innocent self-love, but also of pride; and it may be the seduction of Satan, because when he wants to take a person into his grasp entirely, what better thing can he do than to render him morally callous and fill him with presumptuous self-assurance ?

How are you and I to know? I think the first essential mark of the difference between true and false assurance is to be found in the fact that the true works humility. There is nothing in the world that works such satanic, profound, God-defiant pride as false assurance; nothing works such utter humility, or brings to such utter self-emptiness, as the child-like spirit of true assurance. Surely this can be known. If a person is self-confident, there is self-assurance; if there is any evidence of pride in connection with his claim, it is a most deadly mark—it is the plague-spot which marks death and corruption. But if there is utter humility, you have the sign of the true spirit.

This will manifest itself in connection with another mark. If one is really united to Christ in a union so established that Christ is indeed in possession of the soul, the whole consciousness will be taken up with what I would call Christ-consciousness, and there will be no self-consciousness. Little children are very prompt to show their character. There is a great difference in them. Bring a child into the room. She comes thinking about nothing in particular, looking at her mother, then looking at the guests or anything that objectively strikes her, not thinking of herself. That is pure, sweet, and lovely. She grows older, and she comes to think of herself and what people think of her, and her manner has lost its unconsciousness. A great deal of what you call bashfulness is rottenness at the heart; it is self-consciousness. Nothing in the world so tends to defile the imagination, to pervert the affections, and to corrupt the morals, as self-consciousness. You know it is connected with every diseased and morbid action of the body.

A young woman told me that she wanted the witness of the Spirit, and she talked about it everlastingly; she wanted to tell her own experience and feelings always. I told her she must forget herself, not think of her own feelings. The man who is talking about his love unceasingly has no love; the man who is talking about his faith unceasingly has no faith: the two things cannot go together. When you love, what are you thinking about? Are you not thinking about the object of your love? And when you believe, what are you thinking about? Why, the object that you believe. Suppose you ask yourself, "Am I believing?" Why, of course you are not believing when you are thinking of believing. No human being believes except when he thinks about Christ. Am I loving? Of course I am not loving when I am thinking about loving. No human being loves except when he is thinking about Christ as the object of his love.

In Virginia I once saw one human being in whom there was the perfect work of grace, as far as I could see as her pastor, and I was intimate with her six years. Even on earth she was one of those who had made their garments white in the blood of the Lamb, and she seemed always to walk upon the verge of heaven. I never heard her speak of any one particular of her character or of her own graces. I have come out of the pulpit when the congregation had gone, and have found her upon her knees in her pew, absolutely unconscious of all external objects, so far was she absorbed in worship. When I roused her from her trance, she cried instantly, "Is He not holy? is He not glorious? is He not beautiful? is He not infinite?" She did not speak of her own love or of her feelings.

A great deal of Perfectionism is rotten to the core. All self-consciousness is of the very essence and nature of sin. Then, again, true confidence leads necessarily to strong desires for more knowledge and more holiness, for unceasing advances of grace.

I was told once, in a congregation where I preached, that I need not tell a certain young man anything about religion; he had finished it—that is, that, having finished it, he found nothing else to do. That is what the word "perfect" means. Now, when a man has finished eternal life, when he has finished learning all the revelation of

God, when he has experienced all the infinite benefits of
Christ's redemption, when he has finished all the mysterious
work of the Holy Ghost in his heart, he ought to be
annihilated.   There is no place in heaven or on earth for
such a man.   But a man who really has the love of God
in his heart is always reaching forward to the things
which are before.   The more he loves, the more he wants
to love; the more he is consecrated, the more consecration
he longs for.   He has grand ideas and grand aims, but
they lie beyond him in heaven.

I want to speak now about Antinomianism.   There
are two forms of Antinomianism, but they are the same
thing.   One has been called Neo-nomianism, and the other
Antinomianism.

Antinomianism is the doctrine that Christ has so satisfied the law for us that it is abolished; that having gone
to Christ we are washed and cleansed, and we may do as
we please, because Christ has in every sense so fulfilled the
law that it has no more dominion over us.   That is called
Antinomianism.

It has been very common for Arminians to charge upon
Calvinism the doctrine of Antinomianism.   We repudiate
it.   We say with Paul of the man who says, " Let us continue in sin that grace may abound," his damnation is
sure.

Neo-nomianism is a substitution of a new and lower law
for the infinite law of God.   The law is the absolute perfection which God has put before us, and they lower the standard when they teach a lower doctrine with regard to sin.

The other view is that God has, for Christ's sake, not
abolished the law, but he has substituted a new law, and
that in place of the law of absolute perfection things are
adjusted to the nature of man in his present state.

This is the doctrine of the Roman Catholic Church, and
the doctrine also of many pretenders to perfection; it is

the precise doctrine of the "higher life" under a different name.

Of course, there can be no controversy if you mean really higher life. We all believe in that; we all preach it. "Go on unto perfection;" "leave the things which are behind;" strive after holiness in every direction. But if you say you have attained to it, and that higher life is just what I see embodied in the lives of A, B, and C, I say that is the very opposite. It is not a higher life; it is a lower life.

It is wrong, because it substitutes a lower standard. It is wrong, because it gives you a false idea of sin, for sin means "any want of conformity" to the absolute standard of God. Every one is a sinner. John Wesley admits that; everybody admits that. If you use the word "sin" in the sense of a real, deliberate choice of evil, then perhaps some men may not be sinners in that sense.

But even Dr. George Peck, whose book is a standard with regard to the doctrine of Perfectionism among Arminians, says: "In the life of the most perfect Christian there is every day renewed occasion for self-abhorrence, for repentance, for renewed application to the blood of Christ, for application of the rekindling of the Holy Spirit." What is the use of calling that perfection? We do go on unto perfection, and we grow better and better every day; but every day we come so far short that there is renewed occasion for having recourse to the standard of perfection. We require the renewed application of the blood of Christ and the grace of the Spirit. We do not call this perfection. But you say, Why make a point of telling people they cannot be perfect? I say we do not make a point of telling people they cannot be perfect. I open the Bible and it says, Move on; "forgetting the things which are behind," go forward. When a man can show that he is doing this, he is going on to perfection. I would not preach that you cannot be perfect, but I would preach to you, Have no standard of perfection but Almighty God and Jesus Christ his Son. That is the doctrine. Perfectionism is pernicious and evil, because it is false. It is not true, and every lie does harm. A lie that touches the very quick and centre of religious experience is of the very nature of death itself.

A man recently died in London who held this doctrine. He was once my guest in America. I loved him. I was his guest in London. But I thought he knew no more of theology than a babe; yet he was trying to teach others when he ought to have been taught himself. He said that we all receive Christ twice—we receive him for our justification, and afterward we receive him for our sanctification; and he tried to illustrate it in a great many instances. He spoke of D'Aubigné, Thomas Chalmers, and Mrs. Jonathan Edwards.

Now, it is very remarkable that nearly all the most perfect saints never themselves knew their own perfection. Mrs. Edwards was all the time aspiring for perfection which was beyond her, and never thought for an instant that she was perfect. D'Aubigné never heard of the grace of justification without sanctification. And if you could have talked to Dr. Chalmers, with his great heart and glowing tongue, on such a theme as this, he would have struck it down into the dust. It is not true. You cannot take Christ for justification unless you take him for sanctification. Think of the sinner coming to Christ and saying, "I do not want to be holy;" "I do not want to be saved from sin;" "I would like to be saved in my sins;" "Do not sanctify me now, but justify me now." What would be the answer? Could he be accepted by God? You can no more separate justification from sanctification than you can separate the circulation of the blood from the inhalation of the air. Breathing and circulation are two different things, but you cannot have the one without the other; they go together, and they constitute one life. So you have justification and sanctification; they go together, and they constitute one life. If there was ever one who attempted to receive Christ with justification and not with sanctification, he missed it, thank God! He was no more justified than he was sanctified.

The whole process is the reverse of sanctification in its very essence, for the more a man grows in sanctification the more delicate is his sensibility, the more exquisite his sense of sin. A man who has been in a swoon, utterly dead to sensation, recovers his sensations gradually. As he becomes more and more conscious, he gradually perceives everything that is wrong with him. So the more a man is sanctified the more is there a change in his judgment; it becomes more discriminating, and the more humble will be his estimate of himself. Things which did not appear to be sin at first will be realized as sin afterward more and more.

Those who say, "We have already attained, and are already perfect," lower the standard: instead of sanctification, it is pollution; instead of a higher life, it is a lower life. Again, it necessarily generates increasing self-consciousness and spiritual pride; these things run together, and will go out at last in utter darkness.

You can all understand the ripening of the pear. There is a ripening which goes on in the autumn of the year which is perfect; and perfectly ripe fruit is one of the most perfect and beautiful things in nature. It is a gradual process from the blossom through all the different stages. You could not hasten it. It is growing on in the sunshine and when the dews of heaven descend upon it. The ripening is perfect; and when you take the pear from the limb, you say, "Thank God, this is perfect! It has run through all the stages, it has omitted none ; it has come to the end, it is finished." But you go sometimes and you find pears early ripe, and they have a sweet and luscious self-consciousness of it ; and they fall down flat on the earth and are soft, because there is a worm at the core. My good grandmother used to say, and I think now it is worth repeating, " I do hate the early-ripes."

XVI.

THE SACRAMENTS.

BAPTISM.

A S we have seen before, in Lecture IX., that the Church
and Kingdom of God rest upon a covenant, it is
evidently appropriate that Christ should provide visible
seals by which that covenant should be ratified and its
benefits symbolized to all who accept its terms. We have
seen also, under Lecture XIV., that the true Church is
designed by God to organize itself under his law, under
varying historical conditions, in outward visible communities : it is evident, therefore, that it is to be expected that
Christ should give to his Church certain divinely-appointed
and universally-recognized badges of membership by which
they are to be distinguished from others.

The word "sacrament" is not in the Bible, and therefore the meaning of that term, and of the other terms by
which the class comprising Baptism and the Lord's Supper
have been designated, must be determined from the general
usage of the Church.

I. They have been called "mysteries" by a very natural
association. The mysteries were the secrets of Grecian
religious rites, which could not possibly be discovered by
the uninitiated, but which were, while jealously guarded
from the outsider, gradually revealed to the initiated in

proportion to his grade of membership.   The early pastors
of the primitive Church were surrounded by heathen communities.   On the Sabbath days their congregations at
first consisted of three distinct classes—the heathen in-
quirers, the catechumens, and the communicants.   After
the sermon had been preached, with singing and prayer,
the general audience of the uninitiated heathen were dismissed with the formula, *Ite, missa est!*—" Go, it is dismissed."   Then the catechumens, or candidates for baptism,
the first degree of Christian profession, were instructed,
and afterward dismissed with the same formula, *Ite, missa
est!*   Then only the communicants of the second or highest
grade of Christian profession remained, and they together
celebrated the most sacred rite of the Lord's Supper, at
which none of the uninitiated were allowed to remain even
as witnesses.   Hence the sacraments came by analogy to
be regarded as the Christian mysteries, or innermost secrets
unveiled only to the initiated ; and hence, likewise, the
Lord's Supper itself came to be called the " Mass," from
its being introduced by two repetitions, and followed by a
third repetition, of the dismission formula, *Ite, missa est!*

These rites have more generally and permanently been
called " sacraments," which has mistakenly been taken as
the Latin equivalent of the Greek mystery.   The *sacramentum* was anything that renders sacred or binds, as
a bail or a soldier's oath.   These sacred rites seal and
publicly consummate a Christian's profession of faith and
allegiance.   They bind him to a service, like a citizen's
oath of loyalty, which was obligatory upon him antecedently in consequence of his birth.

In the same general sense these special rites have been
called, especially among Scotch Presbyterians, " sealing ordinances."   By engagement therein the professing Christian
openly signifies and seals his profession of faith and promise of service.   At the same time, by the admission of

the individual to the privilege of participating in them, the Church, through its officers, signifies and seals its recognition of the covenanting believer as an accepted member of the Church. It is for this reason that the right of admitting to or of excluding from these " sealing ordinances " is called " the power of the keys," the power of admission or of exclusion, " of binding or of loosing," of which our Lord speaks in his address to Peter (Matt. xvi. 19). And for this reason also the right of administering these " sealing ordinances," which are the keys that open or shut the doors of the visible Church, has always been rigidly confined to the ordained ministry or highest class of church-officers, thus qualified to act in this matter—not as individuals, but as representatives of the whole body of believers and the executors according to law of their corporate will.

II. It is a more important question to ask, what are the real nature and design of these sacraments in the economy of the Christian Church ?

Sacraments are symbols, symbolical actions, wherein outward physical signs represent inward invisible grace. The signs consist of the elements, and of the sacramental actions of the minister and of the recipient in relation to these elements. They are symbolical transactions, in which Christ and the benefits of his salvation are represented, sealed, and applied to believers. The grace symbolized is purchased by Christ, is conveyed and applied by the Holy Ghost, and is received by faith. That grace, therefore, as inward and invisible, belongs to the spiritual Church as such, whether organized into visible societies or not. But the sacraments, wherein this inward invisible grace is represented by outward physical signs, belong obviously to those visible societies or organized churches into which the spiritual children of God are gathered. They can have no other sphere. They are signs and seals to men in the flesh of things which relate to the spiritual world. But the outward sign has no pertinency except in relation to the condition of men in the flesh, and sustaining the relations of members of visible organized societies. Their need and use grow out of the two facts—(1) that as long as we are in the flesh the most profound impressions are made upon our souls through our bodily senses; and (2) that as long as we are associated together in these outward visible organizations we need visible, easily recognizable badges of fellowship and seals of a common loyalty.

These symbols are, in the *first* place, natural. Circumcision and the washing the body with water in baptism are obviously natural signs, significant of the need of a second birth—a new birth, which will be like life from the dead; a life distinguished from the natural life by spirituality. The sacrifice of the paschal lamb, and the sprinkling of his blood on the doorposts, and the eating of his flesh at a sacrificial feast as people in fellowship with God, and the breaking and eating of the bread and the pouring out and drinking of the wine in the Lord's Supper, are obviously natural signs, significant of our participation in all the sacrificial benefits of Christ's redemption.

In the *second* place, being selected by God as natural symbols of the spiritual graces represented, they are ordained by him to be so regarded and treated on his authority by his Church for ever. Their suggestive and edifying power is due to both of these facts—the natural likeness and the divine appointment.

The design of these sacraments is obvious from their nature and uses, and is, moreover, clearly taught in Scripture.

1st. They are effective objective exhibitions of the central truths of the Gospels. Like pictures, they impressively set forth to the eye and the imagination the same great truths which the Word of God read or preached sets forth to the ear. Their use has proved the wisdom of their appointment. The *rationale* lies in the constitution of human nature as embracing rational spirits incarnate in animal bodies.

2nd. They are badges of church-membership, and hence at the same time of our relation to Christ as our Teacher, Redeemer, and King, and of our relation to one another as beneficiaries of the same redemption, learners in the same school, brethren in the same family, subjects of the same kingdom, and heirs of the same inheritance. They discharge the same offices as do the pass-signs of the secret societies, the uniform of the army, the standards of the battle, the flag of the nation. They give definite visibility to the professing organized Church of Jesus Christ on earth, at once in the eyes of its own members and of all outsiders.

3rd. They were also designed by Christ to be the seals of his covenant with men. Every covenant implies two parties, who mutually give and receive pledges. A seal is an outward visible thing or action attached by appointment of government, which recognizes and consummates a contract, rendering the contract even more sacred by the governmental recognition. In these sacraments Christ seals his mediatorial undertaking for us, and pledges by an objective declaration, in every case audible and visible, our salvation on the condition of our really and spiritually doing what we in appearance do in receiving the sacrament. We at the same time swear a sacred oath, enacted by word and act, to put ourselves absolutely into Christ's hands, to receive his full salvation, and to be consecrated to his service.

4th. They were also ordained by Christ to be means of grace—not the only means, in the absence of which grace is not given, but real, divinely-appointed means, the use of which is obligatory and most useful to all Christians; the appointed instruments in the hands of the Holy Spirit of effecting and distributing grace to men severally as he wills. " The outward and ordinary means whereby Christ communicates to his Church the benefits of his mediation, are all his ordinances ; especially the word, sacraments, and prayer " (Larger Cat., Ques. 154). Christ uses these sacraments, not only to represent and seal, but also actually to apply, the benefits of his redemption to believers (Shorter Cat., Ques. 92). This efficiency as means of grace does not, of course, inhere in the sacramental elements or actions themselves, nor in the merit or intention of the administrator, but always in the present gracious volition of the Holy Ghost, whose instruments they are ; just as the efficiency of the axe or hammer or sword is due to the will and power of the man who wields it. The axe cuts down the tree because it is adapted to cut wood, and because it is energetically and skilfully wielded by a strong man. The sacrament acts as means of conveying grace, because its signs and actions are adapted to affect the mind and the heart and the will of men in the right way at the same time, and because the Holy Ghost, who works in us to will and to do of his good pleasure, uses it as he wills, and to effect his own purpose.

III. It is well known that the Romanists hold that there are, under the new law or covenant, seven sacraments —namely, baptism, confirmation, the Lord's Supper, penance, marriage, orders, extreme unction ; although they have always acknowledged that baptism and the Lord's Supper constitute a pre-eminently sacred class by themselves—as Thomas Aquinas calls them, *potissima sacramenta.* All these, with the exception of penance and extreme unction, are admitted by Protestants to be important divine ordinances. The only question between Protestants and Catholics at this point relates to the proper extension of the word "sacrament," which is not found in the Bible.

The true way of putting the question on the Protestant side is not to raise a controversy as to the meaning of a non-biblical word, but to ask, Are there any other divine ordinances of the same class, possessing the same qualities, and sustaining the same relations, as baptism and the Lord's Supper? We Protestants answer, emphatically, No!

That these special ordinances were designed to be perpetual is as plain as language and reason can make it. In the *first* place, this is antecedently probable, because the reason for their original institution still continues. In the *second* place, this continued use, in the case of each sacrament, is specifically commanded : " Go ye into all the world, discipling all nations, baptizing them," etc., and, " Lo, I am with you alway, even unto the end of this world-age " (Matt. xxviii. 19, 20 ; Mark xvi. 15) ; " Do this in remembrance of me ; " and the inspired comment of the apostle, " For as often as ye eat this bread, and drink this cup, ye do shew the Lord's death till he come " (1 Cor. xi. 26). These are, therefore, to continue until the second coming of Christ. In the *third* place, the apostles practised the use of both sacraments as long as they lived. And in the *fourth* place, the entire Christian Church, under the guidance of the Holy Ghost, has continued their observance in unbroken continuity unto the present time.

IV. BAPTISM.

All the world knows the vast volume of controversy and of controversial literature which has been generated in the Church around this immense subject. We have, on the one hand, the great body of the historical Christian churches, and on the other hand, the Protestants of Protestants, our Baptist brethren. In this point of view the advantage appears to be on our side. But this advantage is very greatly abated when we come to estimate the average quality of the two great contestant bodies in mass, and recognize the fact that these Baptist brethren stand among those occupying the very foremost rank in intelligence, learning, piety, effective usefulness, and universal and strict fidelity to the Word of God. The questions in debate relate to fundamental points. 1st. What is baptism? What, precisely, are we commanded to do when we are commanded to baptize? 2nd. What classes of persons are we to baptize? These Lectures have nothing to do with controversy. We propose, therefore, in the most friendly spirit toward all those who differ from us, to state with perfect simplicity our own belief as to what is the truth on both these subjects.

[I.] We believe that the command to baptize is precisely and only a command *to wash with water* as a symbol of spiritual regeneration and cleansing into the name of the Father, and of the Son, and of the Holy Ghost. The essential parts of the external sacrament are, consequently, (1) the formula; (2) the element; (3) the action; (4) the sense in which the symbol is interpreted.

(1.) It is essential to the validity of this ordinance that it should be administered " in the name of the Father, and of the Son, and of the Holy Ghost." This is certain—(*a*) because of the words of the great commission in Matt. xxviii. 19; (*b*) from the essential significancy of the rite. Besides being a symbol of spiritual purification, it is essentially, as the rite of initiation into the Christian Church, a covenanting ordinance, whereby the recipient recognizes and pledges his allegiance to God in that character and in those relations in which he has revealed himself to us in the plan of salvation. The formula of baptism, therefore, is a summary of the whole Scripture doctrine of the Triune Jehovah as he has chosen to reveal himself to us in all those relations which the several Persons of the Trinity graciously sustain to the believer in the scheme of redemption.

· (2.) The element, as is universally acknowledged, is water. Water is to the physical system of this earth and to the life upon its surface what the blood is in the animal organism. When water is withheld, the whole earth becomes first clouded with dust, and then parched to death, and finally becomes a barren desert. When the water is copiously restored, the face of nature is purified, and the desert is transformed into the garden of the Lord. Water as the universal bearer of life and solvent is the natural type of spiritual regeneration and sanctification. If water, therefore, is absent, there is no baptism, because the command to baptize is the command to wash with water.

(3.) The element and the action by which it is used and applied constitute what is technically called the "matter of baptism"—that is, the thing done by the person who performs the rite. This we believe to be simply a washing with water. The whole rite is a symbol of spiritual cleansing. The thing to be done, therefore, is to wash. The manner of doing it is, therefore, necessarily accidental and outside of the command. This we fully believe—

(a) Because the Greek words used to express the command $\beta\alpha\pi\tau i\zeta\omega$ and $\beta\acute{\alpha}\pi\tau\omega$, although their root-meaning is to immerse in any liquid, have come to mean generally the producing of the effect for the sake of which the liquid is applied—for example, to wash, or to tinge, or to dye—no matter in what manner the liquid is applied to the subject operated upon. The word $\nu i\pi\tau\omega$, to wash, and the word $\beta\alpha\pi\tau i\zeta\omega$, are used interchangeably in the New Testament (Matt. xv. 2 ; Mark vii. 1–15 ; Luke xi. 37–39. See also 2 Kings v. 13, 14 and Titus iii. 5).

(b) These words are unquestionably used in the New Testament in a great variety of connections in which they cannot emphasize any one mode of applying the water, as the "washing of cups, and pots, and brazen vessels, and of tables" (Mark vii. 4), and the baptizing of Moses "in the

cloud and in the sea " (1 Cor. x. 1, 2).   The " divers wash-
ings ". of the first tabernacle (Heb. ix. 10) we know to
have been effected chiefly by sprinkling and pouring
(Heb. ix. 13–21 ; Ex. xxx. 17–21).

(*c*) In all probability, the original manner of applying
the water in Christian baptism was by pouring the water
out of the hollow of the hand, or out of a shell or small
vessel, without any emphasis or special signification attached
to the manner in which the water was applied.   This we
regard as probable, because the prevailing modes of purification among the Jews were the pouring of water and
the sprinkling of blood or ashes (Lev. viii. 30 ; xiv. 7, 51 ;
Heb. ix. 13–22).   The personal ablutions of the priests
were performed at the brazen laver, from which the water
poured forth through spouts or cocks (1 Kings vii. 38, 39 ;
2 Chron. iv. 6).   Pouring water out of a vessel upon the
hands, feet, or head of the person has been the method of
applying water for purposes of purification from the earliest
age to the present time in all the Oriental world from the
Ganges to the Bosphorus.   The earliest rude remains of
Christian art in the Catacombs represent John as baptizing
on the side of a stream of water by affusion.

(*d*) The outstanding essential fact, about which there
can be no controversy, is that baptism with water is a
symbol of baptism by the Holy Ghost.   The one signifies
what the other effects—that is, the cleansing the soul from
the guilt and pollution of sin (John iii. 5 ; Titus iii. 5 ; Acts
ii. 38 ; xxii. 16 ; 1 Cor. vi. 11 ; Eph. v. 26).   It is the
washing of the body corresponding to the " washing of regeneration and renewing of the Holy Ghost."   John and
the apostles baptized, and the modern minister baptizes,
with water ; but Christ baptizes us with the Holy Ghost
(Luke iii. 16 ; Acts i. 5 ; xi. 16 ; xxii. 16 ; 1 Cor. xii. 13).
The one is the shadow, the other is the substance.

(*e*) Everywhere in the New Testament the connection in

which the baptism with water is spoken of indicates the
fact that it symbolizes the baptism of the Holy Ghost, and
implies spiritual purification. In John iii. 22–30 the
question debated between some of John's disciples and the
Jews as to baptism is expressly defined to be a question
concerning purification. Men were exhorted to be baptized
in order to wash away their sins. It is declared that men
must be born of water and of the Spirit, and that baptism
as well as faith is an essential condition of salvation. The
effect of baptism is declared to be purification (2 Kings v.
13, 14; Judith xii. 7; Luke xi. 37–39).

(*f*) The metaphorical representation given in Scripture
of the Spirit's influence, of which baptism is the outward
sign, never implies that the mode of the application is
essential. The gift of the Holy Ghost was the grace signified (Acts ii. 1–4, 32, 33; x. 44–48; xi. 15, 16). The
fire, which did not immerse them, but appeared as cloven
tongues and "sat upon each one of them," was the symbol
of that grace. Jesus was himself the baptizer, who now
fulfilled the prediction of John the Baptist that he should
baptize with the Holy Ghost and with fire. The gift of
the Holy Ghost is set forth alike in the Old and New
Testaments in such terms as "came from heaven," "poured
out," "shed forth," "fell on them" (Isa. xliv. 3; lii. 15;
Ezek. xxxvi. 25–27; Joel ii. 28, 29).

(*g*) The metaphorical illustrations of the effects and
benefits of baptism given in the New Testament do not lay
any emphasis upon nor suggest any importance as attaching to the mode of applying the water in baptism. We
are said "to be born of water and of the Spirit;" to "have
put on Christ" as a garment in baptism; to be "planted
together or generated together;" "to be buried with him
by baptism into death" (John iii. 5; Gal. iii. 27; Rom. vi.
3–5). These, none of them, represent baptism itself, but
all alike refer to the spiritual effects of that grace which

water-baptism symbolizes. In baptism we symbolically and professedly receive the Holy Ghost. The indwelling of the Holy Ghost unites us vitally to Christ. Union with Christ involves our being "generated or grafted together with him into one vital organism;" our putting on Christ as our righteousness; our being united with him federally, so that his death is our death and his rising to newness of life ours also; as he is a Priest, we are priests; as he is a Prophet, we are prophets; as he is a King, we are kings. All this and much more is true, but none of it even suggests the manner in which the water shall be applied in baptism.

(*h*) The Christian Church as a great historic body has always felt itself free in regard to this question. In the Eastern churches pouring has prevailed from immemorial times. The Greek church has always insisted on immersion. The Roman Catholic and Protestant historic churches admit both forms. During all the more modern freer and more evangelical ages the tendency toward baptizing by sprinkling has increased and become more general. The general body of Christians have always felt that as the mode of the application of the water in baptism was not of the essence of the commandment, they were free to do in the matter as convenience or local custom suggested.

(*i*) It is in the highest degree incongruous with the genius of the Christian religion and with the general analogy of its institutions that the mere manner of applying water as symbolical of purification should be considered of any importance. This religion is pre-eminently spiritual and reasonable, and not external or formal. It is designed for all men of all climates, ages, and conditions, and to be applied to individuals and communities under all conceivable circumstances. The external mode of performing a rite is insisted upon in no other instance. Christ and his apostles have left no prescriptions as to the form of church government, nor as to the manner of induction into church offices. No hints even as to a liturgy or form of prayer or order of general service of the sanctuary are given in their writings. Neither posture in prayer nor form of psalmody is prescribed. The questions as to the use of instrumental music, robes, and written or extemporaneous prayers, are left absolutely indeterminate. In the case of the sister sacrament of the Lord's Supper the manner of celebrating it, by absolutely universal consent of all Christians, has been left to the free selection of each ecclesiastical community, some receiving it lying on couches, as the apostles did who received it from the hands of Christ, and some kneeling, and some standing, and some sitting; some using unleavened bread after the original example, and others insisting upon the bread of every-day life.

(*j*) The case standing thus, as we think, as above stated, it is evident that the only point in connection with the mode of baptism is to insist upon it that the mode is an accident of no importance at all. The only serious mistake that possibly can be made in the premises is that of insisting upon some one of the many possible modes as absolutely essential to the integrity of the rite. The essence of the thing is to wash with water as a symbol " of the washing of regeneration and renewing of the Holy Ghost." Everything other than this or more than this necessarily confuses the doctrine and obscures the impression of the truth. The simple command stands, and embraces all Christians : " Go, wash with water into the name of the Father, and of the Son, and of the Holy Ghost ; " and " He who baptizes with the Holy Ghost and with fire will be with you alway, even to the end of the world."

[II.] *Who are to be baptized ?*

There are two principles applying to the solution of this problem which appear to us to be very clear and unquestionable.

The *first* of these principles is, that baptism is a sacramental action representing an inward invisible grace. Consequently, the outward action ought never consciously and intentionally to be applied where the inward invisible grace is absent. There could be no farce more profane, no empty show more ghastly, than that of sealing the form of a covenant where there was no real promise, of applying an outward symbol of spiritual life and grace where all spiritual life and grace are absent. Such mockery would transform the sacred pledges of God's truth into a lie.

The *second* principle, which we affirm to be no less obvious and certain, is, that the baptism with water is itself an outward visible sign, to be applied by human agents who are incapable of reading the hearts of men, and who have no power of conveying, and no authority of absolutely pledging, the spiritual gifts which God retains in his own hand. It follows, consequently, that in practice, while the sign should never intentionally be applied where the grace is absent, there cannot, however, be any infallible connection between the sign and the grace. God alone reads the hearts of men and dispenses the invisible grace, and men who cannot read the heart alone dispense the outward visible signs of the sacrament. It follows that these human ministers of God's will must administer these rites upon certain presumptions—that is, they must follow certain divinely-appointed signs or indications which raise in each case the presumption that the parties concerned are either now or to be hereafter the parties to whom the invisible spiritual grace signified belongs. It is perfectly plain that every human society, whether social, political, or religious, must necessarily be organized and administered on the same principles. Men can judge character only by external indications, and these external indications must be assumed to be presumptive evidence of the reality and genuineness of the character they indicate. And the individual officers of the society, whatever it may be, cannot be allowed to follow unrestrictedly the indications of their own variable judgments in each particular case. The society itself must, through its supreme authority, establish general rules and tests of presumptive evidence upon which its officers must act alike in the admission and in the exclusion of members.

1st. In the case of adults, or persons arrived at the condition of independent responsible agency, the presumptive ground of fitness for admission to the sealing ordinances of the Church is a competent knowledge of the plan of salvation, a credible profession of personal faith, and a walk and conversation consistent therewith. The amount of knowledge requisite must vary with the general intelligence of the subject. But it is evident that no person can be a Christian by profession who is absolutely ignorant of his own guilt and pollution and of Christ's meritorious work in our behalf. And, on the other hand, it is no less evident that multitudes of Christ's children are saved who have attained only to the vaguest and most elementary knowledge of the essentials of the gospel. A "credible profession" does not mean a profession of faith which compels credence, or which convinces the observer that it is genuine; but it is simply the opposite of the incredible—it is a confession that can be believed. Neither ministers of the gospel nor elders are able to read the secrets of the human heart, or to judge of character. Therefore, the great Head of the Church has not laid upon us the responsibility. The responsibility of professing Christ rests upon the individual professor. Every man who has the competent knowledge, and who makes a profession not incredible, and whose life is in conformity therewith, has a presumptive right to come to the sacraments. He does not need to prove his way in. If the session or pastor exclude him, they or he must show sufficient positive evidence of his not being a Christian to keep him out. This plain principle is one of great importance, the violation of which has brought great evil upon the Church. As the minister and church-session have no power of reading the heart of the applicant, so it must be a great evil if they officially form and express any judgment in the case. If they do pretend to listen to and judge of the value of the experience recited, they profanely assume to possess the prerogatives which belong to God alone, and they lead deluded souls to put an unwarrantable confidence in the worthless indorsement of the church authorities. It is by reason of this that so many are asleep in Zion. Each man ought to be thrown back upon his own unshared responsibility, and made " to examine himself, that so he may eat of this bread."

On the other hand, it is the great duty of those church-officers to whom Christ has committed the keys of the visible kingdom of heaven on earth to proclaim the truths of the gospel, to impress the resulting duties upon the consciences of men, and to set forth the high conditions of Christian communion which God exacts. The Romanists baptize all children indiscriminately. All adults who render an outward adherence to the Church are baptized. The State-Church systems of Protestant Europe recognize every reputable citizen of the State as a legitimate member of the Church. The true doctrine is, that no man, whatever his external relations may be, has a right to come to the holy sacraments unless he is duly qualified; and he cannot be duly qualified unless he is a living member of Christ's mystical body, a temple of the Holy Ghost. Unless he possesses this character, his approach to the sacraments is in vain and a sin. But of this fact the man himself is always and only the one responsible judge. The officers and members of the church have no right to go behind his not incredible profession, on the presumptive evidence of which the Master requires all others to receive him and to treat him in all things as a Christian brother.

2nd. The children of all such persons as, on the ground of their own credible profession of faith, are received as members of the visible Church are to be baptized as members of the visible Church, because, presumptively, heirs of the blessings of the covenant of grace. The divinely appointed and guaranteed presumption is, if the parents, then the children. This is not an invariable law binding God, but it is a prevailingly probable law, basing the authorized and rational recognition and treatment of such children by the Church as heirs of the promises. The reasons for our thinking so must be condensed into the fewest words:—

(1.) This presumption is rendered exceedingly probable by the fundamental constitution of humanity as a self-propagative race. A moral government pure and simple presupposes only individuals, and addresses itself to the control of individuals through their reasons, consciences, and wills. But the fact which differentiates the human subjects of the divine government from an ideal realm—as that of the angels, for instance—is that we are a race in which the nature, character, and status of the parent determine those of the child by a universal and inevitable hereditary law. Thus, the apostasy of Adam gave an entirely new direction to the history of his entire race, and thus the character and destiny of families, races, and nations have been always predetermined by the deeds and experiences of their ancestors. The law of heredity is the fundamental law of animal nature, including man; and since the God of nature is identical with the God of grace, it was to be anticipated that his remedial scheme of redemption should conserve and operate through all the laws of nature, while it antagonizes only that false nature which is sin. Hugh Miller, the Christian geologist, says: " Whatever we may think of the scriptural doctrine on this special head, it is a fact broad and palpable in the economy of nature that parents do occupy a federal position, and that the lapsed progenitors, when cut off from civilization and all external civilization of a missionary character, become the founders of a lapsed race. The iniquities of the parents are visited upon the children. In all such instances it is man left to the freedom of his own will that is the deteriorator of man. The doctrine of the Fall in its purely theologic aspect is a doctrine which must be apprehended by faith; but it is at least something to find that the analogies of science, instead of running counter to it, run in exactly the same line. It is one of the inevitable consequences of that nature of man which the Creator ' bound fast in fate ' while he left free his will, that the free will of the parent should become the destiny of the child."

(2.) This presumption is borne out by the analogies of the entire history of God's providential revelations of the scheme of redemption recorded in Scripture. If the parents by an inevitable law bore their children away from God in their apostasy, it is surely to be expected that they shall bring back their children with them Godward in their regeneration. The sin of the parents immediately involved the condemnation and guilt of the family. So when God began graciously to open to men a way of escape, and set up his kingdom in the world, the family was made the first form of the Church. In the entire patriarchal age every family the heads of which professed the true religion was a visible Church. The father was the prophet, priest, and king. By him the morning and evening sacrifices were offered. Wherever Abraham and the other patriarchs went they erected the altar and called upon the name of the Lord. The whole family, including especially the little children, constituted the Church, and were trained in the knowledge and service of God. In all his covenants God explicitly included the children with their parents. The faith of the parents turned the favour of God upon their children, and the promises of the parents bound their children under inalienable obligations. The curse denounced upon Adam and Eve has been in all its specifications inflicted on their seed throughout all generations. So when covenanting with Noah, the second father of the race, God said, "I will establish my covenant between me and thee, and thy seed after thee in all their generations;" and when making his national covenant with the Israelites, Jehovah declared this principle: "For I, Jehovah thy God, am a jealous God, visiting the iniquities of the fathers upon the children unto the third and fourth generation of them that hate me; and showing mercy unto thousands of them that love me and keep my commandments." And in the first great sermon of the New Dispensation, on the day of Pentecost, Peter, when preaching to the people that they must repent and be baptized, gives this remarkable reason for it: "For the promise [the gospel covenant] is unto you, and to your children, and to all that are afar off, even as many as the Lord our God shall call."

(3.) Baptism under the New Dispensation of the covenant of grace in all respects takes the place of circumcision under the Old. It is "the circumcision of Christ" (Col. ii. 11, 12). The one was a mark that was a sign of the necessity of regeneration and a pledge of its gift. In the other, water, the universal element of cosmical life, and the universal instrument of cleansing, is applied to the person with the same significance and design. Each in its own age was the authoritatively appointed door of entrance into the fold of salvation, and the badge of citizenship in the kingdom of God. Viewed as a mere outward rite, neither circumcision nor baptism, nor their absence, avails anything, but the new creature, which both alike signify. Baptism takes the place of circumcision, the seal of the covenant which God made with Abraham: "For as many of you as have been baptized into Christ have put on Christ. And if ye be Christ's, then are ye Abraham's seed, and heirs according to the promise " (Gal. iii. 27, 29). Baptism represents the washing away of sin ; circumcision did precisely the same. For God said, " I will circumcise thy heart and the heart of thy seed to love the Lord with all thy soul," etc. Circumcision, like baptism, represents an inward spiritual grace: " For he is not a Jew, which is one outwardly ; neither is that circumcision, which is outward in the flesh : but he is a Jew, which is one inwardly ; and circumcision is that of the heart, in the spirit, and not in the letter ; whose praise is not of men, but of God " (Rom. ii. 28, 29). Circumcision as well as baptism unites us to Christ. For Paul says (Col. ii. 10, 11): " In whom [that is, Christ, Head of all principality and power] ye are circumcised with the circumcision made without hands, in putting off the body of the sins of the flesh by the circumcision of Christ." Water-baptism is the precise equivalent of " the circumcision of the flesh ; " and the baptism of the Holy Ghost is the precise equivalent of " the circumcision of the heart." The apostle Paul says everything of circumcision that an evangelical pastor would now say of baptism. The condition of the circumcision of an adult under the Mosaic law was precisely the same credible profession of faith which is now demanded as a precondition of adult baptism. But all the children of believers were circumcised ; therefore there is every presumption that the children of believers should be baptized.

(4.) The Church under the Old Dispensation is precisely the same Church with the Christian Church under the New. They bore the same name: the " *Kahal Jehovah* " and the ἐκκλησία κυρίου alike mean the Church of the Lord. Thus, Stephen called the " congregation of the Lord " before Sinai " the *Church* in the wilderness." (Compare

Acts vii. 38 with Ex. 32.) Their foundation in the person and work of Christ was the same. The conditions of adult membership in each were the same profession of faith and promise of obedience. Every true Israelite was a true believer (Gal. iii. 7). All Israelites were at least credible professors of the true religion. The sacraments of this Church under its successive dispensations were of the same significance and binding force. Baptism is the "circumcision of Christ" (Col. ii. 11, 12). The Passover, like the Last Supper, represented the sacrifice of Christ (1 Cor. v. 7). The Christian converts from Judaism were not gathered into a new Church, but were daily added to the already existing Church. The Gentile branches did not constitute a new olive tree, but were grafted into the old Israelitish olive tree (Rom. xi. 17–24). The apostles, who entered the Church by circumcision, and who acknowledged Christ as the Messiah before the excision of the Jews in mass because of unbelief, were never baptized; while Paul and others, who belonged to the exscinded mass, were grafted back to their own olive tree through baptism.

But the infant children of all the members of the Church under the Old Testament were regarded and treated as members of the Church themselves, and their membership was sealed on the eighth day by circumcision.

(5.) Christ and his apostles, members of a Church which had always included infants, and themselves circumcised in infancy, in all respects spoke and acted as Pædobaptist ministers would in their place. Christ blessed little " children," and declared of such is " the kingdom of heaven," or the visible Church under the New Dispensation (Matt. xix. 14 ; xiii. 47). He commissioned Peter to feed his lambs (John xxi. 15–17), and all the apostles to " disciple all nations " by baptizing, then teaching them (Matt. xxviii. 19, 20).

The apostles were not settled pastors in an established Christian community, but itinerant missionaries in an unbelieving world, sent not to baptize, but to preach the gospel (1 Cor. i. 17). Hence we have in Acts and the Epistles the record of only ten separate instances of baptism. In every case, without a single recorded exception where there was a family, the family was baptized as soon as the head of the family presented a credible profession of his faith (Acts xvi. 15, 32, 33 ; xviii. 8 ; 1 Cor. i. 16). And in their Epistles they always addressed children as members of the Church (Eph. v. 1 ; vi. 1–3 ; Col. iii. 20 ; 1 Cor. vii. 12–14).

In the most natural manner, without the slightest hint of change, and with every incidental indication possible of the uninterrupted continuance of the historical church-membership of infants, the narratives of the New Testament church-life grow from those of the Old. The preaching of the New Testament opens with the explicit declaration, abundantly significant as coming from an apostle to a representative national audience, all of whom knew of no Church which had not always embraced children in its sacramentally-sealed membership : " The promise "—that is, the gospel covenant, of which circumcision and baptism were successively the seals—" is unto you and to your children " (Acts ii. 39).

(6.) The universal consent of Christians in historical continuity with the apostles bears unbroken testimony to the immemorial right of the children of Christian professors to be recognized as members of the Church with their parents. It is noticed in the earliest records as a universal custom and as an apostolical tradition. Justin Martyr, writing A.D. 138, says that " there were among Christians of his time many persons of both sexes, some sixty and some seventy years old, who had been made disciples of Christ from their infancy." Irenæus, who died about A.D. 202, says: "He came to save all by him-self—all, I say, who by him are born again unto God, infants, and little children, and youths." The practice of infant baptism is acknowledged by Tertullian, born in Carthage A.D. 160. Origen, born of Christian parents in Egypt A.D. 185, says that it was "the usage of the Church to baptize infants," and that "the Church had received the tradition from the apostles." Cyprian, bishop of Carthage from A.D. 248 to A.D. 258, together with his entire synod, decided that baptism should be administered to infants before the eighth day. St. Augustine, born A.D. 358, declared that "this doctrine is held by the whole Church, not instituted by councils, but always retained." This Pelagius himself was forced to admit, although he had visited all parts of the Church from Britain to Syria; and the point made by Augustine was fatal to the position which Pelagius occupied (Wall's *History of Infant Baptism* and Bingham's *Christian Antiquities*, bk. xi., ch. iv.).

The Church split into several fragments, Roman, Greek, Arminian, Nestorian, and Abyssinian, all differing in much, but all agreeing in support of the custom of recognizing and sealing infants as church-members.

At the time of the Reformation learned and holy men were raised up by God in the midst of every European nation. There were perfectly independent movements in each national centre of reform. Zwingle, the Reformer of the Swiss; Luther, the Reformer of the Germans; Calvin, the Reformer of the French, Cranmer, of the English Church, and Knox, of the Scotch, were all independent, and in some things diverse, yet they all agreed spontane-ously in the recognition of the church-membership of the infant children of believers. And the great historic churches of the Reformation—the Anglican, the Lutheran, the Reformed or Presbyterian in all its varieties, the original branch of the Independents, the world-conquering

Methodists—all unite with the older churches, Eastern and Western, in maintaining this grand historic constitution of infant church-membership. Those who protest against this ancient and ecumenical consensus, however eminently respectable as we affectionately recognize them to be, are certainly a recent growth, and thus far, as compared with the mighty host, but a small minority.

[III.] *What is the Use of Infant Baptism?*

We freely admit that our good Baptist brethren, who refuse to recognize and treat their children as members of the Church of Christ from birth, nevertheless enjoy with us the very benefits which infant baptism asserts and seals. The mistakes of God's true children will never make him unfaithful to them, nor defeat the blessings he intends for them. Precisely the same is true of the truly Christian Quakers. They enjoy all the blessings signified and sealed by the outward sacraments, although they neglect all of them entirely. Nevertheless, our Baptist brethren being judges, the obedient use of the sacraments is the more excellent way.

The use of "infant baptism" is precisely the use of any sacrament—that is, the incomparable benefit of externally signifying and sealing the benefits represented.

1st. In the baptism of every infant there are four parties present and concerned in the transaction—God, the Church, the parents, and the child. The first three are conscious and active, the fourth is for the time unconscious and passive.

2nd. In the act of baptism the use is found at the time in the benefit resulting from binding the parents and the Church to the performance of all their duties relating to the child, and from binding upon the child those special obligations and sealing to the child those special benefits which spring from the gospel covenant as it includes the children with the believing parent. The faith involved is that of the parent and of the Church, while the unconscious and passive beneficiary is the child himself.

3rd. Subsequently, when the child is taught and trained under the regimen of his baptism—taught from the first to recognize himself as a child of God, with all its privileges and duties; trained to think, feel, and act as a child of God, to exercise filial love, to render filial obedience —the benefit to the child directly is obvious and immeasurable. He has invaluable birthright privileges, and corresponding obligations and responsibilities.

4th. It is evident that this should be supplemented by a rite of confirmation. Of course I do not here refer to the unauthorized Romish and prelatical sacrament of the laying on of the hands of one of the changed successors of the apostles. I refer simply to the historical, universally-practised Christian ordinance observed in bringing the Christianly instructed and trained children before the Church "when they come to years of discretion: if they be free from scandal, appear sober and steady, and to have sufficient knowledge to discern the Lord's body, they ought to be informed it is their duty and their privilege to come to the Lord's Supper" (*Directory for Worship*, ch. x., § 1). Then they who have been members of the Church from their birth are admitted to full communion, and are confirmed in their church standing, upon their voluntarily taking upon themselves the vows originally imposed upon them by their parents in baptism. This is the CONFIRMATION, separated from the abortive mask of the so-called sacrament, that John Calvin declared was an ancient and beneficial custom, which he earnestly wished might be continued in the Church (*Institutes*, bk. iv., ch. xix. 12, 13), and which Dr. Charles Hodge declared to be "retained in some form or other in all Protestant churches" (*Princeton Review*, 1855, p. 445). As far as we misunderstand or ignore this beautiful ordinance of confirmation we abandon to the mercies of our Baptist brethren the whole rational ground and reason of infant baptism.

[IV.] Mar Johanan, the Nestorian bishop, when solicited by high-churchmen to separate himself from non-prelatical Christians, exclaimed, "All who love the Lord Jesus Christ are my brethren." Above all the narrow, meagre patriotism on earth is the large, free, ecumenical patriotism of those who embrace in their love and fealty the whole body of the baptized. All who are baptized into the name of the Father, and of the Son, and of the Holy Ghost, recognizing the Trinity of Persons in the Godhead, the incarnation of the Son and his priestly sacrifice, whether they be Greeks, or Arminians, or Romanists, or Lutherans, or Calvinists, or the simple souls who do not know what to call themselves, are our brethren. Baptism is our common countersign. It is the common rallying standard at the head of our several columns. It is our common battle-flag, which we carry forward across the enemy's line and nail aloft in the heights crowned with victory. We will be confined in our love and allegiance by no party lines. We follow and serve one common Lord. Hence there can be only "one Lord, one faith, one baptism," and hence only one indivisible, inalienable "sacramental host of God's elect."

XVII.

THE LORD'S SUPPER.

WE now enter the innermost Most Holy Place of the Christian temple. We approach the sacred altar on which lies quivering before our eyes the bleeding heart of Christ. We come to the most private and personal meeting-place, appointed rendezvous, between our Lord and his beloved. We are here to have discovered to us the Christian mysteries which have been carefully reserved for hundreds of generations for the initiated alone. To all else the wide world is invited without limit and without condition, but to this sacred rite the covenanted brethren alone. It marks the central, vital epochs in the believer's life and intercourse with heaven. It marks hence the successive stages of his pilgrimage along the King's highway toward the New Jerusalem and the banqueting-halls of our Father's house. It is consequently the central ordinance in the whole circle of church life, around which all the other ministries of the Church revolve, and through which we have exhibited to the outward senses the indwelling of God with men, the real presence and objective reality of "the holy catholic Church," and the reality and power of "the communion of saints." It will be our place to rehearse succinctly its biblical and ecclesiastical names, its genesis, its matter (including its elements and sacramental actions), its design and significance and effect, and its future promise.

I. 1st. It is called by the apostle (1 Cor. xi. 20), and after him by the Christian Church in all ages, by the familiar and touching title, " the Lord's Supper.". The Greek word δεῖπνον, here translated " supper," properly designated what we would now call the dinner, or the principal meal of the Jews, taken by them and by all Eastern nations generally late in the afternoon or in the evening of the day. The sacrament inherited this name by natural descent, because our Saviour instituted it while he and his disciples were partaking of this meal. It is called the *Lord's* Supper, because it was instituted at his *last* supper with his disciples to commemorate his death and to signify and to convey and seal his grace.

2nd. It is also called by the apostle (1 Cor. x. 21), and after him by all Christians, " the Lord's Table." The word " table " here of course stands for the gracious provisions spread upon it, and for the entire service connected with it. It is the " table " to which the precious Lord invites his guests, and at which he himself graciously presides.

3rd. It is called also by the apostle " the Cup of Blessing " (1 Cor. x. 16), the cup blessed by Christ, and so consecrated to be the vehicle of supernatural blessings graciously conveyed to men worthily partaking. In Christ's name and in virtue of his commission the ordained minister now " blesses "—that is, invokes the divine blessing upon —these elements, that they may be made the instruments of conveying this blessing to the worthy partakers of them.

4th. This service is also called " the Communion " (1 Cor. x. 16). This and " *the* Sacrament " are the titles most commonly given by the way of eminence to this sacred rite. The act of partaking of these holy symbols, if intelligent and sincere, involves the most real and intimate communion—that is, a mutual giving and receiving —between Christ, the Head and the Heart of the Church, and his living members, and consequently a vital interchange of influences between all the living members of that spiritual body of which he is the Head.

5th. The evangelist Luke also calls this sacrament on one occasion (Acts ii. 42) "the Breaking of Bread," because the symbolical action of the officiating minister in breaking the bread signifies the precious truths that the flesh of Christ, torn for us sacrificially, purchased our redemption, and that, as we all partake of one bread as we receive one Christ, so we shall all be one in the most vital and spiritual sense in time and eternally.

6th. This holy ordinance is also called by our Lutheran brethren, in their symbolical books, "*Sacramentum Altaris,*" the Sacrament of the Altar, because they have accepted so far the Romish tradition, retained also in the Anglican Church, which has transformed the "communion table" of Christ and his apostles into an altar. This of course the Lutherans, who are strict Protestants, use only in a figurative, commemorative sense, because this sacrament is in no sense an atoning sacrifice, except in so far as it is the commemoration of the one all-perfect, all-satisfying sacrifice which our Lord offered in his own body on the cross eighteen hundred years ago.

7th. In the ancient Church, as among some of the moderns, *agapæ* or "love feasts" were held, at which all the Christians of a community assembled and feasted in common. At these the consecrated elements of the Holy Supper were distributed and received. The name of the feast thus came to be applied to the sacrament which was the crown of the whole.

8th. It was called in the ancient Church often "a sacrifice, an offering." But it was never understood to be a real sin-expiating sacrifice in itself. It was given this name, since so sadly perverted in the Roman Church, only because it represents commemoratively the one finished sacrifice of Christ, and because it is connected with the

spiritual sacrifices of the worshipper's heart and life (Heb.
xiii. 15), and with an accompanying collection and oblation
of alms for the poor of the church.

9th. One of the most beautiful of all the designations
this sacred service has borne is that of " Eucharist," from
the Greek word εὐχαριστέω, *to give thanks.* To " ask a
blessing " upon our food and " to give thanks " for it have
always been intimately associated in Christian practice.
According to Matt. xxvi. 26, 27, our Lord is represented as
" having blessed " the bread, and then as having given
thanks when presenting the cup. It is both " the cup of
blessing " upon which we have invoked the divine blessing
(1 Cor. x. 16), the cup of thanksgiving, " the cup of salvation," which we take in the house of the Lord, calling
upon his name, and giving thanks for his salvation (Ps.
cxvi. 13).

II. *Its Genesis.*—This is essentially and immediately the
personal sacrament of Jesus Christ. It was immediately
instituted by him in person while partaking of the last
supper with his disciples. It immediately commemorates
his death. It is always administered by his direct
authority. The worthy communicant immediately communicates with the present Christ. The reality of the
sacrament depends entirely upon his being really immediately present in the act. Take away either its original
institution by Christ or the immediate presence of Christ
in every repeated celebration of it, and it is no sacrament
at all. Nevertheless, like every other scriptural ordinance, it was not suddenly thrust into existence without
any foregoing preparation. All things, divine sacraments
as well as others, obey the law of continuity, and grow
under the special providence of God out of long-prepared
roots or seeds. The divinely-prepared historic root of the
Lord's Supper was, as is well known, the Passover. The
nation of Israel was the type of the Christian Church.

The deliverance of that nation from the bondage of Egypt, and the redemption of her sons from the slaughter which overtook the first-born of every Egyptian household, were types of our redemption from sin. The paschal lamb was a type of Christ. The paschal supper with its attendant rites represented, under the Old Economy, the external redemption already accomplished, and no less the future perfect redemption to be afterward accomplished when Christ the true paschal Lamb was sacrificed. The Lord's Supper commemorates the same redemption, looking backward to the already accomplished fact. The Christian Sunday is an historical continuation of the Jewish Sabbath, only the day of the week changes, and runs back in absolutely unbroken continuity through the ages—through the ages before the Flood, through the years before the Fall—it and matrimony being the only monuments of the golden age of innocency. Each recurrent holy day stands to us, *first*, as a monument of the sovereignty of Jehovah as Creator, and, *secondly*, as a monument of our redemption consummated in the resurrection of our Lord. Every Lord's day when we celebrate the Holy Supper we repeat in a chain of unbroken continuity the memorial of his sacrificial death. And in the beautiful circle of the Christian year, Holy Week, Good Friday, Easter, we repeat in a far longer chain of unbroken continuity the Christian sacrament of the Supper, looking back over a vista of nearly eighteen centuries and three-quarters to its institution, and also over a vista nearly twice as long, of nearly three thousand five hundred years, to the institution of the first Passover and the redemption of Israel from the bondage of Egypt.

When God delivered the children of Israel from their bondage in Egypt, he sent forth his angel commissioned to destroy the first-born in each Egyptian household. He commanded the Israelites by families or small groups of families to select a male lamb of the first year without blemish, and slay it at the setting of the sun, and with a sprig of hyssop sprinkle the lintels and side-posts of the doors of their houses. The blood was to them as a token upon the houses where they were; for when the Lord saw the blood he passed over them, so that the plague which destroyed the Egyptians did not come upon them. They were also commanded to roast the flesh of the lamb that night, and to eat it entirely before the morning, with unleavened bread and bitter herbs ; with their loins girded, and their feet shod and their staves in their hands: they were to eat it in haste, ready to depart (Ex. xii. and xiii.).

Hence the Lord appointed the Passover, or Feast of Unleavened Bread, as a sacramental memorial in their generations, as an ordinance for ever. On the 14th of Nisan the house and all the utensils were diligently searched and purged of leaven, which, as incipient putrefaction, was the symbol of moral corruption. At evening, the beginning of the 15th of Nisan, the paschal lamb was sacrificed, and his blood sprinkled on the altar, and the fat burned (2 Chron. xxx. 16 ; xxxv. 11). The lamb was roasted whole, and eaten entirely by the assembled household, with unleavened bread and bitter herbs. Four cups of wine, the Mishna tells us, were always drunk. Two of these are distinctly mentioned in Luke xxii. 17–20. Our Lord, Luke says, took one cup and gave thanks, and said, " Take this, and divide it among yourselves." " Likewise also he took the [second] cup after supper, saying," etc. They also always sang the Hallel, or praise Psalms, consisting of all the Psalms in our Bible from the 113th to the 118th inclusive. The first part, including the 113th and 114th Psalms, was sung early in the meal, and the 115th, 116th, 117th, and 118th Psalms at the close, after the fourth or last cup of wine had been drunk.

This is the "hymn" alluded to (Matt. xxvi. 30; Mark xiv. 26) when it is said, "And when they had sung an hymn, they went out into the mount of Olives."

After the filling of the second cup of wine, and just before the eating of the paschal lamb began, the son or some other member of the family asked the father, who presided as the prophet and priest of his household, what was the meaning of the peculiar arrangements of this feast (Ex. xii. 26). Then the father rehearsed the history of their great national redemption, and expounded the symbolical and commemorative and the moral and religious significance of the traditional observance. The whole service was at the same time a pious memorial of the redemption of the lives of the first-born of Israel and of the nation itself from the bondage of Egypt, and a type or prophetical symbol of the redemption of men by the sacrifice on the cross of the body of Jesus Christ.

Therefore Christ came up to the feast of the Passover on purpose to be offered up a sacrifice for the sins of the world. When many came up out of the country to be purified before the Passover, "they sought for Jesus, and spake among themselves, as they stood in the temple, What think ye, that he will not come to the feast?" They little knew the significance of their own question. Of course he would come. If he did not, the entire historical development of the Jewish people for nearly two millenniums would have been a failure. The meaning and fruition of the entire line of prophets and of priests, of sacrificial offerings and of periodical feasts, depended upon his coming up to this particular feast—fulfilling the promise, giving reality to the symbolical representation of all that had gone before. Therefore he at once fulfilled all the prophecy of the past, and inaugurated the future of realized redemption. He ate with the disciples the flesh and bread of the typical Passover, and while doing so he gave to the elements a new and higher significance, and thus developed out of the paschal supper of the past the Lord's Supper of the incomparably more glorious future. So he took the bread—the same unleavened bread which had been eaten from the beginning for sixteen hundred years—and gave thanks, and brake it, and gave unto them, saying, "This is my body, which is given for you : this do in remembrance of me." As if he had said, You will no more need to kill and eat the paschal lamb, for I, Christ, am your true Passover, sacrificed for you (1 Cor. v. 7). But this bread I appoint to be the symbol of my sacrificed body : take and eat it, until I come again, in remembrance of me. Likewise also he took the last or fourth cup after supper—the same cup which had been drunk for ages uncounted at the close of the paschal supper. This ancient cup, with all its historical associations, he took up, and instantly glorified it with new meaning. THIS cup hereafter you are to continue to drink until the end. It is henceforth the new testament in my blood, which is shed for you : drink ye all of it (Matt. xxvi. 26–28 ; Luke xxii. 20). And from that awful night until to-day, for upwards of eighteen hundred and fifty years, the disciples of Christ of every nation and rite have endeavoured, with more or less success, to keep this feast of the Christian Passover with the unleavened bread of sincerity and truth (1 Cor. v. 8).

III. The matter of the Lord's Supper consists (1) of the elements used, and (2) of the sacramental actions which are performed in their use. The elements consist, as all Christians are agreed, of bread and wine.

1st. The bread used in the original sacrament was the unleavened bread which had been used by divine command in the paschal feast from the time of Moses to that of Christ. But Christ speaks of it, in instituting the sacrament, not as " unleavened," but as " bread." The point of the symbolism is that as bread—our daily bread—is the staff of life and nourishes the body, so Christ in his divine-human Person and mediatorial offices nourishes our souls when apprehended by faith. It is evident, from the allusions to its observance throughout the Acts and the Epistles, that the apostles commemorated the communion in connection with ordinary social meals, and in the use of whatever bread happened to be present, which on such occasions we know to have been the common leavened bread. Although it is obviously a matter of indifference what particular form of bread should be used, a controversy sprang up between the Greek and Roman Churches as to the kind of bread it is proper to use in the Eucharist. The Greek Church insisted that the bread used should be leavened, and maintained that the continued use of unleavened bread was a remnant of Judaism. The Roman Church insisted upon the use of unleavened bread. The Lutheran branch of the Protestant Church adheres to the practice of Rome in this particular. The great body of the Reformed churches, including the Anglican Church, on the contrary, maintain that the kind of bread is not essential, but that the wafer used by the Romanists is not properly bread, which is the staff of life, the ordinary food of man. We therefore, by an eminently proper tradition, use ordinary leavened loaf bread, so prepared that the unity of the " one bread " of which all partake is visibly set forth, and this is broken before the people into parts, so that they, being many, all partake of one bread.

2nd. The contents of the cup were wine. This is known to have been " the juice of the grape," not in its original state as freshly expressed, but as prepared in the form of wine for permanent use among the Jews. " Wine," according to the absolutely unanimous, unexceptional testimony of every scholar and missionary, is in its essence " fermented grape juice." Nothing else is wine. The use of " wine " is precisely what is commanded by Christ in his example and his authoritative institution of this holy ordinance. Whosoever puts away true and real wine, or fermented grape juice, on moral grounds, from the Lord's Supper, sets himself up as more moral than the Son of God who reigns over his conscience, and than the Saviour of souls who redeemed him. There has been absolutely universal consent on this subject in the Christian Church until modern times, when the practice has been opposed, not upon change of evidence, but solely on prudential considerations. Many Christians have, however, mingled water with the wine because it was an ancient custom probably practised by Christ himself, and also by some because water mingled with the blood flowed from his broken heart (John xix. 34).

But the Lord's Supper is not a material object, something, like the "host" in the Roman Catholic worship, that can be enclosed in a box, carried about, lifted up, and worshipped. It is in its essence a transaction, something performed in time, having a commencement, a progress, and a conclusion. Hence we Presbyterians hold that the consecrated elements cannot be carried from the church after the celebration of the communion by the minister to sick and absent communicants. If a person is not present at the communion, he does not commune, no matter how much he partakes of the bread or wine which remains. The only proper way to meet the cases of sick communicants is for the minister to take representatively the Church with him to the sick-room, and there go through the service in all its parts.

Since, then, the communion is a transaction, the sacramental actions involved are as essential parts of it as the elements of bread and wine. These are—

1st. The "blessing," or consecrating prayer, in which we ask God to set apart as much of the elements as we shall consume to their sacramental use, to bless them to us, and us in their use; in which, moreover, we invoke the presence of Christ, the great Master of assemblies, as one of us in our midst, and of the Holy Ghost in our hearts.

2nd. The "breaking of bread," symbolical of the sacrificial breaking of the body of Christ upon the cross, and also of the oneness of believers, who, being many, all partake of one Bread. This is so prominent that the entire service is once designated from this one feature (Acts ii. 42).

3rd. The distribution and reception. In these acts the whole communion culminates and concludes. The sacred character of the elements does not consist in themselves, but in their use. As soon as this use is completed, the bread and wine, whether in the body of the recipient or remaining in the vessels of the service, are no more holy than any other specimen of their kind in the world. In the Roman, Anglican, and Lutheran Churches the minister in person conveys the bread and wine carefully to the mouth of each communicant. In the Reformed churches, on the contrary, the elements are distributed by elders, or "representatives of the people," who carry the elements and set them before the communicants, each one of whom is expected to receive and appropriate them with his own hands. The Lord says to each of us, "Take, eat." The communion always implies an active attitude upon the part of each recipient. Each communicant for himself transacts with his present Lord. Each one receives and appropriates to himself by faith Christ and all the sacrificial benefits of his redemption. It is, therefore, a cruel and an injurious perversion of this ordinance when the minister, not satisfied with all his other opportunities of preaching, throws his fellow-communicants into a passive attitude at the Lord's Table by his ceaseless addresses, fencing of tables, and charges and preachments of whatever kind. Christ is present. Every believer at the table should be left alone with his Lord. All that one fellow-communicant, minister or other, can do for his fellow in such a case is to stimulate and direct his activities Christward. This can be done only by leading in direct acts of worship, in *appropriate* hymns and prayers, or in the simple, quiet recitation of the words of Christ himself. Who besides Christ should dare to discourse at the communion ? All that the minister can possibly have any true call to say, in the way of instruction, exhortation, or warning, can surely be delivered previously in the " preparatory services " or in the " action sermon."

IV. *The Design or Meaning of the Sacrament.*—This, of course, is the heart of the whole ordinance. The one necessity for us is to have clear and comprehensive views as to what meanings the sacrament bears, and as to the uses it is designed to serve for us. Comprehension here is as much to be sought as clearness, because this consummate means of grace has many sides, like a diamond cut with many facets, and sustains many relations and accomplishes blessings for us in many different ways. The real truth here, as elsewhere, is to be found only in the view which takes in the whole on all sides.

Let us begin, therefore, with the surface meanings and lower uses, and rise gradually toward the heart and inner mystery of the whole.

1st. This sacrament is, in the first place, avowedly and self-evidently a commemorative rite. The Master said when he instituted it, " This do in remembrance of Me." And ever since that awful night endless successions of disciples have gathered to perform these sacred rites with the intention of " showing forth his death till he come."

The great mass of men pass away in indistinguishable throngs, falling like the leaves of the forest in mass, their individuality lost to human recollection in this world for ever. The memory of some few men out of the thousands lingers long and fades slowly into the night of oblivion. A very few epoch-making men, as Moses, Paul, Augustine, Luther, change the course of human history and live for ever in the new world they inaugurate. But it is only Christ, the incarnate God, Christ, the perfect Man, Christ, the bleeding Price of man's redemption, Christ, the resurgent Victor over death and hell, whose ever-present memory is the condition of all progressive thought. and life. The memory of Christ as the great character of all history has become omnipresent in all literature, philosophy, ethics, politics, and life. All experience, all existence, witness to him. The whole universe repeats his story and keeps him eternally in mind. Monuments (*monere*) exist to keep persons and events in mind. They are of many kinds—as of earth or stone or brass, or changes wrought in the forms of human speech or action, or other observances to be repeated for ever at intervals. This latter kind are incomparably more effective and imperishable as memorials than the others. The Tower of Babel, the Pyramids of Egypt, the most stupendous material monuments the world has ever seen, have either perished or are far gone in decay, while the history they were erected to commemorate is lost beyond the rational guess of critics. And yet the Sabbath-day monument of creation, thousands of years older than the Pyramids, and the Lord's Supper, which in its historic roots in the Passover was brought into being at the very feet of the then young Pyramids themselves, remain as fresh and as articulate with their original significance as at their birth. These observational monuments are likewise omnipresent the world over, as well as imperishable. The Sabbath day and the Lord's Supper, preserved and disseminated with absolutely unbroken continuity down the ages and throughout the nations, keep the memory of Christ alive just as it was at the first, because their very existence and their constant repetition are the unfaded testimony of Christ's contemporaries, the accumulated testimony of all the ages, that Jesus Christ was in very fact delivered sacrificially for our offences and raised again for our justification (Rom. iv. 25).

2nd. It is no less obvious that the sacrament is an object-lesson addressed to the eye, a picture of the essential central verities of the gospel to be seen accompanying and enforcing the preached or read Word addressed to the ear. God has so constituted us as composed of soul and body that all impressions made on the senses naturally compel the attention and excite the corresponding emotions more powerfully than abstract ideas expressed in words. This is the source of the power of all music and poetry and art, which appeal to the senses, the imagination, and the feelings. Experience has proved that when men invent improved methods of exhibiting the gospel beyond the narrow limits of illustration explicitly authorized by the Master, infinite corruption is the swift result. But certainly we are safe as long as our liturgical scheme keeps accurately within the limits prescribed by the positive commands of Christ and the example of his apostles. The excess of the Papists and Ritualists, on the one hand, is not more dishonouring to Christ and injurious to the spiritual interests of his Church than the unauthorized restrictions of the Quakers on the other.

This pictorial exhibition of the central truths of the gospel presented in the elements and sacramental actions of the Lord's Supper is of course reinforced and rendered many times more effective by the fact that all the worshippers take part personally, each one for himself, in those sacramental actions. Not only is the mind exercised with divine truth, not only are the senses appealed to, and the emotions through the senses, but the will is immediately called into action, and the outward acts of taking and of eating and drinking correspond in the consciousness immediately with the inward acts of receiving and appropriating Christ and the benefits of his redemption. It is for this reason that the Reformed insist so emphatically upon the communicant actively taking and appropriating the elements with his own hands, and that we so urgently exhort the minister not to throw the worshippers at the communion into a passive attitude by his instructions and exhortations, but to confine himself to the legitimate office of stimulating and guiding their spiritual activities by leading them in direct acts of worship and covenanting with the Lord.

3rd. It is also obvious, and universally recognized, that this holy communion service is a visible mark or badge of Christian discipleship—an appointed form whereby repentant rebels are to lay down their rebellion and take up and profess their new allegiance to their Lord—and a conspicuous sign whereby the Church and her members are to be distinguished from the world. Every human society finds such a visible, easily-recognized sign or badge indispensable, and this especially when the members of the society in question are commingled in hostile relations with foreign elements. And it is obvious that every such badge of membership and pledge of loyalty to be effective must, like the flag of the nation, be authoritatively imposed by the central sovereignty.

True living faith in the Lord Jesus Christ is the only absolutely necessary condition of salvation, because if a man exercises true faith in the very article of death, as did the thief upon the cross, he shall be certainly saved. Nevertheless, it is evident that in the social state true faith, if it exists, must express itself in full and open acknowledgment of the Lord, and that salvation must be conditioned upon open loyal confession and upon open loyal obedience, as much as upon an internal principle of faith. The faith is the root. It comes first, and the true profession and obedience depend upon it, and cannot exist without it.

Nevertheless, in the advanced stage the fruit is just as essential as the root, and the tree that finally fails to bear fruit will be cut down and cast into the fire. The judgment asserted by Christ is unavoidable : " Whosoever therefore shall confess me before men, him will I confess also before my Father which is in heaven. But whosoever shall deny me before men, him will I also deny before my Father which is in heaven " (Matt. x. 32, 33). Hence the conditions of salvation as proclaimed by the Master himself include public confession as well as faith : " Go ye into all the world, and preach the gospel to every creature. He that believeth and is baptized shall be saved ; but he that believeth not shall be damned " (Mark xvi. 15, 16). This principle is explicitly emphasized by the apostle Paul: " The word of faith, which we preach : that if thou shalt confess with thy mouth the Lord Jesus, and shalt believe in thine heart that God hath raised him from the dead, thou shalt be saved. For with the heart man believeth unto righteousness ; and with the mouth confession is made unto salvation " (Rom. x. 8–10).

It is true that a true believer, who for any reason is prevented from confessing Christ by wearing publicly his sacramental badge, may just as efficiently confess him by other significant words and deeds. And it is further true that if a communicant is indeed a true believer at heart he will constantly confess Christ in other ways—indeed, in all conceivable ways—in all his life. Nevertheless, a loyal citizen cannot choose his own flag. The public and official signification of loyalty cannot be left to the accidental choice of individuals. Above all, in a state of active war no loyal soldier can for one moment fail to hold aloft the one battle-flag which his leader has intrusted to his care. He covers it with his body, he shields it with his life, he carries it aloft with streaming eyes and heaving breast at the head of the host. So do we with solemn joy, with reverent love and passion, carry in sacred pomp this sacramental flag of confession and of challenge high in the face of the world which crucified our Lord.

But before we can go any further we must answer this question : Is Christ really, truly, personally present with us in the sacrament ?   Do we therein covenant and commune with him in person, touch to touch, immediately and really; or is this only a show, a symbol of something absent and different from what it seems ?

The gross perversions of the Romanists and Ritualists, who have made it altogether a question of the local presence of Christ's flesh and blood, have occasioned much confusion of thought and many prejudices on the subject. Nevertheless, as a matter of fact, every believer knows that Christ *is* present in the sacrament—that he has, as a matter of fact, experienced his presence.   If he is not present really and truly, then the sacrament can have no interest or real value to us.   It does not do to say that this presence is only spiritual, because that phrase is ambiguous.   If it means that the presence of Christ is not something objective to us, but simply a mental apprehension or idea of him subjectively present to our consciousness, then the phrase is false.   Christ as an objective fact is as really present and active in the sacrament as are the bread and wine, or the minister or our fellow-communicants by our side.   If it means that Christ is present only as he is represented by the Holy Ghost, it is not wholly true, because Christ is one Person and the Holy Ghost another, and it is Christ who is personally present.   The Holy Ghost doubtless is coactive in that presence and in all Christ's mediatorial work, but this leads into depths beyond our possible understanding.   It does not do to say that the divinity of Christ is present while his humanity is absent, because it is the entire indivisible divine-human Person of Christ which is present.

When Christ promises to his disciples, " Lo, I am with you alway, even to the end of the world-age," and, " Where two or three are met together in my name, there am I in the midst of them," he means, of course, that he, the God-man Mediator they loved, trusted, and obeyed, would be with them. His humanity is just as essential as his divinity, otherwise his incarnation would not have been a necessity. His sympathy, his love, his special helpful tenderness, are human. He is able to be our perfect High Priest, " being touched with the feeling of our infirmities," because he " was in all points tempted like as we are, yet without sin " (Heb. iv. 15).

But what do we mean by " presence " ? It is a great mistake to confuse the idea of " presence " with that of nearness in space. This may be a condition of presence, or it may not, but it is never " presence " itself. If you walk abroad at noonday in the tropics, the most overwhelmingly present thing to you in the universe is the intolerable sun, although it is ninety-three millions of miles distant. If another person is only one foot distant, but separated from you by a wall which cuts off all sight and sound, he is as absent as if in the centre of a distant star. But if the same person, a hundred feet from you in an audience-room, sees you face to face, and hears every vibration of your voice, he is as truly present as if he touched you at every point. When Whitefield's preaching was fully heard and its power felt across the Delaware River, he was present really and truly wherever his voice was heard and his matchless eloquence felt. " Presence," therefore, is not a question of space ; it is a relation. Personal presence is such a relation of persons that they are conscious of each other as imme- diate objects of perception and sources of influence. We know nothing as to the ultimate nature of the union of our souls and bodies, yet we no less are certain of the fact. We know nothing as to the ultimate nature of either sight or hearing, whereby we make our mutual presence felt in social intercourse, yet we are absolutely certain of the facts. So we need not speculate how it is that Christ, the whole God-man, body, soul, and divinity, is present in the sacrament, but we are absolutely certain of the fact. He has promised it. We have hundreds of times experienced it. We can neither see his face nor hear his voice with our bodily senses; nevertheless, when we exercise faith, he, the whole Christ, speaks to us, and we hear him; we speak to him, and he hears us; he takes all we give him, he gives us and we receive all of himself. This is real, because he is present. And this is not confined to the sacrament. He makes manifest to our faith the reality of his presence with us, and communicates the same grace to us, on many other occasions. But here and now and thus is his appointed rendezvous. Whatever may be our fortune under other conditions and at other times, here and now and in this breaking of bread we have a personal appointment to meet our Lord. And he never disappoints those who thus seek him with faith and love.

The Romanists and Lutherans and Ritualists have confused this question and greatly lowered its tone by insisting that the real presence in this sacrament is the literal flesh and blood of Christ, and that the object we really eat and drink when we partake of it is the same literal flesh and blood. This view, as far as it has any scriptural foundation at all, rests on two assertions of Christ.

(1.) In the Gospel of John (vi. 53, 54) he says, "Except ye eat the flesh of the Son of man, and drink his blood, ye have no life in you. Whoso eateth my flesh, and drinketh my blood, hath eternal life." Two great mistakes have been made: (*a*) this language has been interpreted literally instead of spiritually; (*b*) it has been held to refer to the Lord's Supper. Now, neither of these interpretations is true. In ver. 63 Christ explains the sense of the entire passage when he says, "It is the spirit that quickeneth, the flesh profiteth nothing; the words that I speak unto you, they are spirit, and they are life." The literal interpretation is senseless, useless, and revolting. No eating of any flesh can give spiritual life or holiness to man. The spiritual sense is full of light and sweetness. What is present in the sacrament is not literal flesh and blood, to be eaten and drunk, but the whole divine-human person of our Lord, to be loved, worshipped, communed with, covenanted with, and enjoyed in every form of use and fellowship. Eating and drinking is not by the mouth and digestive organs of our bodies, but it is the believing reception and self-appropriation to our souls of the spiritual grace offered. What we do thus eat and drink is not literal flesh and blood, but all the sacrificial benefits of Christ's redemption, all the blessings of every kind he purchased for us by his sacrifice—justification, adoption, sanctification, life, peace, joy, victory, himself and the fulness of his love and grace. Besides, this language does not refer to the Lord's Supper. The words were spoken before the Lord's Supper was instituted, and no allusion is made to that Supper in the entire passage. Besides, "the eating of the flesh" and "the drinking of the blood" spoken of in that passage are declared to be absolutely necessary to salvation, which no Christian, whether Papist or Protestant, ever believed to be true of the Lord's Supper.

(2.) The second assertion of Christ upon which this revolting doctrine is made to rest is his word of institution: "Jesus took the bread......and gave to his disciples, and said, Take, eat; THIS is my body." Now, remember that Christ was sitting in the actual flesh at the table, eating and drinking the bread and wine with the rest. According to all the laws of language and common sense, he could only have meant, "This bread represents, signifies, my body." Thus, in Gen. xli. 26, 27, it is said, "The seven good kine are seven years; and the seven good ears are seven years." Thus it is said in the symbolical language of Daniel (vii. 24), "And the ten horns are ten kings;" and in Rev. i. 20, "The seven stars are the angels of the seven churches, and the seven candlesticks are the seven churches." And so we now say, when tracing on a map the progress of an historic battle, "These are the British forces, and these are the Americans," or, "Here are the Federal forces, and here those of the Confederates."

On such an unsubstantial basis as this has grown up the Romish doctrine of transubstantiation—that when the priest pronounces the words of consecration the whole substance of the bread is changed into the very body of Christ, and the whole substance of the wine is changed into his blood, so that only the sensible qualities (appearance, taste, smell, etc.) of the bread and wine remain, and the very substances of flesh and blood remain without their appropriate qualities. This conversion of substance is permanent, so that the flesh and blood in the form of the wafer and wine, as long as they are visible, are to be kept and adored as the very flesh and blood of Christ. And, the blood being insepa- rable from the flesh, and the human spirit inseparable from the blood, and the divine Spirit from the human, whoso- ever either eats the bread or any portion of it, and he who drinks the wine or any portion of it, eats or drinks the entire person of the God-man. Hence when the Romanists withhold the cup from the communicant he suffers nothing, because, eating the bread, he receives the whole Christ. Hence the minister is a priest, and when he, turning toward the altar, elevates and waves the host toward God, he offers a real expiatory sacrifice, expiating the sins and purchasing gracious favours for the living and the dead. Thus Romanists make the mass a sacrifice as well as a sacrament. On the same unsubstantial ground even the Lutherans insist that while the bread and wine remain just what they appear to our senses to be, nevertheless the literal flesh and blood of Christ, though invisible, are really in, with, and under the bread and wine, and are really eaten and drunk together with them. And even Calvin tried to mediate between the two extremes by maintaining that though the flesh and blood of Christ are, as to their essence, absent in the distant heavens, nevertheless they are dynamically present (as, for example, the sun throughout the sphere of its radiance) to the body and soul of the believing communicant.

Discarding all such materialistic and mechanical conceptions, we maintain our unshaken faith, not in abstract, material flesh and blood, but in the actual objective, effective presence with the believing communicant of the whole divine-human Person of Christ. We are unable, and we do not care, to explain the nature of the fact scientifically; but we do know that he is as fully and as really with us in the sacrament as the minister or the fellow-communicant sitting by our side. Face to face and heart to heart and hand to hand, he recognizes and speaks to us, and we recognize and speak to him; and when we speak he hears, and when he hears his whole divine-human heart responds.

4th. Since, then, Christ is personally and immediately and literally present, our communion with him is direct and real. The Greek words κοινωνία, the act or state of copartnership, the having all things in common, and μετοχή, participation, are in the New Testament indiscriminately translated "communion" and "fellowship." In the one body all the vital organs have communion. The brain and the heart and the lungs and the stomach reciprocally live in and through each other. Communion between is copartnership and fellowship. The most entire, unlimited, and intimate of all human communions is between husband and wife in a true marriage. The most absolute and intimate of all communions in the universe is between

Father, Son, and Holy Ghost in the one Godhead. The most absolute and intimate communion between God and the creation is that established through the divine-human Person of Christ with his believing people. This is both symbolized and actually effected in the Lord's Supper— symbolized in our eating bread and drinking wine; actually effected by our immediately receiving into our souls, through faith, the actually-present Christ, his whole Person and all the benefits his blood purchases, and by our unreservedly giving to him and his taking our whole selves as consecrated to him. There is no figure in the world which expresses more adequately this absolute entire reception, appropriation, and assimilation of another than that of eating and drinking. We incorporate the whole Christ entire and all his offices and work into our personal characters and lives. We freely give and Christ takes immediate possession of our whole selves, all our potentialities and activities, for ever. Throughout every octave of our spiritual nature every chord is attuned and brought into exquisite harmony in response to the transcendent mind and spirit of Christ. Hence the Lord's Supper is characteristically called the "Communion;" "for the cup of blessing which we bless, is it not the communion (κοινωνία, copartnership) of the blood of Christ? the bread which we break, is it not the communion of the body of Christ?"

And if we have communion with Christ, the common Heart and Head of all, we must have communion one with another. All at the same table, all in the same ecclesiastical fellowship, all of every name and rite now living on the face of the earth and eating of one bread and drinking of one cup, all of all ages and dispensations, through these sacred elements receive the universal Christ, both theirs and ours, and experience that eternal life, that undying joy, which from the Head flow to and through all his members. Herein, on every Communion Sabbath, we visibly proclaim

our faith and fellowship with the one everywhere present
Christ, and in him with "the holy catholic Church, the
communion of saints."

5th. And, finally, this holy Supper is, in conformity
with its inner nature, called by way of eminence "*the*
Sacrament." The *sacramentum*, in classical Latin, came to
mean specially the soldier's oath. The army, halting under
the shadows of the great primeval forests, gathered in its
new recruits, and by the terrible ceremonial of the soldier's
oath they were bound to an unconditional loyalty to their
imperial leader, who reigned from his seat at the head of
the host. A victim having been offered in sacrifice, his
blood was poured into the hollow of their convex shields.
The new soldier, plunging his right hand into this sacrificial
blood and raising it to heaven, swore by all most sacred to
be faithful, heart and act, to his master through life and
through death. This, of course, implied a reciprocal pledge
of protection and benefit from the lord to his loyal follower.
So Jesus went in person to the feast, and taking the broken
bread and poured wine, the symbols of his crucified body
and shed blood, he swears to each of us to fulfil for us and
in us his whole mediatorial work—to secure for us, body
and soul, his complete salvation culminating in the bosom
of God. And we, with streaming eyes, taking in our hands
and mouths the same tremendous symbols, swear, looking
straight into the face of our present Lord, to keep back no
part of the price, but to place on the altar of his service all
we are and all we possess, without reserve or change for
ever. Take the shoes from off your feet and step lightly,
for the place is most holy on the inner side of the veil.
And when you go down and out into the world again, remember that the binding sanction of this great sacrament
rests on you every moment of your lives.

V. Our blessed Saviour told us, when he instituted this
holy Supper just before his death, "I will not any more

eat thereof [of this Passover] until it be fulfilled in the
kingdom of God" (Luke xxii. 16); and again, "I will not
drink henceforth of this fruit of the vine, until that day
when I drink it new with you in my Father's kingdom"
(Matt. xxvi. 29).

[The MS. shows that the conclusion of this Lecture was
left unwritten.]

XVIII.

THE STATE OF MAN AFTER DEATH AND THE RESURRECTION.

WE come now to the fourth and last department of systematic theology, usually designated by the common term *Eschatology*, or the science of last things. The great departments of Anthropology and Soteriology relate to events and matters of personal experience which have come to pass. The topics embraced in the department of Eschatology relate to events and experiences yet future to us. This fact, of course, accounts for the comparative vagueness and absence of uniformity which characterize the faith of the great historic Churches upon the several points involved in this department. The whole region lies entirely beyond our experience. We can know anything on these points only as it is definitely revealed in the Word of God. And it must ever be remembered that this revealed Word was not given us to satisfy our curiosity or to afford us the material for speculation, but simply to afford us a practical ground of faith and hope and a guide to the performance of duty. Beyond this information thus afforded the Scriptures will not carry us. One of the wisest reflections ever made on the matter of biblical prophecies was that by the great Sir Isaac Newton—namely, "that prophecy was not given in order to make men prophets." And it is just as profoundly true that no amount of study, no brilliancy of interpretation, will ever make the future hemisphere of Eschatology as clear to us in this life as we have already found to be the departments of the person and work of Christ, of the Spirit's application of the same, and of our practical duties on the line of our earthly pilgrimage.

The main essential points, such as the fact that human probation is closed at death, the second coming of Christ, the resurrection of all men, the general judgment, and the final award of endless happiness or misery, all are clearly taught in Scripture, and all are firmly held with unvarying consent in all the creeds of the great historical Churches. Dissentient opinions on these points are in the strict sense of the word heresies, and have been confined to individuals or small and transient Church parties.

On the other hand, as to all other points involved—as to the time in which some of the events will occur, or as to the order in which they will come to pass, and as to the intermediate state—Christians, otherwise orthodox, differ from one another and hold various views. Within these limits we must tolerate difference and respect the mental independence of our brethren. In a few matters of detail, not settled in any way in our Confession of Faith, I shall be forced to differ from brethren whom I hold in great respect and affection. I do so with reluctance and with sincere deference to their opinions, and only because I am convinced that the views I shall present are more consistent with the statements and language of the Bible, and that they offer a far stronger polemic position from which to defend our common faith than that occupied by the brethren who will most emphatically dissent from me.

I. The *first* point explicitly and emphatically stated in Scripture is, that human probation ends with death—that the relation then established between a man and God remains unchanged for all eternity. Everything the Scriptures say on the subject plainly implies this fundamental fact, and there is nothing in the sacred Book which, in its plain interpretation, carries an opposite meaning. " Blessed are the dead which die in the Lord, that they may rest from their labours ; and their works do follow them " (Rev. xiv. 13). It is the earthly life, " the things done in the body," which are finally to determine character and destiny at the judgment-seat of Christ (2 Cor. v. 10). Our blessed Saviour, in the parable of the rich man and Lazarus, declares explicitly two capital facts : (1) that immediately upon death the good man goes to a state of holiness and happiness, and the bad man to a place of torment ; and (2) that these states and the characters they imply are permanent and irreversible. Abraham evidently voices the divine judgment when he says to the importunate subject of instant perdition, " And beside all this, between us and you there is a great gulf fixed : so that they which would pass from hence to you cannot ; neither can they pass to us, that would come from thence " (Luke xvi. 19–31). Christ's commission to his original apostles, which defines the only and the entire ground of authorized hope, reads thus, " Go ye into all the *cosmos*, and preach the gospel to every creature. He that believeth and is baptized shall be saved ; but he that believeth not shall be damned ; " " And, lo, I am with you alway, even to the consummation of the age "—to the end of this world, period, or dispensation (Mark xvi. 15–17 ; Matt. xxviii. 20). Thus the commission and the offer of the gospel it carries extend only to the present age of the gospel on the earth. They who do not believe here and now in this life shall be damned. Paul beseeches the Corinthians that they " receive not the grace of God in vain," because " *now* is the accepted time, *now* is the day of salvation " (2 Cor. vi. 1, 2). The same lesson is enforced by all our Lord's various parables of the kingdom of heaven—as, for instance, the parable of the

Ten Virgins and of the Talents. The Lord comes to each of us at death. His coming is always sudden, and the person who is found without oil in his lamp is excluded from the marriage supper.

II. The teaching of Scripture upon the other points included in the immediate destiny of every soul after death is admirably summed up and clearly stated in the answers to the thirty-seventh and thirty-eighth questions of our Shorter Catechism—" The souls of believers are at their death made perfect in holiness, and do immediately pass into glory, and their bodies, being still united to Christ, do rest in their graves till the resurrection;" " At the resurrection, believers being raised up in glory, shall be openly acknowledged and acquitted in the day of judgment, and made perfectly blessed in the full enjoying of God to all eternity."

The wicked Dives was immediately upon death cast into Hades, and " lifted up his eyes, being in torment," doubtless in the same prison-house wherein, according to Jude (sixth verse), " the angels which kept not their first estate, but left their own habitation, he [God] hath reserved in everlasting chains under darkness *unto the judgment* of the great day."

III. All these points are settled. Concerning these there ought to be no longer any debate. But it is abundantly evident, although constantly overlooked by Christians, that the Scriptures settle nothing as to the place or location in space of either heaven or hell. Unquestionably, these terms must designate place or definite location in space, because all created spirits, good or bad, can exist only under the limitations of space. But the particular places are defined neither absolutely nor relatively. Whether these places are far apart or contiguous in space; whether they each always continue to occupy the same portions of space, or are occasionally or frequently moved from one portion of space to another; whether each of them occupies a fixed region or is carried about on revolving spheres like the suns and their planets; whether relatively to us they are up or down,—all these questions are unanswered in Scripture, and with regard to them all opinion is absurd and speculation vain.

It is true that the Scriptures characteristically represent the destination of the good as upward and that of the bad as downward, and in the Old Testament the latter is spoken of as under the surface of the earth. But it is unquestionable that this language is purely metaphorical —that it refers not to relation or direction in space, but to moral differences of honour, happiness, and the reverse. In this sense the language is perfectly natural and consistent with the general manner of thought and language characteristic of Oriental people, and especially of the biblical writers. But it is plain that, when used from the point of view of the inhabitants of a revolving and rotating globe like this earth, the literal interpretation of this language is absurd.

To say, moreover, that heaven is where the infinite and omnipresent God is, is evidently to contribute no definite information with regard to its locality, since essentially he is just as much in hell as in heaven. The New Testament beautifully settles this question to the perfect satisfaction of every Christian heart—"To be absent from the body is to be at home with the Lord" (2 Cor. v. 8, Revised Version). Heaven, as a place, is defined to be where the incarnate God-man is.

IV. But this at once demonstrates the fact that the condition of Old Testament saints before Christ's death was in some essential respects different from that which all the redeemed dead share together since his death and ascension. To us and to all the redeemed the essence of heaven is to be with Christ, to be where he is. The vision of God in the incarnate Word, the intimate fellowship with the risen and glorified God-man, our merciful High Priest, is the very essence of the blessedness we seek. Now, whatever else may have been true of the place, the state, or the blessedness of the redeemed dead in Old Testament times, they could not have enjoyed *this crowning* grace. As the Old Testament believer, in the use of the ceremonial system of symbolic worship, looked forward trustingly and longingly to a Christ to come hereafter as the goal of his desire, as we New Testament believers look forward with trust and joy and longingly hasten unto the second coming of our Lord, so must the happy, holy redeemed dead in the Old Testament age have looked forward trustingly, longingly to the fulfilment of all their desires, the goal of all their hopes, to the coming and dwelling among them for ever of their incarnate Lord in his sacrificed body, beautified and glorified.

Therefore, it follows that when, on the evening of Friday, the soul of the then dead Christ, personally united for ever to his divinity, entered Paradise, he must have irradiated it with a sudden light never seen there nor in all the universe of God before. That one moment consummated heaven and revolutionized the condition of the redeemed for ever. How much more then, when some forty days afterward, in his completed person, his risen and glorified body united to his glorious soul and Godhead, he ascended and sat down on the right hand of the Majesty on high, must the seats of bliss have been transformed and glorified for ever, and made the central temple and cosmopolitan eye and crown of the universe! "For the Lamb is" now henceforth "the light thereof."

V. It is also very plainly the teaching of the *Word of God* in both Testaments that the condition into which the souls of men, either good or bad, depart immediately after death, although fixed and irreversible in its general character, is nevertheless intermediate and not ultimate in the character or degree either of the misery on the one hand or of the blessedness on the other.

1. In the first place, although the souls of believers immediately after death are made perfect in holiness, and pass into a state properly called glorious, nevertheless the intermediate state is a condition of *death*. The spirits of men, while their bodies remain in the graves, are ghosts or disembodied souls. The condition of even the redeemed dead, although completely delivered from sin and at home with the Lord, is one in which they are not yet completely delivered from *all* the consequences of sin. They look forward to the resurrection of their bodies and to the consummation of their salvation consequent upon the second advent of Christ on earth and its immediate consequents, just as the Church on earth does. Christ, although his soul was in Paradise, continued " until the third day under the power of death." The same is true of Abraham, Isaac, and Jacob, and of all the dead until the morning of the resurrection. The Bible always speaks of the " resurrection of the dead ; " therefore they are called " dead," although their souls are in heaven before the resurrection. The Scriptures characteristically point the faith and hope of believers forward, not to the hour of death, but to that of the resurrection, as the crisis of our complete redemption. The day of resurrection is called " the day of redemption " (Eph. iv. 30). Paul (Phil. iii. 11) declares it to be his great object of desire and of effort " if by any means I may attain unto the resurrection of the dead." The hope of the gospel, as Paul and all the apostles preached it, was the hope of the resurrection of the dead. When the hour comes, it is the *dead* in Christ, still dead, who are to rise first (Acts xxiii. 6 ; 1 Thess. iv. 16).

2. Spiritual death is not here in question. As far as

unbelievers are concerned, they continue spiritually dead from their birth through all eternity. As far as the believer is concerned, he is spiritually alive from the moment of his regeneration (John vi. 54). But death, in its common sense, is precisely defined as the suspension of the personal union of soul and body. It continues precisely as long as this union is suspended. It ends the instant this union is re-established by the resurrection. The human soul is essentially constituted for this personal union with a material body. This union conditions all its sensibilities and all its activities. When absent from the body the personality is incomplete; the ghost-life, however happy, must be intermediate and provisional. It is only in the reconstructed personality consequent upon the resurrection of the body, and its glorification in the likeness of Christ, that the person is ready for final judgment or for the consummation of salvation.

This view certainly does not depreciate the state of the disembodied dead with Christ in heaven during the present age. It is perfectly true that the believer at death "is made perfect in holiness, and does immediately pass into glory." But that is not final. There is something incomparably higher and more complete to look forward to— when all the redeemed shall pass for ever from under the power of death, and each entire person, instinct with life and glorified, shall be completely conformed to the likeness of his Lord and adjusted to his environment in the new heavens and the new earth.

VI. In connection with this we are brought to the question as to the true meaning of the Hebrew and Greek words *Sheol* and *Hades*, in the Old and New Testaments. This question is rather of exegesis and of biblical theology than of positive doctrine. We hold, as has been shown, precisely what our Catechism and Confession of Faith teach as to what becomes of the souls and bodies of men imme-

diately after death.   Nevertheless, the revelation of truth,
communicated by God to the fathers, and recorded in the
Scriptures, has been a gradual one, and it is of importance
for us to know, not only what the truth finally revealed is,
but also to trace the history of its gradual communication
through past dispensations.   It is only in this way that we
can rightly interpret the Scriptures in their true historic
sense.   And, above all, it is only in this way that we can
maintain the true historic ground of our faith in controversy
against all who deny its truth.

It is true that the Scriptures must be interpreted according to the analogy of the faith, and that the general design
and fixed principles of the whole must guide us in the
interpretation of the parts.   Nevertheless, the dogmatic
method of interpretation, whereby it is insisted that the
fullest development of doctrine gathered in the apostolic
writings shall be found in the earliest writings of the Old
Testament, may be carried very much too far, and be a
great occasion of weakness when assaulted by the enemies
of truth.   The question is not how we do now conceive of
heaven and hell, but what did the sacred writers mean by
Sheol and *Hades*.

The English word " hell " is of Saxon origin, and originally meant " a concealed place," and hence either the "grave,"
where the body goes at death, or the " invisible world,"
" the spirit world," where the soul goes.   But it has come
now to have the fixed sense of " the place of perdition,"
where the devil, his angels, and the lost souls of men are
in torment.   This last sense is so general and so firmly
established that no attempt should be made to alter or
confuse it.   We use, therefore, the term " hell " for the
place of the punishment of lost souls.   Many scholars have
held that the words *Sheol* and *Hades*, in the original
Scriptures, sometimes mean " hell " and sometimes " the
grave."   I believe that modern Hebrew and Greek scholars,

free from mere traditional trammels, unite with almost absolute unanimity in maintaining that these words never on a single occasion in the Bible mean either "hell" or "the grave," but always and only the invisible spirit world, in which the disembodied souls of men, whether good or bad, abide after death and before the resurrection, while they remain under the power of death for a season. This view is certainly consistent and uniform. It permits a simple and natural exegesis of all the passages in which the words in question occur, and it does not in the least modify or weaken the dogmatic positions assumed in our Confession.

The word "heaven" often occurs in the Old Testament, but is never used to express the place or the condition into which believers are introduced at death. The single exception (2 Kings ii. 1) proves the rule, because Elijah, of whom alone it was said that he went to heaven, was translated in his body, and did not die at all. The word "heaven" always designates in the Old Testament the dwelling-place of God. Heaven is his throne, while the earth is his footstool. He is always represented as reigning, looking, hearing, answering, acting, coming from heaven. But, on the contrary, all men, good and bad alike, go when they die to *Sheol* (Dr. C. Hodge's *Systematic Theology*, Part 4, ch. i., sect. 1).

Sheol occurs sixty-five times in the Old Testament, and, with two or three exceptions, is represented in the Septuagint by the Greek equivalent *Hades*. *Hades* occurs also eleven times in the New Testament, and throughout both Testaments the two words have one single, plain, uniform meaning. They mean the spirit or ghost world, in which the disembodied spirits of all men are gathered before the resurrection while they remain under the power of death. It is part of the realm of death. Residence in it, like death, is part of the consequences of sin. Irrespective of

the atonement of Christ, its condition would be purely
penal and hopeless.   But in view of that atonement *Sheol*
or *Hades* was to all true believers the vestibule of heaven.
The fact that all men, good and bad, were represented as
going to *Hades* or *Sheol* of course did not imply that they
all went to the same place, or to the same or to a like condition, any more than it does now when it is said that all
men go down to the grave or to death, or than it is when
it is affirmed of different emigrants from Europe that they
are going to America.   All went to *Sheol* or *Hades*—that
is, *all*, good and bad alike, went out as disembodied spirits
into the ghost world, precisely as all, good and bad alike,
died, though death is the penalty of sin.   And all alike
continued under the power of death in the disembodied
state until the resurrection.   But the good were rendered
perfect in holiness, and taken to seats of bliss called " paradise " or " Abraham's bosom ;" while the wicked, abandoned
by the spirit of grace and sealed until the day of perdition, went to *Gehenna*, a place of torment.   And between
these two there was a great and utterly impassable gulf
fixed.

It naturally follows that *Sheol*, *Hades*, and *death* are
generally spoken of in the Old Testament as dark and
dread-inspiring, as the consequence of sin.   The fulness
and completion of salvation had not then been brought
fully to light.   Even believers, while anticipating salvation with calm faith, yet shrank from death and their
continuance in *Sheol* or *Hades*, and looked forward with
longing to the completion of salvation in the *resurrection*,
which was the ultimate goal of their hope.   The Psalmist
exultantly affirms, " Thou wilt not leave my soul in Hades "
(Ps. xvi. 10).   Thus Peter, filled with the Holy Ghost, declares that the patriarch David spoke of the resurrection
of Christ, God having promised that he would "not leave
his soul in *Hades*."   Thus Martha, the weeping sister of

Lazarus, confessed at his grave the common faith and hope of a believing Jew: "I know that he shall rise again at the resurrection of the last day." And thus, in the *resurrection*, when the salvation of the redeemed and the condemnation of the lost are finally consummated, it is foretold in Rev. xx. 13–15, "The sea gave up the dead which were in it; and death and *Hades* delivered up the dead which were in them......And death and *Hades* were cast into the lake of fire." Then the lost will suffer the second death. Then the redeemed, complete in soul and body, and in both bearing the glorious image of Christ, shall be delivered from all the power and influence of death for evermore.

VII. This explains perfectly the much-disputed phrase in the most ancient and universal creed of the Christian Church, wherein it is asserted of Christ, "He was crucified, dead, and buried; he descended into hell." In the original it stands, "He descended into *Hades* ;" and since the changed sense acquired by the English word "hell," the original and accurately-correct and biblical word "Hades" should be restored. This creed, as it stands, is a part of the binding standards of our Church, to which every minister and elder solemnly subscribes, and it is, after the Scriptures, the most ancient, venerable, and generally recognized of all the historic literary monuments of the Christian Church. It seems to me a dreadful violation of the bonds which connect us with the history of Christian faith and life, and of the common ties which still connect the divided segments of "the body of Christ," for any one branch of that Church to agitate for the mutilation of the venerable creed which belongs to the whole brotherhood, and to all the sacred past as well. This is rendered the more clear and forcible by the obvious fact that the natural and most generally accredited meaning of the clause objected to is perfectly true, and that it can have no objectionable doctrinal implications. The true meaning is that given it in our Confession of Faith—that is, " continuing in the state of the dead, and under the power of death, until the third day." That is precisely what going into *Hades*, the world of the disembodied spirits of dead men awaiting their resurrection, means. The soul of Christ, personally united to his divinity, went, the moment he gave up the ghost, to the very same place and condition as that to which the souls of all redeemed men from the beginning had gone. But on the first day of the week Christ arose, and thus became the first-fruits of them that slept; and afterward ascended, carrying captivity captive (1 Cor. xv. 20 ; Eph. iv. 8).

VIII. Man consists of soul and body. The entire person, reintegrated by resurrection after death, is the only possible subject of complete and final judgment—the only possible subject upon which complete and final punishment can be inflicted, or to which complete and final rewards can be granted. Unless man is judged, acquitted, and acknowledged in the body, and in the body made perfectly blessed in the full enjoying of Christ to all eternity, the whole and complete historical person is not justified or saved. Unless the sinful man is judged, condemned, and damned in the body, the whole and complete historical person of the sinner is not dealt with according to law and justice, and the supreme holiness, truth, and justice of God are not fully shown forth. Resurrection is equally necessary in the case of the finally saved and of the finally lost, and for the same reason—that is, in order to complete the full personality, as a subject of judgment, and hence of reward or of punishment.

It hence follows that the resurrection of the redeemed is (1) the consummation of their personal salvation ; (2) therefore, in their case, gracious, for Christ's sake, a consequence of Christ's resurrection. On the other hand, the resurrection of the reprobate is (1) the necessary antecedent to their final judgment and endless perdition ; (2) and hence, in their case, judicial and punitive. It seems very clear that it is not logical to reason from the fact that Christ's true people are everywhere encouraged to look forward to the "resurrection of life" as the crowning of their redemption, that therefore the "resurrection of damnation" must be redemptive also (John v. 29). The latter is to lead "to everlasting punishment," but the other "to life eternal" (Matt. xxv. 46).

IX. The ground of the resurrection of the reprobate will be judgment—the demands of the perfect law which they have broken. As to the nature of their resurrection bodies we have no revelation.

The ground of the resurrection of the saints is the already accomplished resurrection of Christ, the "first-fruits of them that slept." We are to rise because he rose. We are to rise as certainly as he rose. And we are to be like him when we awake, because "he will change our vile body, that it may be fashioned like unto his glorious body, according to the working whereby he is able to subdue all things unto himself" (Phil. iii. 21).

1. The same bodies are to rise again which are deposited in the grave. This is expressly asserted in every way : " It is sown in weakness ; it is raised in power : it is sown in corruption ; it is raised in incorruption." We are to rise in the same sense that Christ rose. But his identical body rose again and was identified. Our " vile bodies are to be made like unto Christ's glorious body." We know not what the essential principles of bodily identity are, but we know, certainly, that we have identically the same bodies from the cradle to the grave, although the material constituents of these bodies are continually changing. It is enough for us to be absolutely sure that the bodies we shall rise with at the resurrection will be in the same sense identical with the bodies we lay aside at death, as the

bodies we lay aside at death are identical with the bodies with which we were born.

2. But our bodies, although identical, will be changed, modified (not exchanged), so that they will then be perfectly adapted (*a*) to the instincts and faculties of our glorified souls, and (*b*) to the physical conditions of the new heavens and new earth wherein dwelleth righteousness.

The body of Christ is now material, as Thomas proved when he thrust his fingers into the print of the nails, and as Christ asserted when he said, after his resurrection, " A spirit hath not flesh and bones, as ye see me have " (Luke xxiv. 36–40). If so, it must have a material home to live in. Hence the material universe, in some form, will be as everlasting as the spiritual world. Therefore our bodies will be material like his.

The essential definition of a body is " a material organism personally united to a soul, to be the organ of that soul in perception, in volition, and in expression." Every body, as an organism, therefore, must be constructed of matter, and must be adjusted in every case to the appetites, instincts, and passions of the soul to which it is united, and to the physical conditions of the environment in which it exists. It is plain that the soul of a sheep never could exist in the body of a lion, nor the soul of a lion in the body of a sheep. It is just as plain that if a body is to inhabit any element, it must be physically adjusted to its conditions. Thus, if it is to inhabit the water, it must have the body of a fish ; or if it is to inhabit the air, the body of a bird. So our new body must be transformed into complete adjustment to the glorified spirit and to the glorified world it is to inhabit, and in which it is to act.

In this life our body is called " animal," *psuchikon* (1 Cor. xv. 44). In the new life it will be what the New

Testament calls "spiritual," *pneumatikon.* The established meaning of that phrase in the New Testament is, that which has been made the temple of the Holy Ghost, and which consequently has been transformed by his indwelling (1 Cor. ii. 12–15). The "spiritual body" will therefore be our very same material body, modified by the indwelling of the Holy Ghost so as to be no longer "animal," but rather so as to be a fit temple for the divine Guest, and a fit organ for the perfectly sanctified and spiritualized soul.

3. Our bodies will be rendered perfect as the organs of our souls in *perception.* Here we possess but five bodily senses, and hence come into contact with the material world only on five sides. We can take knowledge only of its tangible, visible, audible, and odoriferous properties. Beyond doubt, the world, even as at present constituted, possesses far different properties and presents other aspects, perhaps far deeper, grander, larger, than any now open to us. At present our existing senses are feeble and of narrow range, and we need to increase their powers by the use of instruments, such as the microscope, the telescope, and the spectroscope, whereby new spheres are opened to us.

For illustration, imagine the case of Laura Bridgman, born without the sense either of sight or of hearing, and of course utterly unable to conceive the use or the essence of either experience. Suppose that her teacher, endowed with supernatural power, should have placed her some day of the year, in the spring days of her life, on some central tower in the harbour of Boston. At first she would stand in absolute isolation, teeming with force and life and mind, touching the world only through the soles of her feet and the zephyr which fanned her cheek, yet enveloped in darkness and silence infinite, alone and apart as really as if sunk in the abysses of night beyond the orbit of the nethermost sun. Suppose then her teacher should touch her and say, " Daughter, hear ! " and at once there should flow into her open soul all the myriad voices of the globe. Suppose, again, the teacher should touch her and say, " Daughter, see ! " and suddenly that hitherto isolated soul should pass out in one instant into the infinite world, and take into her irradiated consciousness all the visions of the sea and earth under the stupendous sky. Without moving herself, or any change of environment, the mere opening of ear and eye would widen her horizon infinitely and bring her face to face with a thousand worlds, all new.

Some such experience will be yours and mine when we are clothed upon with our glorified bodies on the morning of the resurrection. Coming up from rural or urban grave-yards, rising before the awful whiteness of the throne and the intolerable glory of Him that sits thereon, and passing through the interminable ranks of flaming seraphs and diademed archangels, the perfect senses of our new bodies will bring us at once into the presence of the whole universe, of the music of all its spheres, and of the efful-gence of all its suns—of the most secret working of all its forces, and of the recorded history of all its past.

4. Our new bodies will be no less perfect as the organs of our souls in *volition*. At present our volitions have direct control only of a few voluntary muscles and of the course of our thoughts. Besides this, our physical energies need constant reinforcement from nutrition and sleep, and are rapidly exhausted by fatigue, and in a few years en-tirely decay. Man in this world could not stand the competition of any but the weakest of the lower animals if it were not for his superiority of intellect, and for the characteristic fact that he alone is a tool-making and tool-using animal. It is by machinery, to which he harnesses all the forces of material nature, that man maintains his lordship of the world.

But completely redeemed humanity is symbolically represented in the ancient ritual by the cherubim which surrounded the ark of the covenant, the throne of Jehovah over the mercy-seat, and which were inwrought in all the walls and curtains of the tabernacle and the temple. This composite symbol consisted of the ox, the lion, the eagle, and the man. Here were symbolically gathered into one focus, and set forth as the attributes of every redeemed man, all the energies now distributed through all the provinces of the animal world. The *ox* represents brute strength, the power that cultivates and renders fruitful the earth, and that bears the burdens of mankind. The *lion* is the king of beasts, at whose voice and tread all the denizens of the forest tremble. The *eagle* is the king of birds, who soars upward to the seats of the sun, and who sleeps in perfect equilibrium upon his inexhaustible wing. *Man* is the sovereign intelligence, who gathers all the energies of the physical world and sways them to his use.

Taken together, they constitute the type or prophetic symbol of our resurrection bodies. There will be there no need of grosser nutriment and no need of sleep. Our energies will not flag with fatigue, nor will they be exhausted with age. Our wills will not be confined to indirect and difficult action through cumbrous machinery, but the whole soul will act directly upon every subservient force. Without inertia or friction our purposes will be spontaneously executed by inexhaustible energies, to which all exercise will be pleasure, and continuous activity the unshadowed rapture of an immortal life.

5. Our new bodies, finally, will be perfect as the organs of our souls in *expression*. The expression of mental characteristics and states is a great mystery. Yet we are absolutely dependent upon it for all our knowledge of and for all our communion with each other. In some ex-

ceptional cases the power of expression acquired by some souls through their bodies opens to us a grand conception of what in the resurrection may become the common property of all saints. We have all of us experienced something of the magic power wielded by the great masters of the art of expression—the poets, painters, singers, and orators of all time. Yet even in these the present body of flesh is only a coarse and opaque medium for the spirit's light. I have no doubt that the resurrection bodies of the saints will be of more than crystal translucency, through which each glorified soul will dart his rays through myriad facets. The recognition of friends, then, will not be the recognition of souls through the remembered features of the body, but rather the recognition of persons through irradiating characteristics of their souls. When we rise on that great Easter morning, and our new senses sweep the historic generations of the redeemed, we will know the great masters of thought and song and the great leaders of the sacramental hosts in instant glances, from our long knowledge of their thoughts and deeds. And when, in the centre of the hosts, we meet the Object to which all thoughts and hearts converge, there will be no need of introduction between the glorified Lord and his glorified servant, however humble he may be. The instant rapturous recognition will be mutual and spontaneous: " Rabboni !" " Mary !"

XIX

FINAL REWARDS AND PUNISHMENTS.

I T is a very striking infelicity that so many of our
systems of theology end as their last words with
"hell" and "eternal punishment," as if these were the
climacteric categories in which the study of the nature,
purposes, and works of the Lord must find its final and
characteristic goal. Such an arrangement has little influence upon the substance of the doctrine held; but it mars
the symmetry of truth, it misrepresents the real facts of
the case, and it must depress the enthusiasm of the believer and give unnecessary occasion of stumbling and of
offence to the unbeliever.

We will, therefore, purposely reverse the common order,
and consider, first, what the Scriptures teach us as to
the future of those who depart this life finally impenitent; and after that close with a short study of the
glimpses they afford us into the endless blessedness of
the redeemed.

I. It seems to be very clear that there are only seven
distinct views as to the final destiny of man which are
possible, one or other of which, with very slight modification, must be held by all who think upon the subject.

1. It has been held by many that one end happens to
man in common with all other animals—that his conscious
intellectual life is inseparable from his body, and that

when the one falls to pieces and decays at death, the other ceases absolutely and for ever. Against this materialism human nature in all its varieties and throughout its entire history has protested. The false religions have here joined voices with Christianity in holding before all the inhabitants of the earth the certainty of a future life.

2. Again: many parties with whom the sense of sin and its ill-desert is vague and slight have flattered themselves that the benevolence of God was his only characteristic moral attribute, and the universal happiness of his creatures his one chief end. These have consequently held an indiscriminate Universalism, including the immediate happiness of all men after death, without reference to distinctions of moral character or to the redemptive work of Christ.

This, of course, is abhorrent to an enlightened moral sense, and derogatory to the personal holiness and governmental rectitude of God. All who bear, however loosely, the Christian name must repudiate this view, since it absolutely repudiates Christ and the value and dignity of his mediation.

3. Universalists, who have at the same time endeavoured to justify their claim to being a Christian sect, have maintained that since Christ died for all men, all men must be saved; that this salvation, depending as it does upon what Christ has done and will do in man's behalf, cannot be rendered of no effect by what men themselves may do or experience on earth; that in some way and at some time, and probably sooner and with far less difficulty than we are apt to fear, Christ will draw the spirits of all men to himself, and secure for them the conditions of perfect happiness for ever.

This view, although it names the name of Christ, and professes to rest all its hopes upon his mediatorial achievements, nevertheless is essentially as anti-Christian as those we have just dismissed. It puts a higher estimation upon happiness than upon holiness. It puts mere benevolence on a higher rank among the attributes of God than purity and righteousness. It regards deliverance from the mere punishment of sin as of greater importance than deliverance from the pollution and power of sin itself. It is founded not in the least upon positive revelations of God's purposes, but is maintained upon grounds of human sentiment and reason exclusively, against evident testimony of God's inspired Word and the uniform belief of God's historic Church.

4. In latter times the view has been entertained by many that although the Scriptures plainly teach that all who reject Christ and die finally impenitent shall be condemned in the judgment of the great day and condignly punished, yet two immutable facts remain which must always afford a rational basis for an eternal hope with regard to all men:—(1.) They are essentially free agents, and as such possess an inalienable power of self-determined choice. As soon as they cease to be moral agents they must cease to be proper subjects of punishment. As long as they continue to be moral agents they continue (so it is claimed) to possess the power of repentance and the will (at least) to reform. No one can predict (it is argued) that penal sufferings will be unending, because no one can be certain of any sinner, in any state or in any world, that he will not repent and return. (2.) God is immutably and before all things merciful. All his government, penalties as well as blessings, looks to promoting the excellence and happiness of all his creatures. He has sought by temporal dispensations to bring men to repentance in this life; so he will ceaselessly continue to seek to bring the condemned and suffering spirits of lost men in the world of penal inflictions to repentance by means of those more tremendous and more cogent disciplines. Reason and conscience will

always be pleading with men to repent and throw down the weapons of rebellion. The sufferings of perdition will afford the most powerful arguments conceivable to induce men to close their ears to the suggestions of sinful passion and to open them obediently to the influence of reason and conscience. And all the while the eternal God is eternally the God of mercy and grace, and to the latest moment yearning to receive the prodigal with open arms upon the first indication of his willingness to return. Immediate punishment after death of all who reject the gospel and die unreconciled to God, and the ultimate restoration of all during the future ages, are the hope of many.

5. Others, who cannot admit that the Scriptures leave any opening for the indulgence of this eternal hope in behalf of all souls, nevertheless maintain, both on the ground of justice and upon that of harmony with the characteristics of God as revealed in nature and in revelation, that hereafter, at some time between death and the final judgment, the gospel will be offered under favourable conditions and with hopeful results to all to whom it was not clearly revealed and upon whom it was not urgently pressed in this life.

6. Many others, who cannot disguise to themselves the obviously anti-scriptural character of this so-called "eternal hope," admit that the Word of God plainly teaches that all human probation, in every sense, ceases with the close of the present life; that the sentence pronounced on the reprobate in the judgment of the great day is absolutely final and irreversible; that those upon whom the sentence is pronounced will never be restored. But they claim that continued conscious existence after death and after judgment is no part of man's natural inheritance and no part of the sinner's doom. They hold that immortality is conditioned upon the personal attainment of eternal life, and that it is a gift which Christ graciously bestows only upon

his redeemed. The penalty of eternal death, which will certainly be inflicted upon all who depart this life impenitent, is just the ceasing to be, the being cast utterly and finally out of existence, as the penalty exacted of the sinner by the law of God.

7. There remains room in this series of alternative hypotheses only for the catholic doctrine of the entire historical Church : (1) that the probation of man in every sense, under both gospel and law, terminates with death ; (2) that the state of the relations subsisting between any man and God at that crisis will remain absolutely irreversible for ever ; (3) that neither during the intermediate state between death and the resurrection, nor after the judgment at any time through the endless ages, will any conditions of restoration be offered, or efficient grace extended ; (4) that all the lost will continue conscious rebels and sufferers through absolutely unending duration.

II. It appears that this classified statement of opinion is absolutely exhaustive. Any possible opinion on the subject of man's future destiny must be capable of being brought in under one or other of these heads. Such a position can differ from the corresponding statement here made only in the details. Leaving aside the first three views as plainly beyond the pale of Christianity, it seems that the choice is necessarily confined to the following positions : (1) either universal restoration of all to holiness and happiness ; (2) or the offer of the gospel in the future world under more favourable conditions to all those who were left to live and die ignorant of it in this world ; (3) or the annihilation of all the finally impenitent ; (4) or the Church doctrine of the eternal conscious misery of all those who depart this life unreconciled to God.

III. In preparing ourselves for an examination of the testimony of the Word of God on this subject, we should, in the first place, seek to be profoundly impressed with its

vital importance.   Before any other knowledge attainable
by us in the compass of the universe, it is most essential
for us to know what our Creator and sovereign Lord intends to do with us after death—whether deliverance from
the sin and misery and the fearful looking-for of judgment
which afflict us in this world is possible for us, and upon
what conditions.   If any preparation is to be made for the
future, it must be made now.   If there await us any future
dangers which are in any way avoidable, the present time
affords us the only possible opportunity of avoiding them.
What we need above all other things that God can give us
is a clear, certain knowledge of the actual truth.   It is very
natural for us to shrink from facing the truth boldly and
to turn away from the evidence of coming danger, and to
fix our attention upon every flattering light which appears
to promise some relief from danger.   If we really wish to
be safe, we must be honest with ourselves.   If we really
wish to be honest with ourselves, we should suspect our
natural tendency to shrink from the evidence which
threatens danger, and to resist it with all our might.

More than all this, we should recognize the superficiality
and essential cruelty of that mock charity which makes
so many professed theological reformers disguise from
sinners or explain away the real facts as to the attitude
of the Word of God on this subject.   Even if mistakes
should be made in the way of rendering the aspect of
scriptural teaching more menacing than it really is, while
it might give unnecessary pain for the present, it could
not betray souls to unexpected dangers hereafter.   But
there is no more deadly injury, no more wanton cruelty,
which any man can perpetrate upon a fellow-creature,
than that which the theological reformer is in danger of
when, against the apparent meaning of God's Word, against
the unanimous judgment of Christ's Church, he softens the
emphasis of warning, and assures the incorrigible sinner

that it is not, after all, so certain that he must die the second death of eternal pain and shame.

IV. Unquestionably, every Christian who understands his own heart will recognize the fact that he sympathizes profoundly with the feeling of his brethren who, from a mistaken philanthropy, seek relief from the plain teachings of Scripture as to the fearful doom of the finally impenitent. To human view the conception of never-ending, hopeless sin and misery is absolutely overwhelming. If we could realize its tremendous meaning it would paralyze our minds and hearts. We think and speak of it so calmly because it is so far off and so vague that it fails to impress us as an actual reality. There is nothing on earth more outrageously vulgar and profane than the coarse and careless shouting out of threats of damnation against heedless sinners by an orthodox ranter. When we declare the terrible judgments of our Lord against our fellow-sinners, of our own flesh and blood, who by nature are no worse than we are, we should do it tremblingly and with tears. We should remember that in all respects we deserve the same fate ourselves, and that it is only infinite, undeserved grace which has made us to differ. We should seek to treat all impenitent sinners with the yearning tenderness with which our blessed Lord wept over Jerusalem, with outstretched arms and heaving breast—"If thou hadst known, even thou, at least in this thy day, the things which belong unto thy peace; but now they are hid from thine eyes."

V. Our appeal must be made exclusively to the Scriptures. We accept these as the infallible rule of faith because they are the very Word of God. They were designed to furnish us all the information which is needed by us, and all that God intends us to have, on this subject.

We must come to the study of this Word in a teachable spirit, with a mind open to receive all that it has to convey to us, with simplicity and godly sincerity, without prejudice. What we need above all things to know is, not what we think or what other men think ought to be, but what is, in fact, the real, plain meaning of God's declaration on this subject.

The question is not, What can we, with skilful exegetical management, get out of the Bible on this question by breaking up the text and bringing the stress of our strong wills to bear against the natural sense of each separate clause ?—the question is not, What may the several passages possibly mean in the way we wish ? but, What, upon the whole and along the entire line of Scripture, did God the Holy Ghost intend us to believe, what impression did he intend to make upon us, as to these stupendous subjects by the language he has chosen, by the general method in which he has conducted the argument ?

1. Remember that it was "the Lamb of God," the tender and compassionate Saviour, who gave himself to die for the sins of men, who taught the most frequent and the most terrible lessons upon this subject. He addressed the common people in common language, and his representations, statements, and metaphorical descriptions were of one consistent tone from the beginning to the end of his ministry, without the least variation or modification of view. They must have understood him in the common meaning of terms as then currently received. Josephus (*Antiq.*, xviii. ch. i. 2 ; *Bell. Jud.*, ii. ch. viii. 14) says that the Pharisees of that day taught that the souls of the wicked after death were consigned to an everlasting imprisonment, to be punished with eternal vengeance. Christ, therefore, knew perfectly how his hearers, holding these opinions, would understand his frequently repeated "Gehenna of fire" (Matt. v. 22, 29, 30 ; x. 28 ; xviii. 9 ; xxiii. 15, 33 ; Mark ix. 43, 45, 47 ; Luke xii. 5).

2. As to either the restoration or the annihilation of

those who depart this life impenitent, the Scriptures say absolutely nothing. There is no single passage in the whole New Testament which indicates or suggests either of these views when frankly and reasonably interpreted. On the contrary, the ceaseless, hopeless, conscious suffering of those who die impenitent, both during the intermediate state before the resurrection and in the final state after the resurrection and judgment, is asserted over and over again in every form, in the most definite language, and with the greatest emphasis possible.

(1.) In the first place, it is explicitly declared that the sufferings of the wicked shall have *no end*—Their fire is not quenched, and shall never be quenched, and "their worm dieth not" (Mark ix. 44–46). Because the fire is unquenchable (Matt. iii. 12)—"The smoke of their torment ascendeth up for ever and ever, and they have no rest day nor night" (Rev. xiv. 11).

(2.) In the second place, the Word of God explicitly affirms that this suffering shall *last*, shall *endure* for ever—"The children of the kingdom shall be cast into outer darkness: there shall be weeping and gnashing of teeth" (Matt. viii. 12). Jude, in verse 13, says the wicked "are wandering stars, to whom is reserved the blackness of darkness for ever." And Peter (2 Pet. ii. 17) says of them, "To whom the mist of darkness is reserved *for ever*."

The fire (which is the metaphor expressing their torment) is declared to be "everlasting" (Matt. xxv. 41–46; Mark ix. 43), and the wicked are declared "to suffer the vengeance of eternal fire" (Jude 7). It is an "eternal judgment" which comes *after* the resurrection of the dead (Heb. vi. 1, 2). Those who obey not the gospel "shall be punished with everlasting destruction from the presence of the Lord, and from the glory of his power" (2 Thess. i. 9). "And many of them that sleep in the dust of the earth shall awake, some to everlasting life, and some to shame and everlasting contempt " (Dan. xii. 2).

It is never said that the *effects* of this punishment are everlasting, which might be true if that punishment were a condign annihilation of the sinner once for all. The effects would continue for ever, even although the punishment itself was inflicted in one act. But, on the contrary, the Scriptures declare that *not* the effects only are everlasting, but that " the condemnation," " the punishment," " the contempt," " the torment," " the fire," " the worm," " the chains," are everlasting, are never to cease to be. What is the sense of " everlasting " " torment," " chains," " fire," " worm," of " no rest day nor night for ever," if the sinner himself has ceased to be, or if the sinner himself has in the meantime been restored to the divine favour ?

This, we assert, is the general, uniform, and characteristic language of the Scriptures on this awful subject. It is the most intensely practical of all subjects, and as far removed from a merely theoretical and speculative interest as the heavens are above the earth. This is language addressed by God to plain, practical people of all classes, who would only be deceived by any subtleties of language. It is addressed to Jewish hearers and readers, who, God knew, understood this very same language in their ancient Hebrew Scriptures to mean definitely and surely this awful doctrine of endless conscious suffering, and this only.

Now, we charge you that God is always true and frank. He speaks, not to frighten, but in order to be understood. And he means what he says—just what he says. Is it not infinite blasphemy for man to dare to modify his words on such a subject ? Is it not the utmost reach of human folly to attempt to erect flimsy gauze barriers to shut out the approach of the intolerable fires he declares it to be his purpose to pour out ? Is it not the last refinement of cruelty to administer to bewildered sinners moral anæsthetics, assuring them of an "eternal hope," only that they may meet "the vengeance of God's eternal fire" with drugged consciences?

3. As to the supposition that to those to whom the gospel has not been plainly offered in this life it must in justice be offered hereafter, there are two things to be said, very plain and very certain :—

(1.) And, *first*, this supposition, even if it should turn out to be true, would bring no relief to us who have had the gospel offered to us in this world. It would still remain true, what God so terribly affirms, that "if we sin wilfully after that we have received the knowledge of the truth, there remaineth no more sacrifice for sins, but a certain fearful looking-for of judgment and fiery indignation, which shall devour the adversaries " (Heb. x. 26, 27).

(2.) The *second* thing to be said is that the Scriptures from beginning to end do not afford any ground for this "supposition." We are told to believe in Christ *now*, or we shall be damned. We are told to take our lives in our hands and make every sacrifice to preach the gospel to every creature in this life, in order that he may be saved. Christ promises to bless the preaching of the gospel in *this* world unto the end of the present age. But there is not the slightest suggestion that if men die without hearing the gospel in this life it will be preached to them in the next.

(*a*) It is not promised. (*b*) The presumptions are all against it. The circumstances of the unregenerate in the next world are all unfavourable. The world into which they pass immediately after death is everywhere and uniformly described in Scripture as a place of awards, and not of probation, and as the scene of sufferings absolutely endless. (*c*) The Bible always speaks of death as closing probation: "*Now* is the accepted time; *now* is the day of salvation;" "After death comes the *judgment;*" "For as many as have sinned without law, shall also perish without

law " (Rom. ii. 12). Remember that the term "law" with
Paul included the sum of all God's revelations to men, the
"gospel" as well as the moral law. The matter of the
judgment is to be "the deeds done in *the body*." The
question, as Christ puts it, is the treatment we extended to
him in the persons of his disciples in *this* life. (*d*) Christ
owes the unevangelized nothing, absolutely nothing. Salvation is of grace. The gift of Christ to expiate the sins
of men was wholly and simply gratuitous. If God *owed*
salvation, then *expiation* was a farce. If God *owed* salvation, then it was the height of false pretences for him to
pretend that "he *so* loved the world that he gave his only
begotten Son." If he did not owe it to all, he did not owe
it to any. He is thus absolutely free to grant it to *none*,
or to *all*, or to *few*, or to *many*, as he pleases, "according
to the good pleasure of his will."

Considering what we are and what Christ is, and what
he, out of his *infinite* love, has done for us, it is the last
and meanest insult that either man or devil can give, to
cast in his face that his amazing self-sacrifice was the
payment of a debt—that he ought to have made it—that
we had a right to expect it for ourselves, and have a right
to expect, independent of all promise on his part, that he
will send the knowledge of it to others, either in this life
or in that which is to come.

4. The Greek words and phrases in the New Testament
aion, aionios, eis ton aiona, eis tous aionas, etc., translated "eternal," "everlasting," "for ever and ever," and
applied to the never-ending sufferings of the lost, mean in
the usage of the Greek language precisely what their
English equivalents mean in the usage of the English language. The attempt of a class of Bible interpreters to
establish a new sense to the term "eternal" or *aionion*,
shows how far scholarly men, otherwise honest, may be
warped by a determined bias of desire in representing the

plainest and most certain and universally-known matters of fact. They maintain that these terms, as used in the Bible, do not express measures of duration, but express only the *quality* of the things of which they are predicated.

It is a simple matter that endless duration should also carry with it, because endless, an added idea of quality. If a man believes in Christ, he has "eternal life" already abiding in him. This life is not without either beginning or end in us, but it is without beginning or end in God; it is self-originating, self-existent, and inexhaustible and endless in God, from whom we receive it, and therefore it is called eternal. And in us also it will prove inexhaustible and endless.

It is simply absurd to deny that these terms originally, naturally, and always mark duration, and duration corresponding to the nature of the object of which they are predicated. Applied to God, they express his infinite duration as the metaphysical eternity without beginning, end, or succession. Applied to the soul of man and his future experiences, they express the strictly everlasting, that which has beginning but no end. Applied to the "everlasting mountains" (Hab. iii. 6), they express the duration of mountains.

They are the very words used in the New Testament to express the eternal duration of God (Rom. i. 20; 1 Tim. i. 17; Rom. xvi. 26; Heb. ix. 14), and the endless reign of Christ (Rev. i. 18), and the unending duration of the happiness of the redeemed (Matt. xix. 29; xxv. 46; Mark x. 30; John iii. 15; vi. 57, 58; Rom. ii. 7; 2 Cor. ix. 9), as well as the unending duration of the miseries of the lost.

They always express the idea of "unending continuance." The existence of God, the glory of God, the reign of Christ, the blessedness of the saints (Gal. i. 5; Eph. iii. 21; Rev. i. 18; iv. 9; x. 6; xv. 7; xxii. 5), all continue for

ever. So, of course, will the suffering of the impenitent
continue for ever (Rev. xiv. 11 ; xix. 3 ; xx. 10). These
terms are used to express a state of things opposed to this
present life as one that passes away, that ceases to be
(Luke xviii. 30), and they are used as synonymous with
apthartos, incorruptible, immortal, that which never ceases
to be (Rom. i. 23 ; 1 Tim. i. 17 ; 1 Cor. ix. 25 ; 1 Peter
i. 4), and with *akatalutos, indissoluble,* and hence endless,
enduring for ever (Heb. vii. 16).

VI. Human reason is not qualified to judge of the
absolute justice or of the governmental propriety of eternal
suffering as the penalty of sin.

1. In comparison with God, the human intellect is very
narrow in its range and imperfect in its processes.

2. In comparison with God, our point of view is infinitely inferior. We see from beneath, he sees from
above ; we see only in part, his vision comprehends the
whole sphere, and discerns all objects in their true proportions and relations. He alone can judge of the real evil
of sin and of the measures proper to its punishment and
restraint.

3. We are ourselves the malefactors. It is self-evident
that self-interest, that moral blindness and callousness, for
ever render every criminal an utterly incompetent judge of
the measure of guilt attaching to his own wrong-doing.
All experience proves this in criminal jurisprudence and in
private life. If this be true when we judge of the heinousness of our offences against our fellow-men, how much
more must it vitiate our judgments as to the heinousness
of our sins against the infinitely holy God !

We are not required to assent to the abstract metaphysical dictum that every sin, being committed against an
infinite God, is essentially an infinite evil, and intrinsically
deserves an infinite penalty. It is perfectly sufficient, in
order to establish the abundant justice of eternal suffering,

for us to recognize the common-sense principle that never-ending sin richly deserves never-ending punishment. Every sin continues as long as it is unrepented of. And every sin continues unless the wrong-doer not only repents, but also reforms. But sinners in hell never repent nor reform. Even if a sinner, by a miracle, did repent and reform, it would still remain that his guilt would demand condign punishment or vicarious expiation. But in that case, on the hypothesis of a sinner's repenting and reforming, God has never revealed to us that the guilt of his temporal sin, now repented of and reformed, deserves or would be punished with unending suffering. But that is a purely hypothetical case, which never, absolutely never, occurs. Surely a Christian who has lifted his eyes to the divine Victim upon the cross can never feel any difficulty in recognizing the perfect justice of the unending suffering of the finally impenitent. Surely sinners who never repent nor reform, who continue in a course of never-ending sin, deserve, yes, demand imperatively from justice, never-ending punishment.

The plea is now frequently offered that the stern doctrine of unending punishment is offensive to the sense of justice of an enlightened age, and is the exciting cause of a great deal of the infidelity now prevalent. This is utterly false as a fact, and as a plea is most unworthy and degrading in spirit. Infidelity has its source, not in the injustice of God, but in the rebellious will and impenitent blindness of men. Men doubt about eternal punishment because they are blind to the infinite evil of sin; and they are blind to the infinite evil of sin because they have inadequate and unworthy views of the absolute holiness of God. In an age of general peace and epicurean luxury, when, in the whole sphere of human thought, the supernatural has been overcast and hidden by the natural, God appears to us "altogether such an one as ourselves." We conceive of him as confederate with us in our pleasures and as connivent with us in our sins.

What is needed to break down rebellion is not the lowering of the claims of the government. What we need to render infidelity impossible is surely not a further obscuration of the awful majesty and holiness of God. What we need to render moral evil infamous is surely not the lowering the standard either of the law's demands or its penalties. There will be no infidelity in hell, nor before its opened mouth in judgment. And there will be far less infidelity when all who speak for God in the pulpit or in the press cease from human sentiment or speculation, and conform their utterances, both in matter and form, to the frank, explicit, majestic, though terrible, utterances of God's Word.

VII. We have in support of this doctrine also the true and genuine witness of the "Christian consciousness." The organ of this "Christian consciousness" cannot be any particular age of the Church, nor any self-appointed school of Christian thinkers, no matter how cultured or self-conscious of their own superiority. The presumption is ten thousand to one that the Bible does teach that God wills the finally impenitent to suffer endlessly. The Old Testament was in the hands of the Jews centuries before Christ came. They uniformly understood these Scriptures as teaching that the wicked are to suffer for ever (Josephus, *Wars*, ii., ch. viii. 14 ; *Antiq.*, xviii., ch. i. 2 ; *Philo Judæus*, i. p. 65 and p. 1391). The New Testament has been in the hands of Christians for eighteen hundred years. All the great Church fathers, Reformers, and historical churches, with their recensions and translations of the sacred Scriptures, their liturgies, and hymns ; all the great evangelical theologians and biblical scholars, with their grammars, dictionaries, commentaries, and classical systems, have uniformly agreed in their understanding of the teaching of the sacred Scriptures as to the endlessness of the future sufferings of all who die impenitent. And this has come to pass against the universal and impetuous current of human fears and sympathies.

The only exception to this unanimous judgment of the Christian Church of all ages consists of relatively a few men, who, hating this doctrine, have beforehand determined that the Bible *cannot* teach it, and so afterward easily persuade themselves that it *does not.*

VIII. Heaven!

Of heaven, the final home of Christ and his people, and of the eternal rewards of well-doing, we are told far more in the Scriptures than we are told of the final punishment of the wicked. The facts are no surer, but the details are much clearer. And yet we do not need to say much on the subject. There is prevalent no prejudice against the doctrine of heaven, as there is in this day against that of hell—no array of objections to the Church doctrine to be refuted. It is sufficient for Christians that, with the Bible in their hands, they set their affections on things above, and seek, through grace and the diligent observance of all means and duties, to grow constantly in meetness for the inheritance of the saints in light.

The main points embraced within our present knowledge can easily be stated.

1. Heaven, *as a place,* is where Christ, the God-man, is. Heaven, *as a state,* is one of intimate knowledge of him and of the whole Godhead in him, and of fellowship with him. Although we shall be perfectly holy and confirmed in grace, so that we shall never more be liable to sin, nevertheless the atoning, sin-expiating blood of Christ will for ever be the only foundation of our claim and our only plea for life or blessedness. It will always be our "purchased possession." As Christ is inexhaustible, so heaven is inexhaustible. There is room and verge for every capa-

city, for every idiosyncrasy, and indefinite progress in all directions, through the eternal ages.

2. Heaven, as the supreme centre of divine revelations and communications through Christ, must pre-eminently bear the characteristics of God. It will be absolutely pure, majestic, holy, noble, in all its elements and characteristics. Everything that is impure and that defileth will be excluded. Its inhabitants will all be arrayed in linen *fine and white*, which has been washed and made white in the blood of the Lamb. Everything, therefore, that encompasses our life on earth, which is narrow, dark, selfish, petty, ungenerous, untrue, unclean, must be faithfully cut away at every cost. There can absolutely be no compromise between light and darkness—between the candidate for heaven and the spirit and fashion of this world.

3. Heaven, as the eternal home of the divine Man and of all the redeemed members of the human race, must necessarily be thoroughly human in its structure, conditions, and activities. Its joys and its occupations must all be rational, moral, emotional, voluntary, and active. There must be the exercise of all faculties, the gratification of all tastes, the development of all latent capacities, the realization of all ideals. The reason, the intellectual curiosity, the imagination, the æsthetic instincts, the holy affections, the social affinities, the inexhaustible resources of strength and power native to the human soul, must all find in heaven exercise and satisfaction. Then there must always be a goal of endeavour before us, ever future. It will never be said there that we have already attained or have already *finished;* but, forgetting the things which are behind, and reaching forth unto the things which are before, we will press toward the ever-advancing mark for the prize of the high calling of God in Christ Jesus. Ever upward and onward the pathway of the redeemed and glorified will always be, with Christ Godward.

4. The constitution of heaven will be related not only to human nature, redeemed and glorified, but also to angelic nature in all its grades and orders. Christ and the commonwealth of his redeemed kindred after the flesh will be central. But with us all holy intelligences in all their infinite varieties of rank and gifts and functions will be comprehended. Heaven will prove the consummate flower and fruit of the whole creation and of all the history of the universe. Every sun and all the stars will send tribute. All nations and generations of mankind, all varieties of rational spirits, all angels and archangels, all cherubim and seraphim, will send representatives. For this is "the mystery of God's will, according to his good pleasure which he hath purposed in himself : that in the dispensation of the fulness of times he might gather together under one Head all things in Christ, both which are in heaven, and which are on earth ; even in *him*" (Eph. i. 9, 10).

5. Although heaven can only be entered by the holy, yet such, we are assured, is the infinite provision made for human salvation, and such the intense love for human sinners therein exhibited, that the multitude of the redeemed will be incomparably greater than the number of the lost. My father, at the close of his long life spent in the defence of Calvinism, wrote on one of his conference papers, in trembling characters, a little while before he died, "I am fully persuaded that the vast majority of the human race will share in the beatitudes and glories of our Lord's redemption." Remember that all who die before complete moral agency have been given to Christ. Remember that the vast populations of the coming millenniums are given to Christ. Then shall the promises of Christ to the great "father of the faithful" be fulfilled to the letter : "Thy seed shall be like the sands of the sea-shore ;" "Thy seed shall be like the stars of heaven for multitude," and recollect that when God made this promise, while

Abraham saw only with the naked eye, God took in far more than even the telescopic heavens in magnitude.

6. While heaven is thus infinitely comprehensive, and all the more blessed because it is so, yet each individual, however humble and useless, will have his special individual place prepared expressly for himself. Every glorified body will be articulated to the idiosyncrasies of each individual soul. Every glorified person will be exactly adjusted to his personal friends, associations, relations, and personal work. Paul said of Christ in his personal relation to himself, " Who loved *me*, and gave himself for *me*." We will never, not the least one of us, be lost in the crowd. Our infinite-sided Saviour will have his special recognition, his special communion, and his special tokens of love for each of us. We will all be exalted by being parts of an infinite whole. But we will none of us be lost in the mass. Each will retain his personal value, and in Christ his private life. " To him that overcometh will I give a white stone, and in the stone a new name written, which no man knoweth saving he that receiveth it " (Rev. ii. 17).

And now these Lectures are ended. We shall not meet together here any more. Let us pledge one another, as we part, to reassemble in heaven. We are now parting from one another, as pilgrims part upon the road. Let us turn our steps homeward, for if we do we shall soon—some of us now very soon—" be at home with the Lord." Adieu ! *

* So ended this course of Lectures delivered by Dr. Hodge in Philadelphia, Tuesday, May 30, 1886. The propriety of leaving this conclusion unchanged is obvious. How sadly the words were verified ! Dr. Hodge died on the 12th November 1886.

INDEX

INDEX.

ABBOT, Dr. Ezra, 70.

Abrahamic Church, 179.

Advocate, Christ an, 203.

Agnosticism, 15, 29.

Alexandria, school of, 193.

Angel of Jehovah the second Person of the Trinity, 226.

Angels, probation of, 167.

Annihilation, 386, 390.

Anthropology, 139.

Antinomianism, 308.

Antioch, school of, 193.

Apollinaris, 193.

Apostolic succession, 176, 261.

Arians, 192.

Arminianism, 122, 126, 134, 136, 308.

Assurance of faith, 303.

Athanasius, 192.

Atonement, the day of, 212.

Augustine, St., 161, 268.

Augustinianism, 23, 43, 137.

BAPTISM, 319–338; form of, 320; subjects of, 325; qualifications for, 327; of infants, 329; use of infant, 336.

Bible. See *Scriptures*.

Body, the resurrection, 377.

Breath of life, 142, 144.

Brentius, 196.

CALVINISM, 23, 120, 126, 134, 136, 137, 308.

Canon of Scripture, 61; how ascertained, 64–72.

Catholic Church, the Holy, 259.

Cause, second, 18, 38, 51, 85, 132; and effect, necessary and educational, 132.

Chalcedon, Council of, 194.

Chance, 44, 135.

Character and personal choice, 166.

Chemnitz, 196.

Cherubim, symbols of the glorified body, 381.

Christ, the two natures of, 104, 198; Christianity centres in the Person of, 184; the Person of, 184–220; the offices of, 201–248; a Mediator, 201; Advocate and Paraclete, 203; a Prophet, 205; a Priest, 208.

Christ, a King, 223–248; his kingdom of power, 230; of grace, 232; of glory, 235; the only Head of the Church, 233; the allegiance due to, 245.

Christ-consciousness, 306.

Christian consciousness, 69, 398.

Chronology, 151.

Church, what is the? 174–183, 258; the visible and the invisible, 174, 260; marks of the, 176; of Rome, 176; organization, an accident of the, 177, 261; began in the family, 178; composition of the, chronologically, 178; unity of the, 181, 258, 264; and State, 235.

Circumcision and baptism, 331.

City of God, 250, 268.

Communion, 339–363.

Communicants, relation of, to population of United States, 240.

Concupiscence, Romish doctrine of, 293.

Confirmation, rite of, 337.

Consciousness, the Christian, 69, 398; reveals God, 10.

Constantinople, Council of, 194.

Council of Nice, 192; Laodicea, 193; Ephesus, 194; Chalcedon, 194.

Covenant, fitness and history of the term, 164; nature of a, 166; of works, 166–171; of grace, 171–174; of redemption, 172; of redemption and Christ, 172.

Covenants of God with man, 163–183.

Creation, 32, 49, 141; of man, 140; providence and redemption, 44; Scripture doctrine of, and the plan of salvation, 145.

Crises of history, 287.

DEATH, state after, 364–382; believers at, 367; probation ends at, 365, 387.

Deism, 15, 17, 19, 29, 107.

Destiny of man, seven possible views of the, 383–387; of the wicked, 387–399; solemnity of this subject, 387, 388; false sentiment about the, 388.

Discrepancies in the Scriptures, 82, 83.

Dispensation preferred to the term covenant, 173.

Dispersion of races reversed by the kingdom of Christ, 287.

Docetæ, 192.

Dominion over the creatures, 155.

EDUCATION and religion, 241–245.

Edwards, Jonathan, 135.

Election, 120, 123–127.

Ephesus, Council of, 194.

Eschatology, 139, 364.

Eternal hope, the, 386, 393.

Eucharist, 342.

Eutychianism, 192, 194.

Everlasting punishment, 391–398; origin of scepticism about, 397.

Evolution, 43, 145.

FABER, Mr. Stanley, 126.

Faith and prayer, 91; the source of, 127; and assurance, 303–306.

Fatalism, 136.

Foreknowledge of God and election, 129.

Foreordination, 124, 132.

Fourfold state of man, 188.

Freedom of man and predestination, 128, 134, 158.

Free-will, 156–162; and responsibility, 160.

Friends, the, 291.

GENESIS, 146.

God, his nature and relation to the universe, 9–28; agnostic view of, 15, 29; the Abyss, 15, 27, 109; definition of, impossible, 10; the deist's view of, 15, 29; the efficiency of, in the universe, 21; eternal and omnipresent, 13; extramundane, 17, 25, 29; the Father, 30, 101, 108, 111; the First Cause, 11, 19, 25; the government of, 42; holiness and justice of, 13; immanence of, 18, 23–25; intelligent and has a plan, 163; is there a? 9; our idea of, defined, 11, 25; and the laws of nature, 85–88; moral and religious view of, 17; only one, 101; the pantheist's view of, 17, 29; a Person, 10; a personal Spirit, 11, 30; has other perfections besides benevolence, 14; the perfections of, expressed in providence, 36; his preservation of his creatures, 42; the plan and purpose of, 42, 163; the providence of, 29; the relation of, to the universe, 14; how revealed, 9, 33; revealed in three Persons, 97–117; the Son, 101–104, 109–111; the sinful actions, 23; the transcendence of, 16, 27; the Unitarian God playing solitaire, 106; the universe reveals, 21; is unknowable, 15; what is? 9.

Good works, 290–312.

Grace, prevenient, 23.

Green, Professor W. H., 150.

Guyot, Professor, 150, 152.

HADES, 371–376.

Head of the Church, Christ the only, 233.

Heaven, 399–402; a place, 399; place of, undetermined, 361; dying infants go to, 259, 401; meaning of, 368; and Old Testament saints at death, 368.

Hell, place of, undetermined, 361; Christ's descent into, 369, 375; meaning of, 372, 376.

Heresy, 191; partial truth, 15.

High-Churchism, 177, 182.

Higher criticism, 66, 67.

Higher life, 309.

Hodge, Dr. Charles, 80, 401.

Holiness of God and predestination, 130.

Holy Catholic Church, 259.

Holy Ghost, 105, 112–116, 203, 205, 256, 304.

Hume, David, 55.

Huxley, 148.

IDENTITY of the resurrection body, 377.

Illumination, spiritual, 76.

Illustrations:—The Copernican system, 131; the increasing boundary of darkness, 15; how a botanist comprehends a flower, 16; vital principle in plants illustrates the divine immanence, 19; St. Peter's at Rome as a creation, and Michael Angelo the directing genius, 21; bodily changes expressions of the spirit, and God revealed in changes of the universe, 27; the musician the cause of the sound but not of the discord of the instrument out of tune, or God's relation to sinful acts, 23; Dr. Witherspoon and special providences, 34; the musician articulating air, and God articulating nature, 40; Charleston earthquake and providence, 41; the missionary in Siam making ice before the court did no miracle, 47; miracles related to natural law, as man's agency in the electric telegraph, 53; Bible an organic whole like a cathedral, 74; inspiration analogous to the man at the helm, 78; the sculptor and statue, and the vital principle of a tree, 94; parable of light, 110–117; view of a battlefield from the strategic centre, 131; looking eastward in the morning and in the evening, the difference, 131; a chronometer illustrates foreordination, 132; picture perspective, and chronology in history, 151; Adam created mature, illustrated by Dr. Plumer's account of a strange case, 154; free-will illustrated, 156, 157; logic like a ladder, 156; fiddle out of tune, and origin of sin, 161; seeing the Church like seeing the earth—too near the planet to see it, 175; unity of the Church not like drops of water in the ocean, or grains of sand that make the desert, but like the cathedral, 181; orchestra illustrates Church unity, 181; soul and body illustrate Christ's humanity and divinity in one Person, 189, 199; telescopes of highest power have the narrowest field, and simple minds the deepest revelations, 208; sacrifices like paper promises to pay, 213; kingdom of Christ and kingdoms of this world, like gases, vacuums to one another, 234; the little child unconscious, 306; "I do hate the early-ripes," 312; Laura Bridgman, illustration of the glorious body of the resurrection, 379; cherubim, symbols of the glorious body of the resurrection, 381.

Image of God, 155.

Immanence of God, 18.

Incarnation of the Son, 109, 164, 197.

Infants dying in infancy go to heaven, 259, 401, 460.

Infidelity, source of, 397.

Inspiration, 78; verbal, 79.

Intermediate state, 365, 370.

JEHOVAH, the second Person of the Trinity, 226.

Jewish Church, 179.

Justification, 292; Protestant doctrine of, 292, 295; Romish doctrine of, 292; precedes regeneration, 294.

KENOSIS, 196.

Keys, power of the, 315, 328.

King, Christ a, 223–248.

Kingdom, universality of the mediatorial, 228; Christ's, of power, 230; of grace, 232.

Kingdom of Christ and kingdoms of the world, 234; Christ's, of glory, 235; of Christ, 241–270; three names for the, 249; of God, heaven, and Christ, 250; growth of the, 256; law of the, 271–289; and the United States, 287.

LAODICEA, Council of, 194.

Laura Bridgman, 379.

Law, of the kingdom, 271–289; and gospel, how mutually exclusive, 281; channels for revealing the divine, 278; use of, 282, 301.

Laws of nature, 39, 41, 53, 86; and prayer, 93.

Logic a ladder, 156.

Logical unfolding of the covenant from Moses to Christ, 180.

Lord's Supper, 195, 339, 363; names for the, 340–342; genesis of the, 342; matter of the, 346; bread and wine of the, 346, 347; sacramental actions of the, 348–350; meaning and design of the, 350; Christ's presence in the, 355.

Lutherans, 122, 194, 357, 359.

MAN, the original state of, 139–162.

Man, scriptural account of the origin of, 140; made of dust, 140; the soul of, not divine spirit, 142; antiquity of, 150; created mature, 153; made in the image of God, 155; his dominion over the creatures, 155; and free-will, 156; fourfold state of, 160; God's covenants with, 163–183; his moral character and personal choice, 167; probation of, 168; destiny of, seven possible views of the, 383–387.

Materialism, 383.

Mediator, Christ a, 201.

Mill, J. Stuart, 37, 53, 125.

Miller, Hugh, 169.

Miracles, 46–60; what is a? 26, 32, 46, 51; and moral government, 54; the use of a, 50, 57, 86; not impossible, 52, 54; and laws of nature, 52; does not betoken defect, whim, or change of plan, 54; not improbable, 55.

Morality, 17, 25, 27, 272.

Moral government and miracles, 55.

Mosaic Church, 179.

Mysteries, 97, 161, 313, 339.

NATURE, laws of. See *Law.* Definition of, 48.

Natures, two, in Christ, 190.

Natural, what is? 48; law, 87.

Necessity, doctrine of, 135.

Neo-nomianism, 308.

Nestorians, 192.

"New Departure," the, 23.

Nice, Council of, 192.

OFFICES of Christ, 201–248; two meanings of word "office," 201.

Origen, 193.

Original sin, 121, 169.

Orthodoxy always catholic, 15, 25, 27, 40, 107, 136, 191.

PANTHEISM, 17, 24, 27, 29, 40, 107.

Parable of light, 110–117.

Paraclete, Christ a, 203.

Parker, Theodore, 54.

Passover and the Lord's Supper, 343–346.

Patriarchal Church, 178.

Patriotism, false, 246.

Pelagianism, 121, 290.

Penance, Romish doctrine of, 293.

Perfectionism, 301, 307.

Persons in the Godhead, 97–117; order of the, in the Trinity, 103, 188.

Person of Christ, 184–200; doctrinal difficulties of the, 186.

Person of Christ, heresies relating to, 190; Lutheran doctrine of, 194; Reformed doctrine of, 195; the lesson of all ages, 207.

Polytheism, 107.

Power of the keys, 315, 328.

Prayer, 84–96; and rationalists, etc., 87.

Prayer, what is acceptable? 89; answer to, 90; and foreordination, 92; and laws of nature, 93; experience testifies to the need of, 95; Professor Tyndall's "test," 95; for President Garfield, 95; and use of means, 90.

Predestination, 118–138; a subject unavoidable and important, 118; Calvin's way of presenting, 120; and freedom, 128; and God's holiness, 130; not antagonized by other truth, 134; opposite of fate, 135.

Presence, Christ's, in the Lord's Supper, defined, 355.

Priest, Christ a, 208–222.

Priesthood, the ministry not a, 220.

Probation, 167–169; ends with death, 365, 386, 387; second, 385, 393; as it was offered, the best chance, 168.

Profession, what is a credible? 327.

Prophet, Christ a, 205–208.

Providence, Scripture doctrine of, 29–45; the execution of one plan, 33; universal, 34; natural and ordinary, supernatural and gracious, 35; special, 35; the expression of God's perfections, 36; facts of nature and religion reconcilable with, 36–42; to be interpreted by light of Scripture, 42; and redemption, 44.

Public schools and religion, 241–245.

Punishment, everlasting, 391–399.

RATIONALISM, 99, 272, 290.

Rationalists and prayer, 87.

Reason and revelation, 99.

Regeneration precedes sanctification, 295.

Religion, 17, 25, 27; and education, 279; and science, 27, 39; and State, 237.

Renan, 62.

Repentance, 293; the first motion of, from God, 120.

Responsibility and free-will, 160.

Resurrection, 376–382; of the wicked, 376, 377; of saints, 377; of the body, 378; identity of the body in, 377, 378.

Revelation by word or book not impossible, 62; and reason, 99; the nature of, 77, 279.

Rewards and punishments, the final, 383–402.

Ritualism and Romanism, chief error of, 221, 357.

Romanism, 291–294, 303, 355, 357.

Rome, Church of, 176.

Rule of faith, 61, 279.

SACRAMENTS, 313–319; meaning of the word, 313; called mysteries, 313; nature and design of the, 315; means of grace, 317; Romish view of, 291; of the Romish Church, 318; of perpetual obligation, 319; the sacrament of baptism, 319–338; the Lord's Supper, 339–363.

Sacramentum, 341, 362.

Saints of the Old Testament at death, 368, 373; resurrection of the, 377.

Salvation, essential parts of, 204.

Sanctification and good works, 290–312; and justification, 294; standard of, 300.

Schism, 182, 267.

Science, why men of, cannot see traces of God, 10, 39; and religion, 26, 27, 39, 41, 141, 147, 150.

Scriptures, the, 61–83; the genesis of the, 72; a human book, 73; a divine book, 74; an organic whole, 74; are the Word of God, 20, 75, 79, 82; God's part in producing the, 75; discrepancies in the, 82.

Sealing ordinances, 314.

Self-consciousness, 306.

Semi-Pelagianism, 121, 290.

Sheol, 371–374.

Sin, effects of, 278; universal sense of, 209; the measure of, 396; nature and origin of, 161, 300; original, 121, 169.

Sinful acts foreordained, 124.

Smith, Dr. H. B., 81, 82.

Soteriology, 139.

Soul, the living, 142; created, 143.

Sovereignty of Christ, 224.

Spencer, Herbert, 15, 135.

Spiritual-mindedness, 208.

State and religion, 237 ; and Church, 234.

State after death and resurrection, 364–382.

Supernatural, the, 27, 40, 48 ; and miracle not coextensive, 47.

System, God's plan regarded as a, 163, 169 ; of human redemption, 170 ; place of humanity in God's, 164.

TABERNACLE, the service of the, 210.

Text of Scriptures, how ascertain the true, 65, 70 ; one, not convincing, 145.

Theism, Christian, 15, 17.

Theology, order of topics in, 139.

Transcendental theology, 119.

Transubstantiation, 359.

Trinity, the, 97–117, 187 ; known only by revelation, 97 ; the most reasonable view of God, 99, 107 ; order of Persons in the, 103, 188 ; illustrated by a parable of light, 110–117 ; and the doctrine of the Person of Christ intimately associated, 186.

Tyndall and a prayer-test, 95 ; and evolution, 148.

UNITARIANISM, 106, 187, 192.

United States a Christian nation, 240 ; proportion of church members in, 240 ; and the kingdom of God, 287.

Universalism, 384.

Usher, Archbishop, and the Westminster Assembly, 165.

VITAL principle of plants illustrates the divine immanence, 19.

WATER the symbol of spiritual regeneration, 321.

Westminster Assembly, 165.

Whately, Archbishop, 126.

Wicked, destiny of the, 383 ; solemnity of the subject, 387.

Wicked, false sentiment about the destiny of the, 388.

Wine of the Lord's Supper, 347.

Woman created, 144.

Word, Christ the, 205.

ZWINGLE, 119.